Oracle Application Express 3.2

The Essentials and More

Develop Native Oracle database-centric web
applications quickly and easily with Oracle APEX

Arie Geller

Matthew Lyon

[PACKT] enterprise
PUBLISHING
professional expertise distilled

BIRMINGHAM - MUMBAI

Oracle Application Express 3.2
The Essentials and More

First published: June 2010

Production Reference: 1250510

Published by Packt Publishing Ltd.
32 Lincoln Road
Olton
Birmingham, B27 6PA, UK.

ISBN 978-1-847194-52-7

www.packtpub.com

Cover Image by Vinayak Chittar (vinayak.chittar@gmail.com)

Credits

About the Authors

Arie Geller is an independent IT consultant, with more than 30 years of experience with systems analysis, software development, IT infrastructure, etc. He started to use HTML DB 1.6 (the former name of APEX) to develop data centric Web applications in the Oracle environment, and continue doing so, with all the following versions, until today.

Arie has specialized in developing Right-To-Left-oriented applications, and he brings his expertise and experience in this field into the book. Arie is also an active member of the APEX community on OTN, where he assists other members and shares his knowledge and experience as much as he can.

> I would like to thank my surrounding family for their great patient and support, and also to my friends and customers for their understanding, during the very demanding period of writing this book.
>
> I would also like to thank Joel Kallman and Scott Spadafore (RIP) from the APEX development team, for their invaluable help and insight on APEX, over the years.

Matthew Lyon is a Senior Consultant at SRA Information Technology in Adelaide, South Australia. His involvement in enterprise software development extends across analysis, design, development, architecture, and project management, giving him a deep appreciation of the effective use of software technology. He has experience with a wide variety of technologies but has a passion for Oracle APEX and Java. Matthew runs APEX training courses for clients and is active in the Oracle community as a presenter and as a committee member of the South Australian Oracle User Group. Matthew has more than 10 years experience in software development and has been using APEX since HTMLDB version 1.6.

> I would like to thank my lovely wife Zoe and beautiful baby girl Rose for their help and support while writing this book.

About the Reviewers

Ashish Agarwal has the distinct privilege of being one of the less than a few hundred Oracle Certified Masters in the world (`http://www.oracle.com/technology/ocm/aagarwal.html`). He is also a certified Project Management Professional from PMI, USA & Oracle Certified Professional in Oracle 10g, 9i, 8i, and 8. With a total industry experience of more than 12 years in Information Technology Field, exhaustive experience and Knowledge in Managing Oracle Databases and Oracle Applications (ERP and CRM Suites), administration is his expertise. Participating in the design of Infrastructure Architecture for Oracle Products and managing data centre kind of environment with multiple databases and servers are some of his other experience areas.

Ashish has worked with companies like Panasonic, Oracle, Sapient, and Mercer across the geographies of India, Singapore, Malaysia, Canada, and the UK, and is now currently running DBCON—a Database & Oracle APEX consulting company based in Singapore. DBCON leverages on the power of the Internet to provide live online training, application development, management and maintenance, support, and troubleshooting in Oracle technologies to anyone in the world. DBCON also leverages on the power of the Internet to engage the best people in their respective areas from across the globe.

Attracted to Oracle Application Express because of its simplicity and productivity, Ashish regularly conducts live online training in Oracle Application Express through his company DBCON. Anyone from anywhere in the world can attend this training with just a PC and internet connection. To learn more about live online training in Oracle Application Express please visit `http://www.dbcon.com` or e-mail at `ashish.agarwal@dbcon.com`.

Ben Burell is an Oracle developer currently based in the Isle of Man. He is an active contributor to the Oracle APEX forum as 'Munky' and sporadically blogs about APEX related tips and tricks at `http://munkyben.wordpress.com`.

He enjoys problem solving while listening to music, meaning that he quite enjoys his job!

Katie McLaughlin is a software developer and consultant who has been working with Oracle Apex for many years, developing enterprise applications as well as for smaller business requirements. She currently works for an international software house, developing financial applications for some of the largest companies in the world.

> I'd like to thank my partner, Karl, for all his kindness and for bringing many a cup of tea during the time I worked on this book.

Penny Cookson has been working with Oracle products since 1987. Penny is the Managing Director and Principal Consultant for SAGE Computing Services, an Australian company which specializes in providing Oracle education and consulting services. She has written and conducted training courses and provided expert advice in a wide range of products, including Application Express, and is a regular presenter at Oracle and User Group conferences. She was Oracle Magazine's Educator of the Year in 2004 and is an Oracle ACE.

Table of Contents

Preface

Oracle Application Express—APEX for short, or by its former name, HTML DB, is a declarative, Web-based RAD (Rapid Application Development) tool. APEX runs inside an Oracle database, tightly integrated with its internal resources, and utilize them optimally. Using a Web browser, it allows us to develop, test, and deploy a Web based, data-centric application in a declarative manner, but on the same time it doesn't limit our abilities to manually enter specific and tailored code, both on the client and server side, that will answer our most specific needs and demands.

Developing data centric Web applications can be a real challenge as it's a multi-disciplinary process. There are many technologies involved in the client side (HTML, CSS, JavaScript, etc.); the interaction with the database, in the server side; the typless nature of the Web environment; and above all, the need to put it all together, in a manner that will allow the end users to do their job, in the simplest and most efficient way, while enriching their user experience. If you are working in the Oracle environment, APEX can be your best solution.

What is the aim of the book

With this book, you'll learn how to easily develop data centric Web applications for the Oracle environment, using the APEX RAD tool.

This book is not a recipes book, although it includes many working examples. You will learn to understand the basic principles behind the APEX building blocks, and how they operate. It will allow you to take advantage of existing "APEX recipes" but more importantly to create your own.

The book covers the development cycle of an APEX application. It starts with the design phase, including building your necessary database objects infrastructure; continue with ways to implement the application logic (on the server side) and the User Interface (on the client side), whilst showing you how to enhance your applications features and functionality, according to your specific needs; and it ends with application deployment.

The book includes dedicated chapters that deal with the Globalization and Localization aspects of developing APEX applications, with dedicated chapter for developing Right-To-Left oriented applications.

Who this book is for

This book is for developers, in general, and web developers, in particular, who wish to learn how to develop data-centric web applications in the Oracle environment. It is also for novice APEX developers, who wish to learn how to use and best utilize the APEX environment, as well as for more experience APEX developers who wish to improve their knowledge and understanding of APEX and its capabilities and learn from the experiences of others.

Developers who work in a multi-lingual environment, in general, and in a Right-To-Left environment, in particular, will be most beneficial from the dedicated chapters on these subjects, which include issues that we believe are documented for the first time.

The book assumes basic knowledge of HTML, SQL, and PL/SQL. Basic JavaScript understanding is an advantage, and in general, can make your life much easier as an APEX developer. The book includes a dedicated chapter which gives a general review of these issues.

What this book covers

Chapter 1, An Introduction to APEX gives an introduction of APEX architecture and technology, while explains some of the above-mentioned terms in the APEX context.

Chapter 2, What we need to know to effectively use APEX reviews. Some of the basic skills we should have in order to better utilize the Web development aspects of APEX. It talks about HTML, the DOM, CSS, and JavaScript.

Chapter 3, APEX Basic Concepts discusses some of the major APEX concepts and explains how they can help us in our developmental efforts.

Chapter 4, The Application Builder Basic Concepts and Building Blocks explains the major building blocks of the APEX application, and how to create them using the APEX Application Builder.

Chapter 5, APEX Items discusses the major building blocks of the application page—the application items. We'll review **application items** and **page items** and learn how they can serve us in our applications.

Chapter 6, APEX Buttons explains different types of buttons that a developer can place on an APEX page, creating/editing them, assigning attributes and using the REQUEST feature

Chapter 7, APEX Computations reviews the computation mechanism and sees how we can use it in our applications.

Chapter 8, APEX Validations discusses APEX validations, which help us to maintain the integrity and consistency of our data by making sure that only correct and consistent data will be used and saved into the database.

Chapter 9, APEX Processes reviews the main concepts of APEX processes and how they can help us to implement our application logic. It includes discussions on application level processes (including on-demand processes), page level processes, and the various types and options APEX provides us with to implement them.

Chapter 10, APEX Branches discusses APEX Branches, which are responsible for the flow of the application.

Chapter 11, APEX SQL Workshop reviews some APEX IDE built-in utilities that will help us define our application database infrastructure, either declaratively or by using DDL commands and scripts.

Chapter 12, APEX Forms reviews the various sources that we can use to create an APEX form. How to use the APEX Create Form wizard to generate a new form and manually create an APEX form.

Chapter 13, APEX Reports discusses how we can create and modify reports in APEX applications.

Chapter 14, Tabular Forms describe the APEX tabular form concept, with a very detailed discussion on how to generate one using an APEX wizard, or in more complex scenarios, doing it manually, using specific APEX APIs.

Chapter 15, Calendars looks at how we can use calendar components in our applications.

Chapter 16, Interactive Reports looks at how we can use Interactive Reports in our applications.

Chapter 17, AJAX with APEX looks at how we can utilize the APEX AJAX framework, both on the client and server side, to integrate and support this important technology in our APEX applications.

Chapter 18, Globalization and Localization With APEX Applications deals with the Globalization and Localization aspects of APEX applications. It include detailed discussion about the APEX built-in translation mechanism and sees how we can develop multi-lingual APEX applications.

Chapter 19, Right-To-Left Support in APEX review the specific actions we need to take in order to generate and support APEX Right-To-Left applications.

Chapter 20, Deploying APEX Applications discuss the means APEX provides us to deploy our developed applications.

Chapter 21, The APEX Runtime Environment explains what the APEX Runtime Environment is all about and how we can manage it.

Chapter 22, Security looks at APEX Security and how it can be used in our applications.

Chapter 23, Application Conversion looks at how we can convert Microsoft Access and Oracle Forms applications to APEX.

Chapter 24, APEX Best Practices looks at the best practices for developing APEX applications.

Appendix deals with APEX installation, upgradation, and configuration issues.

Standards and assumptions

This book assumes basic knowledge in the main technologies and programming languages that we are using while working in APEX. These include, for the client side, HTML/XHTML, CSS, and JavaScript; and for the server side SQL and PL/SQL.

You can practice developing APEX application using the Oracle hosted site on apex.oracle.com. APEX is also included in the free ORACLE XE database version, which can be downloaded from the Oracle OTN site (otn.oracle.com). You can also download the latest version of APEX, and use it to upgrade the built-in version in the Oracle XE.

Conventions

In this book, you will find a number of styles of text that distinguish between different kinds of information. Here are some examples of these styles, and an explanation of their meaning.

Code words in text are shown as follows: "On a page level, we define the `<style>` tag in the `<head>` section of the HTML code."

A block of code is set as follows:

```
<head>
. . .
<link rel="stylesheet" type="text/css" href="myCSS.css" />
. . .
</head>
```

When we wish to draw your attention to a particular part of a code block, the relevant lines or items are set in bold:

```
select *
from emp t
where t.deptno = v('P1_DEPTNO')
and t.hiredate = (select max(hiredate) hiredate
from emp t1
where deptno = v('P1_DEPTNO'))
```

New terms and **important words** are shown in bold. Words that you see on the screen, in menus or dialog boxes for example, appear in the text like this: "APEX includes some wizards and tools, such as the **Wizard Report** and **Query Builder**."

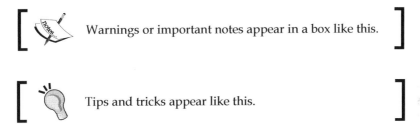

Warnings or important notes appear in a box like this.

Tips and tricks appear like this.

Reader feedback

Feedback from our readers is always welcome. Let us know what you think about this book—what you liked or may have disliked. Reader feedback is important for us to develop titles that you really get the most out of.

To send us general feedback, simply send an e-mail to feedback@packtpub.com, and mention the book title via the subject of your message.

If there is a book that you need and would like to see us publish, please send us a note in the **SUGGEST A TITLE** form on www.packtpub.com or e-mail suggest@packtpub.com.

If there is a topic that you have expertise in and you are interested in either writing or contributing to a book on, see our author guide on www.packtpub.com/authors.

Customer support

Now that you are the proud owner of a Packt book, we have a number of things to help you to get the most from your purchase.

> **Downloading the example code for the book**
>
> Visit `https://www.packtpub.com//sites/default/files/downloads/4527_Code.zip` to directly download the example code.
>
> The downloadable files contain instructions on how to use them.

Errata

Although we have taken every care to ensure the accuracy of our content, mistakes do happen. If you find a mistake in one of our books—maybe a mistake in the text or the code—we would be grateful if you would report this to us. By doing so, you can save other readers from frustration and help us improve subsequent versions of this book. If you find any errata, please report them by visiting `http://www.packtpub.com/support`, selecting your book, clicking on the **let us know** link, and entering the details of your errata. Once your errata are verified, your submission will be accepted and the errata will be uploaded on our website, or added to any list of existing errata, under the Errata section of that title. Any existing errata can be viewed by selecting your title from `http://www.packtpub.com/support`.

Piracy

Piracy of copyright material on the Internet is an ongoing problem across all media. At Packt, we take the protection of our copyright and licenses very seriously. If you come across any illegal copies of our works, in any form, on the Internet, please provide us with the location address or website name immediately so that we can pursue a remedy.

Please contact us at `copyright@packtpub.com` with a link to the suspected pirated material.

We appreciate your help in protecting our authors, and our ability to bring you valuable content.

Questions

You can contact us at `questions@packtpub.com` if you are having a problem with any aspect of the book, and we will do our best to address it.

1
An Introduction to APEX

Oracle Application Express—APEX for short, or by its former name HTML DB – is a **declarative**, **Web-based RAD** (Rapid Application development) tool. It is used to develop **native** Web-based, **data centric** applications.

Let's clarify some of these terms, and understand what they mean in the APEX context.

Web-based

The term **Web-based** appears in the description of both the development tool and its product—the APEX application. We are using a Web browser to both develop and run our applications. The advantages are obvious. Web browsers are installed, almost by default, on most of the workstations we are using, independently of the workstation hardware or operating system. It means that on the client side, we don't need anything else to start developing with APEX, or to run APEX applications. Moreover, it means very easy access to our applications, both internally – using Intranet – or externally, using the Internet. If we add all the modern smart phones and other PDAs on the market today, which include built-in Web browsers, we'll come to the conclusion that the range of options to access our APEX applications is very wide.

Another important advantage when using a Web browser is the ability to free us from hardware and local operating system dependencies. As the APEX Application Builder actually generates HTML code, we (as developers) don't have to worry about the hardware specifications, or the local operating system our end users will be using, to run our APEX application. As long as they have access to an HTML supporting Web browser, we are covered.

However, Web based application development can also be a drawback. Unfortunately, not all Web browser manufacturers have fully adopted all the international standards in this field. As a result, there are cases in which different Web browsers will display the same code page differently. The variety of Web browsers in the market today, like Internet Explorer, Firefox, Chrome, Opera and Safari, just to name a few, support and implement HTML, XHTML, CSS and JavaScript versions and levels, in different ways and styles. There are known cases where even the same Web browser brand, but in different versions, or across local operating systems, delivers different results with the same code. We need to be aware of this, and take actions to resolve it—if we want to ensure cross-browser compatibility code for our applications (which will apply to greater numbers of potential users). Sometimes we need to take hard decisions and waive the support of certain web browsers in order to keep our code simple and maintainable.

A list of supported Web browsers can be found in the APEX release notes. For version 3.2, which is the latest APEX version at the time of writing this book, it can be found at `http://download.oracle.com/docs/cd/E14373_01/relnotes.32/e13365/toc.htm#BGBCEGBI`

Native Web based

APEX, in all its previous forms, was always designed to operate in the Web environment. The final product of the APEX Application Builder is HTML code that can be run directly on any Web browser that supports the HTML 4.0 and above standard. APEX Application Builder also incorporates special features into generated applications, as a direct result of operating in the Web environment. Further on, we will discuss APEX architecture and its main features, but for now we will mention **session state** and **Optimistic Locking**, as distinguished Web environment features which help us overcome the stateless nature of this environment.

The APEX Application Builder fully supports **CSS (Cascading Style Sheets)** and JavaScript, as integrated components of APEX applications. That includes built-in CSS files as part of a wider page layout and format mechanism, which we'll address later in the book, and a JavaScript library. The JavaScript library also includes, among a variety of general and APEX related functions, an **AJAX (Asynchronous JavaScript and XML)** framework. This allows even novice developers to utilize this advanced technology, and produce high quality applications, compatible with the latest trends in the market like Web 2.0, etc.

Data Centric

APEX was designed to produce applications that store, retrieve, manipulate, and display data, from Oracle Databases. This means that if your application's main logic doesn't revolve around data manipulation, it may be that APEX is not your optimal application development tool. However, if data manipulation is at the heart of your application, APEX could be your best bet.

APEX is actually a collection of PL/SQL packages, which "live" inside the Oracle database. It means that APEX automatically inherits all the outstanding features, often mentioned with regards to the Oracle database environment: high performance, robustness, reliability, enhanced security, scalability, and more. In addition, APEX can natively utilize the very rich SQL and PL/SQL environment, including the built-in packages that the Oracle database has to offer, and use them to manipulate the data in the optimal ways a RDBMS can offer.

Moreover, APEX can utilize special functionality features that are included in the various database versions and editions, like Oracle XML DB, Oracle Text, and Oracle Multimedia.

Another advantage in this context is that, like the client side which relies on Web browsers to gain hardware independence, (alongside operating system independence), the APEX engine relies on the database platform for the same purpose. As long as we have a proper running version of an Oracle database, starting with Oracle database 9.2.0.3 and above (including the free version, Oracle XE), we can ignore the hardware and operating systems aspects of the server.

A declarative development tool

APEX is a declarative tool. It means that we, as developers, concentrate more on the "What needs to be done", and less on the "How to do it". Think, for example, about SQL. In a SELECT statement, when we are using the ORDER BY clause, we are actually telling the database what we need—a sorted data result set, but we don't tell it how to actually do the sorting. In fact, the entire SELECT statement, just like SQL itself, is a declarative statement. In APEX, we are telling the Application builder that we need to lay out an HTML item on the page, or retrieve certain records from the database, and the APEX engine generates the proper code for doing that, both on the server side and the client side.

Working declaratively in APEX means that we are not generating traditional (3 GL) program code. Instead, we are working with a series of wizards and property sheets, which allows us to define all the metadata we need in order to generate an application page's code. APEX includes sets of pre-defined wizards, supported HTML objects, supported database objects and data types, page rendering options and procedures, after submit processes and DML options, navigation and branching options, and more. We can use all of these to declare our application page's forms, reports, charts, etc., with their layouts and application/business logic. The APEX engine translates it all into an HTML code for the client side, and SQL and PL/SQL code for the server side. Whenever the predefined options don't give us the exact solution we need, APEX allows us to use our own SQL and PL/SQL code for the server side, and HTML/XHTML, CSS, and JavaScript code, for the client side. As mentioned before, it also allows us the use of AJAX technology, within a built-in framework, to query the server side, while running on the client side without submitting the page.

RAD tool

APEX provides us with a full development environment, allowing us to develop, test, and deploy our applications. APEX includes three modules: Application Builder, SQL Workshop, and Utilities.

Application Builder

The Application Builder allows us to develop and test our applications, without leaving the development environment. While working in the Application Builder, it automatically adds a dedicated **developer toolbar** to every page in our application, making it very easy to toggle between the running page and its code within the Application Builder. The developer toolbar also provides the developer with more options to assist in the development process, like checking **session state**, running in **debug mode**, etc. Moreover, the Application Builder allows us to manage, monitor, and control all the application's **shared components**, **supporting objects**, and **deployment scripts**. In addition, the Application Builder includes tools for exporting and importing applications and application components.

 Some of these terms might be unfamiliar to you at this stage, but don't be alarmed as we'll cover them all further down this book.

SQL Workshop

The SQL Workshop includes a series of tools which allow us to create, manage, and inspect our application data infrastructure. This including wizards to create and manipulate database objects, scripts and queries, and the SQL Commands facility, which allows us to run SQL and PL/SQL code in the context of APEX. This can be very useful, as some of the APEX features and APIs are not available outside the APEX context (e.g. SQL*Plus) for security reasons.

Utilities

The Utilities module includes a number of tools to help us manage the APEX development-surrounding environment, especially regarding the database. It includes tools for the import and export of data into and out of the database, the APEX data dictionary, and several database monitoring and reporting tools.

The APEX environment also includes a special administration module, which allows us to define the APEX working environment, developers, and users.

All these modules include declarative, wizard-based tools, which makes the application development cycle a very rapid one. These development environment allows us to quickly define a prototype of our application, and then expand it with all the finer details.

Globalization, localization, and NLS

APEX was designed with globalization, localization, and NLS (National Language Support) in mind. To begin with, the APEX interface is translated into nine languages, other than English. The languages are German, Spanish, French, Italian, Japanese, Korean, Brazilian Portuguese, Simplified Chinese, and Traditional Chinese.

APEX can utilize all the globalization, localization, and NLS features that the Oracle database has to offer, and add some of its own. The *Application Builder* **Shared Components** module includes a **Globalization** section, which allows us to define relevant parameters for globalization, localization, and NLS. It also includes a wizard to guide us through the process of translating our entire application into secondary languages.

APEX takes into account the client side NLS settings when dealing with the import and export of data into and out of the database. It also takes into account the database NLS settings, in order to properly sort data, display dates, number format (e.g. decimal point or comma) and the local currency, among others.

APEX supports the **XLIFF (XML Localization Interchange File Format)** standard, which allows us to translate an entire APEX application into any language we need, without re-writing the application code. APEX provides a built-in mechanism to simultaneously run the same application in multi language User Interfaces, giving us several options to determine the application language, including the option of matching the APEX application language to the end user's browser language preferences. Moreover, if we need to support a language which is not included in the native supported languages list, this mechanism will allow us to specifically translate the built-in APEX engine strings and messages into that language, allowing us to develop and support APEX application in any language that our database can support.

 Since version 2.0, the client side communicates with the server side, using the AL32UTF8 character set, **regardless** of the database character set. Due to some of the advanced technologies APEX is using (like AJAX), this setting is mandatory. If you are going to work in a multi-language environment, it would be optimal to set your database character set to AL32UFT8. This will ensure a true multi-language environment, while eliminating the need to employ any character set conversions between the client and the server. Oracle is advising users to use AL32UTF8 as their default choice for the database character set.

Throughout this book, we will devote special attention to globalization, localization, and NLS issues in the APEX environment, including **RTL** (Right-To-Left) support examples.

APEX architecture

The core of APEX is a collection of PL/SQL packages, written using the **PL/SQL Web Toolkit**, and several hundred database tables, in which all the metadata regarding developed applications are stored.

The PL/SQL Web Toolkit is a collection of Oracle supplied database packages, which allow us to produce Web page code, directly in the database, using PL/SQL stored procedures. During run-time, and in real-time, the APEX engine queries the metadata tables and retrieves all the relevant information for a specific application page. Next, it uses the PL/SQL Web Toolkit to generate the application page's HTML code. This page's code also includes the proper linkage to the CSS and JavaScript resources that support proper page functionality, layout, and styles. Some internal tests run by the APEX development team, showed that the APEX engine performs all the real-time rendering processes, with an average overhead of less than 0.04 seconds per page. Pretty impressive in my opinion, and the APEX engine includes a server side caching mechanism, that can help us reduce that further.

It is important to understand that although the final product of *APEX Application Builder* is an HTML page code, no static files with any related HTML file extensions, are stored on the server. Each page is created upon demand—a specific URI request. That, of course, gives us considerable flexibility with constructing the pages, e.g. the same page can be displayed somewhat differently for various users, or include conditioned components, depending on the user's security privileges, or role in the company, etc.

So, on one side we have the APEX engine, a collection of PL/SQL packages, running inside an Oracle database, and on the other side we have the application user, using a Web browser. How can we connect, and communicate between the sides? As we are in a Web environment, we are going to use the HTTP protocol, implemented in two technologies.

The first way is by using the **Oracle HTTP Server (OHS)** technology. OHS is based on the well-known (open source) Apache HTTP server, in its 1.3 or 2.0 versions. What interests us, for the APEX environment, is the Oracle plug-in module for this HTTP server, called **mod_plsql**.

OHS, with the *mod_plsql* module, is located between the client's Web browser and the Oracle database server. The *mod_plsql* module communicates with the database by mapping the Web browser request into PL/SQL stored procedures in the database. In turn, the PL/SQL stored procedures can manipulate the data in the database tables and generate HTTP responses, which can include HTML code, to be displayed on the client Web browser.

In order to communicate with the database, *mod_plsql* is using a **DAD (Database Access Descriptor)** file, which contains configuration parameters on how to connect with the database, which user and password to use, NLS parameters, and others.

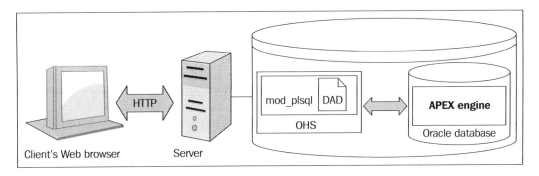

The second technology to implement the HTTP communication protocol utilizes the **Embedded PL/SQL Gateway** running on the XML DB HTTP server, which is an integrated feature of the Oracle Database. Using the DBMS_EPG package, the Embedded PL/SQL Gateway can implement the core functionality of the OHS *mod_plsql* module, without installing it. This technology was first supported by APEX in the embedded version (2.1) of the Oracle XE database. Today, it's also supported by APEX 3.0 and above versions, running on Oracle 11g databases. APEX 3.0, which uses the embedded PL/SQL gateway, is installed by default as part of the 11g database installation process, and can be upgraded to any higher APEX version.

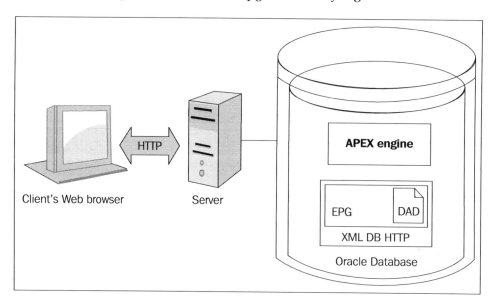

Summary

APEX is a RAD tool, running inside an Oracle database. Using a Web browser, it allows us to develop, test, and deploy a Web based, data centric application, in a declarative manner.

Although APEX is a declarative tool, we need to be familiar with some other programming technologies and resources, in order to optimally utilize it. That's in the next chapter.

2
What we need to know to effectively use APEX

APEX is a declarative tool. As such, we are working with wizards and properties/attributes sheets. However, in some cases, the declarative wizards don't support all the technologies, options, and finer details that are available to us in the environment in which APEX operates and are important to achieve the tasks and business logic of our APEX application.

Whenever we want to enhance the generic result of a declarative wizard, such as in some of the following cases:

- Generating complex reports
- Having better control over the page layout, format, and styling
- Enhancing the functionality of the APEX application page, utilizing advanced technologies (like AJAX)
- Fully utilizing the Oracle database resources

and more, we need to have some basic skills and a knowledge of relevant programming languages and technologies.

When and where appropriate or needed, whether mandatory or optional, the APEX wizards and property sheets will allow us to use our skills to develop snippets of real code to achieve what we want.

The following are some of the skills and technologies that we believe will help you the most while developing with APEX.

SQL and PL/SQL

SQL is essential where reports, charts, and calendars are concerned as it defines the scope and the conditions of the fetched data from the database. APEX includes some wizards and tools, such as the **Wizard Report** and **Query Builder**, which can greatly assist novice users in creating SQL queries, but basic SQL knowledge is still an advantage. The same can be said about PL/SQL, especially when we want to enhance the APEX built-in wizards and pre-defined processes capabilities, or when we use AJAX (on the server-side). For example, the APEX built-in wizards and the declarative pages natively support working with a composite *Primary Key* of up to two segments. Working with compound *Primary Keys* with more than two segments, is possible, but we will have to write our own DML code for that.

In this book, we'll assume that you have the basic skills and knowledge to handle the APEX tasks that involve SQL and PL/SQL.

HTML and CSS

HTML and CSS skills will help us a lot with enhancing and enriching the APEX built-in wizards and tools that are dealing with the look and feel of our applications. APEX allows us to define our own HTML templates or add our own CSS files, built from scratch or based on the existing HTML and CSS pre-built libraries (*Theme* in the APEX terminology). This will allow us to create applications with the exact look and feel that we need, for example, to maintain consistency with other Web applications in our environment.

JavaScript

JavaScript can give us the ultimate control over our pages, allowing us to change their layout and content dynamically and in real-time. JavaScript is also the client-side component of AJAX, which is a crucial technology in all the modern Web applications.

However, we must bear in mind that JavaScript can be banned from our client's Web browsers due to strict security policies, for example. JavaScript is also not fully supported on many of the low-end smart phones and PDAs. We should check the target environment for our APEX application and then decide how to use JavaScript.

Mastering JavaScript will make your life as a Web application developer much easier, regardless of which specific development tool you choose to use. Spending time learning it will definitely be worth your while, and the Internet is filled with JavaScript tutorials that can greatly assist in the learning process.

APEX includes a built-in JavaScript library. As of version 3.x, this library is documented in the APEX User's Guide. You should use this documentation to familiarize yourself with that library.

```
http://download.oracle.com/docs/cd/E14373_01/apirefs.32/e13369/
javascript_api.htm#CDEEIGFH
```

Globalization and National Language Support (NLS) note:

JavaScript is a crucial element for APEX non-native supported language applications, especially in the RTL (Right-To-Left) environment. It's the only technology that allows us to adapt compound built-in APEX components to the NLS and RTL orientation environment. We will elaborate more on these issues, further in the book.

In the following sections I'll explain some specific issues pertaining to HTML, CSS, and JavaScript that I find useful and important to working effectively with APEX. I strongly believe that enhancing your skills and knowledge in these issues will give you a better understanding of how the APEX *Application Builder* is working and will allow you to develop better APEX applications right from the start.

HTML

We already know that the final product of the APEX Application Builder is an HTML code, so the importance of this **H**yper **T**ext **M**arkup **L**anguage (and its successor, the e**X**tensible version, XHTML) can't be overrated.

The DOM (Document Object Model)

Every element that we are placing on our application page is being translated by the APEX engine, into a combination of HTML, CSS, and in some cases, JavaScript code. As such, all the elements of the page are being arranged in a **DOM (Document Object Model)** structure—a **hierarchical**, **tree**-like model. The DOM standard, formalized by **W3C (World Wide Web Consortium)**, allows us to access and manipulate every node on the tree, whether by direct access or by walking up (or down) the tree.

The main building blocks of the DOM are the DOM objects. Every DOM object has a series of properties and methods, and it can include other objects and even a collection of objects (e.g. an array of all images or links on the page).

The two highest objects in the DOM hierarchy are the DOM **window** object and the DOM **document** object.

- DOM window—this object is located at the top of the DOM tree, and can be seen as representing our Web browser window.
- Dom document—this object is part of the DOM window object, and it represents our HTML document

Every HTML element is represented by a DOM object with its own attributes and methods. Every such object is represented by one or more nodes in the DOM tree.

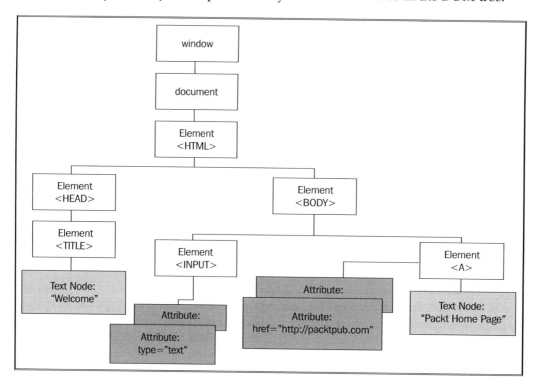

The DOM document object can include other DOM objects, which represent various HTML tags—e.g. `<A>`, `<INPUT>`, `<BUTTON>`, `<IMG>`, etc. Each such DOM object has a set of attributes and methods according to its type and functionality.

One of the most useful attributes of the DOM elements is the **ID** attribute, which uniquely identifies the element, within the document object. Other attributes allow us to name the element (a non-unique attribute), read or set its value, status (e.g. disabled, read-only, checked, etc.), and appearance (e.g. style, class etc.).

DOM walking

The DOM is a hierarchical, tree-like model. As such, by using hierarchical terms like parents, children, and siblings we can walk the DOM up and down, reaching every node on the tree even if it does not contain a means of identifications, such as ID or name. This allows us more direct access. Using some of the specific DOM walking node object properties, such as **parentNode, firstChild, lastChild, nextSibling,** or **previousSibling,** can bring us anywhere we need on the DOM.

DOM methods

The DOM also includes several built-in methods for easy access to the DOM elements. In APEX we are usually using these methods in JavaScript code. The following are the most common built-in DOM methods that we will be using:

- `document.getElemetById('id')`: This method will return the element uniquely identified by the `id` parameter. For example, `document.getElementById('P1_NAME')` will return the DOM element with the ID attributes of `P1_NAME`.

- `document.getElementsByTagName('tag_name')`: This method will return an **array** of elements defined by the same HTML tag. For example, `document.getElementsByTagName('select')` will return an array with all the `<select>` elements in the HTML document.

- `document.getElementsByName('HTML_name')`: This method will return an **array** of elements sharing the same HTML name. For example, `document.getElementsByTagName('f01')` will return an array with all the elements with an HTML name of `f01`.

Bear in mind:
- The names of the DOM methods are case sensitive.
- The APEX built-in JavaScript library includes a function, `$x(pId)` or `html_GetElement(pId)`, which simplifies the use of the `document.getElementById()` method. I'll elaborate more in the JavaScript section.
- The `document.getElemetsByTagName()` and `document.getElementsByName()` methods are **always** returning an **array**, even if it includes only one member.

Specific DOM objects can also have methods according to their type and functionality. For example, the window object has a method called `print()` which allows us to call the local OS (Operating System) print services, or the `open()` and `close()` methods, which allow us to open a popup window and in turn, close it. Most of the DOM objects that represent HTML page elements have a method called `focus()` which allows us to focus the application cursor on the element. Some of them have functionality dependent methods like `click()` for the DOM checkbox item, which emulates a mouse click on that item. You should familiarize yourself with all these methods as they can make some of your tasks easier.

DOM events

HTML 4.0 introduced the option of including HTML event handlers as part of the DOM elements. The standard defines a set of events that we can use as attributes of the various HTML tags. The events are fired in the Web browser as a result of the actions performed on the document such as moving the mouse cursor around, using the keyboard, changing the value of an element, navigating across the page, etc. We can trap these events and use them to invoke snippets of code, like JavaScript, in the Web browser.

The following is a list of some common events that we will be using while working with APEX:

- `onload`: This event allow us to fire a JavaScript code just after the page has been loaded into the browser and the construction of the DOM has finished.

- `onfocus, onblur`: These events allow us to associate our code with the focus status of the item—the item just got focused, or the focus was just shifted to another page element—and fire our code accordingly.

- `onchange`: This event allow us to fire our code if the value of the element has been changed.

- `onmouseover` and `onmouseout`: These events allow us to fire our code based on the position of the mouse cursor in relation to the object that initiated the event. For example, open a drop-down menu list when the cursor is parking on the menu element, and close it when the cursor leaves the element.

 The correct syntax for the HTML events is **all in lower-case** and **NOT** like onLoad, onChange, etc.

The APEX context

As we'll see in the next chapter, APEX provides us with basic **Themes**, a collection of HTML templates that include basic layout options for key elements on the application pages such as layout regions on the page, forms and reports regions, labels, lists, etc. The HTML code in these templates is easily accessible and can be modified to meet our needs.

The APEX Application Builder, as a default behavior, sets a unique ID to every application page item we define. This ID is actually the name of the item in the Application Builder. It also groups items with a common denominator, e.g. items on the same table column, or all the options of a checkbox item, under the same HTML name attribute. This allows us easy direct access to these items. In addition, the wizards and properties sheets of the Application Builder allow us to use, and define, specific HTML attributes and events per application page (e.g. the onload event) or per specific items on the page (e.g. the onchange event).

The APEX built-in JavaScript library includes several functions that help us in manipulating the DOM objects, based on direct access or DOM walking. I'll elaborate on these in the JavaScript section.

A good understanding of the DOM, and how APEX is using it, is a key element in utilizing more advanced development options such as applying your own CSS to a specific application page component or manipulating it using JavaScript.

CSS

The **C**ascading **S**tyle **S**heets allow us to control the look and feel of our HTML pages and achieve the page design we want. The CSS language allows us to set or change the format, style, position, and other visual properties of the HTML page elements. Combined with JavaScript, it allows us to do that dynamically at run-time, even after the DOM is fully constructed.

The CSS standard is relatively new and is not being implemented to the same level, or in the same manner, across the various Web browser versions. When we are talking about different display results of the same HTML code across various Web browsers, it is usually because there are different ways of supporting (or not supporting) and implementing the CSS standard. We have to bear this in mind and always check if the CSS code we are using is supported in our target client's environment. Sometimes we have to add specific CSS code for a specific Web browser, most notably for MS Internet Explorer. We should always favor using common, supported CSS code as it will make our support and maintenance efforts easier.

The cascading effect

The cascading effect of the style sheets is responsible for the high flexibility and fine-tuning we can achieve using CSS. It means that we can have more than just one CSS resource for our HTML page, and each CSS resource can include contradictable styling instructions for the same HTML element. The client, in our case the Web browser, must calculate, at run-time, the precedence of all the styling instructions pertaining to the same HTML element and determine which one to apply. The style with the highest precedence is not always obvious, or easy to calculate, because of all the rules involved in these calculations. There are elements of hierarchy and inheritance, loading order, inline or external code, and other factors that can influence the style precedence. At large, we can say that the order in which the CSS resources are being loaded into the page is very important (the last one to be loaded has a higher precedence over the previously loaded ones). Inline code takes precedence over external code and, specifically, more targeted styling instructions have precedence over more general or inherited ones. On top of all that, we have the option of setting the highest precedence style ourselves in case we need to ensure that a specific style will be the one to be applied.

The style sheets

We are applying the CSS styles to the HTML elements on the page. Each style has two components. The first is the CSS **selector**, which identifies and sets the applied scope of the style—which HTML elements will be affected by this style. The second CSS style component includes the style **properties**—how the HTML element will be styled. We are using the following syntax to define a CSS style:

```
selector [, selector] {
    property: value;
    . . .
    property: value;
}
```

 The new-lines are not mandatory; however, they make the CSS code more readable.

The CSS code can be defined **inline**, as part of the HTML page or element code using the `<style>` tag, or as an **external** file, which the HTML page loads as part of the page rendering process using the `<link>` tag.

On a page level, we define the `<style>` tag in the `<head>` section of the HTML code. The syntax should be similar to the following:

```
<head>
    .  .  .
<style type="text/css">
selector [, selector] {
    property: value;
        .  .  .
    property: value;
}
    .  .  .
</style>
    .  .  .
</head>
```

On the HTML element level we don't have to use the selector component (it's implied by association), so the style becomes just another attribute of the HTML element. For example:

```
<tag_name style="property: value; ... ;property: value;" ... >
```

In order to load an external CSS file, we are using the `<link>` tag as part of the HTML `<head>` section. Let's say we have an external CSS file called `myCSS.css`. We can load it into the HTML page by using the following code:

```
<head>
    .  .  .
<link rel="stylesheet" type="text/css" href="myCSS.css" />
    .  .  .
</head>
```

 Inside an external CSS file we are using the same basic style syntax, without the `<style>` tag.

Using an external CSS file allows us to centralize the control over the entire application's look and feel. Instead of writing the same styling code repeatedly for the various application pages, we can maintain a single file with all the styling instructions we need. Besides saving us a lot of code typing, maintaining a single source of styling instructions ensures a unified look and feel, throughout the application.

CSS properties

The CSS properties are actually the styling instructions for the HTML elements. These properties deal with visual aspects of the HTML elements such as borders, tables, text, fonts, colors, background, etc. The CSS properties can determine whether the element will be on display or remain hidden; the layout nature of the element, e.g. an inline element or a block one; its relative or absolute positioning on the page; and much more.

The values of the CSS properties can include absolute values, e.g. "12px", or relative values, e.g. "50%". They can include numeric values or string values like **thin** or **red**. Each value, according to its nature, can include measurement units like **px** for screen pixels; **pt** for print points; **em** for relative fonts; or **in, mm**, and **cm** for absolute distance measurements.

CSS selectors

The CSS selector component defines the target and scope of the CSS properties that we want to apply. There are several options to define the CSS selectors, varying from a very general target and scope, to a very specific one. The following is a description of some of the common CSS types of selectors we can use:

HTML tags selectors:

As we are applying the CSS to HTML elements, it only makes sense to use HTML tags as CSS selectors. Using HTML tags as a CSS selector means that all the HTML elements of this tag on the page will be styled in the same way, using the CSS properties. For example (using external CSS file syntax):

```
p {
    font-family: Times New Roman;
    font-size: 12px;
    color: #000000;  /* Black */
    text-align: left
}
```

This style will be applied to all the paragraphs on the HTML page and style the content to use a black, 12 px, Times New Roman font with the text aligned to the left.

Pseudo-class selectors:

The HTML tag <a> has four displayed options: default **link** display, **visited** link, **hover** state, and **active** state. The CSS pseudo-class selectors allow us to define different styles for the different link statuses:

```
a:link {color: #0000FF; }      /* Blue   */
a:visited {color: #A52A2A; } /* Brown */
a:hover {color: #00FFFF; }     /* Aqua   */
a:active {color: #FF0000; }  /* Red    */
```

These CSS styles will initially color all the links (<a> elements) on the HTML page in blue. Links that we visited will be colored brown, and while hovering over them, they will be colored in aqua. When the link becomes active (the moment the mouse is clicked on it), it will be red.

HTML ID selectors:

We can apply a CSS style to a specific HTML element identified by its ID. The CSS selector will include the ID prefix with the Number-sign (**#**) character.

Let's say we have the following HTML code snippet:

```
<p id="paragraph1">Welcome to the APEX world. In the next ...</p>
```

We can style this specific paragraph using the following CSS code (using external CSS file syntax):

```
#paragraph1 {
   font-size: 14px;
   color: Aqua;
}
```

Because the #paragraph1 style is more specific regarding the target and scope of the style than the general p style, it will take precedence over it and will be the chosen style to be applied to the paragraph using a font size of 14px, colored in Aqua. Because this style does not include any properties regarding the font-family or text-align, these properties, along with all the other relevant, but not specifically defined, properties will be inherited from other CSS styles higher in the CSS hierarchy.

 The *HTML tag selectors* and *HTML ID selectors* don't require any changes in the existing HTML code. They use existing elements and attributes.

Class selectors

The HTML tag selectors give us a very wide and repetitive scope of styling, while the ID selectors give us a narrow scope—a specific element to style. The class selectors give us a bit of both. They allow us to set classes of styles, which we can specifically apply to every HTML element we associate with them. The targeted elements don't have to be of the same HTML tag or be identified by any means. The same class can be attached to a `<p>`, `<div>`, or even an `<a>` element by becoming the `class` attribute of the HTML element.

We can freely define the name of the class, and in the CSS code it will be prefixed with a dot (.), e.g. `.chapterHeadline`, `.mainParagraph`, etc. Let's go back to our paragraph, but this time we will style it using a class (for this example, I'm using inline, page level, syntax):

```
<style type="text/css">
.bold12 {
  font-size: 12px;
  font-weight: bold;
}
</style>

<p class="bold12">Welcome to the APEX world. In the next ...</p>
```

This class will make the paragraph using the default font, but in 12px size, and bold typeface.

 Using CSS classes does require us to change the HTML code adding the *class* attribute to the HTML elements we want to style.

Compound (nested) class selectors:

The element we chose to style, using a CSS class, can contain other HTML elements. For example, a paragraph can include a link, like in the following example:

```
<p class="firstP">welcome to the Packt Publishing web site -
<a href="www.packtpub.com">www.packtpub.com</a></p>
```

The paragraph itself is being styled according to the `firstP` class. But what about the `<a>` element nested in the `<p>` element?

One option is to style this tag specifically by associating its style with the parent element class. The CSS style can look similar to the following:

```
a.firstP:link {color: #0000FF;}
a.firstP:visited {color: #A52A2A;}
```

For this CSS style to be applied, we need to change the HTML code to include the class attribute with the `<a>` element:

```
<p class="firstP">welcome to the Packt Publishing web site - <a
class="firstP" href="www.packtpub.com" > www.packtpub.com </a></p>
```

This CSS style is very targeted. What will happen if we have several links, or other HTML elements, nested in the parent element? Do we have to define the class to each and every one of them? We can widen the CSS style scope, regarding these nested HTML elements, by using contextual selectors.

Contextual selectors:

We can use the CSS selectors that we have already defined in a specific CSS context. The CSS context will set the initial affected scope, and the contextual selectors will be limited to this scope only. For example:

```
.firstP a:hover {color: orange;}
```

This CSS style will affect all the `<a>` elements within the `firstP` class. This type of selector simplifies the HTML code for us by allowing us to only define the class attribute for the parent element (in our example, the `<p>` element) without repeatedly doing the same for every `<a>` element it includes.

The !important keyword

As I mentioned before, the CSS style precedence calculation, taking into account all the cascading rules, can be very complicated at times. The CSS language helps us to set the highest precedence of a specific CSS property using the **!important** keyword. For example, the following style for `<h1>`

```
h1 {
   color: LightBlue !important;
}
```

will make sure that every `<h1>` element on the HTML page will be colored light blue, regardless of any other potential CSS styles with the same property but higher precedence. This is a very powerful option, but we need to use it very carefully and very wisely, otherwise we'll sterilize the cascading effect, which is one of the most important and powerful features of the CSS language.

The APEX angle

The APEX environment includes a central CSS library, which includes several external CSS files. These files control and style the look and feel of all the shared components in the APEX environment, both for the development tools and the developed applications. According to the APEX version and configuration that we are using, these files are stored on the local OS file system of the machine hosting the Oracle HTTP Server; or loaded into the Oracle XML DB server (as part of the Oracle database itself) if we are using the Embedded PL/SQL Gateway. More details on that can be found in the installation and configuration appendix.

In addition to the central CSS library, each APEX *Theme* also includes a specific CSS file. This file is responsible for the unique look and feel of the *Theme*. The name of this CSS file is version-dependent, for APEX v3.1/3.2, it's called `theme_3_1.css`.

Where to store our external CSS file?

If we are using our own external CSS file, we have two major options for storing it. The first is to store it on the local OS file system of the machine hosting the **Oracle HTTP Server (OHS)**, alongside the CSS files that came with APEX. The other option is to store it on the database, as a static file, using the APEX dedicated built-in upload mechanism. Until version 3.1, the best option, performance wise, was to store the CSS files on the OS file system because that was the only way the Web browser could have cached them. Database-stored CSS files had to be repeatedly downloaded to every application page. The use of a new set of HTTP Header parameters, allowing the Web browser to also cache database-stored CSS files (along with other static files we can upload to the database), was introduced in version 3.1. This option can dramatically improve the loading time of pages using database-stored static files, and it's very important if we are working on a hosted environment where we don't always get access to the OS.

 In order to utilize the caching option of database-stored static files we need to add some new parameters to the DAD we are using, for both the Oracle HTTP server or the Embedded PL/SQL Gateway. We'll discuss that in the APEX installation appendix.

Personally, if both options are available I believe that using the local OS file system to store our static files is the best option.

How to load our CSS code?

If we are going to use an external CSS file we need to load it into every page of our application. In APEX, the best way of doing so is by using the **page template**. We already know that we should use the `<link>` tag, and that the tag should be part of the HTML `<head>` element. Hence, in the *page template* we'll add the proper `<link>` into the *Header* section.

> **Attention:**
> As we want our CSS file to take precedence over the APEX Theme CSS file we must place our `<link>` tag **after** the `<link>` of the theme CSS file.

If we are going to use an inline CSS code, with the `<style>` tag, we should also locate it in the `<head>` element of the page. However, in this case, as we are dealing with a specific page code we'll be using the *HTML Header* field in the *Page* section of the *Page Rendering* column, in the *Page Definition* page of our application.

> Sounds complicated? All these terms and locations (e.g. page template, HTML Header field, etc.) will become very clear once we start developing with the APEX Application Builder.

Globalization and NLS

CSS is a crucial component in adding RTL (Right-To-Left) support to our APEX applications. The initial change of page orientation is being done through a CSS property - **direction** - of the `<body>` element. If we are using an external CSS file, we can add this style into it. If not, we can add it as inline code to all the page templates of the application.

Because of the cascading effect we can use a specific style for the RTL support without changing any other CSS properties associated with the `<body>` element:

```
body { direction: rtl;}
```

JavaScript

JavaScript is an **Object-Oriented Programming (OOP)** language, which runs in the Web browser.

JavaScript is not Java, despite the similar names. While Java can be a client-side and server-side programming language, running on the Oracle database, using the Oracle JVM, and utilizing a Java stored procedures, JavaScript is a client-side, interpreted script language only. It is running in the Web browser and has access only to some local resources, mainly the current active DOM (parent window can also access its popup windows DOM and a popup window can access its parent window DOM). Server-side resources, like PL/SQL blocks (anonymous or others) can't fire JavaScript code. However, the other direction, which is the JavaScript code triggering a server side processes, is possible, and this direction is one of the reasons JavaScript is so important and useful. JavaScript is the 'J' component in AJAX—a technology that can dramatically improve the way our applications function, and enhance the user experience. We will talk about AJAX later in the book, but in a nutshell AJAX technology allows us access to server-side resources without submitting the page.

JavaScript allows us to manipulate the DOM of our HTML page dynamically and at runtime. We can use JavaScript as part of the HTML page rendering process by using the `<script>` tag. With the **src** attribute of `<script>` we can also load an external JavaScript file into the page. We can use the `onload` event to trigger JavaScript code right after the Web browser has finished building the initial DOM and all the HTML page components have been loaded. At runtime we can use the various HTML events to trigger JavaScript code, and with the `href` attribute of the `<a>` element by using the keyword **javascript:**.

During runtime, JavaScript can also help us control the page flow by allowing us to conditionally branch to different locations on the current page or on other pages.

JavaScript features

JavaScript is an interpreted script language, which means its code is being parsed at runtime by the JavaScript engine, which is part of the Web browser software. The following is a list of features that we should be familiar with, and be aware of, while working with JavaScript.

Object-Oriented

JavaScript is an object-oriented programming language, although not all the features of an object-oriented environment are fully implemented by it. JavaScript includes some built-in objects with specific properties and methods, and it allows us to define our own objects with properties and methods.

All the pre-defined data types that JavaScript uses, such as **String, Number, Date,** and **Array**, are actually JavaScript objects, with pre-defined properties and methods to deal with these properties. When we talk about JavaScript helping us the to manipulate the DOM, we are actually referring to JavaScript DOM objects which represent the HTML elements and the DOM nodes.

JavaScript uses the keyword **new** to create a new instance of an object. The following will assign a **Date** object reference to the `newDate` variable:

```
newDate = new Date();
```

As a novice, I always wondered what the difference between a function and a method is. A method is a function, that is associated to a specific object, and can operate on the properties of this object.

Case sensitive

JavaScript is case sensitive. It's important to remember this when dealing with variables and function names, both for the built-in functions and methods, and for the ones we are naming ourselves.

JavaScript names must begin with a letter or the _ (underscore) character. The naming convention is that variable names start with a lower case, while object names (like Date, String, etc.) start with a capital letter. We can use the case sensitive feature to create names that are more readable—'thisIsAnExample' is easier to understand than 'thisisanexample'. This technique of increasing readability is also known as 'camelCase' (because of the hump in the middle).

JavaScript variables

JavaScript variables do not have to be declared, however, it is considered 'good practice' to do so. We declare a JavaScript variable using the keyword **var**. As part of declaring the variable, we can also initialize its value.

The following are all legal JavaScript statements:

```
var x;
var y = 3;
z = 'Hello World';
```

JavaScript variables are not declared with a specific data type. The data type is derived from the value of the variable and its syntax. For example:

```
x = 3;
```

will set x to be a numeric variable while

```
x = '3';
```

will set x to be a string variable.

JavaScript arrays

JavaScript supports multi-dimensional arrays and includes some very powerful methods to deal with them. JavaScript uses square brackets [ ] for the array element index, starting with **zero**. `myArray[0]` will include the first element of the array, `myArray[1]` will include the second element, and so forth.

Some of the built-in DOM methods, e.g. `getElementsByTagName()`, return arrays as a result. Let's say we want to collect all the images on the HTML page. We can use the following within the JavaScript code:

```
var pageImages = document.getElementsByTagName('IMG');
```

The `pageImages` variable is actually a JavaScript array, containing object references to all the DOM nodes of type `<img>` on the HTML page. Now, we can loop through this array and print all the sources for the page images:

```
for (i=0; i < pageImages.length; i++) {
  document.write(pageImages[i].src + '<br />');
}
```

 We can use the **length** property of the JavaScript array object to get the number of elements the array includes. This property is automatically set and updated by the JavaScript engine.

JavaScript operators

JavaScript includes operators for arithmetic, assignment, comparison, and logical operations. You can find the full list of available operators in the JavaScript tutorial of the W3Schools site at `http://www.w3schools.com/js/default.asp`.

Because JavaScript variables' data types are determined by the variable content, using some of the operators requires special attention to the actual data types of the involved variables, and the data type of the results. Check the following snippet of HTML code and its results:

```
<body>
<h1>JavaScript Operators</h1>

<h3>x = 3;</h3>
<h3>y = '3';</h3>

<script type="text/javascript">
    var x = 3;
    var y = '3';
    var z;

    z = x + x;
    document.write('x + x = ' + z + '<br />');

    z = y + y;
    document.write('y + y = ' + z + '<br />');

    z = x + y;
    document.write('x + y = ' + z + '<br />');

    if (x == y) {
       document.write('x == y => True' + '<br />')
    } else {
       document.write('x == y => False' + '<br />')
    }

    if (x === y) {
       document.write('x === y => True' + '<br />')
    } else {
       document.write('x === y => False' + '<br />')
    }

</script>

</body>
```

JavaScript Operators

x = 3;

y = '3';

x + x = 6
y + y = 33
x + y = 33
x == y => True
x === y => False

As you can see, JavaScript can take the data type of the variable into account (e.g. the === operator) but can also perform some data type conversions, by default, like in the case of using the + operator on numeric and string variables. As the example shows, strings take precedence over numbers.

 If you want to be sure you are performing an arithmetic operation on your variables, especially if they originated from the DOM, you can use the JavaScript's built-in functions Number(), parseInt(), or parseFloat().

Blocks of code

JavaScript is a block-structured language. We can use blocks of code to arrange the code in logical units. We can condition the execution of these blocks and repeat them as much as we need. JavaScript uses the curly brackets { } to mark a block of code.

Conditional blocks of code:

JavaScript supports nested 'if ... else' and 'switch ...' statements:

```
if (condition1){
   Block of code 1;
} else
  if (condition2) {
     Block of code 2;
  } else {
   block of code 3;
  }
else {
  block of code 4;
}
switch (variable) {
  case 1:
     Block of code 1;
     break;
  case 2:
     Block of code 2;
     break;
   . . .
  Case n:
     Block of code n;
     break;
  default:
     Default block of code;
}
```

Repetitive (loop) blocks of code:

JavaScript supports several options of repetitive (loop) blocks of code:

```
for (initial loop index; loop condition; end of iteration code){

    Block of code;

}


while (condition) {

    Block of code;

}
```

Detailed examples of how to use these blocks of code will be available throughout the book.

JavaScript functions

As we saw in an earlier example about JavaScript operators, we can use JavaScript as an inline code, using the `<script>` tag. However, JavaScript also supports functions. We can define all the JavaScript functions we need as part of an inline code, however, we can also store them in an external file. We can load this file as part of the HTML rendering process, and by doing this, make all the JavaScript functions in it available to us in the HTML code.

```
function functionName (parm1,...,parmn){

    Block of code;

    return(variable);

}
```

The APEX angle

The APEX environment includes a JavaScript library, which includes several JavaScript files. These files contain JavaScript objects, methods, and functions for the APEX development environment itself and the developed applications. It also includes an AJAX framework, which allows us to utilize this advanced technology more easily, and makes it accessible even to inexperienced developers.

Similar to the APEX CSS files, JavaScript files are also stored, either as part of the OS file system of the Oracle HTTP server, or in the Oracle XML DB server if we are using the Embedded PL/SQL Gateway.

The APEX built-in page templates include loading statements for the basic JavaScript files, making them available on every page of the application. In version 3.x the basic JavaScript files being loaded are:

- `apex_ns_3_1.js`: includes APEX namespace objects, methods, and functions.
- `apex_3_1.js`: includes all the non-namespace objects, methods, and functions. This is the main JavaScript library for the developers and the one documented as part of the APEX APIs (starting with version 3.0).
- `apex_get_3_1.js`: includes the APEX AJAX framework infrastructure for the client-side.
- `apex_builder.js`: includes JavaScript resources for the APEX Application Builder environment.

As of version 3.x, the APEX JavaScript files are distributed in two formats. The first format is compressed files, and we load these files into our application pages to reduce their size (hence speeding up the loading time). The second is regular (text) JavaScript files which we can use for learning and debugging purposes.

Advanced Note:

The APEX engine automatically generates the loading statements of the basic JavaScript files as part of the #HEAD# substitution string. As of version 3.0, we can declaratively decide if we want to include the standard CSS and JavaScript files in our page. This can be very useful if we want to reduce the total size of the HTML pages, like in the case of developing for PDAs.

Where to store our external JavaScript file?

The same consideration we applied to the storage place of our external CSS files, is also applicable to our external JavaScript files.

How to load our external JavaScript file?

Similar to an external CSS file, we are going to use the APEX *page template* to load our external JavaScript file into every page of our application. We are going to use the `<script>` tag with the `src` property to specify the location of the JavaScript file. Assuming we are also using the APEX JavaScript directory to store our file, the loading statement can look similar to the following:

```
<script src="#IMAGE_PREFIX#javascript/myJS.js" type="text/javascript">
</script>
```

Although I believe that the preferred option of storing the external JavaScript file is on the HTTP server OS file system, sometimes (as in the case where we are using hosting services) we aren't allowed access to it. In these cases we can upload the JavaScript file into the database as a static file, using the dedicated APEX mechanism for that. When referencing such a file we should use a proper APEX built-in *substitution string* to note the location of the file. The loading statement should look similar to the following:

```
<script src="#WORKSPACE_IMAGES#myJS.js" type="text/javascript"></
script>
```

Bear in mind:

We will discuss APEX *substitution strings* later in the book. For now, just remember that although the *substitution string* mentions 'IMAGES', it also refers to static files like CSS and JavaScript files that were uploaded into the database.

Globalization and NLS

JavaScript is a crucial element in the APEX globalization and NLS, especially for non-native supported languages and Right-To-Left (RTL) oriented languages.

JavaScript is the only means we have to alter pre-defined APEX components such as built-in items, built-in system messages, etc. Not all of these built-in components can be easily translated using the APEX translation mechanism.

A notable example is the built-in **Shuttle** item. This is a compound item, which includes some images that act as the item controls. These images will not change their content if we change our page orientation. For example, an image of a right arrow pointing to the center of a Left-To-Right oriented page will remain a right arrow image in the Right-To-Left oriented version of the page, only this time, upon changing its layout position, it will point to the right border of the page and not to the center of it. This is not the functionality it was intended for. JavaScript is the only way we have to change the internal code of the item and put a left arrow image, with the correct functionality instead of the original image. A full example of using JavaScript in that manner will be part of a discussion about the APEX Shuttle item, in a chapter that will be dedicated to Right-To-Left support.

PL/SQL and JavaScript (advanced)

A PL/SQL block, running on the server-side, can't fire JavaScript code, but it can generate it using the PL/SQL Web Toolkit. We can use the functions of the toolkit within the APEX Application Builder as part of an On-Load PL/SQL process to generate a `<script>` tag containing a valid JavaScript code. According to the firing point of the On-Load PL/SQL process we are using, this code will be embedded into the application HTML page code generated by the APEX engine, in locations corresponding with the firing point. While the page will be loaded into the Web browser, this JavaScript code will be fired as an integral part of the page HTML code.

Don't be confused by the coincidence of the events. For inexperienced users, it might look as if the PL/SQL code is running the JavaScript code. It is not. The JavaScript code is being created on the server-side using PL/SQL, but it will only run on the client-side, when the page is loaded into the Web browser.

JavaScript and server-side resources (advanced)

Running on the client-side, JavaScript can only access items rendered on the page—rendered but not necessarily displayed-as JavaScript can access hidden items. It means that JavaScript doesn't have direct access to server-side resources such as the APEX application items or the APEX built-in global variables (e.g. APP_USER, APP_ID, etc.). In order to allow us easy access to some of the server-side resources while using JavaScript, the APEX engine automatically defines, on every application page, at least four hidden items, and sets their values to the corresponding server-side variables. The following is a list of the item's IDs and descriptions:

- pFlowId: The application ID number. Corresponds to the built-in substitution string APP_ID.
- pFlowStepId: The page ID. Corresponds to the built-in substitution string APP_PAGE_ID.
- pInstance: Session number. Corresponds to the built-in substitution string APP_SESSION (or SESSION).
- pRequest: The REQUEST value (if it was specifically set prior to branching to this page).

Advanced Note:

We can use the same technique to allow JavaScript to access other server-side APEX variables, and not necessarily the built-in ones, by using the substitution string &ITEM. notation. I'll use it as an example when I talk about substitution strings.

The APEX JavaScript API

As I mentioned at the beginning of this chapter, APEX includes a built-in JavaScript library, which is loaded automatically to every application page and includes a variety of objects, methods, and functions that can greatly assist us in utilizing the power of JavaScript, especially to the novice or the inexperienced JavaScript developers. As of version 3.0, the JavaScript API is documented in the APEX user's guide, which makes the use of this library even easier.

The following are examples of some of the most basic JavaScript functions in this library:

$x(pItemId)

This function is a smart shortcut to the DOM method `getElementById(pItemId)`. The smart part is that the `$x()` function will return `false` in case the `pItemId` element is not found on the page. That means we can use it in a condition. For example:

```
if ($x('P1_ITEM1')) {
    alert ($x('P1_ITEM1').value);
}
```

Advanced Tip:

There are times when we are not sure if a specific element has been rendered on the page (for example a conditioned item). Using the `$x()` function can allow us to avoid using the "try ... catch ..." JavaScript statement in order to avoid an error message. This will make our code simpler and readable.

$v(pItemId)

This function will return the value of the `pItemId` element.

```
var applicationId = $v('pFlowId');
```

`applicationId` will be set to the value of the running application ID.

$s(pItemId, pValue)

This function will set the value of the `pItemId` element to `pValue`.

```
$s('P1_ITEM2',$v('P1_ITEM1'));
```

The value of the item `P1_ITEM2` will be set to the value of the item `P1_ITEM1`.

$x_UpTill(pItemId, tagName, className)

This function has DOM walking capabilities. It will start from the `pItemId` node, and will walk up the DOM tree until the first node of type `tagName`, or until the first node with the `className` class.

```
var row = $x('P1_ITEM1','TR');
```

This will set the `row` variable to point to the `<tr>` node, which contains the `P1_ITEM1` element (item).

$x_Show(pItemId) , $x_Hide(pItemId)

These functions will show or hide the `pItemId` node.

```
if (flag) {
  $x_Show('P1_ITEM1');
Else {
  $x_Hide('P1_ITEM1')
}
```

If `flag` is true, the `P1_ITEM` node will be displayed on page, otherwise it will be hidden.

redirect (location)

This function will allow us to redirect to any valid URL. Later in the book, we'll get to know the APEX '**f?p**' URL notation. We can use the `redirect()` function to branch to anywhere in the application directly from JavaScript.

General Note:

Although the parameter name we are using, `pItemId`, includes the string 'Item', all the relevant functions will operate on any legal DOM ID and not just on APEX item nodes.

I'm repeating my strong recommendation of taking the time to become familiar with the content and the capabilities that the APEX JavaScript built-in library has to offer.

Summary

In this chapter, we reviewed some of the basic skills we should have in order to better utilize the Web development aspects of APEX. We talked about HTML, the DOM, CSS, and JavaScript. This chapter is not meant to teach you all these skills, but merely to give you a glimpse of what they are, what you can do with them, and what you should be looking for in order to continue learning and mastering these skills. One of the best resources to learn more about the issues in this chapter can be found in the following site `http://www.w3schools.com/default.asp`.

The APEX development environment is not equipped with dedicated tools for handling HTML, CSS, or JavaScript. It's important, and can be a major time saver, to find the proper tools for that. Both Firefox and MS IE have some very good add-ons to help us understand the DOM structure and effective CSS and JavaScript problems. Other commercial or free utilities can also assist you in your developmental efforts. Search the Internet, or ask around your friends or others who already have some experience in this field. The important thing is that you find the proper tools for you.

 This chapter includes some advanced sections and tips. If you are a novice, please don't be alarmed. You should return to this chapter after you have finished reading the book, when all the terms and concept of APEX will be clearer to you.

Now it's time to start focusing on APEX. That's in the next chapter.

3
APEX Basic Concepts

Anyone can open a cookbook, follow the recipes, and produce a decent meal. But only those who know their way around the kitchen can produce a great meal, and can do even better by improving the current recipe, or even inventing a new one. So, before getting to the APEX recipes, let's try to learn a bit more about the APEX kitchen.

Knowledge and understanding can be very powerful. If you become familiar with the APEX environment, and understand the APEX concepts and capabilities, you'll be able to design and develop better, faster, and more optimal applications utilizing advanced technologies to give your users better and improved UI experiences right from the start.

In the following sections we'll discuss some of the major APEX concepts and learn how they can help us in our developmental efforts. These concepts will include:

- Session state
- Substitution strings
- Shortcuts
- Themes and templates
- The f?p URL notation
- APEX multi-lingual support

Later in the book, when we discuss specific tasks in the APEX environment, then we'll use these concepts with more detailed examples.

Session state

APEX runs in the Web environment. The Web environment is, by nature, a **stateless** environment. In a traditional client-server environment, the client establishes a permanent connection with the server and can rely on the historical results of previous actions to perform the current ones, hence, a *stateful* environment. On the other hand the Web browser, for instance, only establishes a short-term connection with the Web server, for the duration of one specific request, and such as that request does not rely on any results of previous requests. Each such request must be independent of other requests, hence, a *stateless* environment. For example, if you are logged into legacy accounting software and ask it to print a report, the system can rely on the fact that you were already authenticated in the past (during the login process) and will not ask you to do that again. If your accounting software was running on the Web, it would not have been able to rely on past actions and their results, and you would have had to supply the result of authentication for each request to the Web server. One of the solutions to overcome the *stateless* nature of the Web is to use cookies in order to preserve some history about previous actions. APEX also uses cookies as part of the login process. However, APEX is taking a step forward in order to help us overcome the *stateless* nature of the Web—**Session state**. A built-in mechanism works automatically (although we can also use it manually) in the background of the application and saves some of the history pertaining to APEX page requests, thus mimicking some degree of a stateful environment.

The session state mechanism, which acts transparently, as far as the end user is concerned, saves all the values associated with an application page into an Oracle table, which is part of the APEX schema (the schema that holds all the APEX metadata tables). It does so at pre-determined firing points in the application page life cycle. We can use session state values to populate the current page items; it allows us access to item values on previously run application pages, and it allows us access to APEX items, from outside the APEX engine, e.g. in stored procedures.

Session state firing points

The session state has several firing points. Some of them are transparent to the user and are triggered by the APEX engine, others can be manually triggered by the developer.

The following are the major firing points and manual options to trigger the session state:

- **After submitting a page**: The main point of setting the session state is after submitting the page and before any of the other processes that might be involved in this phase (e.g. validation, computation, processes, and branching . We'll discuss all of them in dedicated chapters, further down the book).

- **Explicit value assignment to APEX items**: Using *Computations* and *Processes* to assign values to APEX items, either as part of the page rendering phase or its submit phase, also sets the session state.

- **Using the** `APEX_UTIL.SET_SESSION_STATE` **procedure**: This procedure is part of the APEX APIs. It allows the developer to save the session state of a specific item in the application while working with PL/SQL.

- **Using the built-in JavaScript method** `add()`: This method is part of the APEX AJAX framework. It allows the developer to set the session state of a specific item in the application while working with JavaScript.

- **Using the** `f?p` **notation**: The `f?p` URL notation, which we'll discuss later in this chapter, allows us to set the values of items while redirecting to a new application page.

 During the "after submit" firing point, **all** the active items associated with the page are saved into session state. All the other options allow us to only save a specific *item-value* pair into session state.

Session state and the application page life cycle

The APEX engine has two major procedures pertaining to the life cycle of an application page, which we'll explore in greater detail in the next chapter. For now, let's say that the first procedure—SHOW—deals with the **Page Rendering** phase of the page, while the second procedure—ACCEPT—deals with the post-submit operations in the **Page Processing** phase of the page. Session state is heavily involved in both these procedures, which include major firing points for the session state.

Session state and the page rendering phase

Session state has two modes of operation. The first is temporary by nature and the second is the persistence mode. The temporary mode is held in memory using PL/SQL arrays, and acts like uncommitted data. Values are displayed on the page and you can reference them, but only for the duration of the page view. If you are not submitting the page, and as such, committing the data, these values will not be saved. The session state temporary mode is only used during the *Page Rendering* phase.

While defining a page item we can decide how this item will be initialized. Later in the book (Chapter 5) we'll review the available options we have when defining an APEX item. In general, for every item, we can define a specific way of computing its initial value. This can include several stages, but for now, we'll refer to it as the item source.

The computed value, using the item source, is stored in the temporary session state and will be displayed on the page. However, the session state persistence mode can influence this value. One of the options we have while defining an APEX item is to decide that the item value will be determined under the condition of "**only when current value in session state is null**". This means that when the session state includes a value for the item, that value will take precedence over any other way of computing the item value (i.e. item source) and it will be used to set the initial value of the item.

The other option is to ignore the session state and use the item source "**always, replacing any existing value in session state**". This option gives precedence to a new value, which was computed during the SHOW procedure using the item source over any stored value in the session state. This value will be stored in the temporary session state, but for now, it will not update the persistence part of the session state. This can lead to a situation where the displayed value of the item is different from the value stored in the persistent session state.

The displayed value of an item can be different from the corresponding item value in the persistence session state. That includes a situation where the displayed value will be null and the persistence session state will include non-null value. This is a perfectly valid situation.

Using computations in the page rendering phase

The Page Rendering phase, as we'll see in the next chapter, also includes options for using *Computations*. We'll discuss this APEX component later in the book, but for now, let's say that *Computations* allow us to use a wizard-driven set of options for assigning values to APEX items, without necessarily writing actual code, either at the application or the page level. *Computations* will **always** set the session state for the specific items being computed.

Although Computations will always set the session state, the computed value will not necessarily be displayed on the page. If we chose the option of "**always, replacing any existing value in session state**", the displayed value will be the one that was computed using the item source. This is another example of where the displayed item value will not be equal to the corresponding session state value.

Using processes in the page rendering phase

Processes are also APEX components that allow us to define specific APEX actions by simply choosing from wizards-driven lists of options, or by manually coding snippets of PL/SQL code in the form of PL/SQL anonymous blocks.

Within the PL/SQL anonymous blocks we can reference every APEX item by using its name and the bind variable notation. For example, if we have an item called P1_ITEM1, then we can reference it in the code using :P1_ITEM1. If we specifically assign a value to this item, like in the following code, then this value will be set in the persistence session state:

```
:P1_ITEM1 := 100;
```

Using bind variable notation allows us to reference values of page items in the temporary mode of session state. If we set a page item to a default value, then this value will be available to us during the *Page Rendering* phase using the item name with bind variable notation.

Another way of specifically assigning item value, and by doing that, setting it in session state, includes the use of the SELECT ... INTO statement. If we are using an APEX item in the INTO clause, its value will be set in the persistence session state.

Lastly, using APEX item as an OUT parameter in a PL/SQL procedure will also set its value in session state.

Special session state processes

The **Processes** section includes a special sub-section named **Session State**. This sub-section includes several declarative options to deal with various aspects of the persistence session state, mainly to clear session state for specific items, pages, or even the entire application.

The **Session State** sub-section also includes some options to maintain APEX **Preferences**. Preferences is a built-in APEX persistent repository, which holds pairs of name-value parameters that we can set/use in the APEX application. Unlike session state, which persists for the duration of a single user APEX session, the data in the Preferences repository is saved on the APEX metadata tables and as such, can persist across APEX sessions. User preference will remain the same across all the APEX sessions of the user until specifically changed.

Session state and the page processing phase

The *Page Processing* phase includes the most important firing point for session state. In this phase, we are only populating the persistence mode of session state.

Before the APEX engine starts processing the page using the ACCEPT procedure, it saves all the values of all the active items on the page into session state. This action comes before any other APEX actions pertaining to the *Page Processing* phase. In the current context, saving session state comes before *Validation*. We'll discuss *Validations* later in the book, but for now, let's say that the *Validation* section allows us to check the validity of the submitted data prior to any further actions with it. In case of a validation error—the data doesn't meet the conditions we set for it—the APEX engine will issue a proper error message and will return us to the original page, allowing us to correct the problem. The APEX engine uses session state values to re-populate the page with the original data prior to submitting the page.

 This description of using the session state in case of validation errors is correct for regular forms only. For more complex forms, such as updatable reports (also known as Tabular Forms), session state is not used.

Computations and processes in the page processing phase

The assignment of explicit values during *Computations* and *Processes* in the *Page Processes* phase also updates the session state, just like in the *Page Rendering* phase.

Manually saving to session state

The session state firing points we reviewed so far are triggered automatically, and transparently, by the APEX engine. In addition to these firing points, the APEX engine allows us to manually save individual pairs of *item-value* into session state.

Using the APEX_UTIL.SET_SESSION_STATE API procedure

This procedure is part of an APEX built-in package that we can access using the APEX_UTIL synonym. The procedure is defined as follows:

```
APEX_UTIL.SET_SESSION_STATE (
   p_name IN VARCHAR2 DEFAULT NULL,
   p_value IN VARCHAR2 DEFAULT NULL
);
```

where p_name is the name of any APEX item in the application or page level.

As you can see from the definition of this procedure, the values in session state are not being saved according to the data type of the items, but as strings. The column of the session state table, which holds the session state values, is actually a CLOB column.

The main reason to use this API is when we want to update session state as a result of data manipulation in stored procedures. Another reason can be when popup pages, where we want to rely on values from the parent page prior to submitting it.

Session state and AJAX

Session state is a server-side process and, as we mentioned before, its main firing point is when we are submitting the page. However, sometimes we want to save the session state while on the client side, especially when using AJAX.

AJAX technology allows us to poll the server and manipulate the data on our page according to the received results. However, as we didn't submit the page, no values were saved into session state.

The APEX AJAX framework includes a built-in method called add(), which allows us to save an *item-value* pair into session state. We will explore the APEX AJAX framework in greater detail, in Chapter 17, but for now the following JavaScript function is an example of how we can save session state from the client side:

```
function setSessionStateValue(pItem, pValue) {
    var get = new htmldb_Get(null, $v('pFlowId'), null,0);
    get.add(pItem, pValue);
    get.get();

    get = null;
}
```

where pItem is the name of the item we want to set, and pValue is the value we want to set it to.

This version of the function is compatible with APEX V3.1.x and higher. In any earlier version, you should replace the use of $v('pFlowId') with $x('pFlowId').value or html_GetElement('pFlowId').value

Using the f?p URL notation

Later in this chapter we'll have a detailed discussion about the **f?p** URL notation. This special URL syntax also allows us to specify the items and the values that we want to set when redirecting to a new application page. These items will also be saved on *session state*.

Advanced note:

While using the f?p URL notations we can't set item values that include the colon character (:). One of the options to overcome this limitation is to use the add() method, as was described in the previous section. Another option is to replace the colon character with another character prior to the redirection to the target page, and on that page, revert it to the original colon character. Bear in mind though that the value which will be saved in the *session state,* will include the replaced character and not the original colon character. We'll see an example of that in the f?p section, later in the chapter.

The f?p section will show us that this syntax can also allow us to clear portions of session state, starting with a single item on the page and ending with the entire application session state.

Referencing persistence session state

As we saw, we can reference the values of the temporary mode *session state* in the *Page Rendering* phase using the bind variable notation. We can use the bind variable notation to also access the values in the persistent session state. Moreover, as we are talking about persistent values they will be available to us in all the other pages of the application. In the declarative sections of the APEX *Application Builder,* we can simply reference them by their name. In SQL or PL/SQL we can use the item name with the bind variable notation.

For the sake of simplicity and clarity, we will use the term *session state* from now on to reference the session state persistence mode.

APEX includes two built-in PL/SQL functions that allow us access to session state values. The v('item') function will return the session state value of the item, using the VARCHAR2 data type. The nv('item') function will do the same, returning the value as a NUMBER data type.

Session state and stored procedures

The APEX engine renders the application page in real-time, based on all the meta-data defined for the page while it was created. At rendering time, all the session state values are available to the APEX engine and it can use them while running any PL/SQL code.

Stored procedures, on the other hand, are being stored in the database in a compiled mode (which is one of the reasons to use them—better performance). At compile time, and outside the APEX engine, we don't have any access to session state values mainly because they have not been created yet. In order to reference session state values from within a stored procedure, we must use the v() or nv() functions. At runtime, these functions will retrieve the session state values for the stored procedure to use.

Security Note:

The v() and nv() functions will only work in an APEX context. Although it is possible to create an APEX context outside the APEX environment, you must have a proper login and password on the database level for the schema associated with the APEX application. This technique is outside the scope of this book. In our context, the v() and nv() functions will work properly as long as they are being called from the APEX environment—the *Application Builder*, the *SQL Workshop*, or an APEX application.

Using the v() and nv() functions wisely

The v() and nv() functions are also available to us within the PL/SQL snippets of code that we are creating in the APEX *Application Builder*. The following SQL query (which can be used as a report source) will give us the details of the last hired employee(s), in a department of our choosing. In the example, we are using a page item called P1_DEPTNO, which holds the department number we are using as a filter to the report.

```
select *
from emp t
where t.deptno = v('P1_DEPTNO')
  and  t.hiredate = (select max(hiredate) hiredate
                     from emp t1
                     where deptno = v('P1_DEPTNO'))
```

The $v('P1\_DEPTNO')$ function will fetch the session state value of the item, and it will be used in the evaluation of the WHERE clause and in the sub-query. However, the $v()$ function will be called for every row in the EMP table. The demo EMP table only includes a few rows, but in the real world, a table can contain many thousands of rows. Calling the $v()$ function many times can add a considerable overhead to the performance time of the query.

If we are using this code within the APEX *Application Builder*, where session state values are available to us by using bind variable notations, wiser and faster code will look like the following:

```
select *
from emp t
where t.deptno = :P1_DEPTNO
and t.hiredate = (select max(hiredate) hiredate
                    from emp t1
                    where deptno = :P1_DEPTNO)
```

All we did was replace the call to the $v()$ function with a bind variable. This is a simple change, that saves us the overhead of repeating calls to a function.

But what about using a query as part of a stored procedure or a function where session state values are only accessible through the $v()$ and $nv()$ functions?

Let's change our query to the following:

```
select *
from emp
where instr(hr.last_hired('P1_DEPTNO'),to_char(empno)) > 0
```

We are using a function called last_hired() that was defined in a package called hr. The function takes the name of our filter item as a parameter and returns a comma delimited string of the last hired employee(s) in the chosen department. Please review the following function code:

```
function last_hired(p_deptno_item in varchar2) return varchar2 is
  l_empno   varchar2(100) := '';
  l_deptno number;
BEGIN
  l_deptno := nv(p_deptno_item);

  for rec in (select empno
                from emp t
               where t.deptno = l_deptno
                 and t.hiredate = (select max(hiredate) hiredate
                                     from emp t1
                                    where t1.deptno = l_deptno)) loop
```

```
    if l_empno is null then
      l_empno := to_char(rec.empno);
    else
      l_empno := l_empno || ','||to_char(rec.empno);
    end if;
  end loop;

  return l_empno;

END last_hired;
```

In this function, we are using a local variable, `l_deptno`, to hold the session state value, which was retrieved using the `nv()` function. We can use this local variable in the same manner that we used the bind variables in the inline query. In this way, the unavoidable `nv()` will be called only once.

> The use of any function, `last_hired()` in our example, as part of a
> WHERE clause, is not recommended because the function is called for
> every row in the table. Whenever possible it should be avoided. I only
> chose this example for its simplicity. The point is, that even if we must use
> the `v()` or `nv()` functions in stored procedures or functions, we should
> do it smartly by minimizing the number of calls to these functions.

Session state scope and persistence

Session state data is available to us during the **APEX session** in which it was saved.

An APEX session is created with every request sent from the Web browser to the server if a valid APEX session doesn't exist. The APEX engine checks if it can use an already existing and viable APEX session to serve the coming request. If the answer is positive, like in the case where the request includes correct information about an active APEX session, then it will use the existing session. If not, then a new session will be created; it will be assigned a unique session ID, and according to the security features of the application, the user will be asked to authenticate (i.e. perform a login) or will be granted access to the application (e.g. in the case of a public application).

> An APEX session is not created only as a result of a successful login. An
> APEX session is created for the login page itself, prior to any knowledge
> of the results of the login process. An APEX session is also created for
> public applications where no login process is performed.

An APEX session is a logical unit of time, which can last as long as the user sends requests that contain a valid session ID. In a typical secured application, an APEX session can last from the login process until the logout process, or until some idle time, which we can determine, has passed. The APEX engine periodically runs a purge procedure, which purges non-active APEX sessions, older than a time frame that the APEX admin user can set. The default time frame is '**1 Day**'. The APEX Admin user can also purge session state information manually, using the Manage Services reports and tasks.

Advanced Note:

APEX sessions have nothing to do with the database sessions. The HTTP server and the mod_plsql module (or the equivalents in the Embedded PL/SQL Gateway) handle those. Database sessions in the APEX environment are very short and last only for the duration of a single request from the HTTP server to the database. During one APEX session you might use numerous database sessions, and there is no way you can force the system to use the same database session throughout the same APEX session. That is the reason why we can't use global package variables in our APEX PL/SQL code, which have the lifespan of a single database session. This limitation makes session state even more important and useful.

Reviewing session state from the application builder

While working in the *Application Builder* environment, the APEX Engine attached a special developer toolbar to every page of the application we are running.

| Home | Application 250 | Edit Page 5 | Create | Session | Activity | Debug | Show Edit Links |

Clicking on the **Session** box will open a popup window, which allows us to see the current session state of the current page we are working on, and also the entire session state for the current APEX session. These values here are part of the persistent session state, and as such, might be different from the displayed value of the corresponding items.

The APEX Admin user can gain access to session state information pertaining to older (non-active) APEX sessions that have not been purged by the APEX engine using the Manage Services reports.

Substitution strings

Substitution strings are part of an internal APEX engine mechanism, which allows us to use pre-defined strings, and substitute them with their value, as part of the page rendering process.

As substitution strings are part of an internal mechanism, we can only use them within the *Application Builder*. We can't use substitution strings as part of an external JavaScript file or PL/SQL stored procedures/functions.

The *Application Builder* supports three types of substitution strings: APEX engine built-in substitution strings, application substitution strings, and the application or page items.

 Substitution strings must be named using CAPITAL LETTERS only. In any other notation, the APEX engine will treat them as regular strings.

APEX engine built-in substitution strings

The APEX engine includes a series of built-in substitution strings. Some of them contain data, like a regular variable, and some of them include pre-defined snippets of HTML code usually used in **templates** (which we'll discuss later in the chapter).

Some of the *substitution strings* are available to us throughout the *Application Builder*, while some of them are only available to use within certain templates. Other substitution strings are only available in certain **page regions**, like the footer of a report.

 page region is an application page logical container that supports specific functionalities. We'll discuss page regions in the next chapter.

While generating the application page HTML code, the APEX engine scans the relevant metadata, e.g. templates, region sources, headers, and footers of the application page, etc. Each time it encounters a substitution string, it replaces it with its value—data or code. This means that the content of the substitution string must be known at the time when the APEX engine starts the page rendering process.

Substitution strings that contain data

Some of the substitution strings represent documented global APEX variables. These substitution strings are available to us throughout the *Application Builder*. The following table includes some very useful and popular substitution strings that contain data:

Global APEX variable	Substitution string	Description
apex_application.g_user	APP_USER	The name of the current application user.
apex_application.g_flow_id	APP_ID	The current application ID.
apex_application.g_flow_step_id	APP_PAGE_ID	The current page ID.
apex_application.g_flow_owner	OWNER	The owner of the parsing schema.
apex_application.g_request	REQUEST	Special APEX variable, which we'll discuss when we review APEX buttons.

The following table includes some substitution strings that are available to us in templates or page regions:

Substitution string	Available in	Description
REGION_STATIC_ID	Region template	A region static ID, if one was assigned. Otherwise it will include the internal region ID.
TIMING	Footer of report region	The time it took the APEX engine to render the region.
ROWS_FETCHED	Footer of report region	Number of rows (records) that were fetched by the APEX report engine.
CURRENT_ITEM_NAME	Label template	The current page item name that the label is for.
CURRENT_ITEM_ID	Label template	The current page item internal ID (Its primary key in APEX metadata tables).

Whenever some special substitution strings are available to us only in specific locations within the *Application Builder*, it will inform us about it through part of the *Application Builder* page we are working on, or through the help window of a specific field that can hold such substitution strings.

The following is an example of a substitution string informative section as part of a definition page for label template:

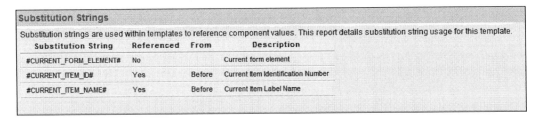

The following is an example of a help window for a field that can include substitution strings. In this case, the **Region Footer** field of a report region:

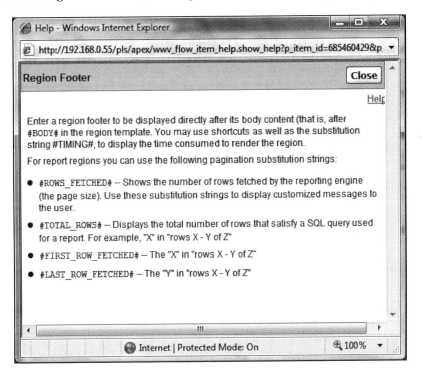

Substitution strings that contain HTML code

Some of the substitution strings contain pre-defined HTML code. These substitution strings are being used mostly with templates.

In some cases, the APEX engine determines the content of the substitution string and we can't change it. For example, the substitution string HEAD is used as part of the page template **Header** field. This substitution string includes the code that handles the loading of the APEX built-in JavaScript and CSS libraries. We'll see a detailed example of that in the templates section later in this chapter.

In other cases, the content of the substitution string reflects the configuration of the APEX environment. For example, the substitution string IMAGE_PREFIX contains the location of the **images** directory (which we'll discuss in the APEX installation and configuration appendix).

Another group of substitution strings reflects the content of various fields in the page definition page. The APEX engine uses the substitution strings to position the content of these page definition fields in the right places, in the HTML code of the application page. For example, the TITLE and ONLOAD substitution strings are respectively reflecting the content of the **Title** and **Page HTML Body Attribute** fields in the **Page** section of the *Page Definition* page. Another important example in this group is the REGION_STATIC_ID substitution string, which reflects the **Static ID** filed in the **Identification** section of the **Edit Region** page. We'll discuss this specific substitution string when we discuss page regions in Chapter 4.

Application substitution strings

We can define up to twenty application-specific substitution strings as part of the **Edit Application Definition** page.

Substitutions	
Substitution String	Substitution Value
NOT_IN_PAGE	:APP_PAGE_ID not in (2,3,5,28,52,57,66,68,70,75,101,1
NOT_NULL	Field must contains a avlue
DATE_VALIDATION	onchange="dateValidation(this);"
MY_VERSION	0.96.10

As we can see from the previous screenshot example, the application *substitution strings* can include snippets of PL/SQL or SQL code, such as in the case of NOT_IN_PAGE; a static string to include HTML tags and entities, such as in the case of NOT_NULL and MY_VERSION; or any other snippets of code, such as in the case of DATE_VALIDATION, which includes an onchange event code, which fires a JavaScript function.

> The application substitution strings can include references to APEX built-in substitution strings, like in the case of NOT_IN_PAGE, which include the built-in substitution string APP_PAGE_ID.

Application or page items

We will discuss application and page items in Chapter 5, but for now, you should remember that we could use any application or page item as if it was a substitution string, using the proper substitution strings reference notation, which we'll cover in the next section. The APEX engine will substitute the item substitution string with its session state value.

Using application or page items as substitution strings allows us to expose them to JavaScript code although they are not rendered on page. We'll see an example of it in the next section.

Referencing substitution strings

We can reference substitution strings in several ways, depending on their type and functionality. We can use the:

- #ITEM# notation
- &ITEM. notation
- bind variable notation
- APEX built-in v() and nv() functions

Using the #ITEM# notation

While working with templates, we are using the # (number sign) as both the prefix and suffix to the substitution string name (which, as was mentioned earlier, must be in capital letters). This notation is available only to template substitution strings.

The following screenshot is an example of using APEX engine built-in, pre-defined substitution strings in the **Header** field of a page template:

```
Definition

# Header

<!DOCTYPE html PUBLIC "-//W3C//DTD XHTML 1.0 Strict//EN"
    "http://www.w3.org/TR/xhtml1/DTD/xhtml1-strict.dtd">
<html lang="&BROWSER_LANGUAGE.">
<head>
<title>#TITLE#</title>
<script src="/i/javascript/testScript.js" type="text/javascript"></script>
<link rel="stylesheet" href="#IMAGE_PREFIX#themes/theme_10/theme_V3.css"
type="text/css" />
#HEAD#
</head>
<body #ONLOAD#>#FORM_OPEN#
```

Using the &ITEM. notation

For substitution strings that are not confined to templates, we can denote a substitution string by prefixing its name with ampersand sign (&) and suffixing it with a period (.), for example, &ITEM1.. The trailing dot is an integral part of the substitution string notation and should not be forgotten.

We mentioned that we could use application or page items as substitution strings. Let's say we have an application item called F250_STARTING_TIME, which contains a time reference that we want available throughout the application. Now we want to display an elapsed time on our application page using a JavaScript code. An elapsed time will be computed relative to the F250_STARTING_TIME, but this application item is not available on page. We can use a local JavaScript variable, and with the substitution string mechanism, assign it the value of the application item:

```
<script type="text/javascript">
var startingTime = "&F250_STARTING_TIME.";
</script>
```

We can also use the &ITEM. notation in templates, like in the case where we want to include the application substitution string MY_VERSION in a page template. The following is a snippet of HTML template code that will do that:

```
<div class="t5Copy"><!-- Copyright -->Demo Application (&MY_VERSION.)
copy;</div>
```

The &ITEM. notation is also a very simple and convenient way to reference substitution strings in the f?p URL syntax where we can't use bind variables because of the prefix colon character. We'll see examples of that use in the f?p section later in this chapter.

 You must pay special attention to the trailing period as part of the substitution string notation. Without the trailing period, the APEX engine will treat the substitution string as a regular string and will not perform the substitution.

Referencing substitution strings in SQL and PL/SQL code

We have several options for referencing substitution strings in SQL or PL/SQL code.

The bind variable notation

We can use the bind variable notations—prefix the substitution string name with a colon (:)—with substitution strings that represent APEX built-in global variables.

The following is an example of using the substitution string APP_ID in a PL/SQL code to retrieve data from the APEX dictionary:

```
select label,item_help_text
into :ITEM_LABEL, :ITEM_HELP
from apex_application_page_items
where application_id = :APP_ID
  AND  item_id = :ITEM1;
```

This code retrieves the label text and the help content of a specific page item. We will use it in a future example about using AJAX.

The APEX built-in v() and nv() functions

When applicable, we can reference the substitution string value by using the APEX v() or nv() functions. Let's say that we want to use the previous example code as part of a packaged function. In this case, it can be similar to the following code:

```
select label,item_help_text
into l_item_label, l_item_help
from apex_application_page_items
where application_id = nv('APP_ID')
  AND  item_id = v('ITEM1');
```

Learning Note:

The APEX User's Guide is available with the APEX distribution file, or online as part of the APEX home page on OTN at http://apex. oracle.com/. The Application Builder help windows contain much more information about the various substitution strings that we didn't mention here. You are encouraged to explore these resources as substitution strings can help you a lot in your daily development work.

Shortcuts

Shortcuts can be considered as a private case of substitution strings, or an extension of them. Shortcuts are included in the *Shared Components* module, and they are defined as part of the **User Interface** section.

Shortcuts act in a similar manner to substitution strings—special string notation, in this case, is an all capital letters string wrap in quotation mark ("), which is being replaced, by the APEX engine, with a content associated with it. However, shortcuts allow us a greater degree of flexibility than plain substitution strings with regard to their content options and its functionalities. When we are using substitution strings, the APEX engine replaces the substitution string with its exact content. While using shortcuts, the APEX engine can replace the shortcut with the products of its content (and not just the content itself) and it can also interact with the APEX built-in translation mechanism, which we'll address later in this chapter.

The following example will show the difference between using a substitution string and a shortcut. I defined a substitution string and a shortcut using the same name, CURRENT_DATE_EUR and the same content—a PL/SQL expression:

```
return to_char(sysdate,'DD/MM/YYYY HH24:MI:SS');
```

This expression returns the current date of the database, using European date notation. I placed them both in an appropriate page region, as seen in the following screenshot:

Source
Region Source
Current date: "CURRENT_DATE_EUR" `  ` Current date: &CURRENT_DATE_EUR.

The following is a screenshot of the result:

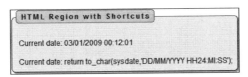

In the case of the shortcut, the displayed result is the product of processing the shortcut content—the result of the PL/SQL expression. And in the case of the substitution string, the displayed result is the actual content of the substitution string—the PL/SQL expression itself.

By utilizing this shortcuts feature, we can build a repository of shortcuts containing snippets of SQL or PL/SQL code, and re-use them throughout our application without the need to re-code repeating code segments.

Defining a shortcut

We define Shortcuts in the **User Interface** section of the *Shared Components* module. The following screenshot is from the **Edit Shortcuts** page:

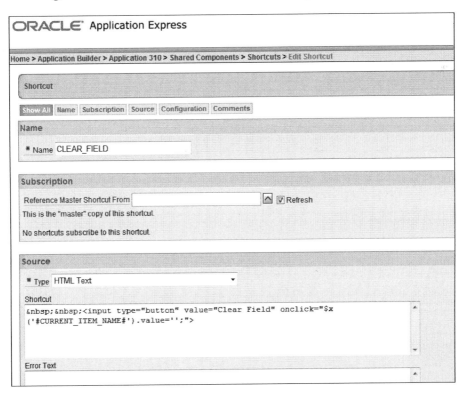

The name field

The **Name** field is mandatory. Shortcuts names must be in capital letters.

The type field

The **Type** field is also mandatory. The shortcuts mechanism supports seven types of shortcut content and functionality:

- **PL/SQL body function**: Using this type the APEX engine will substitute the shortcut with the return result of the function.

- **HTML text**: Using this type will give us similar results as using substitution strings.

- **HTML text with escaped special chars**: Using this type the APEX engine will escape special HTML characters, while doing the substitution.

- **Image**: Using this type the APEX engine will generate the appropriate HTML code for displaying an image. This type supports images stored on the **images** directory, or images that were uploaded into the database, using the APEX built-in images import wizard (part of the *Shared Component* module).

- **Text with JavaScript escaped single quotes**: This type allows us to use shortcuts with JavaScript code. The JavaScript code must be defined within the *Application Builder*, in the fields that support shortcuts (these will be reviewed in the next section).

- **Message**: This type of shortcuts interacts with the APEX built-in translation mechanism, allowing us to define our own repository of translatable messages. We'll discuss APEX multi-lingual capabilities in a dedicated chapter (Chapter 18).

- **Message with JavaScript escaped single quotes**: This type also interacts with the APEX built-in translation mechanism, allowing us to define translatable messages we can use in a JavaScript code.

The shortcut field

This field usually contains the shortcut content. As can be seen in the screenshot, this field is not marked as mandatory. The reason is that for the messages shortcuts types, this field remains empty. The content of the shortcut in these cases is determined in the APEX translation system (which we'll review later in this chapter).

In the screenshot we can see an example of an HTML text shortcut, in this case code for defining an HTML button:

```
  <input type="button" value="Clear Field"
onclick="$x('#CURRENT_ITEM_NAME#').value='';">
```

We can see that we can use substitution strings within the content of a shortcut. In Chapter 5, we'll use these shortcut, this shortcut as part of an item definition.

Shortcuts availability

Shortcuts are only available to us in specific locations within the *Application Builder*:

- **HTML Header field**: This field includes HTML code, which is part of the `<head>` tag. It can also include the `<script>` tag with JavaScript code that references shortcuts, text and messages.

- **Region templates**: Any region template can include shortcuts.

 Shortcuts are not available in all the other types of templates, including page templates.

- **The Source field of HTML text (with shortcuts) region**: This is a specific type of region (which we will discuss in the next chapter) that the APEX engine scans for shortcuts. In other types of HTML regions, shortcuts will be ignored and they will be displayed as regular quoted string.

- **Region Header and Footer fields**: shortcuts are available in the **Header** and **Footer** fields of any region.

- **Help Text field**: As part of the **Help** section in the *page definition* **Page** section (the page level help).

- **Item Label field**: We can use shortcuts in the **Label** field of the APEX items.

- **Item Pre/Post Element Text field**: These fields can also contain shortcuts.

- **Item Default value field**: This field can also contains shortcuts.

Themes and templates

Themes and **templates** are responsible for the look and feel of the APEX applications. They represent the declarative development approach of APEX. Instead of telling the *Application Builder* how to design and style our pages using HTML, CSS, and JavaScript code, which we don't necessarily master, we can only "declare" the theme we want to use and the APEX engine will do the rest for us. Moreover, the APEX implementation of themes and templates is not close to us (like a black box). The *Application Builder* allows us access to the themes and template mechanism, so that we can define new themes and templates, according to our needs, or amend existing ones. This is a very dynamic and flexible mechanism, which actually allows us to enjoy both worlds—a simple, straightforward, and declarative approach alongside almost full control over the generated code through the options of adding or changing existing components.

Themes and templates are included in the *Shared Components* module and they are defined as part of the **User Interface** section.

Themes

A **theme** is a collection of components that defines the look and feel of our application User Interface—the general layout of the page, the different colors of its elements, navigational aids, etc. Each theme includes templates—snippets of HTML, CSS, and JavaScript code—and specific CSS and GIF files and icons.

APEX 3.2 includes 20 built-in themes and until now, every major version release introduced new themes, so we can expect this number to grow. Each theme represents a different page layouts, styles, and colors. The following is a screenshot from the **Create Theme** wizard. The icons are small, and the book is not printed in color, but one can still get a first impression of the variety of options that we can choose from. Of course, the best way to really get familiar with all these themes is to create small demo applications using the various themes.

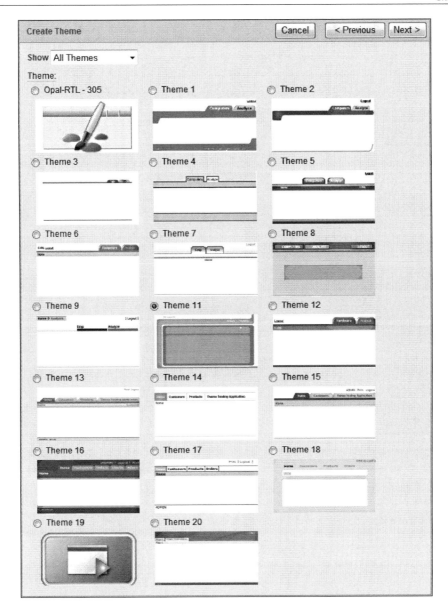

The first theme in this screenshot, **Opal-RTL-305**, is not a built-in theme. This is a theme that was developed to support Right-To-Left applications, a subject we'll discuss later in the book, but for now, it's a good example of the flexibility the *Application Builder* is giving us with regards to our application's look and feel.

Every theme includes a series of templates. As we'll see in the next section, these templates can include any HTML code we need. That means we can generate any look and feel we need, so we don't have to rely solely on the built-in themes. That can be very useful if, for example, we want our APEX applications to mimic other Web-based applications in our environment, such as the corporate standard look.

Templates

A template is a logical container unit that holds various snippets of HTML code. The HTML code can include any HTML/XHTML tag. So, by using APEX templates we can actually achieve any result that can be achieved using HTML in any other Web-based environment. Moreover, because the templates contain regular HTML code, we can easily define our own templates when the built-in ones are not satisfying our needs.

As templates are supposed to be generic, we are massively using substitution strings within their code. At runtime, the APEX engine substitutes them with their content, which is an exact and full HTML code. The combination of all the relevant templates gives us the final application page HTML code to be rendered by the client Web browser.

The templates are divided into nine functional groups. Each such group supports a specific functionality and page layout of the application page.

Page templates

The page templates are setting the main look and feel of the page and its layout options. Each page template includes several layout zones, represented by a built-in APEX engine substitution strings. While we are defining the various page components, we can choose in which layout zone we want to define them and they will be positioned on page accordingly.

The following is a screenshot of a page template layout, in this case, a **One Level Tabs** page template, from theme 5—Opal. Most page templates include the same layout zones:

- **Region position**: The main layout zones on the page. When we define a page region, we can decide where to locate it using these layout zones. Each region position can contain more than one region so our options are quite flexible. Each page template includes eight region position layout zones.

- **Tab cells**: Set the location of the tabs on the page (if the template supports tabs).

- **Navigation bar**: Can include various navigational aids, like breadcrumbs, sidebars, etc.
- **Success message and notification message**: Set the location of the success and notification system messages.

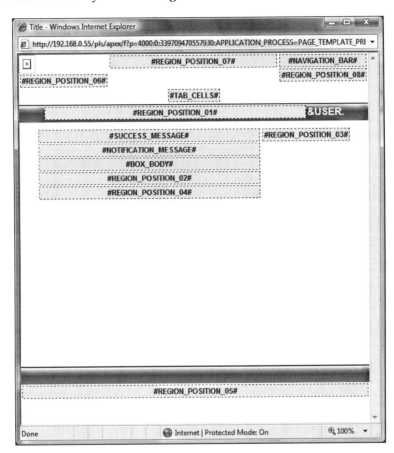

Region templates

Region templates define the main page layout containers. We have a long list of region templates, each with its own functionality support, e.g. **Form Region, Hide and Show Region, Sidebar Region, Reports Region**, and many more.

Reports templates

The reports templates are responsible for the layout of the APEX reports—display as table, single record per page, etc. The reports templates also give us options regarding the conditional display of the column data. They also deal with issues like report pagination, the way data will be displayed (e.g. background colour), etc.

Breadcrumbs templates

APEX supports the use of navigational breadcrumbs. The breadcrumb will be styled and positioned according to these templates.

List templates

APEX supports a variety of list-driven components such as menus and trees. These components will be styled and positioned according to these templates.

Calendar templates

APEX supports several layouts of calendars, including monthly, weekly, and daily views of the calendar. These views can be controlled through the calendar templates.

Label templates

Each application page item has its label, and the appearance and functionality of those can be controlled with the label templates.

Button templates

APEX supports several formats of buttons. One of them is template-driven buttons that allows us to control the look and the functionality of the buttons.

Popup List Of Values template

This template controls the look and feel of the **popup LOV windows**.

 Unlike the other groups of templates, which can have multiple members (templates), there can be only one popup LOV template.

Templates and the APEX upgrade process

The APEX upgrade process installs a new repository of themes and templates, but doesn't upgrade the current themes and templates in the existing applications in order to maintain backward compatibility. This means that if we want to enjoy new features that were added to the theme we are currently using, then we should replace the old theme with the new one, or update the specific templates we are using with the new attributes. We'll discuss a specific example of that when we review page regions in the next chapter.

Theme, templates, and good practice

The *Application Builder* allows us to change any of the existing themes and templates. However, I believe that the original templates should not be changed. If you need to make some changes, and add more features to an existing template, you should make a copy of the original template and make all the changes in that copy. This will ease any future APEX upgrades you'll perform, and it will be much easier for you to track and maintain all the specific changes you have made.

The f?p URL notation

APEX applications run in the Web environment, hence we need to use URLs to navigate around the applications. Each URL includes specific request details to the APEX engine. This engine includes a major procedure called f — yes, a single letter name. The first parameter of the f procedure is called p. According to the URL syntax construction rules, if we want to call procedure f with the parameter p, we get the f?p combination.

The p parameter is a compound one and it includes up to 9 segments. Some of them will not tell you much at this point, but we'll get back to them throughout the book. So, the full syntax of the f?p URL can look like this

```
f?p=App:Page:Session:Request:Debug:CC:itemNames:itemValues:PF
```

The p segments

The p parameter can have up to 9 segments, which are delimited by a colon (:). The location of each segment is **meaningful**, so if you need to use a segment that comes after a segment you don't want to use, you **must** use the delimited character (:), to mark an empty space. For example:

```
f?p=App:Page:Session::Debug
```

In this URL we didn't include the **Request** segment so we can see two consecutive delimited characters instead. This example also shows us that if we don't need to use segments (which follow the last segment we need to include), then we don't have to add the empty delimited segments to the end of the URL.

1—App

It stands for the application ID or alias name. If we want to redirect (branch) to a page in the current application, that we can use the built-in substitution string APP_ID. This segment is also dynamically available through JavaScript, using $v('pFlowId').

Sometimes, it's easier to remember names instead of numbers. We can use the application alias instead of the ID, which has its own substitution string—APP_ALIAS, which can also be used in this segment.

> The first segment is the only mandatory segment in the f?p syntax. If we only use this segment, we'll be taken to the default home page of the application.

> **Advance note:**
>
> If we are using an applications alias, it must be unique within the APEX workspace that the application resides in. However, if the APEX instance includes more than one workspace, and the same alias is being used for an application in that extra workspace, then we must include the parameter c to clearly identify the workspace in which the referenced application is stored. For example:
>
> ```
> f?p=myApplication:Page:Session::Debug&c=WORKSPACE1
> ```

2—Page

Stands for the application page number we want to redirect to. This can be a numeric value or the alphanumeric alias name of the page. If we want to define a self-redirection, meaning we want to reload the current page we are in, we can use the substitution string APP_PAGE_ID. This segment is also dynamically available through JavaScript, using $v('pFlowStepId').

3—Session

It stands for session ID. This is one of the most important segments for maintaining application security and session state. We mentioned before that every APEX session has a unique session ID. If this segment includes a valid session ID, the APEX engine will process the `f?p` URL request and will associate the results with the corresponding session state. Otherwise, if the application is not public the user will be asked to authenticate.

We can reference the current session ID by using the substitution string `APP_SESSION` or in its shorter format—`SESSION`. This segment is also dynamically available through JavaScript using `$v('pInstance')`.

The most commonly used segments in the `f?p` URL syntax are the first three segments. The following are possible combinations of use:

    f?p=&APP_ID.:3:&SESSION.

This will redirect us to page 3 on our current application, using our current session.

    f?p=20:&APP_PAGE_ID.:&SESSION.

This will take us to the same page we are currently in, but on application 20. As we are using the same session ID, we will not be required to re-login to application 20 (provided we have taken a proper configuration measurement for that. More details will be available throughout the book).

    f?p=&APP_ID.:&APP_PAGE_ID.:&SESSION.

This will perform a self branch to the current page, in the current application, using the current session ID.

4—Request

This stands for the `REQUEST` value and allows us to set the `REQUEST` value while branching to a new page. We'll discuss this option in more detail when we discuss Buttons.

This segment is also dynamically available through JavaScript using `$v('pRequest')`.

5—Debug

The *Application Builder* includes an option of displaying debug information while rendering the page. This segment can hold YES or NO as values. As we are using the f?p URL to redirect to a new page, we can use the substitution string DEBUG to maintain the current debug status for the new page. For example:

```
f?p=&APP_ID.:10:&SESSION.::YES
```

This will display page 10 in the current application in a debug mode.

```
f?p=&APP_ID.:10:&SESSION.::&DEBUG.
```

This will display page 10 in the same debug mode as our current page.

6—CC (Clear Cache)

Clear cache stands, in this case, for clear session state values, in several possible resolutions, which we are stating as the sixth segment.

The Clear Cache segment can include a comma delimited list of items (application or page level) or page numbers, and these items or pages (that is, all the items on the page) will be cleared from session state and will be set to null. The following will clear session state for the P1_ITEM and all the items on page 10:

```
f?p=&APP_ID.:10:&SESSION.:::P1_ITEM,10
```

The APEX engine recognizes several key words in the Clear Cache segment:

- **APP**: Clears all the session state data for the entire application we specified in the first segment. All items of the application will be set to null.

- **SESSION**: Clears all the session state data associated with the session specified in the third segment. This is a cross application action. If more than one application shares the same session ID number (and it's only possible by intentional configuration), the session state of all of them will be cleared.

- **RP**: Reset Pagination. If the page we are branching to (including self-branching) contains a report, this will clear all the pagination parameters for this report.

- **RIR**: Reset Interactive Report.

- **CIR:** Clear settings of Interactive Report.

 Interactive Reports were introduced in version 3.1, so the last two key words are only relevant to this version onward.

7—itemName

A comma delimited list of items on the application or page level that we want to set while branching to the new page.

If we are using the `f?p` syntax to link into an Interactive Report, this segment also allows us to pre-define a report filter on a specific column in the report. More details will follow in the chapter about Interactive Reports (Chapter 16).

8—itemValue

A comma delimited list of values, which should correspond exactly to the list of items we specified in the previous segment. For example:

```
f?p=&APP_ID.:10:&SESSION.::::P10_FIRST,P10_LAST:James,Eduard
```

This will take us to page 10 while setting the `P10_FIRST` item to `James`, and the `P10_LAST` item to `Eduard`.

If a value in this segment includes a comma (as in some countries where the comma is being used instead of a decimal point), we must enclose it with backslashes (\).

Using the previous example, the following

```
f?p=&APP_ID.:10:&SESSION.::::P10_FIRST,P10_LAST:James,\Eduard, Jr.\
```

will take us to page 10 while setting the `P10_FIRST` item to `James`, and the `P10_LAST` item to `Eduard, Jr.`. If we are using this URL with JavaScript, then we must escape the backslash as it is considered a JavaScript special character:

```
redirect('f?p=&APP_ID.:10:&SESSION.::::P10_FIRST,P10_LAST:James,\\Edu
ard, Jr.\\');
```

As we are using a colon (`:`) as a delimited character in the `f?p` syntax, we can't use it to pass values that include colons. The obvious example is time, but as we'll see in Chapter 5 about APEX items, some of them also use colon-delimited strings as their value.

> Using segments 7 (*itemName*) and 8 (*itemValue*) to explicitly set the values of page items takes precedence over clearing the page session state using segment 6 (*CC*). The following will clear session state for page 10, and then set the value of `P10_ITEM1` (an item on the page) to `305`:
>
> ```
> f?p=&APP_ID.:10:&SESSION.:::10:P10_ITEM1:305
> ```

9—PR (Printer friendly)

APEX includes some printer friendly templates that allow us to print a page without some of the components that are only relevant on screen, e.g. buttons, navigation bars, etc. If this segment is set to YES, then the APEX engine will use the printer friendly template to render the page.

Item values including the colon character

As was mentioned before, we can't pass values that include the colon character (:) using the f?p URL syntax. If we can't use any other options to set the value of the item, and we need to use the f?p URL, then we must replace the colon character with another character that will not conflict with the f?p functionality. We should choose the replacement character very carefully as it should be a character that will not be naturally included in the value that we want to set. The following is an example of code that we can use to create the f?p URL:

```
javascript: var URL = 'f?p=&APP_ID.:472:&SESSION.:::::P472_TIME:'+
$v('P470_TIME').replace(/:/g,'~'); redirect(URL);
```

The P470_TIME item includes a time value. These values usually include the colon character, e.g. 10:20:15. We are using the JavaScript method replace to scan the value of P470_TIME, and replace every : character with the ~ character. Now we can safely use the f?p URL syntax, to set the P472_TIME value in the target page.

On the target page we must replace the ~ character back to the original : character. We can do that by using the **Post Calculation Computation** field of the item (which we'll discuss in Chapter 5). In this case, we can use the following:

```
replace(:P472_X1,'~',':')
```

The session state value of P472_TIME will include the ~ characters, e.g. 10~20~15, however, the displayed value will include the original : characters.

Don't be confused with the JavaScript replace **method** that we used on the source item and the PL/SQL built-in replace **function** we are using here.

APEX multi-lingual support

The **User Interface** of the APEX IDE is available in 10 languages and dialects—English (the primary language), German, Spanish, French, Italian, Japanese, Korean, Brazilian Portuguese, Simplified Chinese, and Traditional Chinese. With the proper language installation, a single APEX instance can natively support a development environment in any of these languages. However, that doesn't mean that in order to develop a French application we must work with a French *Application Builder*. Every *Application Builder*, in any language, supports developing APEX applications in a variety of other languages that are being supported by Oracle.

We have two types of APEX applications with **National Language Support** (NLS). The first type is a **single language** User Interface application, in **any** of the APEX supported languages, but this language is not the same as the language of the APEX IDE itself. Hence, the need for the NLS. For example, we can use an English version of the *Application Builder* to develop a French User Interface application. Even though French is natively supported by the APEX IDE, because we are using the English version of the development environment, we need to use NLS elements to support French. We can also use the same *Application Builder* version to develop an Arabic or Hebrew application—languages that are written from **Right To Left** (**RTL**), and are not included in the list of languages that the APEX IDE natively supports.

The second type of APEX applications with NLS includes a single application with **multi-lingual** User Interfaces. In this case, we have a primary language, and on top of it, one, or more, translated language(s). The primary language, just like the translated languages, can be any of the languages that are being supported by Oracle.

The APEX built-in translation mechanism

The *Application Builder* includes a very useful translation mechanism to support both types of APEX applications with NLS. This mechanism has a big advantage because it doesn't force us to decide, in advance the NLS nature of the developed application (if any). We can fully utilize the translation mechanism, and add NLS to our application, in any phase of the application development.

Single language applications

The APEX engine (including the reporting engine) is using a series of **translatable messages** in order to display its internal messages. While working with a single language application, which is different from the *Application Builder* language, we can translate these pre-defined internal messages, into the language of our need. Moreover, as we saw in the *Shortcuts* section, we can define our own messages that can interact with the APEX translation mechanism and be displayed in the language of our choice.

Single application with Multi-lingual user interface

The APEX translation mechanism allows us to develop single application logic and use it with the User Interface in multiple languages. This mechanism is using the **XLIFF (XML Localization Interchange File Format)** standard to translate various APEX components, e.g. internal messages, item labels and help information, templates etc. into the languages we need to support.

National Language Support (NLS) in this book

We'll intensely cover Globalization, Localization, and NLS issues throughout this book with special attention given to RTL oriented applications, and many of our examples will revolve around these issues. We'll also devote a full chapter to the APEX built-in translation mechanism (Chapter 18).

Summary

In this chapter, we reviewed **session state** that gives us persistence features in a stateless environment, helping us to effectively manage our application pages data. **Substitution Strings** give us a very useful mechanism for using dynamic content that can be determined at runtime by the APEX engine or by the developer. Substitution strings allow us a higher degree of flexibility in our applications, referencing objects that will only be populated with values at runtime. An extension of substitution strings is the APEX **Shortcuts** mechanism that allows us even greater flexibility in generating dynamic content at runtime, with possible connection to the APEX built-in translation mechanism. **Themes** and **Templates**, which control the look and feel of our application, represent the declarative nature of the APEX *Application Builder* while maintaining a high degree of flexibility, allowing us to add, modify, or change them as we need. The **f?p** URL notation, which allows us to navigate throughout our APEX applications while passing important information around. Finally, we introduced the APEX National Language Support and its multi-lingual built-in translation mechanism.

In the next chapter, we will learn about the major building blocks of the APEX application, and how to create them using the APEX *Application Builder*.

The Application Builder Basic Concepts and Building Blocks

The APEX Integrated Development Environment (IDE) includes four major modules — the **Application Builder**, **SQL Workshop**, **Utilities**, and a special **ADMIN** module. In this chapter, we will start to get to know the *Application Builder*, its basic concepts, modules, and functionality. These include:

- The APEX **Workspace**
- Working with the APEX IDE and the APEX *Application Builder*
- Creating a new application or working on an existing one
- The very basic concepts of the APEX application **Page component**, how to create/edit one, and its major building blocks, such as the *page region*

So let's start by defining the work frame in which we are operating while developing our APEX applications.

The APEX Workspace

This term was already mentioned briefly in the previous chapters, but now it's time to officially discuss it, and make it clearer.

APEX *Workspace* is a **logical** container that holds all the APEX resources needed to develop an APEX application(s). A new *Workspace* can be created by using the APEX **Administration Services**, by the internal ADMIN user, which is created as part of the APEX installation process. The main menu of the *Administration Services*, and the relevant option for creating a new *Workspace*, can be seen in the next screenshot.

More details on how to use the *Administration Services*, including the login URL, can be found in the Installation appendix.

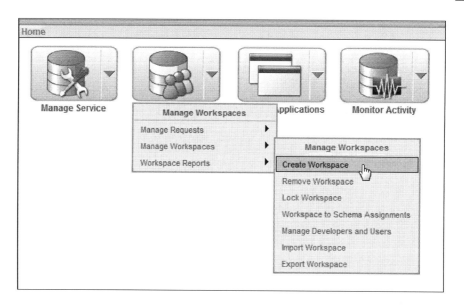

In general, each APEX *Workspace* contains a group of user(s), with different possible security levels and functionalities; associated with one, or more, database schema(s); it holds the APEX applications that are developed within it.

The APEX engine assigns a unique ID, called a **Security Group ID**, to each APEX *Workspace*. This ID number is unique within the APEX instance. Later in the book, we'll learn about situations where we need to preserve the workspace ID across **different** APEX instances.

The **Create Workspace** wizard allows us to supply all the details necessary for the APEX engine to create a new *Workspace*. In the first screen of the wizard, we should name the new *Workspace*, and we can add a short description of it and its purposes (This is definitely a good practice. You should adopt good documentation habits right from the start). In the next screen, which can be seen in the following screenshot, we should supply the details about the initial database schema that will be associated with the new *Workspace*.

We have the option of associating the APEX *Workspace* with an existing database schema, and in this case, we only need to choose its name. The other option is to create a new database schema. In this case, as mandatory fields, we need to supply a new **Schema Name**, a **Schema Password**, and the initial **Space Quota (MB)** for it.

The database schema space quota can be increased later on by using the **Manage Workspaces** wizards.

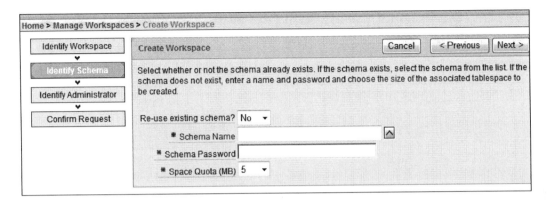

In the next screen of the wizard, we'll be asked to identify the new *Workspace* administrator, assign its password, and note an e-mail address to contact him/her. Similar to the following screenshot, the last screen summarizes all the details and pending our approval, creates the *Workspace*.

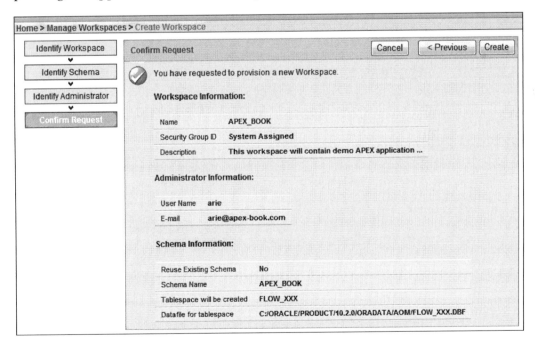

Start working with APEX

The APEX IDE is a secured environment, so we need to log in to it. We can do that as a *Workspace* defined user, in one of the following groups:

- **Workspace administrators:** This group of users has the highest security privileges within the APEX environment (apart from the internal ADMIN user, which we'll discuss later in the book). These group members can manage—create and modify—APEX users and database objects in the *Workspace* associated schema(s); manage APEX related services, e.g. session state, cache, storage request, etc.; have access to various reports, and monitor data pertaining to the development process. In addition to all these management capabilities, *Workspace* administrators can also fully take part in the application's development process.

- **Developers:** These users can create new applications, or modify the existing ones. This group can also create or modify database objects in the *Workspace* associated schema(s). Group members have limited access to system reports, mainly to monitor the development environment.

If we don't define a user as a *Workspace administrator* or a *Developer*, it will become a member of the **End users** group. This group has no development or management privileges, and it's relevant only if we choose to use the APEX built-in "**Application Express**" authentication scheme for our application login. If we are using other authentication schemes, which are using external resources—such as the "**DATABASE ACCOUNT**" scheme, which use the database user accounts—then we don't need to redefine those as users in the *End users* group.

The *Application Builder* allows us to log in to the APEX IDE as users of the *Developers* or *Workspace administrators* groups, and still run the application we are working on as a regular end user, which can be different from the user we used to log in to the *Application Builder*. For example, we can log in to the *Application Builder* using the Developer user 'ARIE', and run the application we are working on using an end user named 'DEMO'. This allows us to check the behavior of the application as it will run under a regular (non-privilege) end user, while still enjoying the option of using the developer toolbar, and without the need to frequently log in/log out under the two user names.

Logging in to the APEX IDE

The following is a screenshot of the login page for the APEX IDE:

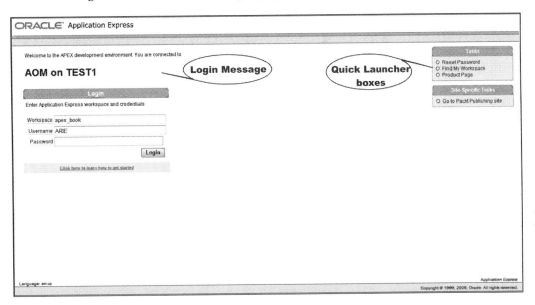

As part of the login process, we need to provide three parameters:

- **Workspace:** The name of the workspace we want to work in. The name is **not** case-sensitive.

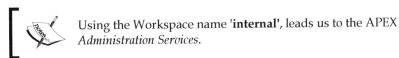

> Using the Workspace name '**internal**', leads us to the APEX *Administration Services.*

- **Username:** A user name, as defined by the APEX ADMIN or a *Workspace* administrator. The name is **not** case-sensitive.

- **Password:** The user password. The password **is** case-sensitive.

   Apex includes several options of maintaining password policies like password strength, expirations date, change on first use, etc. We'll discuss this further in the book.

As can be seen in the login page screenshot, the APEX ADMIN can define a login message, which will be displayed on every login page.

We can also see the **Tasks** box, on the right-hand side of the page, which allows us to quick launch several tasks that can be related to the login process, but do not depend on its results. The APEX ADMIN, using the *Administration Services*, can also define our own quick launch box, called **Site-Specific Tasks**. Remember that these tasks should not be dependent on the results of the login process.

This layout pattern, of using quick launch, context sensitive, tasks boxes, will return in other pages of the *Application Builder*.

The APEX IDE home page

The following is a screenshot of the APEX IDE home page:

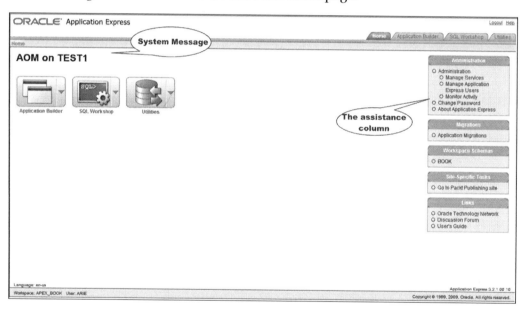

This home page allows us access to the three major modules available to *Workspace administrators* and *Developers*—The **Application Builder**, the **SQL Workshop**, and **Utilities**.

The APEX *Administration Services* module requires a separate login. As we will explain in the APEX installation appendix, we can use a direct URL to its login page, or we can use the regular APEX IDE login page with the built-in workspace holding these services called "**internal**".

We can access each of the modules by either clicking on the module icon or the module tab in the upper right-hand corner of the page. This tab layout will repeat itself throughout all the APEX IDE pages, allowing us quick access to all its modules, wherever we are.

The home page can include a system message, defined by the APEX admin, which can be different from the login message.

We can also see the "assistance column", on the right-hand side of the page. It includes several boxes that allow us to quickly navigate and launch related context and privilege sensitive tasks. For example, the **Administration** box will include different tasks for members of the workspace managers group than for the members of the developer group.

The APEX Application Builder

From the APEX IDE home page, we'll go into the *Application Builder*, which is the main module we are using while developing APEX applications.

The Application Builder home page

The following is a screenshot of the *Application Builder* home page:

We can identify the recurrence layout motives, such as the system message (the same as on the APEX IDE home page), the modules' navigational tabs, and the assistance column.

The *Application Builder* home page includes a list of all the applications within the current *Workspace*. We can display this list using icons (as in the screenshot) or as a detailed list, which includes the elapsed time since the last application update, the number of pages it includes, the name of the developer who last updated the application, and the group the application belongs to. The detail view also allows us to run the application directly from the *Application Builder* home page.

We can define application groups, which can hold applications with a common denominator, using the **Application Groups** in the **Tasks** assistance box. If we define the application groups, then we can display the application list according to these groups.

The *Application Builder* home page includes a "search and display" toolbar. This toolbar allows us to filter the application list using a search string or the application ID:

The filter mimics the Oracle `LIKE` operator with an operand similar to `'%'||search_string||'%'`. This means that we can enter any string we want (part of the application name or ID in the beginning, middle, or the end of it) and we'll get all the application names that fit this search criteria. This mode of operation repeats itself in all the *Application Builder* filter options.

The toolbar also lets us change the way the application list is displayed: icons, details, or group view, and how many list items will be displayed on each page.

The Import button

The *Application Builder* home page includes an **Import** button, which loads the *Application Builder* Import wizard.

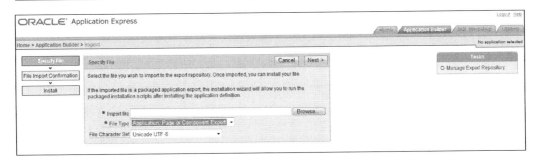

The *Import* wizard allows us to import several types of APEX components into the *Application Builder* IDE. Some of the components can be associated with the *Workspace* we are working on, and as such will be accessible to all the APEX applications within it. Others can be associated with a specific application, and will be accessible only to that application. In our context, the *Import* wizard allows us to import an entire application into the *Application Builder* IDE. This can be very useful when we want to deploy an application that was developed in a different APEX environment, e.g. deploying an application from our development environment into the QA or production environment.

The Create button

The *Application Builder* home page includes a **Create** button, which loads the *Application Builder* **Create Application** wizard:

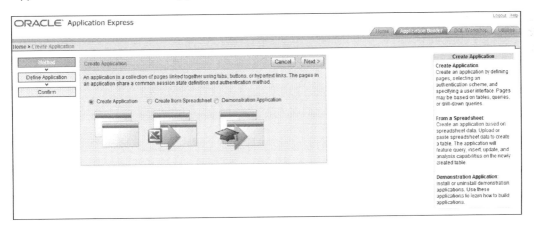

The **Create Application** wizard allows us to create new applications, using the following options:

- **Create Application**: This option allows us to create a new application **From scratch**, or **Based on existing application design model**. The wizard allows us to supply all the basic details that the *Application Builder* needs to create a new application.

- **Create From Spreadsheet**: This option allows us to build an entire application around an existing spreadsheet (or to be more exact, a comma separated (*.csv) or tab delimited file), or part of a spreadsheet, using the cut and paste technique (in APEX versions prior to 3.1, the cut and paste option is limited to up to 32K of data). This option will create the necessary database table, to store the application data, and the series of application pages to manipulate the data and report it.

This is a very simple and quick way of transforming your "database look alike" spreadsheets into a real database application, with all the benefits accompanying this environment, such added security features, simple data sharing, just to name a few. This is an interesting option that you should explore deeper.

- **Demonstration Applications:** The APEX distribution files include demo applications, which can be a very good source of learning. You can install them using this option.

In the **Create Application** wizard screenshot, we can see another common use of the "assistance column" — plain static help text, which is context sensitive. This very basic help information can be of great assistance to the developer, in clearing various options and ways of operations that are available to the developer at this specific point and location.

The Application IDE home page

The most common step in the *Application Builder* home page is to choose the application we want to work with. This will lead us to the application IDE home page.

You should not confuse the application IDE home page, which is a page within the *Application Builder*, with a similar term that we'll use, regarding the developed **application home page**, which is the first application page we'll be redirected to, when running the application. If the application is not public, this is the first page we'll be redirected to, after a successful authentication (login) process.

The following is a screenshot of the application IDE home page:

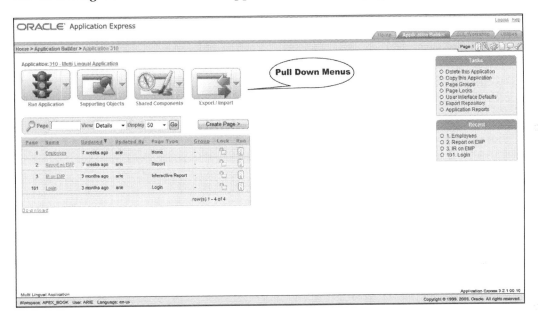

The Pull Down menu section

The upper-left corner includes four **Pull Down Menu with Image** elements, which can lead us to the following functionalities:

- **Run Application:** This allows us to run the application as an end user. If the current application is not public, we'll be asked to perform a login, just as the end user will be asked to do.

- **Supporting Objects:** The APEX IDE excels at developing data-centric applications. As such, the applications are tightly connected to various database objects (e.g. tables, sequences, packages, etc.) which store the application data and support its operation. This menu allows us to navigate to a series of wizards that allow us to include these supporting objects in the application deployment script. More details will follow in the application deployment chapter.

- **Shared Components:** This menu leads us to a series of wizards that allow us to define a variety of APEX components, which we can use, and re-use, throughout the application. Using shared components is a major concept of the APEX *Application Builder,* and we'll discuss many of the options this module has to offer throughout the book.

- **Export/Import:** This menu leads us to the *Application Builder* Export and Import wizards. These wizards allow us to export/import various components of the *Workspace* and application we are working on in different resolutions (e.g. the *Workspace* defined users, the entire application, single pages, specific shared components, etc). We'll have a more detailed discussion on these wizards further in the chapter.

The application pages section

Just below the Pull Down menu section we can find the application pages section, which will lead us to one of the most important building blocks of the *Application Builder* – the application **page**. This section includes a list of all the pages in the current application, and we have four options of displaying it:

- **Icons:** Every application page has an Icon, which represents the type of the page, according to its functionality. This view will display the page icon with the page number and name.

- **Details:** The application pages will be displayed in an eight-columned table, which includes various details on the page. This view will be discussed further in the next sub-sections.

- **by Group**: Similar to application groups, we can define groups of pages and associate the pages with them according to the (logical or functional) criteria of our choice. This view will display our defined groups, and with drill down, we'll be able to see an Icon display of all the pages in the group.

- **by Type:** The *Application Builder* classifies each application page according to its main functionality. These page types include Static HTML, Dynamic Form, Interactive Report, etc. Each type has its own Icon (the same one the Icons view is using), and this view will display these icons, and with drill down, we'll be able to see an Icon display of all the pages of the chosen type.

This section also contains a "search and display" toolbar with a similar functionality (and look) to the one we encountered on the *Application Builder* home page:

The **Page** filter field can accept a string, number, or range of numbers (for example 1, 5, 10-15). In the case of a string or number, it will look for them in both the page ID and the page name. In case of a range, it will display all the pages that have their page ID within that range.

Right next to the toolbar there is a **Create Page** button, which leads us to the **Create Page** wizard. We'll discuss this important wizard further down this chapter.

The detailed list of application pages

The detailed list of application pages includes the following details:

- **Page:** Every application page has a unique ID. This is the value of the APP_PAGE_ID substitution string and the value of the built-in hidden page item with the HTML ID of `pFlowStepId`.

- **Name:** This is a mandatory descriptive name of the page.

 This is not the page alias name, which is not a mandatory page attribute, and can be defined separately.

- **Updated:** A time frame displaying the elapsed time since the page was last updated. The units of the time frame change according to the amount of time it represents — it starts with seconds, minutes and hours; continues with days, weeks, months' and ends up with years.

- **Updated By:** The APEX user name of the developer who updated the page last.

- **Page Type:** The page type as it was classified by the **Create Page** wizard.

- **Group:** The page group this page associates with, if any.

- **Lock:** An icon that will load the *Lock Pages* wizard. Locking a page will prevent other developers from saving any changes to the locked page. This can be very handy in a multi-developer environment, where more than one developer can work on the same application.

- **Run:** An icon that will run the application page within the APEX IDE.

 If we are working on a secure application (where a login is required), then we'll be asked once every APEX session to perform a login to the application. Only upon a successful login process will we be redirected to the page we asked to run. This is the exact behavior the APEX runtime environment will present upon a "deep linking" request.

We can sort the list of application pages according to most of the specified details (Page Type, Lock, and Run are excluded), which can help us with an easy and quick tracing of the page we want to work on.

The Download link

At the bottom of the application pages section, there is a **Download** link, which allows us to download the detailed application pages list into a CSV file.

The APEX IDE doesn't include a built-in version control mechanism. This could be problematic in large development environments, which includes many developers working on large projects. A periodically downloaded CSV file can be a useful source of information, regarding who worked last on each page, which pages were updated and when, etc. This information might help a bit with the project management applicaiton.

The Page component

The application IDE home page usually leads us to the single most important component in our application—the **page**. The following is a basic description of the application page and its main elements. Detailed discussions will follow throughout the book.

While discussing *Session State*, it was mentioned that the application page has two major phases in its life cycle; the **Page Rendering** phase, implemented through the SHOW procedure; and the **Page Processing** phase, implemented through the ACCEPT procedure. These two phases are clearly manifested in the **Page Definition** page layout.

The following is a screenshot of a **Page Definition** page:

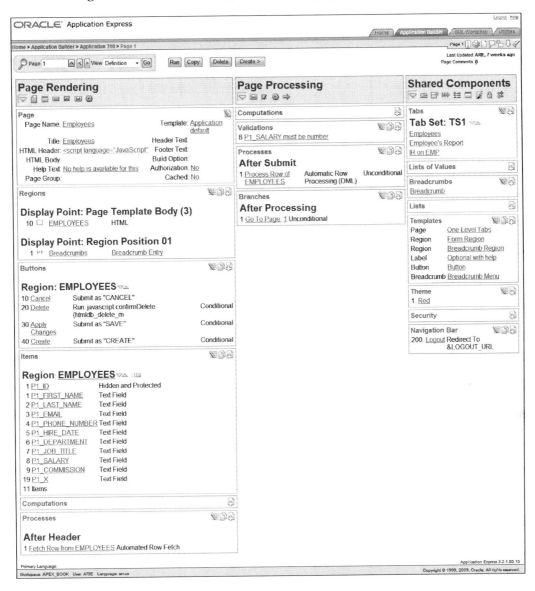

The Page Rendering column

The left-hand column on the *Page Definition* page is all about the page rendering process. It includes six sections—**Page, Regions, Buttons, Items, Computations,** and **Processes**—that allow us, both declaratively and with manual coding, to specify all the parameters and database actions, that will influence the initial page rendering, including the page general layout, the items it will include, and their initial values.

It's important to understand that although we are dealing with page rendering, which ultimately runs on the Web browser at the client-side, all the actions we are initiating in the *Page Rendering* phase are running on the **server-side** by the APEX engine (in the form of the SHOW procedure). In this phase, we are actually instructing the APEX engine how to build the application page HTML code. Only the final result of this phase—an application page code—is running on the client-side. Using JavaScript code can be a good example to clarify the situation. In the *Page Rendering* phase, we can instruct the APEX engine to include JavaScript code in the application page; however, the actual code will only be fired, while the page will be rendered on the Web browser.

The Hide/Show icon bar

The **Page Rendering** column includes a Hide/Show icon bar, which allows us to display a specific section of the column by clicking the corresponding icon, or display them all (the default display mode) by clicking on the first icon (from the left).

The icon bar includes the following icons (from left to right): Show All, Page, Regions, Buttons, Items, Computations, and Processes.

The Page Processing column

The middle column on the *Page Definition* page is all about the page-processing phase. This phase starts when the page is submitted, typically by an end user clicking on a button on the page. This phase includes four sections—**Computations, Validations, Processes,** and **Branches**. These sections allow us to check the validity of the submitted data (and make the necessary changes, if needed); influence the final value of the items, prior to storing them on the database, or passing them to the next application page. This phase is also responsible for the flow control of the application, by instructing the APEX engine where to go next.

Both the **Page Rendering** and **Page Processing** columns include **Computations** and **Process** sections. Although sharing the same internal code, these sections represent different firing points of the associated actions. We can call the **Computations** wizard using the **Page Rendering** section, but if we define a firing point that belongs to the **Page Processing** phase, the APEX engine will automatically relocate the action into the correct column. The reverse direction, from **Page Processing** to **Page Rendering,** is also applicable.

The Hide/Show icon bar

The **Page Processing** column includes the following Hide/Show icon bar:

The icon bar includes the following icons (from left to right): Show All, Computations, Validations, Processes, and Branches.

The Shared Components column

The right-hand column on the *Page Definition* page includes eight sections that represent various shared components—**Tabs, List of Values, Breadcrumbs, Lists, Templates, Theme, Security,** and **Navigation Bar**. Most of these components are responsible for the general *look and feel* of the application, and as such are shared by all the application pages. The **List of Values** and **Security** sections represent programming elements, which can also be shared by the application pages.

The **Shared Components** column on a specific page lists all the various shared components that have been used on that particular page.

The Hide/Show icon bar

The **Shared Components** column includes the following Hide/Show icon bar:

The icon bar includes the following icons (from left to right): Show All, Tabs, List of Values, Breadcrumbs, Lists, Templates, Theme, Security, and Navigation Bar.

The Action Bar

In the upper right hand corner of the *Page Definition* page, just below the APEX IDE modules navigation tabs, we can find the **Action Bar**—a quick access icons bar.

Using this *Action Bar*, we can gain quick access to several useful functionalities (icons from left to right):

- **Run:** Running the current page.
- **Shared Components:** This redirects us to the *Shared Components* module while preserving a link to the page we are working on. The *Shared Component* menu page includes a short version of the quick icons bar, containing an Edit icon, which brings us back to the *Page Definition* page.
- **Application reports**: This is a very useful utility that allows us to gather information about the various application components we are using, where they are located, etc.
- **Developer Comments:** This utility allows the developers to document their work or share important information with other developers on the application level.
- **Page Unlocked/Locked:** This utility allows us to monitor and perform lock and unlock of application pages.
- **Export:** This icon loads the page export wizards.
- **Find:** This is a very useful utility, which opens up in a popup window and allows us to search and inspect various application-related categories such as items, pages, queries, tables and PL/SQL related components, etc.

Creating an application page

We can create a new application page from the *APEX application IDE home page* using the **Create Page** button (screenshot on page 89), or from any existing *Page Definition* page, using the **Create** button (screenshot on page 93). Each button will lead us to the **Create Page** wizard:

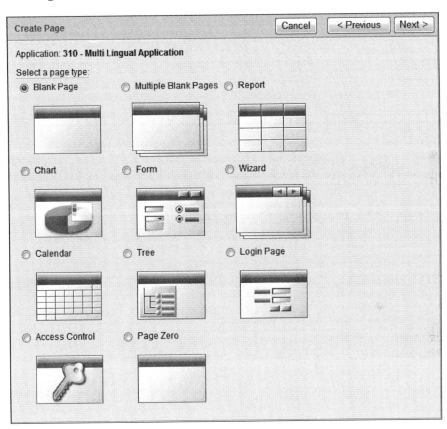

The **Create Page** wizard supports 11 different types of pages that we can use in the developed application. The page type we select here should merely reflect the initial functionality we want for the page, and it will not limit us in adding other possible page functionalities, should we choose to do so, after the initial creation of the page.

The page type selected sets the course of the wizard for the next screens. In addition to the common information about the **Page Name** and **Page Number**, the wizard will ask us to supply relevant information for creating the page according to the page type we chose. For example, if we chose a page type of **Report**, we'll be asked to choose the report type, and according to that, the report source; if we chose a page type of **Form** we'll be asked to choose what kind of form we want to build, its database resources, if any, and so on. If we chose a specific type of page (other than a blank one), then the **Page Create** wizard will create all the specific page components necessary to support the page functionality. The most notable is the appropriate page **Region**, which we'll discuss further down in the chapter.

The **Create Page** wizard supports the following page types:

- **Blank Page:** A blank page without any specific functionality will be created.

- **Multiple Blank Pages**: This option will create multiple blank pages in the application, according to data we can enter, using a *Tabular Forms* (we'll devote a dedicated chapter to *Tabular Forms*, but for now, let's say that *Tabular Forms* allow us a multi-column, multi-row data input mechanism).

- **Report**: This option will create a new page with report functionalities.

- **Chart**: This option will allow us to define a page that displays a chart based on a source query.

- **Form**: This option will allow us to create a form. The wizard supports nine different types, sources, and layouts of a form.

- **Wizard**: This option allows us to create a multi-page wizard in our own application.

- **Calendar**: This option allows us to create a calendar as the main component on the page. As we'll see in the chapter devoted to the APEX calendar, it supports three views: monthly, weekly, and daily, and can be the base for the page functionality (e.g. setting meetings, allocating resources by dates, etc.).

- **Tree**: This option allows us to create a tree on our page. APEX supports various tree layouts and functionalities. Trees are usually used for navigational purposes, while showing hierarchical relationships.

- **Login Page**: This option will allow us to create an alternative login page to the application, with special features that are only relevant to a login page.

- **Access Control**: Apex has a built-in Access Control mechanism, which can grant View, Edit, or Administration privileges to the various end users of the application. We can define and control this mechanism, which is not defined by default, by creating an Access Control page.

- **Page Zero**: This is a special page with a unique functionality. It includes only **Regions**, **Buttons**, and **Items** components, which are only relevant to the *Page Rendering* phase. These components will be integrated into every other page in our application, and will function as if they were defined on it.

 Page Zero is not created by default, and we can create it, at will, using this wizard.

No matter what type of page we chose to create, we'll end up with a *Page Definition* page, similar to the screenshot on page 93, for the newly created page. Some of its fields will contain data based on the information we supplied to the **Create Page** wizard. Now, we can add all the other attributes we'll need in order to fully implement the functionality of the page.

Editing the Page Definition page

Each section on the *Page Definition* page includes one, or more, action icons, which lead us to different editing options:

- **Edit Page Attributes**: — this allows us to edit the fields in the **Page** section.
- **Create**: — this allows us to create a new element in the section.
- **Copy**: — this allows us to copy an element in the section. The target can be the same or a different page in the application.
- **Edit All**: — this leads us to a *Tabular Form*, which allows us bulk editing of all the elements in the section.

The Page section

The **Page** section includes some very important fields we can use to set some general attributes of the application page. We can edit it by clicking on the **Edit Page Attributes** icon, located on the right-hand corner of the section, as can be seen in the following screenshot:

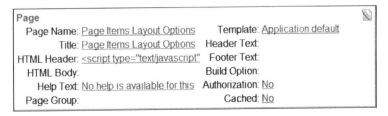

The following is a list of some of the more common and important fields in this section:

- **Name:** A mandatory field, which identifies the page by name. This name will appear in all the *Application Builder* references to application pages.

- **Page Template**: This allows us to set the *page template*.

- **Standard Tab Set**: If the *page template* we chose supports **Tabs**, we can set the tab set for the page, using this field.

- **Title:** This is the title of the page, as it will appear in the Web browser window.

- **Cursor Focus**: This field has two options to set the page cursor, after loading the page. The first option—**First item on page**, will set the cursor on the first active input item on the page. The second option—**Do not focus cursor**, will not set cursor focus.

> If you are going to use the `onload` event on the page, this field must be set to **Do not focus cursor**. If you also need to set the focus on a specific page item, you can use the APEX JavaScript built-in function `$f_First_field(pNd)`, where pNd stands for an item name on the page.

HTML Header

HTML Header

```
<script type="text/javascript">
function checkNotNull (pThis) {
  if ($v_IsEmpty(pThis)){
    alert('This field must contains a value');
    pThis.focus();
  }
}
</script>
```

Include Standard CSS and JavaScript Yes ▾

- **HTML Header**: This field, which can be seen in the above screenshot, represents the HTML `<head>` tag, and as such can hold any HTML code that belongs in this tag. Its content will be added to the content of the #HEAD# *substitution string*, or in some cases (look at the next field on the list) will replace it.

The **HTML Header** field can include the `<link>` tag, which allows us to load our external CSS file(s); it can include the `<style>` tag, which allows us to use inline CSS code; it can include the `<script>` tag, which allows us both to load our external JavaScript file(s), or to define a page specific, inline JavaScript code; it can include the `<meta>` tag, which allows us, among other things, to set attributes in the HTTP header (more information in here at `http://www.w3schools.com/tags/tag_meta.asp`); and it can include *substitution strings* and *shortcuts*.

 Don't confuse this field with the **Header Text** field, which is also part of the **Page** section, however this field includes a header text that will be displayed at the top of the application page.

- **Include Standard CSS and JavaScript**: Setting this select list field to No will exclude the #HEAD# *substitution string* content from the **HTML Header** of the page. It means that the APEX built-in JavaScript libraries, along with the standard CSS file (which pertains to the general APEX environment), will not be loaded into the application page. The specific *Theme* related CSS file will still be loaded with the page.

 This field was added to the APEX 3.0 version. In earlier versions, you needed to delete the #HEAD# *substitution string* from the *page template* to achieve a similar functionality.

- **Page HTML Body Attribute**: The content of this field will be set as the content of the #ONLOAD# *substitution string* and it will be used if the *page template* of the page includes it.

  This is the field to enter our `onload` event code into.

  Help Text: The *Application Builder* allows us to define an application page level help system, which includes a general help description of the page followed by a list of all the page items with their help text (we'll discuss these systems, with some more details, in the page regions section, later in this chapter). The content of this field will be used as the general help description of the page.

- **Comments**: This field can contain your comments as a developer. Software documentation is something most developers tend to neglect, however its importance can't be overrated. Adopt good practice development manners and document your applications.

The **Page** section includes some more sub-sections, such as **Duplicate Submission, Cache**, and so on, which are not included in the scope of this chapter (otherwise, you will need a forklift to carry the book around☺). You are encouraged to look for these issues in the APEX user's guide.

A page region

A **page region** is a logical container unit, which can hold various APEX elements, with common functionality, such as forms, reports, PL/SQL derived page content, etc. The *page region* is also a page layout unit. We can determine the *page region* position on page, according to the layout zones in the *page templates*, and all its elements will be positioned on page accordingly.

Each application page can include as many regions as we need.

Creating a page region

We can use the **Create** icon in the **Regions** section of the *Page Definition* page to create regions on the application page. The **Create Region** wizard supports 11 types of page regions, and we'll be asked to supply the basic and mandatory information that will allow the wizard to create the new region, according to its type:

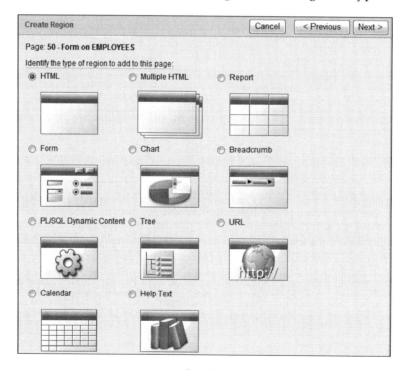

The following is a list of all the page region types:

- **HTML**: This type includes three subtypes:
    - **HTML**: This type of *region* can hold any HTML code and the region will display the products of this code.
    - **HTML Text (with shortcuts)**: This type of region has similar functionality as the HTML *region*; however, it also supports shortcuts. This *region* will display the products of its HTML content, with the products of the *shortcuts* included in it, according to their type.
    - **HTML Text (escape special characters)**: With this type of *region*, the APEX engine will escape all the special HTML characters in its **Source**, as part of the page rendering process. It means that the HTML content of the *region* will be displayed "As Is".

    To clarify the difference between an **HTML** *region* and an **HTML Text (escape special characters)** region, I have defined two HTML *regions* on a page. The first is of type **HTML** and the second is of type **HTML Text (escape special characters)**. Both *regions* share the same **Source** code: `<b>The Look & Feel of the region ...</b>`. The following is the result:

    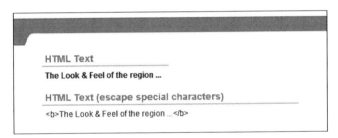

    The first *region* displays the product of its **Source** code—a bold text. The second *region* actually displays the **Source** code itself. The corresponding HTML page code, of this *region*, looks like this:

    ```
    &lt;b&gt;The Look &amp; Feel of the region ...&lt;/b&gt;
    ```

    We can see that all the special HTML character, like '<', '&', or '>', were escaped by the APEX engine. That's the reason why the Web browser didn't parse it as a regular HTML code, and it was displayed as a regular text.

- **Multiple HTML**: This option will allow us to create multiple HTML *regions*, using a *Tabular Form*. The created *regions* are of type **HTML**, but we can change that by editing their **Type** field.

- **Report**: This type supports four subtypes of reports and report wizards. We'll discuss reports later in the book.

- **Form**: This type supports nine subtypes of forms and forms wizards. We'll discuss forms later in the book.

- **Chart**: This type supports three different technologies for displaying charts: Flash Chart (introduced in version 3.0), SVG Chart, and HTML Chart.

- **Breadcrumb**: This type allows us to create breadcrumbs on the application page, and position it in one of the *page template* layout zones.

- **PL/SQL Dynamic content**: This type allows us to use PL/SQL anonymous block, to create dynamic content.

- **Tree**: This type allows us to display a *tree* that was created in the *Shared Component* module, as part of the **Navigation** section.

- **URL**: This type allows us to display any URL we want, including external URLs, directly from the Internet, on our page application.

- **Calendar**: This type supports two types of wizards, which help us to display calendars on our application page.

- **Help Text**: This is a special region, which is part of a dedicated help page we need to create, in order to utilize the page level help system, we can develop for our application. We'll see an example of how to create this help system later in the book.

Editing a page region

After creating a page region, we can edit its features by choosing its name from the **Regions** section in the *Page Rendering* column.

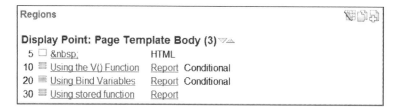

In the above screenshot, we can see four regions on the page: a simple HTML region and three report regions, two of them are conditioned. It means that these regions will be rendered on page only if the condition defined in the region **Conditional Display** section will be evaluated to be true.

The following sub-sections review two of the more important features accessible to us while editing a page region.

Region identification

The APEX engine assigns a unique number ID to every created page region. Then, with the prefix 'R', it uses this ID to create the HTML ID, which uniquely identifies the HTML element that acts as the region container. Usually, this element is an HTML table, and the HTML code for a typical region container looks similar to the following:

```
<table class="t10FormRegion" id="R6058032246644029" border="0"
cellSpacing="0" cellPadding="0" summary="">
```

This ID can be very important to us if we want to use JavaScript to manipulate HTML elements within the APEX page region, as it helps us to set a more targeted scope (than the entire `document` object) to our DOM methods. Unfortunately, this ID is not part of the page region **Identification** section, which can be seen in the following screenshot:

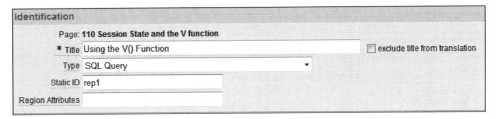

In order to gain more control over the region ID; make it known to the developer without the need to search the page HTML code, to find out the allocated ID, or query the APEX dictionary for the same purpose; and to make sure that the region ID will be the same across all our APEX application deployments, we can set our own region **Static ID**.

The APEX engine will use the content of the **Static ID** item, which can also be a string and not only a number, like the APEX engine generated ID, to create the HTML ID for the region container. We can use this ID with all our JavaScript code pertaining to the DOM element holding the region. If left clear, the APEX engine will resume using its own generated (dynamic) region ID.

Caching

We can use a server-side cache mechanism for our *Page* or *Region*. This type of caching has nothing to do with the client-side Web browser caching. It means that instead of dynamically rendering the page/region from scratch, the APEX engine will use a cached copy of the page/region. This cache copy is saved within the APEX metadata tables, and when used, can save us time and database resources, and thereby increase performance.

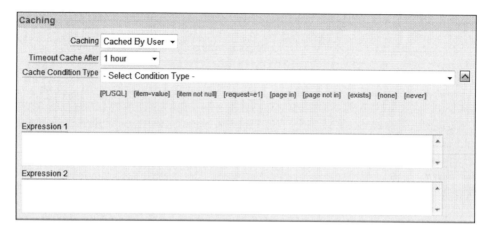

The above screenshot is taken from a region **Caching** section (the page section is very similar).

First, we need to decide whether the region will be **Cached, Cached by User,** or **Not Cached** as the default option. If we choose **Cached**, the same copy of the cached region will be used for **all** the users running the application within the caching time frame we'll set in the next field. For example, if we are using the **Cached** option with a report region, the first user that runs the report will cache it. After that, and within the time frame in which the cache is still valid, every other user that runs the same report will only see a copy of the report as it was rendered for the first user. If, however, we chose to use **Cached by User** then the APEX engine will use the cached copy of the region only for the specific user who actually cached it.

In the next field – **Timeout Cache After** – we can set a time frame in which the cached region will be valid. When this time frame expires, the APEX engine will render the region from scratch. The time frame selected options start with 10 seconds and end with one year, and include various periods of minutes, hours, days, and weeks in between.

In the next field – **Cached Condition Type** – we can set the basic (but not the only) condition for using the cache. The same condition applies to both saving the cache, as part of the ACCEPT process, and retrieving it, as part of the SHOW process.

Advanced note:

Using APEX cache, on the page or region level, can be very useful, but also very tricky and complex. We can't really cover all the intricacies of the mechanism in this section, only give you a taste of them. For example, on top of the **Cached Condition Type** you can define yourself, the APEX engine also uses some built-in conditions of its own. One of them is that the region will not be rendered from cache if its URL has been changed. It means, for example, that a cached report region will be rendered from scratch if its pagination parameters have been changed (as we expect from the pagination functionality).

You should choose very carefully when and where to use the APEX cache mechanism. This mechanism, naturally, fits to more static regions and pages such as the ones holding navigation/menu components, or pages that do not change very often, such as a report of yesterday's sales (it changes once a day), etc.

Summary

In this chapter, we introduced the APEX development environment and its basic components—the *APEX IDE*, and one of its modules, the APEX *Application Builder*. Within the *Application Builder*, we reviewed one of its major components—the *Page Definition* page. We learned how to create a new application page, and how to define its primary attributes, with special attention paid to the page *Regions*.

In the next chapter, we are going to discuss the major building blocks of the application page—the application items.

5
APEX Items

Items are the basic building blocks of our application pages. APEX supports two levels of items: **application items** and **page items**. In the following chapter, we'll review both, and learn how they can serve us in our applications.

Naming conventions and rules

Every APEX item, on the application or page level, must have a **unique name** within the APEX developed application. Some of the naming convention rules that we'll review in this chapter, such as using prefixes that include the application ID or the page ID, help us to achieve this uniqueness. We also need to use meaningful names that will help us to locate and understand the origin and type of APEX items easily.

When dealing with the names of APEX items, we face some ambiguity regarding possible length and case sensitivity. The *Application Builder* allows item names to include up to 255 characters. However, this length doesn't adhere to the Oracle SQL and PL/SQL identifier's naming rules. This can create a problem if we want to use the APEX items in SQL or PL/SQL code, and for the most part we do. Hence, it's a good practice to use the Oracle identifiers rules when we name our APEX items.

Oracle Identifiers naming rules

The following are the relevant rules we should use when naming APEX items:

- The name length must not exceed **30** characters
- The name must start with a letter
- Besides letters and digits, the name can include a $ (dollar sign), _ (underscore), and # (number sign) characters
- The name must not include any "whitespace" characters

Case sensitive APEX item names

There is a greater confusion regarding the case sensitivity of APEX item names. While defining a new APEX item, we can use any combination of case letters, but the *Application Builder* wizard will convert any lower or mixed case item name into an all **uppercase** name.

Within SQL or PL/SQL code, item names are not case-sensitive (just like any other bind variables). This is also the case when we are using them in declarative fields within the *Application Builder*.

If we want to retrieve an item value using the &ITEM. *substitution string* notation then the item name must be in **uppercase**. Otherwise, the APEX engine will treat it as a regular string.

 Personally, I find the case sensitive options to be very confusing. Hence, I'm using only uppercase notations for all my APEX item names. Upper case names work all the time.

Application items

Application items are defined in the *Shared Components* module as part of the **Logic** section. As such, they are available to us throughout the application, like global variables.

Application items are not rendered on the application page and they don't have a specific data type. We are usually using them as part of SQL or PL/SQL code, and they can hold any type of data we choose to store in them. Being used very often in SQL and PL/SQL code, they should adhere with the Oracle identifiers name rules as we specified them earlier in this chapter.

The APEX naming convention recommends us to prefix the *application item* name with the letter 'F' and the application ID. In the following screenshot, we can see the **Create/Edit Application Item** screen of application 250. Hence, the application items will be prefixed, by default, with F250_, e.g. F250_APP_ITEM1. We, of course, can choose any other naming convention or any specific name that we want. Taking into account that changing the Application ID is a viable option when importing an application into an APEX instance, and as such, the current ID number becomes meaningless, it might be a good idea to leave the Application ID out of our naming convention.

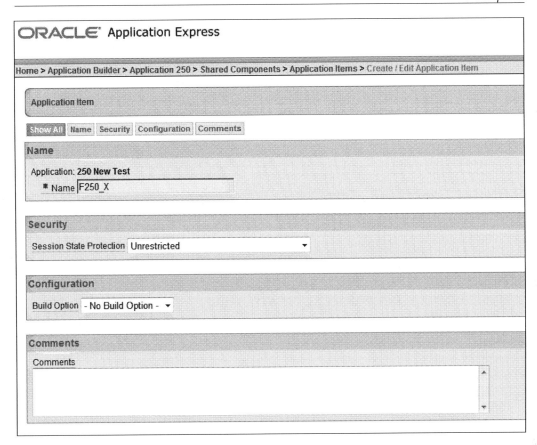

Application items and security issues

As I already mentioned, *application items* are not rendered on page. However, their value can be changed from the client side using the f?p URL syntax. This can make them vulnerable to hacking by malicious end users. In order to prevent this we can define the *application item* to be **Restricted—May not be set from browser**. This will allow us to change the value of this *application item* only by using PL/SQL code (e.g. *Computations* or *Processes*). This restriction will be forced regardless of the *Session State Protection* status. If a client-side attempt to change the value of a protected *application item* is spotted by the APEX engine, it will issue an error message, even if *Session State Protection* is disabled.

Referencing application items

We have several options for referencing *application items*, and we have already mentioned some of them when we discussed referencing *Session State*.

While defining a declarative action that involves *application item* we are using its plain name, e.g. F250_APP_ITEM1. While referencing an *application item* in SQL or PL/SQL code we can use the bind variable notation, e.g. :F250_APP_ITEM1, or the APEX built-in function v(), e.g. v('F250_APP_ITEM1'). Within the *Application Builder*, we can also use the &ITEM. *substitution string* notation to retrieve the *application item* value, e.g. &F250_APP_ITEM1..

> Remember, the first trailing period is part of the *substitution string* notation.

Application items and JavaScript

Application items are not rendered on page, and, as such, are not directly available for use in JavaScript. However, we can use the *substitution string* notation to make them available on page using, for example, a global JavaScript variable. The following code uses a JavaScript global variable and because we are using the *substitution string* notation, it must be defined within the application *page definitions* page (e.g., in the **HTML Header** field of the page):

```
<script type="text/javascript">
var g_app_item1 = '&F250_APP_ITEM1.';
</script>
```

Of course, we can use the same technique to assign an *application item* (or any other *Session State* items that are not rendered on the current page) into a local JavaScript variable (e.g. inside a function).

Page items

At the time of writing this book, the current APEX version is 3.2, and it includes 15 built-in types of **page items**. Almost all of them include various implementation options, which mostly pertain to saving *session state*, data display and format, submitting action, etc. This variety of items and options gives us a lot of flexibility, allowing us to make an optimal choice for the item type we are going to use, and the best way to display its content.

Page items are rendered on the application page. As such, the APEX engine (the SHOW process) translates each of them into HTML code, using the attributes we supply as part of the item definition process. The following sections will include a description of some of the attributes that are available to us while defining an APEX item.

The Name section

The **Name** section includes a **Name** field, which is mandatory (marked with a red asterisk), and a **Display As** field:

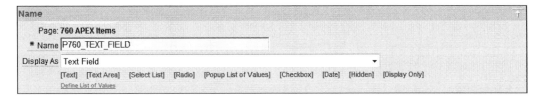

The Name field

The APEX naming convention for a *page item* recommends us to prefix the name with the letter 'P' and the page ID. As a good practice, the name should adhere to all the naming rules we have already specified.

The APEX engine uses the item name as the value of the HTML ID attribute of the rendered item. That gives us a simple and direct hook to every APEX item that was rendered on the page, using the basic DOM method `document.getElementById()`, or any of its APEX built-in JavaScript versions, such as the current `$x()` or `html_GetElement()` in pre-3.x versions.

Until APEX 3.1.x this convention was used with most APEX items. However, for some compound items, such as checkboxes (single items that can include multiple options), the item name was only part of the HTML ID that the APEX engine generated for the various elements of the compound item. APEX 3.1 is introduced using the `<fieldset>` tag to wrap all the compound APEX items. The `<fieldset>` ID attribute is assigned the item name as its value. Now, the item name can lead us to every item rendered on the page, simple as well as compound.

The Display As field

This is a select list field that allows us to choose the type (and sub-types) of the defined item. The **Display As** determines the user interface of the item—whether the user will type in free text, select from a list, check checkboxes, etc. We'll explore all these options when we discuss each of the APEX built-in item types.

Just below the **Display As** field, we can find a quick link row, which allows us to choose directly some of the more popular item type options. We'll encounter this type of functionality in many places throughout the *Application Builder*.

The Displayed section

The **Displayed** section controls the layout of the item on the application page:

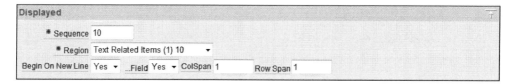

The Sequence field

The **Sequence** field is mandatory and it must include a unique sequence number among all the current page items. This sequence determines the order in which the items will be rendered on page.

The Region field

Each page item must belong to a region so this select list field is also mandatory. The item will be rendered within the selected region according to the region position on page. If we define regions on *page 0*, then these will also appear as options in the select list.

The layout fields

The next four fields give us some fine tuning options about the item layout on the page. APEX uses HTML tables as a helping aid in the page layout, and every item will be part of such a table. The layout fields allow us to position the item on the page using these HTML layout tables:

- **Begin On New Line**: If set to **Yes**, then the item will be positioned on a new table row (`<tr>`) that will be translated into a new line on the application page. If set to **No**, then the item will be positioned on the current table row, which means that on the application page it will share the same line with at least one more item.

- **...Field:** If set to **Yes**, then the item will be laid out in a table cell of its own. If set to **No**, then it will share the same table cell as the previous item.

Note:

By default, each item actually occupies two `<td>` cells—one for the item label, and the other for the input portion (the **Element** in the APEX terminology). If we set the **...Field** value to **No**, the second item (both the *label* and *element* parts) will share the same `<td>` with the *element* part of the first item.

- **ColSpan**: This field will be assigned as the value of the `COLSPAN` attribute of the table cell the item is occupying. It allows us to layout the item as it spans more than one table column.

- **Row Span**: This field will be assigned as the value of the `ROWSPAN` attribute of the table cell the item is occupying. It allows us to layout the item as it spans more than one table row.

Let's examine the following screenshot (using theme 10—Sand):

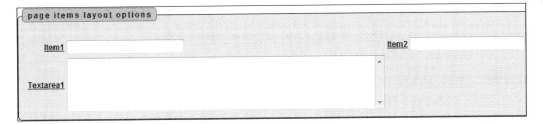

The layout fields for **Item1** are set with the **default values**:

Sequence	10
Begin On New Line	Yes
...Field	Yes
ColSpan	1
Row Span	1

The layout fields for **Item2** are set as follows:

Sequence	20
Begin On New Line	No
...Field	Yes
ColSpan	1
Row Span	1

The layout fields for **Textarea1**, with a **Sequence** of 30, are also set with default values.

In HTML tables, the widest cell determines the width of the entire HTML table column. Hence, in the example, the widest cell in the first column of items is the one occupying **Textarea1**. Because we defined **Item2** to start on the same row as **Item1**, but to be positioned in its own field (table cell), this item is positioned according to the width set by the **Textarea1** item.

If we don't like this layout—usually when we position two items on the same row, we want them close to each other—we have two options to change it. The first is to make **Item1** and **Item2** share the same table cell. We'll do that by setting the attribute **...Field** of **Item2** to **No**. This will yield the following:

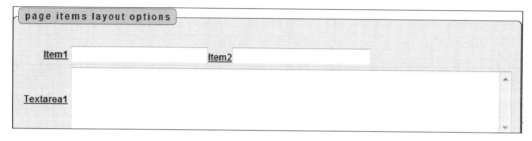

Item1 and **Item2** are now sharing the same table cell with no space between them.

The second option is to set the **Textarea1** item to span over more columns. If we remember that the first item is actually spanning two `<td>` tags (label and element), then we should set the **ColSpan** of **Textarea1** to be at least 3. We'll change the **...Field** value of **ITEM2** back to **Yes** and set the following configuration for **Textarea1**:

Sequence	30
Begin On New Line	Yes
...Field	Yes
ColSpan	3
Row Span	1

The new configuration will yield the following layout:

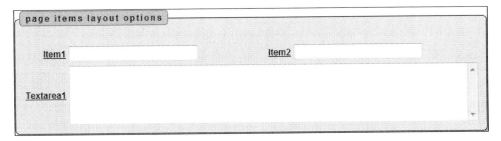

Now that we have learned how to do that, you might want to create an empty application page with several items on it, test all the legitimate combinations of the layout fields, and see how they affect the item's positioning on page.

The Drag and drop wizard

The *Application Builder* offers us another option for arranging items on the application page, using a "drag and drop" technique. We can access the **Drag and drop** wizard through its icon, which is the last icon on the **Region** headline in the **Items** section, as can be seen in the following screenshot. In order for that icon to be visible we must manually define the first item on the region.

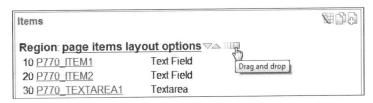

In our "Best Practices" chapter (Chapter 24), we mention this wizard as a productivity enhancer tool, as it makes creating and positioning new items on the application page faster and easier. The best way to learn about the **Drag and drop** wizard is to play with it. Therefore, after reading the corresponding section in Chapter 24, you are encouraged to do so.

The Label section

The **Label** section controls the content, style, and layout of the item label.

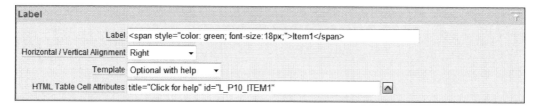

The Label field

The **Label** field contains the text of the label we want to display and can contain any HTML, JavaScript, or APEX shortcut code. This allows us a high degree of flexibility in controlling the content and style of the label. For the label content, by using a JavaScript or APEX shortcut we can make it dynamic. For the style of the label, by using HTML code, we can use any attributes the `<style>` tag supports.

 Using the **Label** field to style the appearance of the label is not recommended on a regular basis. If you need to frequently style the label appearance to a certain look you should define a *label template* for that. It will be easier to maintain the consistency of the labels this way.

In the following example (using Theme1 – Red), the **Label** field was used to change the color (green) and font-size (18px) of the label of **Item1**:

The Horizontal / Vertical Alignment field

This is a select list field that allows us to choose the location of the label relative to the *element* itself—above, left, or below the *element*. If we position the label to the left of the *element* we can choose its alignment within the table cell it occupies.

NLS note:

If we are developing an RTL oriented application, the labels will be positioned to the right of the item *element*.

The Template field

Item labels are template based components, and this field allows us to choose the template we want to use.

APEX provides us two basic characteristics for the label templates. The first one is for mandatory/optional fields, which are marked differently. The second one is for item help. If we choose a label template with help, the label text will be generated as a link to the item's popup help window.

The HTML Table Cell Attributes field

This field allows us to define extra (non-declarative) HTML attributes that will be assigned to the table cell (`<td>`) of the label. By default, the *Application Builder* fills this field with `nowrap="nowrap"`.

The `nowrap` attribute was deprecated in HTML 4.01. If you are changing the default content of this field, or you want to be compliant with XHTML 1.0 Strict DTD, then you should use the `style` attribute, with the `white-space` property: `style="white-space: nowrap;"`.

In the previous screenshot we can see an example of using the `title` attribute to define a simple tooltip for the label—**Click for help**.

Another possible use is with the `ID` attribute. The built-in *label templates* don't attach an ID attribute to the item label. If we need a DOM hook for the label, as in the case of using JavaScript to manipulate the label content, we can define it in this field, as can be seen in the **Label** section screenshot on the previous page.

Note:

This field should be used for assigning an `ID` to a *label* only in sporadic cases. If we need our *labels* to contain `ID` on a regular basis, then we should build a new *label template* that does that. We shall use this *template* whenever we need a *label* with an `ID`.

The Element section

The **Element** section is responsible for the layout, style, and extra functionalities (i.e. in the case of using DOM events) of the data input portion of the item.

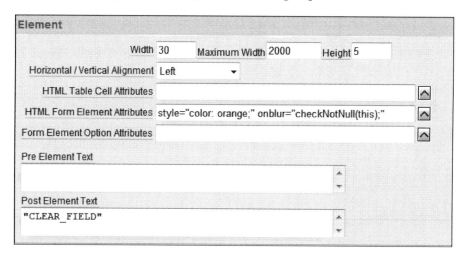

The item dimension fields

The first three fields set the input field dimensions of the item on the page:

- **Width**: This sets the width of the displayed input field **in characters**. This is not the real width of the item, just the width of the displayed field on page. A real limit on the item width is set by the **Maximum Width** item, which is described next.

- **Maximum Width**: This is the maximum number of characters that the browser will allow us to enter into the field. If this number is higher than the **Width** value the data will be scrolled inside the displayed portion of the item. On the other hand, if it's lower than **Width**, the browser will not allow further input of characters even though there is extra space on the displayed field.

Note:

If the defined item is associated with a database table column having a specific length/size/precision restrictions, e.g. VARCHAR2(100) or NUMBER(5,2), it would be a good practice to match the **Maximum Width** field to the max value allowed by the data type declaration (for numbers, don't forget to include the +/- sign and the decimal point in your math). This will prevent us from getting length/size/precision related error messages when saving the data into the database. This is particularly important as this type of error message is generated by the database itself and is not "user-friendly".

- **Height**: This field sets the height, **in lines,** of multi-line items such as the *text area, multi-select list,* or the *shuttle* item. It doesn't have any effect on single-line items.

The HTML Form Element Attributes field

This field gives us control over the element portion itself (compared to the **HTML Table Cell Attributes,** which gives us control over the table cell occupied by the element). This is a very important field, as it allows us to define DOM events for the item.

In the screenshot of the **Element** section we can see this field being used for styling the element—coloring the input text in orange, and attaching to it an onblur event—with the JavaScript function checkNotNull() that we defined as part of the **HTML Header** page discussion (Chapter 4, page 100). The event will fire this client-side validity check function upon leaving the field.

The Form Element Option Attributes field

This field allows us to define extra (non-declarative) attributes for the options of the *Checkbox* or *Radiogroup* items. For example, we can use the following: style="font-weight: bold;" to display the options in bold.

The Pre/Post Element Text fields

These fields allow us to set free text that will prefix or suffix the element input portion in a display only manner. Moreover, these fields can hold HTML, JavaScript, or APEX shortcuts to further control/manipulate the element. In the following screenshot, we can see the use of the APEX shortcut **CLEAR FIELD** (which was defined as part of the *substitution string* and *shortcuts* discussion). This *shortcut* creates a **Clear Field** button, adjacent to the element (using the same table cell).

The results of the **Element** section screenshot can be seen in the following:

The Source section

The **Source** section allows us to define the ways in which the initial value of the item will be computed. We have two options to choose from—computing the item value each time the page is rendered, or relying on the *session state* value of the item.

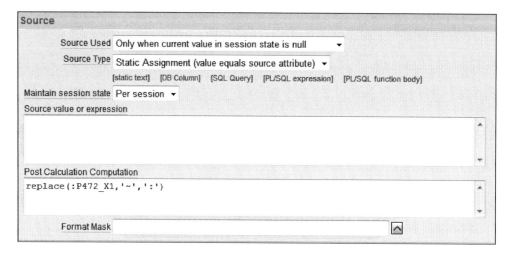

The Source Used field

This select list field sets the precedence of the *session state* value of the item, if it exists, over any other computation means specified by the item **Source value or expression** field.

Only when current value in session state is null

This option gives precedence to the item value stored in the *session state* (in this case, the *persistence* type).

If the *session state* contains a value for the item, that value will be used as the base value to compute the initial and displayed value of the item. If the *session state* contains a NULL value for the item, the **Source value or expression** field will be used.

> You need to be cautious when applying this type of **Source Used** field on an item that serves as a *Primary Key* in the **Automatic Row Fetch** (**ARF**) process (we'll discuss this later in the book). If you want the *ARF* process to fetch a new record, and not the last record that was saved (hence, its *Primary Key* was stored in the *session state*), then you need to clear the *session state* of the item (which, for example, can be done as part of a page branch).

Always, replacing any existing value in session state

This option gives precedence to the value computed according to the **Source value or expression** field over any existing value in the *session state*. As we mentioned when we reviewed the *session state*, this option can lead to a scenario where the displayed value of the item is different from the corresponding *session state* value. However, this is exactly what we need, especially when we are fetching records from the database.

The Source Type field

This select list field determines the type and functionality of the **Source value or expression** field and how the APEX engine should interpret it. We can select from the following options:

- **Always Null:** The item value will always be set to NULL.

- **Static Assignment (value equals source attribute):** The item value will be set to the content of the **Source value or expression** field. The APEX engine will treat the **Source value or expression** field as a *String* variable, and will assign its content as is.

> This option supports the use of the &ITEM. *substitution string* notation. However, APEX *shortcuts* are not supported.

- **SQL Query:** This allows us to use a SQL query in the **Source value or expression** field in order to populate the item value.

- **Item (application or page item name):** This allows us to use an application or page item to populate the item value.

- **PL/SQL Expression or Function:** This allows us to use a PL/SQL expression or to call a PL/SQL function to populate the item value.

- **PL/SQL Function Body:** This allows us to code a PL/SQL body function in the **Source value or expression** field in order to populate the item value.

 A **PL/SQL Function Body** must include a RETURN statement. If we need to use local PL/SQL variables within the function body, the DECLARE statement should be used instead of the IS keyword in a regular PL/SQL function.

- **Database Column:** If we want the item to be populated by the built-in *Automatic Row Fetch* process, or to be manipulated (insert/update/delete) by the built-in *Automatic Row Processing (DML)* process, then we must use this option for the **Source Type**. In this case, the **Source value or expression** field must include the item corresponding table column name.

 The table column name is case sensitive.

- **Preference:** APEX gives us the option of setting user preferences as part of the *session state* mechanism. This option allows us to use the preference as the value of the item. In this case, the **Source value or expression** field should include the preference name.

- **PL/SQL Anonymous Block:** This allows us to use a PL/SQL anonymous block in the **Source value or expression field** to populate the item value.

Just below the input portion of this field, there is a line of quick links, which allows us to set the **Source Type** field to the most common options with only one click.

Maintain session state

This field allows us to set the nature of *Session State* for the item. We can choose from two options:

- **Per session:** The *Session State* value of the item will be retained for the duration of the current APEX session (that is, upon logout, it will no longer be available for the user).

- **Per User**: The *Session State* value of the item will be retained for the current user across APEX sessions (i.e., the next time the current user logs into the application, the item value from *Session State* will be available for him/her, and it will be taken into consideration by the **Source Used** field).

Source value or expression

This field contains the content—data, code, items, column names, etc.—that actually instructs the APEX engine on how to compute the item value. This content must match the selected type in the **Source Type** field. This field can also be left empty (which means it will be set to NULL) in cases where we want to rely on *Session State* values or when NULL is the initial value we need.

Post Calculation Computation

This field allows us to give the displayed value of the item a final fine-tuning. It can hold SQL or PL/SQL expressions or a call to a PL/SQL function. Using the bind variable notation we can reference the item itself, or any other application or page item with *session state* values.

While referencing the item itself we are actually referencing its **temporary** *session state* value as it was computed according to the **Source Used**, **Source Type,** and **Source value or expression** fields. In the case of **Only when current value in session state is null**, temporary and persistent *session state* values will be the same. In the case of **Always, replacing any existing value in session state** they might be different, and the **Post Calculation Computation** code will use the value that was just computed as part of the rendering process.

In the screenshot of the **Source** section we can see an example of using a built-in PL/SQL function—replace—referencing the item itself, using the bind variable notation—:P472_X1. The origin of this example can be found in Chapter 3, page 76, when we discussed an option to pass values that includes the colon character, using the f?p URL syntax.

Format Mask

This field allows us to define a format mask to numbers or dates that were retrieved from, or which are going to be saved to the database. As such, this field is only applicable to items with a **Source Type** of **Database Column**.

The *Application Builder* provides us with an option of setting the date format on the application level. We'll review this in Chapter 18, *Globalization*, but for now, you should remember that the format in the item's **Format Mask** field will take precedence over all other application level date formats.

The Default section

The **Default** section will be used every time the computation result of the initial item value, using the **Source** section, yields a NULL.

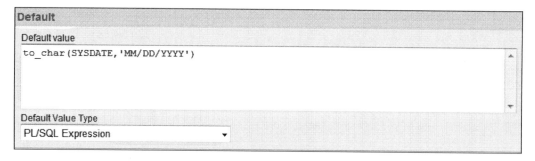

This section supports three options of setting the default value for the item:

- **Static text with Session State Substitutions**: This allows us to assign any text we need to the value. This type also supports the use of both *substitution strings* and *shortcuts*.

- **PL/SQL Function Body**: This allows us to use a PL/SQL anonymous block to compute the default value. As we are talking about a function body, the code must include a RETURN statement.

- **PL/SQL Expression**: This allows us to use PL/SQL expression to compute the default value.

In the screenshot of the **Default** section, we can see an example of setting the default value of an item to the current database date.

Using the **Static text with Session State Substitutions** option, the **Default value** field can be left empty. This means that the initial value of the item will remain NULL if no other value was computed in the **Source** section. However, changing the **Default Value Type** to any of the PL/SQL type options, and leaving the **Default value** field empty, will yield a runtime PL/SQL error message.

The List of Values section

List of Values (**LOV** in short), as the name suggests, is a list of static or dynamic values. All the multi-option APEX items, which we'll review later in the chapter, such as select list, checkbox, radio-group, shuttle, etc., are based on LOV as their resource.

We can define a named LOV—where the LOV is identified by a specific (capital letters) name—as part of the **User Interface** section of the *Shared Components* module, or we can define a page specific LOV as can be seen in the following screenshot of the LOV section:

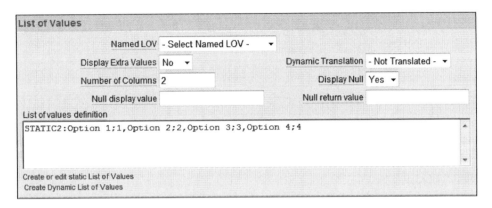

Static LOV

A static LOV includes predefined static pairs of displayed and returned values. The displayed value will be rendered on the page, and the returned value will be assigned as the item value.

 It's a valid option that both the displayed and returned elements will have the same value. In this case, the returned value is optional.

Using the key word **STATIC**, we have two options to control the displayed order of the LOV:

- **STATIC:** This will sort the displayed values lexicographically.
- **STATIC2**: This will display the displayed values according to their defined order in the LOV.

I defined two checkbox items using the following static LOV definitions:

```
STATIC:1,10,12,111

STATIC2:1,10,12,111
```

The following screenshot displays the results:

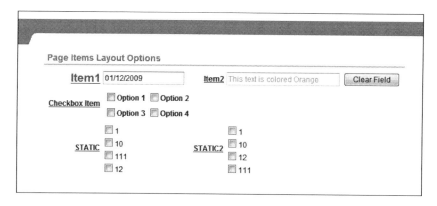

By default, we are using the semi-colon (;) as the delimited character between the displayed and returned values, and the comma (,) as the delimited character between the pairs values of the list. However, we can define different delimited characters if, for example, we want to use displayed values that include commas. In this case, we can use the following syntax:

```
STATIC2(^,-):Red, Green, Blue-1^Black, White-2^Red, Yellow, Green-3
```

The first delimited character '^' separates the members of the list, while the second one, the '-' character, separates the displayed and returned values. The result of such a LOV definition can be seen in the following screenshot:

From this LOV item forward, as long as we are on the same page, the APEX engine will continue to use the alternative delimited characters, until we specifically tell it differently by resetting the delimited characters. If, for example, one of the following items on the application page will include the following LOV definition:

```
STATIC2:1,2,3,4
```

The result will be as follows:

The APEX engine no longer recognizes the comma character as a delimiter, and as a result, the LOV definition is interpreted as including only one value. If we want to display this item differently, e.g. a radio item with four different options, then we should reset the LOV delimited characters to their default values by using the following:

```
STATIC2(,,;):1,2,3,4
```

This time, we'll get the following result:

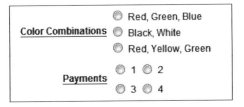

Dynamic LOV

Dynamic LOV is based on a SQL query that returns two values , and they are the displayed and returned values.

Let's say we have a database table called ACTIVE_DAYS, which is defined as follows:

```
CREATE TABLE   "ACTIVE_DAYS"
   ("SNO" NUMBER(1,0) NOT NULL ENABLE,
    "DAY_OF_WEEK" VARCHAR2(15) NOT NULL ENABLE,
    "ACTIVE" CHAR(1) NOT NULL ENABLE,
    CONSTRAINT "ACTIVE_DAYS_PK" PRIMARY KEY ("SNO") ENABLE
   )
```

The first column is the rank of the day in the week (1 for Sunday, 2 for Monday, ..., 7 for Saturday). The next column holds the name of the day and the following column includes active/non-active information. Now we want to define a select-list item that will only display the active weekdays, sorted according to their ranks, and returns the rank value for the selected day. We can use the following dynamic LOV to achieve that:

```
select day_of_week, sno
from active_days
where active='Y'
order by sno
```

As we can see, the dynamic LOV query can include the WHERE and ORDER BY clause. In more complicated cases, it can also include a sub-query in the FROM clause.

Dynamic LOV can also display and return the same value using the same table column. In this case, we need to use an alias for the columns. For example:

```
select ename d, ename r
from emp
```

Defines LOV

The following fields in the LOV section help us to define the LOV we need:

- **Named LOV**: This select-list field allows us to select one of the named LOV we have defined as a *Shared Component*.

- **Display Extra Values**: Multi-option lists include a finite number of possible values. What will happen if we set the value of the item to a value that is not included in the list? This field will determine that. If we set this field to Yes, then the value will be displayed as if it was part of the list. If we set it to No (the default), then the value will not be displayed, and the first value in the LOV will be displayed instead.

- **Dynamic Translation**: This field is only relevant to dynamic LOVs. It allows us to dynamically translate the LOV options as part of the APEX translation mechanism. We'll see an example of this later in the book.

- **Number of Column**: While working with Checkbox or Radiogroup items, we can determine the number of columns to use for displaying the options of the item. An example of it can be seen in the previous screenshot, where the options of the item **Checkbox Item** are displayed in two columns.

- **Display Null**: This field gives us the option of displaying NULL as a valid member of the LOV.

- **Null display value / Null return value**: These fields are only relevant if we set the previous field to Yes. In this case, we can choose the value that represents NULL as a displayed value, and what the returned value will be if NULL is selected.

- **List of values definition**: This field holds the static or dynamic (SQL query) definition of the LOV. If we are using a named LOV then this field will remain empty.

LOV related wizards

At the bottom of the LOV section we have two links to wizards that can help us define the source of the LOV:

- **Create or edit static List of Values**: This wizard uses a two column tabular form to help us define the static LOV pairs of values.

- **Create Dynamic List of Values**: This wizard will help us to create the SQL query for the LOV in a declarative manner.

The Security section

This section, as can be seen in the following screenshot, allows us to set some crude security measures for the item. Chapter 22, which is devoted entirely to APEX security issues, provides us with some more fine tuning options we can use on the item.

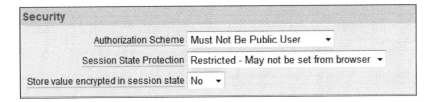

The various fields of the Security section are explained as follows:

- **Authorization Scheme**: The default option of this field is **No Authorization Required**, which means everyone can access the item. The second predefined option, which we can see in the screenshot—**Must Not Be Public User**, allows access to authenticated users only. If, as Chapter 22 explains, we defined our own authorization scheme(s), then we will be allowed to choose from them.

- **Session State Protection**: The default option of this field is **Unrestricted**. However, similar to what we have seen with application level items, we also have an option of restricted changes to the item value, made from the browser. This restriction will be forced even if *Session State Protection* is disabled at the application level.

- **Store Value encrypted in session state**: The default option of this field is **No**. Setting this field to **Yes** will cause the APEX engine to encrypt the value of the item prior to saving it in *Session State*. That allows us to protect sensitive information from other privileged database users that can access APEX metadata tables directly.

The Conditions section

This section allows us to define conditions for rendering the item on the application page in a declarative manner. Only if the condition is evaluated to be **true** will the item be rendered on page.

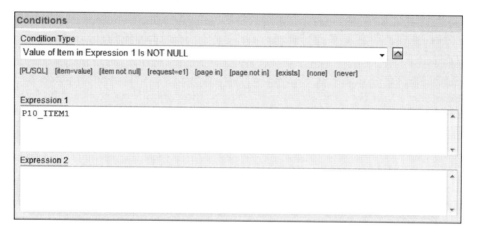

The Condition Type field

This select list item contains a varied list of pre-defined conditions, which can pertain to any application or page level item; runtime parameters such as the **REQUEST** value, the current page identity, validation errors, etc. The conditions can also includes a reference to some environment parameters like the current application language, type of client browser, or some CGI parameters. If we can't find a predefined declarative condition that exactly matches our need, then we can use any SQL or PL/SQL expression or define a PL/SQL function, which returns a Boolean value.

Performance wise, it's always best to use the predefined declarative conditions over the manual coded SQL or PL/SQL expressions or functions. Make yourself familiar with all the predefined declarative options and use them whenever possible. You can find a list of all the available pre-defined conditions for APEX 3.2 at the following URL: `http://download.oracle.com/docs/cd/E14373_01/appdev.32/e11838/condition.htm#BABBBDHI`.

The list of predefined conditions includes the **Never** condition. This condition means that the item will never be rendered on the application page. However, this doesn't mean that the item doesn't exist. The APEX engine will allocate a variable to the item, and we'll be able to reference it using the bind variable notation. The fact that the item is accessible in the APEX engine, but on the other hand it doesn't render on page, makes its behavior similar to an *application item* .

The Expression 1 / Expression 2 fields

The use of these fields is determined by the selected condition we want to apply. Some of the conditions only use the **Expression 1** field, and some of them use both fields. The content of the fields is also dependant on the type of condition we are applying. In some cases, the fields will include item names; in others, they can include data or snippets of SQL or PL/SQL code.

In the screenshot of the **Conditions** section, we can see an example of using a predefined condition to check that the item in **Expression 1** is not NULL.

While referencing APEX items using the predefined declarative conditions, we are using the APEX item name, e.g. P10_ITEM1. If we are referencing the item in a SQL or PL/SQL expression or function, we are using the bind variable notation, e.g. :P10_ITEM1 > 10 .

If we are referencing items on the current page, we are referencing their *temporary session state* value as it was computed in the **Source** section. The values of other items will be taken from the *persistent session state*.

The Read Only section

This section allows us to set the item as **Read Only**, using the same conditions mechanism, as in the **Conditions** section.

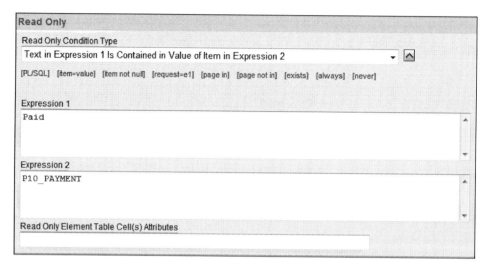

In the screenshot, we can see an example of using a predefined, declarative condition that is using both **Expression 1** and **Expression 2** fields. In this case, the condition is that if the value in **Expressin 1** — Paid — is contained in the value of the item specified in **Expressin 2** — P10_PAYMENT — the item will be set as Read Only.

This section also includes the **Read Only Element Table Cell(s) Attributes** field that allows us to add HTML attributes to the table cell (<td>) occupied by the Read Only item. For example, we can use style="background-color: EDEDED;" to create a light gray background color to the Read Only item.

> The APEX implementation of the Read Only display of the item does not include the use of the ReadOnly HTML property, mainly because some HTML items, such as select list or checkbox, don't support this property. If you want to manipulate Read Only items, you should check the specific APEX implementation for the specific item you are working with.

The Help text section

This single field section allows us to define a specific help text for the item. If we choose to use an item *label template*, which supports item help, then the content of this section will be displayed in the popup help window for the item.

If we implement the page level help system, the content of this section will also appear in the help page as the description of the item.

The Configuration section

APEX allows us to control the availability of its elements through a mechanism called **Build Option**. This single field section allows us to associate the item with a specific Build Option, and by that, it gives us one more parameter to control the availability of the item.

> *Build options* can be defined in the **Logic** section of the *Shared Components* module. This mechanism allows us to have a single APEX application with several different levels of functionalities according to the various build options we defined.

The Comments section

This single field section allows us, as developers, to document anything worth documenting about the item.

APEX pre-defined item types

Until now, we reviewed the common general properties available to us when we want to define an APEX page item. The following is a general description of all the predefined APEX page items we can use on our application page. Later in the book we'll use these items in various examples, emphasizing the unique features of each item type.

Text based items

The following item type's functionality is based on input/output of free text:

 Text

This type of item allows us to input free text. The APEX engine generates a DOM Text object using the HTML <input> tag as part of its implementation.

The **Create Item** wizard supports 5 sub-types of the item, as can be seen in the following screenshot:

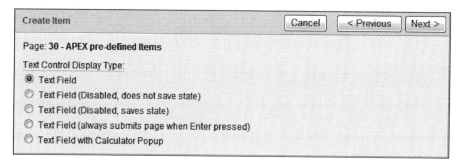

Saves/does not save state refer to *Session State*. Does not save state means that the value of this type of item will not be persistent, as it will not be saved in *Session State*.

 The **Text Field (Disabled, does not save state)** type will create an HTML item without HTML ID, which means the item will not include a hook for JavaScript code. All the other types will include an HTML ID equal to the name of the item.

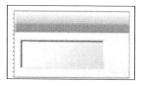 # Text area

This type of item allows us to define a multi-row text area, which allows us to input a large amount of free text. The APEX engine generates a DOM Textarea object using the HTML <input> tag as part of its implementation.

The **Create Item** wizard supports various options for the *Text Area* item type, including the support of a built-in HTML editor (a version of the Web-based FCK editor).

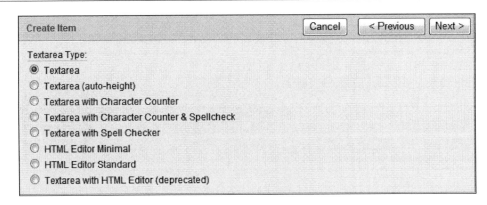

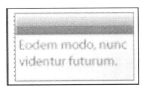

Display Only

This type of item will display the value of the item as Display Only text, not using the format of an input field. The APEX engine implements this type of item in several ways, depending on whether the item should save or not save *session state*.

The **Create Item** wizard supports various options of this type, including the use of LOV as the resource for the display text, and options to save or not save the displayed text in *session state*.

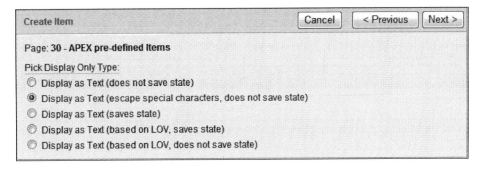

Item types that don't save *session state* will be rendered on the page without the ID property.

Password

This type of item is actually a private case of the Text type. It will display an asterisk instead of every character that will be keyed into the field. The APEX engine generates a DOM Password object using the HTML `<input>` tag as part of its implementation.

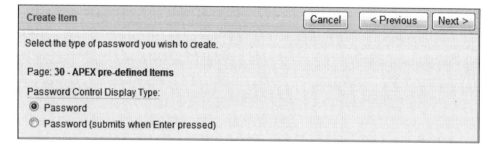

This type also supports the option of submitting the page upon pressing the *Enter* key right after entering the password.

 Security Note:

This item type does **not** encrypt the entered password, it merely masks its value on screen. Without further security measures, the password will be transmitted over the wires using clear text, and if we choose to save the item into a database table, it will be saved as clear text.

Multi-option based items

These types of items allow us to set the value(s) of the item by choosing it/them from a list of options. All these types of items are based on a static or dynamic LOV, as we discussed earlier in this chapter.

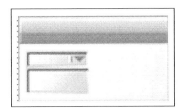

Select List

This type of item allows us to select a single value from a list of values. The APEX engine implements this type with the DOM Select and Option objects, which are generated using the HTML `<select>` and `<option>` tags.

The **Create Item** wizard supports several options for this type:

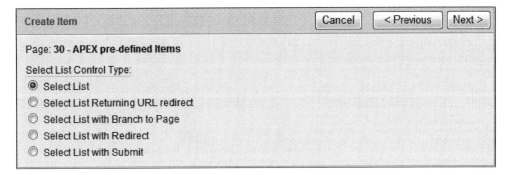

These options are mainly to support cascading select lists (the value of the second select list depends on the selected value from the first select list) without the use of AJAX (e.g. in cases where the client disabled its Web browser JavaScript supports or the browser doesn't support JavaScript as with in some PDAs or smart-phones).

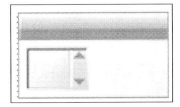

Multiple Select

This type of item allows us to select multiple values from the select list. For this extended functionality, the APEX engine sets the `multiple` and `size` attributes of the HTML `<select>` tag. By default, the `size` attribute is set to '5', which means the item will simultaneously display five options.

APEX uses a colon (:) delimited string of values to represent the selected values. For example, if we selected two options: Red and Green, then the value of the item will be set to Red:Green. If we want to set a default value for this type of item we need to create a colon-delimited list of values. We'll see an example of that later in the book.

Personally, I don't like to use the Multiple Select item because of the way one needs to select multiple values; we need to simultaneously press the *ctrl* key while clicking on the selected options. However, if you forget to press the *ctrl* key, all the previous selections are lost. I find it very annoying. APEX supports the **Shuttle** item (we'll review this shortly), which supports the same functionalities but in a much more user-friendly manner.

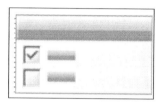

Check Box

This type of item allows us to mark several options as the value of the item. The APEX engine generates a DOM Checkbox object using the HTML <input> tag for every option of the checkbox item. Each such <input> tag has its own unique ID attribute, which is derived from the APEX item name. For example, if the name of the checkbox item is P1_CHECKBOX, the first option of it will be identified by P1_CHECKBOX_0, the next option will have an ID of P1_CHECKBOX_1, and so forth. The APEX engine generates a <fieldset> tag, which wraps the checkbox item, and has an ID attribute equal to the APEX item name.

The use of the <fieldset> tag was introduced in APEX 3.0. In earlier versions the page did not include an ID that exactly matched the item name (in contrast to the default behavior of the APEX engine).

APEX is using a colon (:) delimited string of values to represent the checked options of the item.

The CheckBox item displays a different behavior at submit time, as an unchecked item is not being submitted with the page. This behavior is part of the HTML standard and has nothing to do with APEX. We'll discuss this special behavior in more detail as part of a discussion about using checkboxes in tabular forms.

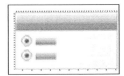

Radio

This type of item allows us to select only one single option from the item options list. In every other aspect, it is implemented by the APEX engine in the same way as the Checkbox item.

The **Create Item** wizard supports two more options for submitting the page or performs self-redirection upon selecting an item option. These options are there to mainly support cascading elements (the value/content of the second element depends on the value of the first element) without the use of AJAX.

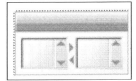

Shuttle

This type of item, which was introduced in APEX 3.0, allows us to manage a multi-option item in a very easy and user-friendly manner. The displayed values of the item LOV source are displayed on the left side component of the *Shuttle*, and we set the item value by moving them into the right side *Shuttle* component. APEX uses a colon (:) delimited string of values to represent the values on the right side component of the item.

NLS Note:

The right and left components of the shuttle are reversed in an RTL oriented environment. However the shuttle controls are not. This item needs special attention if used in an RTL oriented application, and we'll discuss it in more detail, later in the book, with one of the RTL oriented examples.

The APEX engine implementation of the *Shuttle* item is quite complicated, and unlike all the previous types of items we've reviewed so far, which are directly implemented by using corresponding HTML objects, the *Shuttle* type implementation includes an APEX engine internal logic, which operates on two separated select list elements and several control icons.

Popup List of Values

This type of item allows us to manage a large volume of multiple item values by using a popup window that can display predefined LOV, and that can also include a search (filter) mechanism. The item is comprised of a text field, with an adjacent icon that opens the popup window. Selecting an item in the popup window will populate the text field while closing the popup window.

The **Create Item** wizard supports several options for LOV item implementation, which differ by the nature of the returned value, the ways the popup window LOV members are fetched, etc.

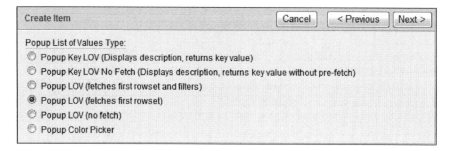

As we can see in the screenshot, the last popup type is a **Popup Color Picker**, which opens a popup window with a pallet of colors, that allows us to choose the color we need without knowing its name or code.

The select list items tends to misbehave, not to mention having high memory consumption if they include too many options. "Too many options" is not exactly an accurate term, but as a rule of thumb, if you have more than a few hundred members in your LOV, you'll be better off using the popup LOV item.

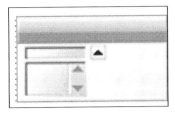

List Manager

This type also allows us to manage a list of values. It can include several components such as a multi-select list, a text input field, a popup icon, and **Add** and **Remove** control buttons, as shown in the following screenshot:

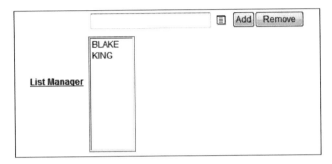

This type of item is also implemented using an APEX engine internal logic. Its value is also represented with a colon (:) delimited string of values.

The **Create Item** wizard supports several options of item functionality for this type:

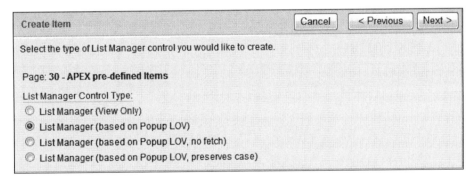

The selected values in the *List Manager* displayed list are all converted to upper case strings; white space is not allowed and it's removed by the item.

Special functionality items

The following types of items have specific functionality.

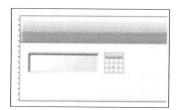

Data Picker

This type of item allows us to open a popup window that includes a calendar that we can use to pick a date (and in some cases a time). The implementation of this type includes a text field with an adjacent icon for the popup calendar. Both elements are wrapped with a `<fieldset>` tag.

This type includes long and varied date and time formats, which are predefined. APEX 3.x also allows us to use self-defined application level formats, and we'll discuss these in more detail in the *Globalization* chapter (Chapter 18).

NLS note:

The popup calendar includes NLS, and the date elements (e.g. days and months) are displayed according to the database NLS settings. The APEX translation mechanism also allows us to translate the calendar buttons.

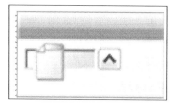

File Brows

This type of item utilizes the HTML DOM FileUpload object. It uses the `<input>` tag to allow us to upload files stored on the local desktop into the database, while presenting a local OS file system browse mechanism. The browse button displayed with the item is an integral part of the HTML implementation of it, and as such, the Web browser itself is responsible for its rendering. This means that the appearance of the button and its label content and language, are Web browser dependent.

Due to some security restrictions in the HTML standard we are not allowed to set a default value to this type of item and we can't clear its content (including through JavaScript). The content of the item will automatically be cleared by the Web browser as part of the page submits process, even if the submits process had failed.

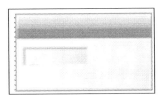

Hidden

This type of item allows us to set hidden items on the page. The APEX engine generates a DOM Hidden object using the HTML `<input>` tag as part of its implementation. Hidden items are rendered on the page, but they are invisible to the users. Nevertheless, every technique that allows us to set the value of a non-hidden item can also be used with hidden items. That is the reason the **Create Item** wizard supports two options when implementing this item:

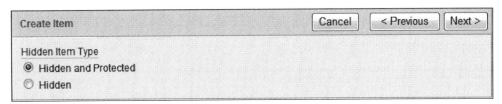

The APEX engine will not allow us to set/change the value of a **Hidden and Protected** item from the client side.

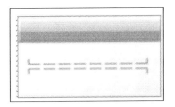

Stop and start table

We have already encountered the potential anomalies of using HTML tables for items layout when we discussed the **Displayed** section of the item. We also reviewed some possible solutions to the situation. However, sometimes a single layout table is not flexible enough for our needs and we want to use more than one. This field allows us to do just that. It closes the current page layout table and it opens a new one. This way, dimensions of previous items on page will not interfere with the layout of the upcoming page items.

The following screenshot shows us a "regular" layout of some APEX items on page:

We can see the **Frequency** field—a *Radio* item with several options, which we chose to display in a single row (using the **Number of Column** field in the LOV section of the item). As a result, the **Finish Date** item, with the attributes of **Begin On New Line** set to **No** and **...Field** set to **Yes**, was positioned far away from the first item on its row—**Start Date**—because of the width of the **Frequently** item.

By inserting the **Stop and start table** item between the **Frequency** item and the **Start Date** item, as can be seen in the following screenshot, we separated the page layout table of the **Frequency** item (and all the potential items that preceded it) from the following items on page:

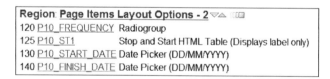

As a result, the widths of the columns of the new page layout table were determined only according to the *Date Picker* items with the higher sequence than the **Stop and start table** item. The new layout looks like this:

If we fill the **Label** field of this item, its content will be displayed on the application page, as a visible separator between the HTML layout tables.

Creating APEX items programmatically

APEX allows us to programmatically create some of the predefined APEX items, as part of SQL or PL/SQL code, using the **APEX_ITEM** API. We'll review this API and see examples of how to use it later in the book, mainly in Chapter 14, which deals with APEX tabular forms.

Summary

In this chapter, we reviewed all the predefined APEX item types and all the declarative fields we can use within the **Edit Page Item** page, in order to define and fine tune them to our needs.

In the next chapter, we'll discuss other very important components on our application page—the buttons.

6
APEX Buttons

APEX buttons are very important components of the APEX application page. They allow us to initiate various page related processes that are responsible for the page functionalities—like submitting the page to the server, and by doing so, starts the page ACCEPT process, or for the flow control of the application—like redirecting to a new page.

The *Application Builder* supports three styles of buttons— an HTML Button, Image based buttons, and Template Driven buttons. Each button must be associated with a page region. Within the region, we can position the buttons based on some predetermined locations in the region template or among the page items in the region.

In this chapter, we will cover:

- The different types of buttons that a developer can place on an Apex page
- Creating buttons and assigning attributes
- Displaying buttons in different regions on the page
- Using the REQUEST feature

Button styles

The *Application Builder* allows us to define three different styles of buttons. As we'll see, the differences between these styles are not only with regards to their looks on the page, but also relate to the measure of control we have over them and their functionality.

HTML Button

This type of button utilizes the HTML `<input>` tag with the `type="button"` property to create the button. As such, the look of the button is Web browser dependent, and will be determined according to the standard look of the said button in each of the various Web browsers we'll use.

The APEX engine uses the `onclick` event to fire JavaScript code to implement the functionality of the button. It also adds the `ID` property and sets it to the button name.

We'll discuss button names later in the chapter, but for now, remember that the button name is an all capital letters string that is not necessarily equal to the button label.

Using this type of button minimizes the HTML page code we need to use. However, it still gives us a high degree of control over the button functionality by using HTML DOM events. At the same time, we lose control over the button appearance, which is Web browser dependent.

NLS Note:

HTML buttons are supported by the APEX built-in translation mechanism, which makes it very easy to translate applications that use this type of button.

Image based button

This type of button utilizes the HTML `<a>` and `<img>` tags to display an image, and gives it a button like functionality.

The APEX engine uses the `href` attribute, with the **javascript:** keyword, to associate JavaScript code with the image to implement the functionality of the button.

Using this type of button gives us full control over the looks of the button and a high degree of control over its functionality. However, we become responsible for supplying the appropriate graphical images to be used as buttons. The APEX built-in *Themes* library includes some generic graphical images, but for most cases they will not be enough.

NLS note:

If our images reflect meaningful messages (i.e. contain text) in the main language of the application, then we'll need to create new images that reflect the same meaningful messages (text) in the language we are going to use for the translated application. If you are going to work in a multi-lingual environment, then you should consider it in advance and check if you can do it (not only from the graphical aspect, but also from a legal point of view). For example, you might be using graphical images that are copyright-protected.

Template Driven button

This type of button is rendered according to theme dependent *button templates*. The button is implemented using a (one row) three-column table. The middle column includes an `<a>` tag and the button label as a text node. The first and third columns include an `<a>` tag that wraps an `<img>` tag. The images used are also theme dependent and we use them to create the right and left edges of the button. Another theme dependent icon is used through a theme dependent CSS class, to create the background of the button body.

The template driven button uses the largest amount of HTML and CSS code, but it gives us a relatively easy way of constructing theme related buttons and creates a more unique and graphically coordinated look and feel to the themes. At the same time, templates give us a high degree of control over button functionality.

NLS Note:

Template Driven buttons are supported by the APEX built-in translation mechanism, which makes it very easy to translate applications that use this type of button. However, unlike *HTML buttons, template driven* buttons are page-oriented sensitive. The APEX Built-in button templates support (out-of-the-box) only the left-to-right orientation. For right-to-left orientation supports, we need to make some changes in the templates or the associated graphical images. We'll discuss all that in a dedicated chapter for RTL support later in the book (Chapter 19).

Button positioning

APEX buttons must be associated with a page region. As an application page can include more than one page region, each button must be associated with the page region in which it's going to be rendered. We have two options for positioning the button within the page region. These options are not just about the layout of the button on page. As we'll see next, these options also affect the "out-of-the-box" functionality of the button. The options are:

- **Create a button in a region position**: This option is based on some predetermined locations, which are defined as part of the region template we are using. This type of positioning supports page submits with redirect, or page redirect only (including page self-redirect, i.e. redirecting to the current page, which is equivalent to refreshing/reloading the page). In both cases, we can either note a specific APEX application page number or use a URL notation to define the target of the redirection.

The option of using a URL allows us to use the f?p notation while utilizing all its options such as setting page item values. However, what is more important in this context is that it allows us to use the **javascript:** keyword to associate JavaScript code with the button. Using JavaScript is not that straightforward with the second type of positioning. This is a major difference in the "out-of-the-box" functionality of these two options.

- **Create a button displayed among this region's items**: This positioning option treats the button as a page item. The button definition will also appear in the **Items** section, and its actual position will be determined according to its sequence number relative to the other items on the page. This type of positioning only supports a *page submit* action. No redirect action is supported out-of-the-box.

Since this type of button doesn't support redirecting, no URL field is provided, hence we can't associate JavaScript code with this type of button. Later in the chapter, we'll see some possible solutions to this limitation.

Create new button(s)

The *Page Definition* page includes a **Buttons** section in the **Page Rendering** column, as shown in the following screenshot:

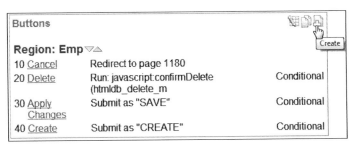

Clicking on the **Create** icon in the upper-right-hand corner of the **Buttons** section will load the **Create Button** wizard, which can be seen in the next screenshot:

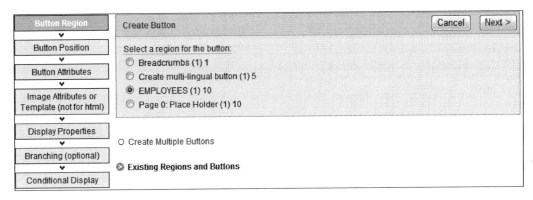

As every button must be associated with a specific region on the page, the first thing we'll be asked to do is to choose a page region to render the button. In our example, the regions list includes four regions—three on the current working page and one on page 0 (I remind you that components on page 0, like page regions, appear on every application page and as such are included in the list of the page regions). The list also includes general information on the layout of the regions on the page. The first number, at the end of the region name, appears in parentheses and indicates the region column. In the example, all the regions are in column (1) so they appear one under the other on the page. If one of them, for example, occupies column (2) it means the regions are rendered side-by-side. Adjacent to the column number is the region sequence on page, which determines the order of rendering the regions on the page.

Very often, when we manually define the page buttons, we need to define more than just one button. For these cases, I want to draw your attention to the **Create Multiple Buttons** link, which leads you to a tabular form like wizard that allows you to define multiple buttons. The following screenshot is an example of this wizard page:

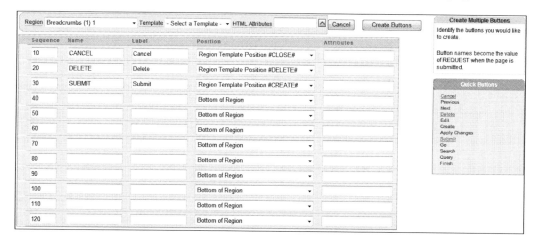

This wizard also includes a **Quick Buttons** assistance box on its right hand side, which includes initial definitions for common buttons like **Cancel**, **Delete**, **Submit**, etc. as the screenshot demonstrates.

The **Create Multiple Buttons** wizard supports only the *region position* buttons, which we'll discuss in the next section. It allows us to define only the initial attributes of these buttons. Later on, we can edit any of the newly created buttons for specific attributes we need to assign.

Button position

Assuming we didn't choose to define multiple buttons, we will be asked next to choose the position of the button within the region. As we discussed already, the position type has an effect on the button attributes and functionality, so the choice we make here will influence the next steps of the **Create Button** wizard.

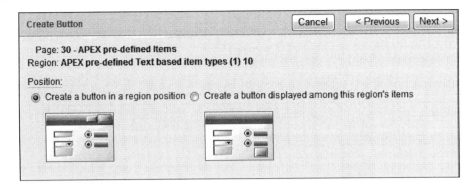

Create a button in a region position

Choosing this option leads us to a series of wizard screens, in which we'll be able to define the features of this type of button.

Button attributes

In this wizard screen, we can define the major (and mandatory) attributes of the button:

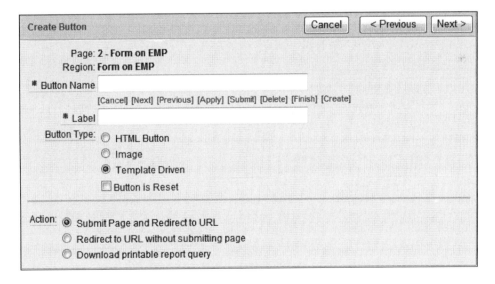

The important fields are explained as follows:

- **Button Name**: This is a mandatory field. The button name is an all capital letters string (and the wizard will convert it into one, if we didn't). This name will be used to set the APEX built-in REQUEST variable. We'll discuss this special variable later in the chapter.

- **Label**: This is also a mandatory field. The value of this field will appear as the button label for *HTML button* and *template driven* buttons.

> **NLS Note:**
>
> As the HTML button and template driven button types are supported by the APEX built-in translation mechanism, we'll be able to translate this field into the translated application languages.

- **Button Type**: This field allows us to choose the button type we want to define.

  In addition to the button style types, we can check the **Button is Reset** checkbox. This will cause the APEX engine to set the functionality of the button to fire the *DOM Form Object* method reset(). This method will reset the content of all the items on the page to their values at rendering time, without reloading the page or changing any session state values. The APEX engine will change the button name to FLOW_RESET_BUTTON.

- **Action**: The **Create a button in a region position** type of button supports three major actions:

  - **Submit Page and Redirect to URL**: This action submits the page, and initiates the page ACCEPT process, which includes setting *session state*, and then the processes defined in the *Page Processing* column. After that, it will redirect to the URL specified (including self-redirect).

  - **Redirect to URL without submitting page**: This action redirects to the specified URL without submitting the page. *Session state* will not be set and the page ACCEPT process will not run.

  - **Download printable report query**: This action was introduced in APEX 3.0 as part of some new and advanced printing options. It will appear only if the application includes *Report Queries* that are outside the scope of this book, so we'll not get into specific details about this action.

The first two *Action* options include **Redirect to URL**. You should remember that it means the option of using JavaScript code or the f?p notation, which allows us to set item values. The latter is especially useful for the **Redirect to URL without submitting page** option, as it doesn't save *session state*.

Image attributes or template (not for HTML)

If we choose to use the *Image* or the *Template Driven* button, we'll be asked next to specify the image or button template that we want to use.

In the case of an image we can use graphical files that are stored in the **images** directory. In this case, we can reference these images using the built-in *Substitution String* #IMAGE_PREFIX#, e.g. #IMAGE_PREFIX#edit.gif . We can also use graphical images that were uploaded into the database. In this case, and according to the images associated with a workspace or application, we can reference them using the *Substitution Strings* #WORKSPACE_IMAGES# or #APP_IMAGES# respectively, e.g. #APP_IMAGES#edit.gif .

Display properties

In this wizard screen we can determine the location of the button in the predefined region positions:

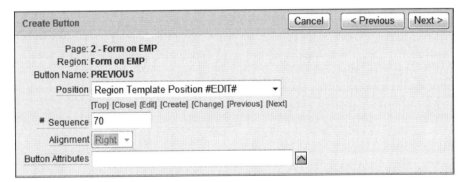

Position

This is a select list field that allows us to choose the location of the button. We can choose a location that is relative to the region itself, like **Above Region**, or **Bottom of Region**; or we can choose a predefined location inside the region that correlates with a specific *Substitution String* in the *region template*, such as **Region Template Position #EDIT#**.

By default, HTML treats multiple white spaces as a single character. Hence, if our region template includes the following sequence of region position *Substitution Strings* `#EDIT##CHANGE##CREATE#`, and we only used the `#EDIT#` and `#CREATE#` positions, then the corresponding buttons will appear adjacently on our application page, in spite of the (empty) `#CHANGE#` position.

Sequence

This is a mandatory field that determines the order in which the buttons will be rendered on the page. This sequence has a positioning meaning and is relevant to when you choose the same region position for several buttons. In this case, the actual order of appearance on the page will be determined by the sequence of the buttons.

Branching (optional)

This wizard screen allows us to choose the application page we'll be redirected to, upon pressing the button and completing its functionality. The wizard will create a branch entry in the *Branches* section of the *Page Definition* page, which will be conditioned by pressing this button. More details about that in Chapter 10, which deals with *Branches*.

Conditional display

This wizard screen allows us to condition the rendering of the button. This is the same mechanism we described for the page items.

Button conditioning is especially useful if the button represents a special functionality that should not always be available. For example, an **edit** button should only be rendered on page if the page contains an existing record in the database. With the same logic, a **create** button should be rendered only for new records.

Create a button displayed among this region's items

Choosing this button position option leads us to a wizard screen that allows us to define the features of this type of button:

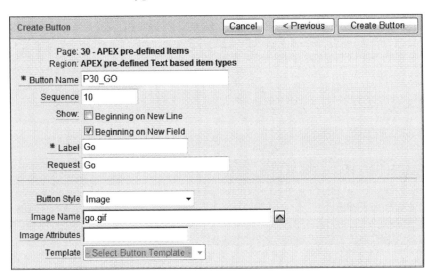

Most of the fields in this screen are familiar to us from the previous button type. Let's review the new ones:

- **Show**: The APEX engine treats the *among this region's items* button as a regular page item. Similar to regular page items, we get to decide whether the button will be positioned on a new line and in a new field.

- **Request**: With this type of button we can define the REQUEST value to be different from the button name. This option allows us to apply the page item naming convention to the button names also, and still associate special reserved REQUEST values with it. We'll discuss this further in the next section.

As seen in the previous screenshot, the *among this region's items* button doesn't include URL field. This means that we can not directly associate JavaScript code with this type of button.

Edit a button

We can edit the attributes of an existing button by clicking on its name in the *Buttons* section. All the attributes we set when we first create the button are open for us to edit. However, the **Edit Page Buttons** page includes a new section called **Database Manipulation Request**, which can be seen in the following screenshot:

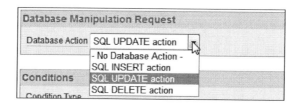

This section allows us to associate the button with a specific database DML action at the **Page Processing** phase regardless of its name or REQUEST value, which we'll discuss next.

If we associate a button with a database action, pressing the button will trigger this action as part of the *Page Processing* phase. We will return to this option in Chapter 9, when we discuss the *Processes* options that APEX provides us.

The REQUEST feature

This is an APEX built-in feature that helps us to determine if, or which button, has been activated (pressed).

Each time we press a button, and this button initializes a page submit process, the APEX engine sets the value of REQUEST to the *Name* of the button, or to the value of the **Request** field in case this is a button displayed among items.

We can also manually set the REQUEST value, either declaratively as part of a page branch, or by using the fourth segment of the f?p URL notation.

The REQUEST scope

Submitting the page initiates the page ACCEPT process, which includes several activities (as can be seen in the **Page Processing** column) such as *Validations*, *Computations*, *Processes*, and *Branches*. The REQUEST value is retained throughout the ACCEPT process and can be referenced in each of its activities. By default, the REQUEST value is cleared—set to NULL—with every branch to a new page (or self-branching).

If we manually set the REQUEST value as part of a page branch, it will retain its value and it will be available to us in the SHOW process of the target page.

Referencing REQUEST

We can reference REQUEST in several ways depending on the type of code we are using:

- **SQL and PL/SQL**: We have several options to reference the REQUEST value from within SQL or PL/SQL code:
    - ○ `apex_application.g_request`: A global package variable (documented)
    - ○ `:REQUEST`: Using the bind variable notation
    - ○ `v('REQUEST')`: Using the APEX built-in function
    - ○ `&REQUEST.`: Using the substitution string notation when the code is stored in the *Application Builder*

- **JavaScript**: Each application page contains, by default, a hidden item with the ID of pRequest. This item will hold the REQUEST value, provided a page branch process sets it.

We can use the fourth segment of the `f?p` URL notation to manually set the REQUEST value. For example, `f?p=&APP_ID.:2:&SESSION.:Go` will set the REQUEST value to Go as part of redirecting to page 2.

> In most cases, the value of REQUEST will be an all capital letters string, but because of the button names naming convention, it can also hold mixed string values, as shown in the example. However, it's important to remember that if you are using the REQUEST value in the *Conditions* section, or with any other manual code, it will be case sensitive. For example, conditioning a button display with a REQUEST value of GO or Go will yield different results.

We can also reference REQUEST in the APEX built-in condition mechanism, as we'll see in the next section.

Condition by REQUEST

We can use the REQUEST value to condition the rendering or firing of various APEX components in both page SHOW and ACCEPT processes.

The APEX built-in condition mechanism includes four predefined declarative conditions that use REQUEST:

- Request = Expression 1
- Request != Expression 1
- Request Is Contained within Expression 1
- Request Is NOT Contained within Expression 1

In addition, we can condition almost all the page ACCEPT actions by pressing a specific button. For example, we can condition a delete process to run only if the delete button is pressed. In these cases, the APEX engine actually checks the REQUEST value—which was automatically set upon pressing the button—and compares it with the process condition.

The **Automatic Row Processing (DML)** process, which we'll discuss in greater detail in the APEX Process chapter, also uses the REQUEST value to determine which of the three supported actions—Insert, Update, or Delete—it should fire. This usually depends on the pressed button that initialized the page submit process.

In the same manner, if we are using the built-in JavaScript function doSubmit() to initialize a page submit, we can use its parameter to set the REQUEST value as if a button was pressed. For example, doSubmit('CREATE') will submit the page as if the create button—a button with the name CREATE—was pressed.

Using REQUEST as a parameter of doSubmit() is optional. It should be used only if we specifically need to set the value of REQUEST.

Using JavaScript with "among this region's items" buttons

As we saw, the **among this region's items** type of button doesn't support redirection, hence doesn't include a URL field. As a result, it makes it harder for us to attach JavaScript code to the button.

We can resolve this limitation in several ways, but here we'll review two of them.

Using this type of button, we usually want to render a button adjacent to an existing page item. Instead of using a dedicated APEX Button, we can use the **Post Element Text** field of the item to define an HTML Button. We can use an `onclick` event to attach any JavaScript code that we need to the button. In the "The Pre/Post Element Text fields" section of Chapter 5, we can see an example of using an APEX *shortcut* to do just that.

If we are using *template driven* buttons in our application and we want to maintain uniform looks among all our buttons, then we can harness the button **Attributes** field to help. Originally, this field was designed to hold the button style attributes, and it associates with the button template `#BUTTON_ATTRIBUTES#` *substitution string*. We can, however, relocate the *substitution string* and use it as part of the `href` attribute of the button link.

The following is an example of button template code, which supports this technique:

```
<table cellpadding="0" cellspacing="0" border="0" summary=""
class="t5Button">
<tr>
<td class="t5R"><a href="#BUTTON_ATTRIBUTES#" tabindex="999">
<img src="#IMAGE_PREFIX#themes/theme_5/button_right.png" alt=""
/></a></td>
<td class="t5C"><a href="#BUTTON_ATTRIBUTES#">#LABEL#</a></td>
<td class="t5L"><a href="#BUTTON_ATTRIBUTES#" tabindex="999">
<img src="#IMAGE_PREFIX#themes/theme_5/button_left.png" alt=""
/></a></td>
</tr>
</table>
```

If we set the content of the **Attributes** field of the button to:

```
javascript: redirect("f?p=&APP_ID.:2:&SESSION.");
```

pressing this button will redirect us to page 2, although originally this type of button doesn't support redirection. Of course, using this technique allows us to attach any JavaScript code we need to this button.

In the following screenshot, we can see an example of using an **among this region's items** button to call a JavaScript function—`printMessages()`—while setting the button REQUEST to PRINTMESSAGES. The template being used in this example is a duplicate of a predefined button template, with amended code, similar to the previous code example:

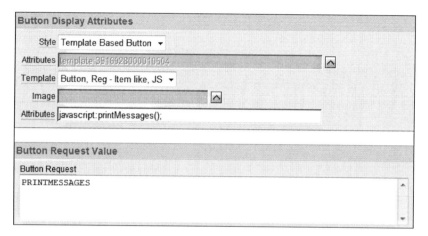

Re-visit the Buttons section

Let's take another look at the **Buttons** section, as we can see it in the following screenshot:

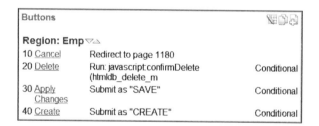

Now, we can have a better understanding of what we see. For each button we can see its sequence; its text label, which also acts as a link to the **Edit Page Buttons** page; the button's main functionality—redirect to a specific page, run JavaScript code; or submit the page. In the latter case we can also see the button REQUEST value. Lastly, we can see an indication of whether the button display is **Conditional**.

Summary

In this chapter, we reviewed the APEX Buttons.

APEX supports three styles of buttons: **HTML Button, Image** based buttons, and **Template Driven** buttons; with two major positioning options: **Create a button in a region position**, and **Create a button displayed among this region's items**. We also discussed the REQUEST feature and how it can help us to use APEX buttons more effectively.

In the next chapter we are going to review APEX computations.

7

APEX Computations

Computations are APEX's declarative way of setting an item's values on the page or at the application level.

On the page level, when we look at the *Page Definition* page, we can see that a **Computations** section appears both in the *Page Rendering* column and in the *Page Processing* column. It's actually the same mechanism, using the same wizard. However, each computation has its own **Computation Points**, and these points determine the computation association with the page rendering phase (the SHOW process) or the page submit phase (the page ACCEPT process).

At the application level, an application computation will run every time a page is rendered or once on a new instance, according to its *Computation Point*.

In this chapter we shall review the computation mechanism and see how we can use it in our applications.

Create a page level computation

Within the *Page Definition* page we can choose either of the **Computations** sections (in the *Page Rendering* or *Page Processing* columns) to create a new computation, using the create icon. The icon will lead us to the **Create Page Computation** wizard:

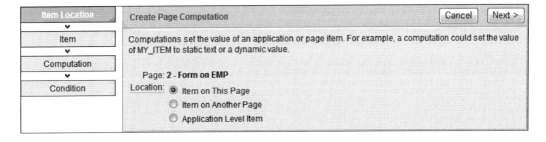

The wizard allows us to create a *Computation* for a specific item on the current page, an item on other pages of the application, or for an application level item. In the next wizard screen—**Item**—we are asked to choose a specific item for the computation:

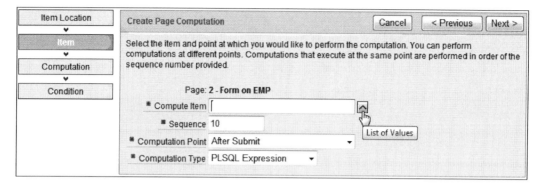

Compute item

This is a mandatory field. Its type depends on the location of the computed item. In the case of an item on the current page we'll see a select list with all the current page items. For items on other pages, or application items, we'll see a popup **LOV (List Of Values)** item, which includes all the relevant items.

Sequence

This is a mandatory field that determines the order in which the computations will be executed within a computation point.

This field doesn't have to be unique, even within the same computation point.

Computation point

This mandatory select list field allows us to choose the firing point of the computation code. The wizard supports eight different computation points; the first seven are related to the *Page Rendering* phase and the last one is related to the *Page Processing* phase.

Page Rendering computation points

It's important to understand that although we are talking about the *Page Rendering* phase, its related computations are server-side activities. They pertain to the different stages of building the HTML code of the application page.

At this stage, we can use the following computation points:

- **On New Instance (e.g. On Login)**: This option will fire the computation every time the user logs in to the application. It will also fire when the session state is being reset on the application or session level.

The following computation points correspond with the matching page components:

- **Before Header**
- **After Header**
- **Before Region(s)**
- **After Region(s)**
- **Before Footer**
- **After Footer**

 As we mentioned in Chapter 3, *Computation* sets the *Session State* and, as such, can influence the displayed value of the computed item in this phase. We are going to discuss this further, later in the chapter.

Page Processing computation point

At this point, we have only one computation point—**After Submit**.

After Submit computations will be executed as the second stage of *Page Processing*—after the automatic and transparent setting of *Session State* that follows the page submit, but before **Validations** (which we are going to discuss in the next chapter). This order allows us to use this computation point to "prepare" the submitted values for the validation inspection.

As computation also sets *Session State*, the session state values that were set during page submit, might be changed according to the computation result.

Computation type

This mandatory select list field allows us to choose the type of code, or assignment, that we want to use in the computation. The following types are supported:

- **Static Assignment**: The actual value we want to assign. This type also supports the &ITEM. *substitution string* notation.

- **PL/SQL Function Body**: We can use PL/SQL function code to obtain the value of the computation. The function body must include a RETURN statement. If we need to use local function variables, then we declare them in a similar manner to a PL/SQL anonymous block. For example:

```
declare
  l_status varchar2(20);
  l_credit  customers.credit%TYPE;
begin
  select credit into l_credit
  from customers
  where cust_id = :P20_CUSTOMER_ID;

  if l_credit >= :P20_CURRENT_PURCHASE then
    l_status := 'Approved';
  else
    l_status := 'Not enough credit';
  end if;
  return l_status;
end;
```

> This option also allows us to call a stored function by using the following notation: return myPackage.myFunctio(x,y);. This way, we can utilize existing functions, or define stored functions that we can reuse in various computations. Defining stored functions is also preferable where large code is involved or when we need to obfuscate the code of the function.

- **SQL Query**: We can use a SQL query to fetch the computation value. For example:

```
select customers_seq.nextval from dual
```

Or:

```
Select discount
from customers
where cust_id = :P20_CUSTOMER_ID;
```

> As each computation can set a value of a single item, we must make sure that the SQL query will return only a single value. Otherwise, a runtime error will occur.

- **SQL Expression** and **PLSQL Expression**: We can use any valid SQL or PL/SQL expression to compute the item value. In this specific context there is no difference between the SQL and PL/SQL expressions, and they are implemented in the same way by the APEX engine. For example:

```
replace(:P20_STATE,'%null'||'%',null)
```

In this example, a value of `%null%` in the `P20_STATE` item will be replaced with a real `null` value.

Or:

```
:P20_FIRST_NAME||' '||:P20_MIDDLE_NAME||' '||:P20_LAST_NAME
```

 The stored function can also be used as a PL/SQL expression such as like `myPackage.myFunction(x,y)`.

- **Item Value**: This type allows us to set the value of the computation to the value of any application or page item. In this case, we are using the item name only and not a bind variable notation.

Computation

This mandatory field, which appears on the next screen of the wizard, holds the computation source according to the *Computation Type*.

Condition

The last screen of the **Create Page Computation** wizard includes the APEX built-in declarative condition system, which allows us to condition the computation with various options.

Create an application level computation

Application level computations are part of the *Shared Components* module under the **Logic** section. Unlike the page level computation wizard, the **Application Computation** wizard includes a single page. The following is a screenshot of the top of this page:

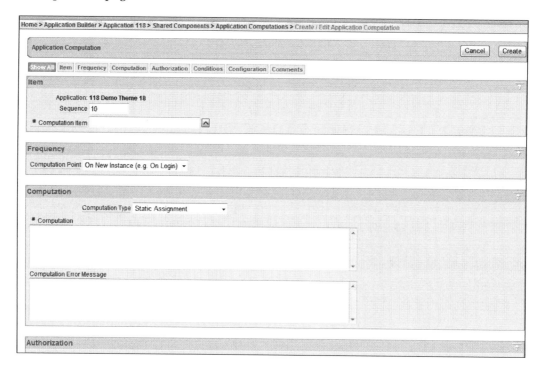

Most of the fields here are identical to the page computation, so we shall just explore the differences.

Computation item

This mandatory LOV field allows us to choose from **all** the items in the application—application and page level alike.

Frequency

This section includes the **Computation Point** for the application computation. These computation points are the same as the page level computation. However the frequency of running differs between page level and application level computations.

Except for the first option, **On New Instance (e.g. On Login),** an application level computation will be fired on every page of the application according to the computation point. For the first option, the computation will run when the user logs in to the application or when session state is cleared.

A good example of using application computation is to display the date and time on each of our application pages. We can define an application item called CURRENT_DATE, and set it with the following *PL/SQL Expression*:

```
to_char(localtimestamp,'DD/MM/YYYY HH24:MI:SSSS.FF').
```

Now, we can embed this application item into the application page templates and each time such a page is rendered by the browser, it will display a current local date and time (in the example, a European date format is used).

 The current local time will be determined according to the session TIME_ZONE parameter.

Edit computations

As usual, we can edit any computation we have defined on both the application and page level.

In the **Edit Computation** page we can define some extra properties that were not available in the wizard. The most important, at least from the UI perspective, is the **Computation Error Message**, which allows us to define our own message in the event of a computation error. Other properties include **Authorization**, **Configuration**, and **Comments** fields.

Computations and Session State

As we already mentioned in Chapter 3, while discussing the APEX *Session State*, using *Computation* in all the firing points, sets the value of the computed APEX item in *Session State*.

If we are using *Computation* to set the value of a page item, while on the **Page Rendering** phase, then the computed value will also be set in *Session State*. However, if the **Source Used** option of the computed item was set to '**Always, replacing any existing value in session state'**, its displayed value on the application page could be different from the *Session State* value, and will be determined by the item source. This is a perfectly valid scenario.

The following table, which also applies to the *APEX Processes* that we'll discuss in Chapter 9, summarizes the possible relationships between computed values (or other specific item value assignments) in *Session State* and the displayed value of the item:

Source Used	Setting Session State	Displayed Value	Session State = Displayed Value
Always	Only by specific assignment	As derived from the item source	Not necessarily
Only ...	Already exist	As in Session State	Yes

Summary

APEX computations allow us to declaratively set the values of APEX application items on both the application and page level, and on various computation points during the page rendering phase or after it was submitted.

In the next chapter, we'll discuss APEX validations, which help us to maintain the integrity and consistency of our data by making sure that only correct and consistent data will be used and saved into the database.

8
APEX Validations

APEX validations are part of the *Page Processing* phase and are fired right after the *Computations* stage. This is an APEX-declarative, server-side mechanism designed to check and validate the quality, accuracy, and consistency of the page submitted data, prior to saving it into the database. In the case of validation errors, we can alert the users and allow them to correct the problems.

APEX has a built-in **Validations** mechanism, which is a server-side mechanism. Currently, APEX doesn't include an out-of-the-box client-side *Validations* mechanism, although it allows us to develop one for ourselves based on JavaScript. It is up to us, as developers, to determine the proper relationship between the client-side and the server-side validation mechanisms.

In this chapter, we are going to review the following issues:

- The APEX concepts regarding data validation
- How to use the APEX built-in server-side *Validation* mechanism
- The main principles of developing our own client-side validations
- Server-side versus client-side validations

Data validation

In the first chapter, we defined APEX to be a data-centric development tool. The data is our most valuable resource, and as such, we should take special measures to ensure it has the following:

- **Quality:** There are many ways to define data quality. For me, it's the ability of the data to serve the purposes for which we are gathering it. For example, if we maintain a customer file in order to be able to send our prospective customers some commercial information, and if our data doesn't include all the options to contact the customer, then the quality of the data is not good enough. If the data should meet certain standards and it does not, then we need to be able to spot it and take corrective measures.

- **Accuracy:** The data must be accurate in order to serve its purpose. It's not enough that we have the customer's credit details. They must be the correct ones, e.g. the correct length of the credit card number, the card is not out of date, etc.

- **Consistency and Integrity:** The data in our database must reflect a real and accurate picture of the real world, and new data entries must co-exist and be consistent with the existing data.

Some of these functionalities should be dealt with as part of the application logic. Some can be dealt with using APEX Validations. After the *Computations* phase (right after page submission) has prepared the data for its final inspection, we can use *Validations* to do just that. Tasks such as checking for the existence of data (e.g. mandatory fields), uniqueness, proper data type and format, validity (such as dates), length, scale, and precision are only a few of the tasks we can define using APEX Validations.

It is true that some of these functionalities can also be performed by database constraints. However, in the case of constraint violation the database will issue its own error message, usually in a terminology (and format) that are not end user friendly. Using validations to detect possible constraint violations prior to sending the data to the database allows us to issue our own error messages, which can be more descriptive, using a friendly terminology for end users. As a result, this helps them locate and correct problems more easily.

How APEX validation works?

As we have mentioned, the APEX built-in *Validations* mechanism is a server-side mechanism. Just after the *Computations* of the *Page Processing* phase completes their run, the validation mechanism kicks in. The APEX engine performs all the validations (subject to their conditions) and accumulates **all** the validation errors, if any (i.e. validation doesn't stop after the first discovered validation error). If validation errors have occurred, then the APEX engine re-renders the page in a **validation error mode**. This means that the error message(s) of the failed validation(s) are displayed according to the error message display option(s) that we chose; the page items are populated from *Session State*, and by default, the *Page Rendering Computations* and *Processes* are not fired. APEX 3.0 introduced two specific predefined and declarative conditions that directly relate to the validations result:

- **Inline Validation Errors Displayed**: This condition allows us to change the default behavior of the APEX engine. The specific conditioned *Page Rendering Computation* or *Process* will be fired only if a validation error occurs.

Bear in mind:

A *Computation* or a *Process* that is conditioned with **Inline Validation Errors Displayed** will not be fired if no validation errors were found. This means that if we want to define a (*Page Rendering*) *Computation* or a *Process* that will run in any case, i.e. regardless of the *Validation* results, then we need to define it twice—first as a regular *Computation* or *Process* and the second time as a conditioned one, using the above condition.

- **No Inline Validation Errors Displayed**: This condition will be set to true if none of the defined inline validations on the page were fired or evaluated to be false, and therefore, no validation error is displayed. For (*Page Rendering*) *Computation* and *Processes*, this condition mimics the default behavior of the APEX engine. However, this condition can be used to condition the rendering of other page elements (e.g. regions, items, etc.) by not having any validation errors.

Creating a new validation

On the *Page Definition* page, press the **Create** icon of the **Validations** section. This will load the **Create Validation** wizard:

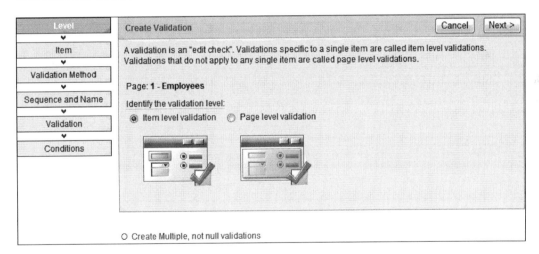

Validation level

In the first screen of the wizard we can choose the validation level we want
to define:

- Item level validation: At this level, we define a validation for a specific item
  on the page.
- Page level validation: At this level, we can define a validation that is not tied
  to a specific item on the page (e.g. validation on a tabular form column).

Create multiple not null validations

A **Not Null** validation is probably the most common validation in use. At the bottom
of the first wizard screen, as can be seen in the previous screenshot, there's a link to a
page wizard. It allows us to quickly define a **Not Null** validation for every item
on the page that we pick.

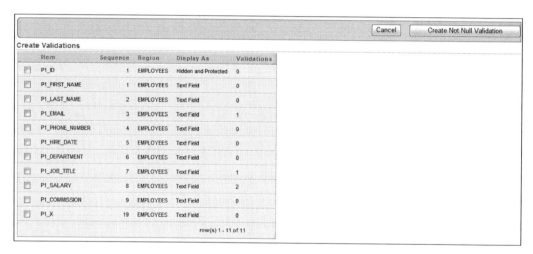

For every checked item, the wizard will create a **Not Null** validation with a generic
error message of **Value must be specified**.

> The **Create Form** wizard automatically creates a **Not Null** validation
> for every item it considers to be a required item. These include items
> that correspond to **Not Null** columns in database tables and items that
> were defined as **Required** with the **User Interface Default** wizard.

Item

If we chose the item level, then the next wizard screen allows us to choose the target item for validation:

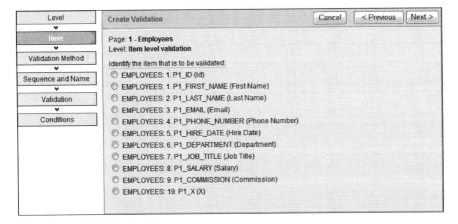

As can be seen in the screenshot, the wizard page lists all the items on the page by their item name and adds their label (in round parentheses) to help us identify the items.

Validation method

The next wizard screen, which both levels of validation share, allows us to choose the validation method we want to define. As can be seen in the following screenshot, the validation wizard currently supports five methods of validations, and we'll review them next:

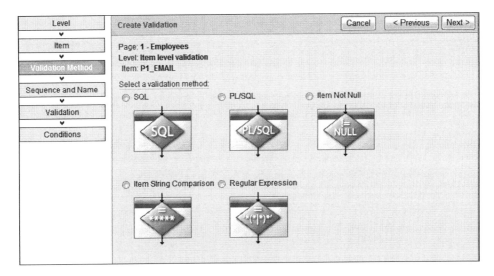

SQL

This method allows us to use SQL code for the validation.

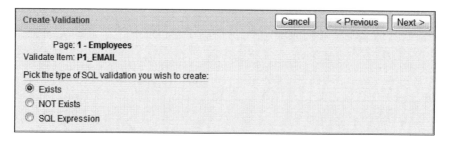

It supports three types of **SQL** validation:

- **Exists**
- **Not Exists**
- **SQL Expression**

Exists

With this type we can use a SQL select statement to check if the value exists in the database. For example:

```
Select 1 from MY_ADDRESS_BOOK
Where email = :P1_EMAIL
```

This validation will return `true` (validation pass) if the value of `P1_EMAIL` exists in the `MY_ADDRESS_BOOK` table, and it will fail with an error message if it doesn't.

 With this type, a **positive** response—fetched rows—passes the validation.

Not Exists

With this type we can use a SQL select statement to check if the value doesn't exist in the database. For example:

```
Select 1 from MY_ADDRESS_BOOK
Where email = :P1_EMAIL
```

This is the same code as for the *Exists* validation. However, in this case the validation will return `true` if the value of P1_EMAIL doesn't exist in MY_ADDRESS_BOOK table, and it will fail with an error message if it does.

 With this type, a **negative** response — no fetched rows — passes the validation.

SQL Expression

With this type we can use a SQL expression as the validation code. If the expression is evaluated to `true` then the validation will pass. Otherwise, it will return the validation error message. For example, let's look at the following SQL expression:

```
Instr(:P1_EMAIL,'@') > 0
```

This will pass the validation if the :P1_EMAIL item includes the character '@'.

Now let's look at the following SQL expression:

```
Instr(:P1_EMAIL,'@',1,2) = 0
```

This will pass the validation if the :P1_EMAIL item doesn't include more than one '@' character.

PL/SQL

This method allows us to use PL/SQL code for the validation.

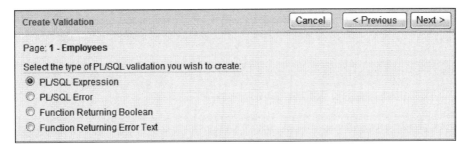

It supports four types of PL/SQL validation, which are explained as follows.

PL/SQL Expression

With this type we can use a PL/SQL expression to validate the item. For example, look at the following:

```
length(:P1_PASSWORD) >= 8
```

This will pass the validation if the length of the password we entered is greater than or equal to eight characters.

 The condition in the PL/SQL expression should reflect a **true** (passing) scenario.

PL/SQL Error

With this type we can use a PL/SQL code that includes the PL/SQL built-in procedure raise_application_error to validate the item. For example, using the following:

```
if length(:P1_PASSWORD) < 8 then
  raise_application_error (-20100,'Password not strong enough.');
end if;
```

This will issue an error message if the length of the password we entered is less than 8 characters. The displayed error message, in this case, is not the one included in the raise_application_error procedure, but it is the error message we defined for the validation (as we'll see later in the chapter).

 The condition in this code should reflect the **error** scenario of the validation.

Function Returning Boolean

With this type we can use more complex validation logic by using a PL/SQL function body that returns true in case the validation passes, or false in case the validation fails and we want to display an error message. For example, we can use the following code:

```
if length(:P1_PASSWORD) < 8 then
  return false;
else
  return true;
end if;
```

In this case, the code can reflect either the validation passing or failing scenario. We could easily use the following code to achieve the same result:

```
if length(:P1_PASSWORD) >= 8 then
  return true;
else
  return false;
end if;
```

With this option, we can also call database-stored functions if we need to implement validations with a higher degree of complexity.

Function Returning Error Text

APEX offers us another option of using a PL/SQL function body for validation. This time, instead of just returning `true` or `false`, we actually return the error message in the case of a validation failure or `null` in the case that the validation passes. For example:

```
if length(:P1_PASSWORD) < 8 then
  return 'The password must include at least 8 characters';
else
  return null;
end if;
```

As you can see in the example code, the text of the error message is hardcoded. If you want to avoid that, you can maintain your own table of error messages and retrieve them using your own stored function. Bear in mind that if you are working in a multi-lingual environment, you'll need to maintain a multi-language table of messages or use the technique we'll describe next.

Multi-lingual support for error messages

In this type of validation (unlike the PL/SQL Error type), the displayed error message is the one we return from the PL/SQL function and not the one in the *Validation* **Error Message** field. As such, the APEX translation mechanism doesn't include it in the XLIFF file it generates (which will be discussed in a dedicated chapter to the APEX Globalization support). However, we can use another APEX API, which is also part of NLS in APEX and allows us to display predefined messages in various languages. The following is an example of using this API:

```
if length(:P1_PASSWORD) < 8 then
  return apex_lang.message('WEAK_PASSWORD');
else
  return null;
end if;
```

In this case, the error message will be displayed in the current language of the application, provided one was defined.

 You should return to this example after reading Chapter 18, which deals with APEX Globalization support. It will make much more sense then.

Item Not Null

This method allows us to define a **Not Null** validation for a specific item. It doesn't have any types, and its code definition is completely declarative.

Item string comparison

This method allows us to use various declarative options of string comparison.

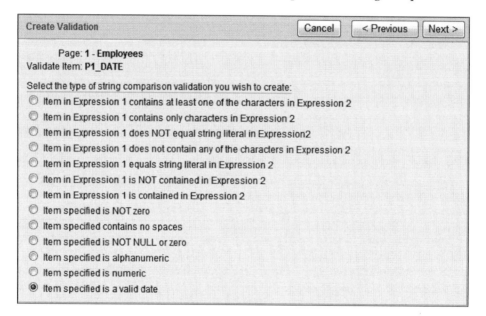

Except for the last option, as shown in the above screenshot, all the other options are self-explanatory. So let's deal with the last one.

Item specified is a valid date

Valid date is a function of the local environment that we are running the application in. There are many date formats supported by APEX. In order to determine if the date we want to validate is indeed legal, we must define a reference format for this date. For example, the string date **29-02-2000** will be a valid one in some European countries, but an illegal date in USA.

The validation code first references the **Item Format Mask**; if that was not defined, then it references the **Application Date Format** (which can be defined as part of the APEX *Globalization* section. We'll review the *Globalization* section further in the book.) The last reference, in the case that none of the previous formats were defined, is the database NLS_DATE_FORMAT parameter.

> This type of validation checks the validity of the date, not whether it matches the date format. For example, if the **Application Date Format** is defined as DD-MM-YYYY, and we fed the validated item with 29-FEB-2000, then the validation will pass.

Regular Expression

This method allows us to use **Oracle Regular Expression** to validate the item. Regular expression allows us to check if the item matches a specific pattern. If it does, then the validation passes. Otherwise, it displays an error message.

Regular expressions are not included in the scope of this book so I'll just present an example code and leave you to explore it (and encourage you to do so because regular expressions, although they can be very complex and difficult to implement, are also very powerful). The following code validates the format of an e-mail address:

```
^[a-zA-Z0-9]{1}[a-zA-Z0-9\.\-]{1,}@[a-zA-Z0-9]{1}[a-zA-Z0-9\.\-
]{1,}\.{1}[a-zA-Z]{2,4}$
```

This regular expression validates the following:

- The first character can be a letter or a digit, followed by letters, digits, and optional dots (.) or hyphens (-)
- Must include the @ character
- The domain name must start with a letter or number, followed by letters, digits, and optional dots (.) or hyphens (-)
- The domain name must end with a dot (.), followed by 2 to 4 letters, only string (for example .uk, .com, or .info)

In the previous section, I mentioned that the declarative built-in validation **Item specified is a valid date** can't be used to check the date format. Regular expressions can be used for that purpose, but they can't be used to check the legality of the date. For example, the string date **30/02/2009** will match a European date pattern, and as such, will pass the regular expression validation, and yet it's not a valid date.

Sequence and Name

This is the next screen on the **Create Validation** wizard and it's common to both page and item level validations:

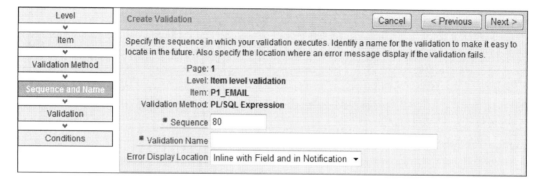

Sequence and Validation Name

These first fields are mandatory. The **Sequence** field determines the order of the validation's evaluation (it doesn't have to be unique, although it's advisable), and the **Validation Name** field can hold a descriptive name for the validation.

Error Display Location

APEX supports two options for displaying validation error messages:

- **On Error Page**: The validation error message(s) will be displayed on a separate error page

- **Inline**: The validation error message(s) will be displayed on the same application page that holds the validated items

On Error Page

The validation error message(s) will be displayed on a separate error page, as can be seen in the following screenshot:

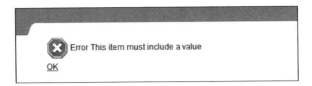

Although the displayed error message is exactly the one we defined, we can see that it's a bit out of context. For example, this is an error message from an **Item Not Null** validation. However, the validated item is not mentioned anywhere. This type of error message display is more appropriate for a page level validation.

Inline

This type of **Error Display Location** supports three options of display locations, all on the same application page that holds the validated items:

- **Inline with Field**: Displays the error message in the same table cell of the item label.

- **Inline in Notification**: All the built-in APEX page templates include a Notification area, which is represented by the #NOTIFICATION# *substitution string*. The validation error message(s) will be displayed at the location of the Notification area and styled by the CSS class associated with it.

- **Inline with Field and in Notification**: The error message will be displayed both adjacent to the item table and in the Notification area.

The following screenshot is an example of an inline error display:

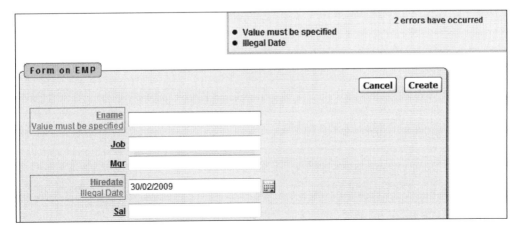

As seen in this case, it's very simple to identify the items that fail validation as the Notification area also draws the attention of the user to the validation errors on page.

 NLS Note:

The **2 errors have occurred** headline in the Notification area is part of the APEX print engine built-in string messages repository. This repository can be translated with the APEX built-in translation mechanism.
We'll add more details on that in the chapter that deals with APEX Globalization support (Chapter 18).

Validation

The next screen in the **Create Validation** wizard allows us to define the validation code (if necessary) and the error message. This screen is dependent on the method and type of validation we chose. For example, the following is a screen for a PL/SQL **Function Returning Boolean** validation:

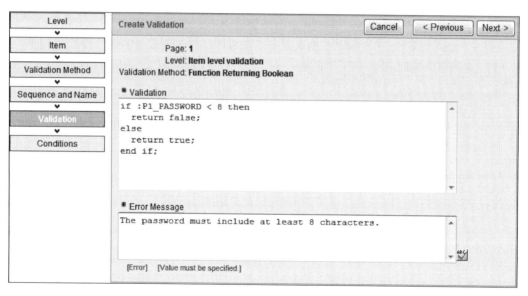

The following screenshot is an example of the **Validation** screen for one of the **Item String Comparison** options:

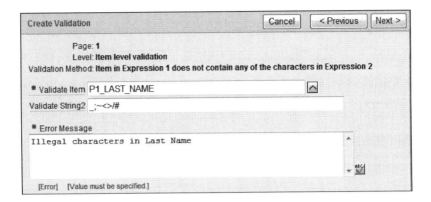

As can be seen, the wizard screen was adapted to allow the input of a comparison expression. In this case it's the **Validate String2** field. In the example, the validation will fail if the validated item includes any of the characters specified in it.

Conditions

The last screen of the **Create Validation** wizard allows us to condition the validation.

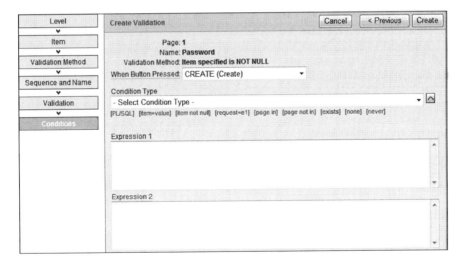

This is the regular APEX built-in *Conditions* mechanism. However, we can see a new element in it—**When Button Pressed**. This option allows us to condition the validation according to a specific button being pressed on page. In the example, we can see a **Not Null** validation called **Password**, which is conditioned by the **Create** button being pressed. The logic is that only a new user/account must be defined with a password. For an existing user/account we can assume that the password already exists on file, so we don't have to re-enter it (hence the item can be null).

The **When Button Pressed** is a **positive** condition—when the validation **should** run following a press of a button. Often we can find ourselves in a reverse scenario—we want to define a **negative** condition—when the validation should **not** run following a press of a button. For example, if the pressed button has a delete functionality, most of the validations will be worthless—we don't care if the item is null because we are going to delete the record anyway. In this case, we can use the REQUEST value to condition the validation. Using the built-in declarative condition **Request != Expression 1** with the REQUEST value of the delete button in Expression 1, we will set a condition for the validation not to run when the delete button is pressed.

Page level validation

Page level validations don't associate with a specific (single) item on the page. For example, we want to make sure that either one of the page items—Address or P.O. Box—will be filled in by the user. As we are dealing with a relationship between two items, we should use a page level validation. In this example, we can use a **PL/SQL** validation method, with the **PL/SQL Expression** type, setting the following code:

```
:P1_ADDRESS is not null or :P1_POBOX is not null
```

 Remember, the PL/SQL expression must reflect a passing condition.

We already mentioned APEX tabular forms. We are going to devote an entire chapter to this feature, but in this context I want to mention that in the current versions (3.2.x and below), tabular forms don't include a built-in declarative validation mechanism. We need to generate our own tabular form validation code, and we do so by using the page level validation. In the tabular form chapter we'll further expand this important issue.

Edit validations

Using the **Validations** section, on the *Page Definition* page, we can edit any validation that we defined. The **Edit Page Validation** page contains three more sections that are not available to us through the **Create Validation** wizard. The **Authorization** and **Configuration** sections allow us another level of validation conditions based on user privileges or the application **Build Options**. The **Comments** section allows us to document the validation.

Client-side validation

Client-side validations can enhance the end user experience by providing an immediate feedback regarding its input. Client side validation can deal with pure local issues that don't relate to the database (the server-side) such as forcing mandatory fields, date format and validity, minimal length, etc. However, with AJAX technology we can expand the scope of local validation to also include database related issues. There is really no need to send all the data to the server and anxiously await its response just to be disappointed by finding out that we are missing a mandatory field, our date is illegal, or the credit card number is too short.

Client-side validation is based on JavaScript. APEX, in its current versions—3.2.x and earlier—doesn't include a built-in declarative, client-side validation mechanism. However, its built-in JavaScript library includes functions that allow us to implement one ourselves.

Implementing client-side validation

The main principle of client-side validation is to run it before submitting the page. We have two options of achieving it. The first option is to attach a proper validation to every item that requires it by using DOM events like onchange or onblur. For example, the **HTML Form Element Attributes** field of a password item can include the following:

```
onblur="if (this.value.length < 8) {alert('Password must include at
least 8 characters');}"
```

When the user moves out from the password field, the onblur event will be fired. In the case of a validation error—password includes less than 8 characters—a proper error message will immediately be displayed to the user.

The second option for local validation is to capture the page submit request, fire a JavaScript validation function, and-if all were validated correctly-submit the page. Otherwise, display a proper error message. With this option we should set the redirect target type of all the buttons that include submit functionality (e.g. submit, save, create, apply changes, etc.) to **URL**. The **URL Target** field should include JavaScript code that fires a JavaScript validation function and, pending a successful validation, submits the page.

For submitting the page from JavaScript we can use the APEX built-in JavaScript library function doSubmit('pRequest'). This function will submit the page while setting the REQUEST value to its parameter value, just as when the page is submitted by pressing a button. For example, the following code can be used as a **URL Target** with a button named 'SAVE':

```
javascript: if (validateColumn('f04')) {doSubmit('SAVE')} else
{alert('Please correct the marked error(s)');}
```

When this button is pressed, it fires a JavaScript function, which we created, called validateColumn(). If this function returns true—no validation errors have been found—the page is submitted with a REQUEST value of SAVE. Otherwise, an error message is displayed to the user

Client-side versus server-side validations

Most users would like to get a prompt response to their actions as part of the data input process, and client-side validations can do that. However, taking into account the nature of the Web environment, client-side validations are very vulnerable and easy to hack. In the APEX environment, the default option is to use open, plain text URLs. Given the very powerful f?p URL options we can easily send data to the server, thus bypassing the client-side validations. Although APEX provides us with some advanced options for preventing that (e.g. Session State Protection), for most cases it should mean that client-side validations are nice and useful to have, but by no means can they replace the server-side validations mechanism.

Summary

In this chapter we reviewed the APEX validation concepts, which help us to preserve the quality, accuracy, and consistency of our data. APEX includes a built-in server-side, declarative validation mechanism that supports both item and page level validations while allowing us to use SQL or PL/SQL code, various pre-defined declarative options of string comparison, and Oracle regular expressions to validate our data. APEX also allows us to implement our own client-side validation mechanism and its built-in JavaScript library includes some functions to support it.

In the next chapter, we are going to review APEX Processes.

9
APEX Processes

APEX **Processes** allow us to implement the application logic. As with *APEX Computations*, *APEX Processes* are also included in both the *Page Rendering* and *Page Processing* phases. The similarity continues with APEX's support of application and page level *Processes*. Some of the *APEX Processes* are fully declarative, while with others, we need to use SQL and PL/SQL code to achieve our goals.

> *APEX Computations* can be considered as a private case of *APEX Processes*. We can use *APEX Processes* to implement **every** *APEX Computation*. So, why do we need *APEX Computations*? Some of the *APEX Computations* declarative options, e.g. **Static Assignment** or **Item Value**, cannot be implemented declaratively with *APEX Processes*, but require the use of PL/SQL code. You can look at some of the *APEX Computation* capabilities as a declarative extension of APEX Processes.

In this chapter, we will review the following issues:

- The main concepts of APEX processes and how they can help us to implement our application logic
- Application level processes
- Page level processes and the various types and options APEX provides us with to implement them
- On Demand processes

Application Processes

Application Processes, which take the form of a **PL/SQL Anonymous Block**, are part of the *Shared Components* module and can be defined in the **Logic** section.

We can distinguish between two major types of *Application Processes*. The first type will be fired, subject to its firing point and conditioning, for every application page. The second type will only be fired on-demand—a specific request to invoke the process.

On the *Application Process* home page, we can see a list of all the defined *Application Processes* (displayed as **Icons**, like in the following screenshot, or as a **Details** list). Pressing the **Create** button will lead us to the **Create Application Process** wizard.

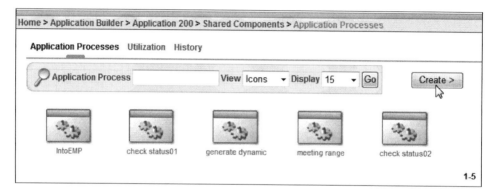

Creating a new Application Process

Using the **Create Application Process** wizard, we can define a new *Application Process*:

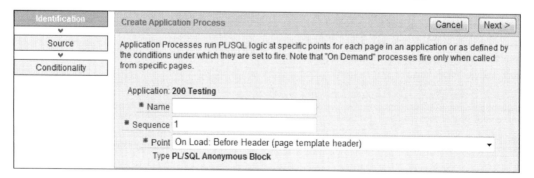

Name

This is a mandatory field that can be used to identify the *Application Process*. We can use this name to invoke an on-demand *Application Process*. In this case, the name is case-sensitive.

Sequence

This is a mandatory field that determines the sequence of firing *Application Processes* with the same **Process Point**. This field is meaningless for on-demand *Application Processes* as they are only being fired for each specific request. As such, the field doesn't have to be unique.

Point

This mandatory select list field allows us to determine the process point of the *Application Process*. We can select one of the following options:

- **On Load**: There are six processing points that are correlated with the page building phases as part of the *Page Rendering* phase:
    - **Before Header (page template header)**
    - **After Header (page template header)**
    - **Before "Body" Region(s)**
    - **After "Body" Region(s)**
    - **Before Footer (page template footer)**
    - **After Footer (page template footer)**

- **On Submit**: There are two processing points as part of the *Page Processing* phase:
    - **After Page Submit—Before Computations and Validations**
    - **After Page Submit—After Computations and Validations**

- **On New Session: After Authentication**: Unlike the previous options, this type of *Application Process* will not be fired for every application page, but only for new sessions.

- **On Demand: Run this application process when required by a page process**: This type of *Application Process* can be called, by a page level process, at any of the **On Load** or **On Submit** processing points. In addition, this type can be invoked using the f?p URL syntax and within the APEX AJAX framework. We'll discuss these options later in the chapter.

Source

The next screen of the **Create Application Process** wizard allows us to define the source code of the *Application Process*.

The **Process Text** field takes the form of a PL/SQL Anonymous Block, and the APEX engine will automatically wrap the code with the BEGIN and END statements. However, if we need to use local variables, then we must use a DECLARE statement. In this case, it's our responsibility to manually add the BEGIN and END statements.

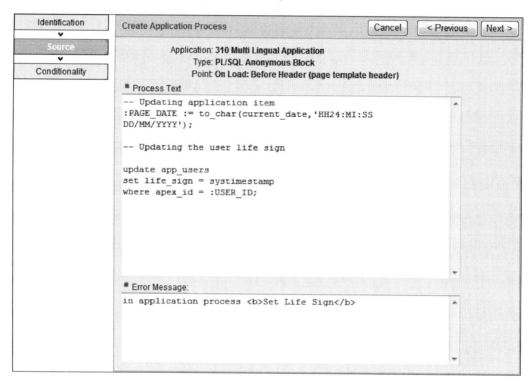

In the above screenshot, we can see an example of using an **On Load: Before Header (page template header)** *Application Process*. According to its firing point, this process runs just before the page header is generated for every page in our application. In the example, we are using it to set an *Application Item* — PAGE_DATE — to an up-to-date local time stamp. We can use this *Application Item* in our page template (using the &PAGE_DATE. notation) and the result will be a display of a current local date and time on every application page.

NLS Note:

Look at the date format in the example: `'HH24:MI:SS DD/MM/YYYY'`. This date format supports a date and time display on a **Right-To-Left** oriented page— this is typical to Arabic and Hebrew, where text is written from right to left but numbers, including date and time, are written from left to right. Using this format, displaying the page in the **RTL** orientation will result in a proper display of the date and time.

If the first part of the example code, setting a value to an *Application Item* can also be done with *Application Computation*; the second part—updating a database table—can only be done with an *Application Process*.

One of the problems we are facing, as a direct result of the stateless nature of the web connection, is to determine whether a user connection is valid/active. Because a **new** connection between the client web browser and the web server is established for every client-side request from the web server, the definition of an active connection is actually up to us. We can decide on a time window in which a user connection will be deemed valid/active. However, in order to do that, we must track the user activities in the application so we'll be able to check if we are still within the time window we set. The second part of the code in our example updates a database table called `app_users` with a time stamp (a `systimestamp` value) every time the user requests a new application page. We can use this information in our algorithm to determine a valid/active connection for that user.

APEX 3.2 introduced some new control options on **Session Timeout**. One of the options is to define a **Maximum Session Idle Time in Seconds**. This option actually implements the principles in our example.

Error message

This field is marked as mandatory. It is for all the *Application Processes* that are not on-demand and will not be displayed for any on-demand *Application Process*.

In the case of an error while running the *Application Process*, the APEX engine will generate an error page that includes the text of the database error message with the text from this field. As can be seen in the last screenshot, the error message text can include HTML tags to style its appearance.

Conditionality

The last screen of the **Create Application Process** wizard includes the *APEX Conditions* mechanism. It allows us to exclude certain page(s) from the default behavior of running the *Application Process* on every page, using an appropriate condition.

As on-demand *Application Processes* are fired only according to a specific request, the *Condition* mechanism does not apply to them. It's our responsibility, as developers, to call on-demand *Application Processes* according to our needs and conditions.

In the next screenshot, we can see an example of using the built-in, predefined condition **Current Page Is NOT in Expression 1 (comma delimited list of pages)** to prevent the defined *Application Process* from being fired on page 101 (by default, this is the login page of the application):

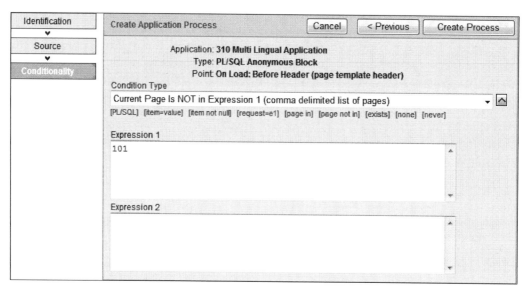

Edit Application Processes

Clicking on any *Application Process* icon or link on the *Application Process* home page leads us to the **Edit Application Process** page, which allows us access to some extra sections that were not available to us in the **Create Application Process** wizard. The **Authorization** and **Configuration** sections give us fine tuning options to control the availability of the *Application Process*. The **Comments** section allows us to save our developer comments. The **Subscription** section will display a list of all the pages that specifically reference the *Application Process*, using a page level process. This list can be empty. However, the process can still be used as an on-demand process by other means (which we'll discuss in the on-demand processes section later in the chapter).

Localization and Application Processes

Application Processes can be used to alter NLS parameters and adapt them to the specific local environment that the application runs in. If you look at a typical APEX application page in a **debug** mode, you'll see that the APEX engine is doing it for us automatically, based on the database NLS parameters. The following screenshot was taken from a page that runs on apex.oracle.com:

```
0.01:
0.01: S H O W: application="50888" page="1" workspace="" request="" session="3068208510630438"
0.01: Application 50888, Authentication: CUSTOM2, Page Template: 5631455530033423225
0.01: ...Session ID 3068208510630438 can be used
0.01: ...Application session: 3068208510630438, user=ARIE
0.01: Fetch session state from database
0.02: ...FSP_LANGUAGE_PREFERENCE v('FSP_LANGUAGE_PREFERENCE')="en-us" (ARIE): wwv_flow.g_browser_language=en-us maplang=en-us
0.02: alter session set nls_language="AMERICAN"
0.02: alter session set nls_territory="AMERICA"
0.02: NLS: CSV charset=WE8MSWIN1252
0.02: ...NLS: Set Decimal separator="."
0.02: ...NLS: Set NLS Group separator=","
0.02: ...NLS: Set date format="DD-MON-RR"
0.02: ...Setting session time_zone to -06:00
0.02: Setting NLS_DATE_FORMAT to application date format: DD/MM/YYYY
0.02: ...NLS: Set date format="DD/MM/YYYY"
0.02: NLS: Language=en-us
```

We can see that in this case, the database of the hosted site is using **DD-MON-RR** as its date format, and that the time_zone parameter is set to **-06:00**. Sitting in Birmingham (UK), for example, using a date standard format of DD/MM/YYYY won't do with these parameters.

We can define an *Application Process*, with a firing point of **On Load: Before Header (page template header)** that includes the following code:

```
execute immediate 'alter session set NLS_DATE_FORMAT=''DD/MM/YYYY''';
execute immediate 'alter session set TIME_ZONE=''+00:00''';
```

This process will run for every page in our application, setting the NLS parameters according to our needs. Moreover, if we are part of a global enterprise, then we can use the *Application Process* conditions system to limit this process to run only for the relevant users. In this case, we can also define a set of conditioned *Application Processes* that can serve different global areas, time zones, or local date and currency standards.

 The alter session statement pertains to a database session (and not APEX session) and remains in effect only for the duration of this database session. As every APEX application page uses at least two database sessions—one for SHOW and another for ACCEPT—we should define a second *Application Process*, identical to the first, but with a *Process Point* of **On Submit—After Page Submission—Before Computations and Validations**, in order to maintain data format consistency.

Advanced Note:

Similar functionality can be achieved using the APEX VPD feature. The APEX engine runs the VPD code prior to every page request. It will save us the need to define two separate *Application Processes*, but we won't enjoy the built-in declarative condition system. VPD is not within the scope of this book, so just remember that it's there, and that we don't have to use it just for pure security needs.

Page level processes

APEX supports page level processes as part of the *Page Rendering* and *Page Processing* phases. The association of the process with one of these phases is determined by its *Process Point*. The page level processes are **all** server-side components, including those that belong to the *Page Rendering* phase.

It's important to understand that the *Processes* associated with the *Page Rendering* phase are run by the APEX engine on the server side as part of building the HTML code for the application page. As such, these processes can't directly access any of the client-side resources. Now, let's take a look at a typical client-side resource like JavaScript. As the JavaScript engine is found only in the client-side Web browser, we cannot directly invoke JavaScript functions from the page level *Processes*. However, within the proper type of APEX *Process*, as we'll soon see, we can use server-side resources like the PL/SQL Web Toolkit to generate and embed specific HTML code into the application page code that the APEX engine builds. In turn, this HTML code (and not the APEX *Process*) will invoke the client-side resources. For example, a page level process, with one of the **On Load** process points, can generate an HTML `<script>` tag that includes a JavaScript code. The embedded JavaScript code will be fired by the Web browser when it runs the application page.

Creating a new page level process

We can invoke the **Create Page Process** wizard from either of the **Processes** sections in the *Page Rendering* column or the *Page Processing* column on the *Page Definition* page. The final association of the *Page Process* will be determined according to its firing point.

Process Type

Unlike the *Application Process* level, which only supports one process category—PL/SQL anonymous block—the *Page Process* level supports several categories of processes. Some of them are fully declarative. In the following sections, we'll review these supported categories:

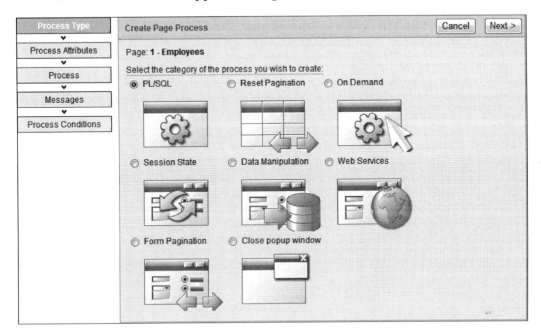

PL/SQL

This category is similar to the *Application Process* level and it supports PL/SQL anonymous blocks. From within the PL/SQL anonymous block, we can call stored procedures/functions, in cases where we need to use a large amount of code and implement very complex logic. We can also call stored procedures/functions when we need to be able to obfuscate our code, or just want to increase the efficiency by using a pre-compiled code.

The following is an example of how we can use this type of *Process* to utilize a server-side resource—the PL/SQL Web Toolkit—to generate JavaScript code that will be fired when the client-side Web browser runs the application page:

```
htp.p('<script type="text/javascript">');
htp.p('window.opener.location.reload();');
htp.p('window.close();');
htp.p('</script>');
```

This code, which can be part of a conditioned **On Load — Before Header** *Process* of a pop-up application page, will reload (refresh) the parent (calling) window and will close the pop-up window.

 This technique can be helpful in cases where the popup window updates items on the parent (calling) window. If the data was saved in *Session State*, either manually or by submitting the pop-up page, reloading the parent window can refresh its display of the data.

The **PL/SQL** category only supports the **On New Instance, On Load,** and **After Submit** process points. The **on-demand** process point is not included in here and has its own category.

Reset Pagination

This category is only relevant to pages that include a report region. Chapter 13 deals entirely with APEX reports and it will cover report pagination in more detail. For now, let's say that the *report engine* tracks the report pagination status in order to be able to present the correct result set for the current report.

In the following screenshot, we can see an example of a typical report using a search field to filter its results. For the first time that we'll hit the **Search** button, the *report engine* will fetch and display the first result set of the report. We can paginate through the entire report result set, while the *report engine* tracks our pagination actions. Now, we want to initiate a new search. After pressing the **Search** button for the second (or more) time, the *report engine* will fetch a new set of results to be displayed. However, the *report engine* still works according to the current pagination status, which is no longer valid as it reflects the pagination status of the previous report.

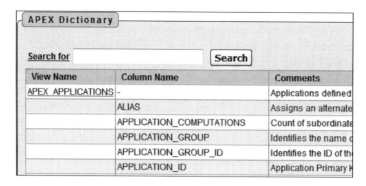

To avoid these kinds of problems, we can create a **Reset Pagination** process, conditioned by the button that launches the new report execution (like the **Search** button in our example).

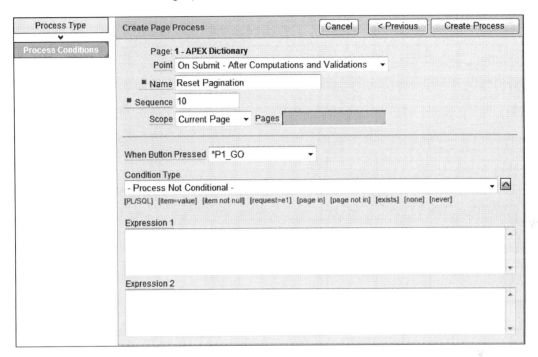

Beside all the fields we have already encountered in previous wizard screens (which therefore won't be described here again), I want to draw your attention to the **Scope** field. This field allows us to reset pagination for the **Current Page**, **Multiple Pages** (using the comma-delimited list of pages in the adjacent field), and **All Pages** of the application.

Bear in mind:

The **Scope** field will not be available to you in the **Edit Page Process** page if you didn't pre-set it in the **Create Page Process** wizard. If this functionality is relevant to you, then you must set it in the wizard. If you did set the **Scope** item, then it will appear in the **Edit Page Process** page, under the **Source** section, and you'll be able to edit it.

On Demand

This category allows us to invoke an on-demand *Application Process* at one of the process points available on the page level. The page level **On Demand** process must reference an already-defined, on-demand *Application Process*.

After setting the mandatory attributes of **Name**, **Sequence**, and **Point** on the **Process Attributes** wizard screen, we'll be asked to choose the on-demand *Application Process* we want to invoke.

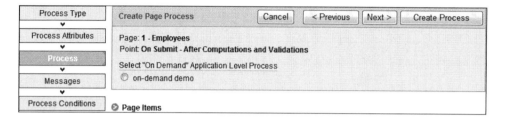

The next two screens allow us to define a **Success Message** and **Failure Message** for the **On Demand** process and to condition it. The condition determines the terms in which this process is in demand and will be fired.

> **Bear in mind:**
>
> Unlike the **On Demand** processes on the *Application Process* level, which can't be conditioned by the APEX *Conditions* mechanism, the **On Demand** *Page Process* is subject to the *Conditions* mechanism. In fact, it actually sets the calling scenario for the **On Demand** *Application Process*. This means that the **On Demand** page level *Process* is not a true independent process (with its own logic); it only serves as a calling mechanism to the **On Demand** *Process* we defined on the application level.

Session State

This category allows us to manage, declaratively, some aspects of the *Session State* mechanism, including the built-in **Preferences** repository.

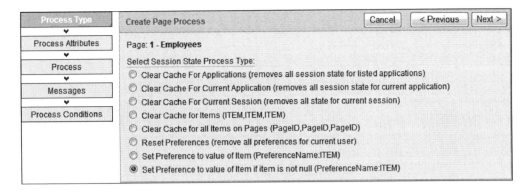

After setting the mandatory attributes of **Name**, **Sequence**, and **Point** on the wizard **Process Attributes** screen, we'll continue to the next wizard screen—**Process**. This screen will be adapted for the *Session State* process type we chose and the expected input for it. For example, the next screenshot is for the **Clear Cache for Items (ITEM,ITEM,ITEM)** type:

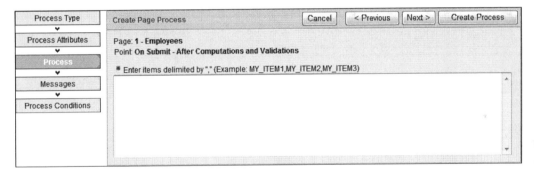

As we'll see in the next chapter on **APEX Branches**, some of the **Clear Cache** activities can also be defined declaratively as part of the *Branches* mechanism.

Data manipulation

This category allows us to manipulate data declaratively. If we use one of the APEX wizards to create a form, then the APEX wizard automatically adds the appropriate DML *Processes* for us, based on the functionalities (buttons) of the form. We will only need to add these *Processes* manually if we have created the form manually.

The **Data Manipulation** category contains several sub categories, as can be seen in the following screenshot:

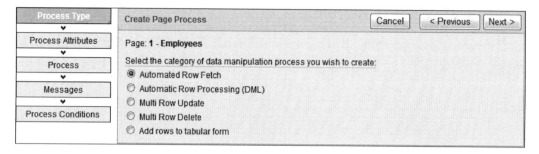

Automatic Row Fetch

This category allows us to declaratively define a process (also known as ARF process), which fetches a record (row) from a database table and populates correlated items on the application page. These correlated items must be defined as **Database Column** in their **Source Type** field and include the name of the correlated table column in the **Source value or expression** field. If we want the newly fetched record to take precedence over *Session State*, then we should set the **Source Used** field to **Always, replacing any existing values in session state**.

After setting the mandatory attributes of **Name**, **Sequence**, and **Point** on the wizard **Process Attributes** screen, we'll continue to the next wizard screen—**Process**—in which we'll set the details about the database table we are going to fetch from, and a mapping between the table's primary key(s) and the page items that contain this data.

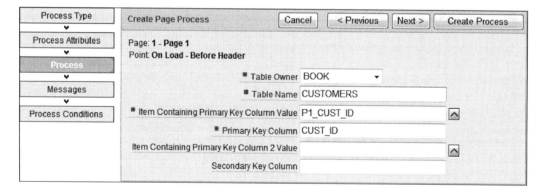

As can be seen in the screenshot, the built-in declarative ARF process only supports a single table with up to two columns in the Primary Key. If our table contains a Primary Key with more than two segments, or our page includes items from more than one table, then we'll need to fetch our data manually by writing our own PL/SQL code, or by creating a view, which will mask the compound Primary Key or the multiple tables. Although the labels on the screen clearly state **Table Owner** and **Table Name**, this process also supports views.

The next wizard screen allows us to define a **Success Message** and **Failure Message** for the process, and the next screen after that allows us to condition it.

 Usually, we should condition an *ARF process* by using a `not null` condition applied to the item(s) holding its Primary Key.

Automatic Row Processing (DML)

This category allows us to declaratively **insert**, **update**, or **delete** data from a table. All the required definitions for the page items, as we specified them for the *ARF process*, are also applied to the **Automatic Row Processing (DML)** process (*Automatic DML* by its short name).

The first two wizard screens are similar to the screens we have described already. The third screen—**Process**—allows us to choose the supported DML actions of this process by checking the **Allowed Operations** checkbox item options:

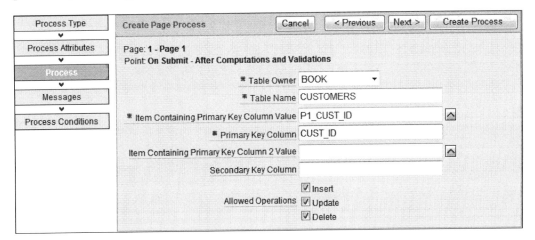

The *Automatic DML* process also supports views. However, bear in mind that applying DML operations on a view requires you to define appropriate INSTEAD OF triggers.

The Automatic DML processes should be conditioned by a button in a manner that will allow the APEX engine to differentiate between the three supported DML actions. We'll discuss this further in the *Edit Page Process* section later in this chapter.

The **Update** functionality of the declarative *Automatic DML* processes can be very important and helpful, as it was designed to support concurrency control and detect lost updates while implementing the **Optimistic Locking** algorithm that APEX uses in its Web environment. These technologies can be very complex to implement by yourself, so you should try to use the declarative *Automatic DML* processes whenever you can. We'll discuss Optimistic Locking and concurrency control issues in more detail, as part of a discussion about manually building tabular forms in Chapter 14.

Multi Row Update, Multi Row Delete, and Add rows to tabular form

These three categories are only relevant to tabular forms that were generated using the **Create Tabular Form** wizard. We'll discuss tabular forms in Chapter 14. So for now, let's just say that this wizard allows us to define DML action related buttons on tabular forms, and it creates the corresponding, button-conditioned, multi row DML processes. If, for any reason, we chose not to create any of these buttons and their related DML processes, then we can do it manually with these categories.

For the **Multi Row Update** and the **Multi Row Delete** processes, we need to supply the **Table/View Owner** and **Table/View Name** of the tabular form basic table with its **Primary Key Column Name**.

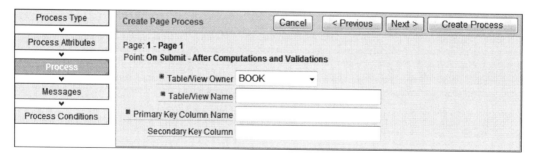

For the **Add rows to tabular form** process we need to set the number of empty row(s) we want to add each time.

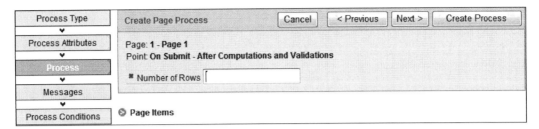

 Each process should be conditioned by its corresponding button on the tabular form. It's logical to assume that if we needed to manually define these DML processes, then we also need to manually define their corresponding buttons.

Web Services

APEX version 3.0 introduced Web Services support. As Web Services are not included within the scope of this book, let's say that we can define a **Web Service Reference** as an APEX shared component (under the **Logic** section) and invoke it on the application page by using a **Web Services** process.

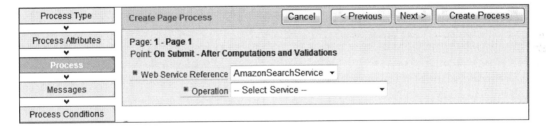

In the above screenshot, we can see an example of a *Web Service* process that is based on the **AmazonSearchService Web Service Reference**.

The *Web Service* processes are usually conditioned by a button that invokes them when necessary.

Form Pagination

This category allows us to create form pagination buttons that can help us navigate (forward and backward) through our form data. These *Form Pagination* processes can be very handy in a master details form, where we need to paginate between (possibly) multiple records that are related to a single master record.

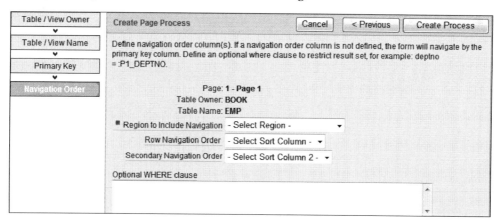

Besides the table/view owner, name, and primary key details, we also need to supply the region that will include the navigational buttons, the order in which we would like to navigate in the table, and an optional where clause to filter our navigation (e.g. in a master details form, it can include the master key).

Close pop-up window

This category allows us to create a declarative process that generates a JavaScript code script, which is embedded in the application page HTML code according to its firing point. The script can close a pop-up window.

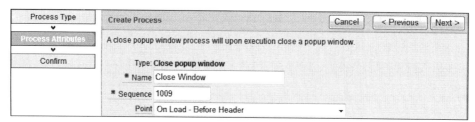

The APEX engine generates the following code for this process:

```
<script type="text/javascript">
<!—
if (self != window.opener) window.close();
//—>
</script>
```

The relevant process points for this process are only the **On Load** process points, and it should be conditioned so the code will be generated only when we intend to close the popup window. Using a REQUEST value that we set as part of a page self-redirect can be a good solution.

> Don't be confused; this is a server-side process that embeds an HTML `<script>` tag, which includes JavaScript, into the application page HTML code. The JavaScript code will only be fired when the page is rendered by the client Web browser.

Edit page level process

From the **Processes** sections on the *Page Definition* page, we can edit every defined process.

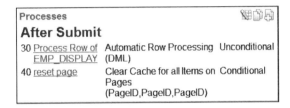

The **Edit Page Process** page contains all the sections we have encountered already. So I want to focus on the following, which is relevant to the *Automatic DML* process.

Source: Automatic Row Processing (DML)

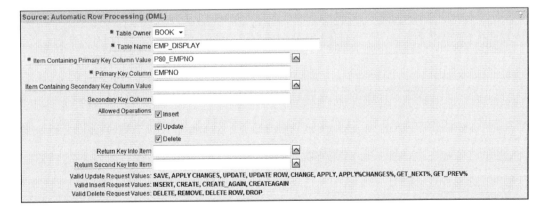

This section includes two fields that are not available to us in the **Create Page Process** wizard: **Return Key Into Item** and **Return Second Key Into Item**. In these fields we can enter the page items that hold the Primary Key(s) of the record we just inserted. This is a declarative implementation of the RETURNING clause in the INSERT statement and can be very useful in cases where the Primary Key is generated by a trigger. In fact, if we want to re-display the newly inserted record on our form using the ARF (Automatic Row Fetch) process, then we must populate these fields so the APEX engine will know which form item(s) should be updated with the newly created Primary Key. Without the Primary Key, no record fetching can be performed.

I would like to draw your attention to the last three informative lines in this section, which include a list of valid REQUEST values for the Insert, Update, and Delete actions. As was mentioned before, the *Automatic DML* process should be conditioned by a button in order to allow the APEX engine to differentiate between the supported DML actions. By default, this differentiation is based on the REQUEST value of the button that initiated the process. If the REQUEST value of that button is included in one of the valid REQUEST lists, then the correlated DML action will be fired. For example, the REQUEST value of an **Apply Changes** button is set to SAVE. As you can see in the previous screenshot, the SAVE value is included in the **Valid Update Request Values** list. This means that pressing this button will trigger the **Update** functionality of the *Automatic DML* process.

Bear in mind:

These REQUEST values don't condition the running of the process, but only its functionality. The process will run and will end successfully, even if no valid REQUEST value has been found. A successful process message will be issued, even though no actual DML took place. If you want to condition the actual running of an *Automatic DML* process, then you should use the *Conditions* mechanism.

I can hear you think to yourself, should I memorize all these REQUEST values and their associated DML actions? I will take you back to Chapter 6, where we discussed *APEX Buttons*. A screenshot from the chapter is as follows:

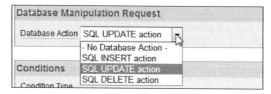

APEX allows us to associate a specific button with a specific **Database Action**. If we choose to do that, then the associated DML action of the button will trigger the correlated DML functionality in the *Automatic DML Process*, regardless of the value of REQUEST. No memorizing is needed.

On Demand processes

As we saw in this chapter, APEX supports on-demand processes at the application and page levels. We saw that we could invoke an on-demand *Application Process* by using a page level **On Demand** process. However, there are two more options we can use to invoke on-demand processes.

The first option is to use the `f?p` URL syntax. We can use the keyword `APPLICATION_PROCESS=` in the fourth segment (the `REQUEST` segment) to invoke an on-demand process. The keyword value can be the application process ID or name. As the process ID might change when we deploy the application into a new APEX instance, it seems safer and simpler to use the process name (just remember that the name is case-sensitive). For example, the following will invoke an on-demand application process called `check_status`:

```
f?p=&APP_ID.:2:&SESSION.:APPLICATION_PROCESS=check_status
```

In this case, the page number is meaningless but still mandatory. If, for any reason, the `check_status` process does not end successfully, then no visible error message will be issued.

The second option to use an on-demand Application Process is with the APEX AJAX framework. The on-demand *Application Process* contains the server-side code of the AJAX event. We'll discuss this issue in greater detail in the APEX AJAX chapter (Chapter 17).

Summary

In this chapter, we reviewed *APEX Processes* that allow us to implement the logic of our application, either by declarative processes or with manually coded SQL and PL/SQL processes.

APEX supports *application level* processes, which will run for every page in our application unless we conditioned them or defined them with an on-demand process point. In this case, they will be fired only upon a specific request.

APEX also supports *page level* processes, which can be fired as part of the *Page Rendering* or *Page Processing* phases. We can also use *page level* processes to invoke an *application level* on-demand process.

In the next chapter, we will discuss APEX Branches, which are responsible for the flow of the application.

10
APEX Branches

APEX branches allow us to implement and control the flow of our APEX application while using either declarative or manually coded options.

The **Branches** section is part of the Page Processing column, and in most cases it will be the last stage of the application page ACCEPT phase. Every application page must include at least one valid **Branch** option, so that the APEX engine will know where to go, after the current ACCEPT procedure has run its course.

In this chapter, we are going to review the following major issues:

- The logic behind an APEX branch
- The types of APEX branches that are available to us
- How to create/edit an APEX branch
- The other things we can do while branching
- Other ways to control the application flow

Bear in mind:

As already hinted in the last bullet, the Branches section is not the only way to define and control the application flow. As we'll see, we can also use tabs, buttons, links, PL/SQL, and JavaScript code to set the flow of the application.

Application flow

A typical application starts with a login page that will automatically redirect us to the application home page upon successful login. In the case of a public application (no login required), we also need to start from a "first page". This home page can be the only page in our application, or the first of many. In a multi-page application we naturally have multiple options of branching. However, as was mentioned before, every application page must include at least one valid branch option, and our single application page is no exception. In this case, we'll define a self branch—a page that branches to itself.

Self branching—branching to the same page is a legitimate and valid branch.

If, for any reason, the APEX engine is not able to detect a valid *Branch* to use at the end of the ACCEPT procedure, then it will issue a runtime error. This runtime error will be displayed as an error page, which can be seen in the following screenshot:

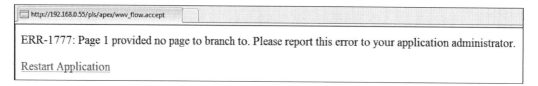

Creating a new branch

On the *Page Definition* page, in the **Page Processing** column, we can use the **Create** icon of the **Branches** section to create a new branch. This will lead us to the first screen of the **Create Branch** wizard.

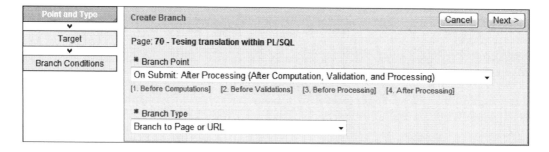

Branch point

APEX supports four **On Submit** firing points, and although the **Branches** section is part of the *Page Processing* column, it also supports one **On Load** firing point. The following is a review of the supported branching points:

- **On Submit: Before Computation (Before Computation, Validation, and Processing)**: With this option, the branch takes place before any of the ACCEPT phase operations. That can be useful in cases where these operations are not relevant or required. A typical use of this firing point is with **Cancel** buttons, where all we really care about is the redirection itself and nothing more.

- **On Submit: Before Validation (After Computation and before Validation and Processing)**: With this option, the branch takes place after *Computation*, but before *Validation*. We can use this firing point when we want to use results from the *Computation* stage with the branch, e.g. computing a next/previous primary key, or when the branch depends on a *Computation* result.

- **On Submit: Before Processing (After Computation, Validation, and Before Processing)**: In this option, the branch takes place after *Computation* and *Validation*, but before *Processing*. As the *Session State* is being saved, we can use the *Validation* stage to make sure it includes valid data and only then branch. A typical use of this firing point will be with **Previous/Next** buttons on wizard pages. On each wizard page we want to validate the user input, but the final processing will only take place on the last wizard page.

  The APEX engine also uses this branching point to perform a page self-branch upon *Validation* failure. In this case, a rollback is performed that brings the page to its pre-submit status while cancelling the *Computation* results. This is a built-in feature, so we don't need to manually define any branches for failed Validations.

- **On Submit: After Processing (After Computation, Validation, and Processing)**: This branching point is probably the most common one. It takes place as the last step of the ACCEPT process, and the APEX engine is ready for its next step.

- **On Load: Before Header**: Unlike the previous branching points, this one is part of the page SHOW phase. It will be fired after the current page **On Load-Before Header Computations and Processes**, but before the page is actually rendered by the browser. This means that the branched page is the one that the user will see, and not the current page. This also means that you can use the SHOW *Computations* and *Processes* results to condition the branch, or to set its parameters.

Branch type

APEX supports several options to define the final destination of the branch. Some of the options are purely declarative and some of them allow us to use manually coded PL/SQL or JavaScript.

In general, there are two options to define the branch target. One is to use a specific application page ID (page number), and the other is to use a URL. The URL usually takes the form of a `f?p` URL.

The following is a review of all the supported branch type options.

Branch to Function Returning a Page

This option allows us to use a PL/SQL function body to generate the branch target. The function should return a valid application page ID. The following screenshot shows an example of the **Target** definition of this type:

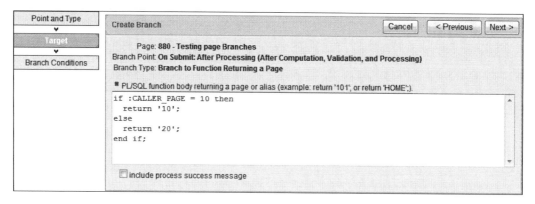

In this example, we dynamically set the branch page target according to the value of an application item called CALLER_PAGE. Of course, regular page items can also be used.

In the above screenshot, we can also see the checkbox **include process success message**. Checking this box will make the APEX engine display any defined success messages of the APEX processes in the current page on any target branch page that the code generated. This option can also be set later, when editing an existing branch.

Branch to Function Returning a URL

With this type, we are also using a PL/SQL body function to dynamically generate the branch target, only this time, it's in the form of an f?p URL. The following screenshot shows an example of the **Target** definition of this type:

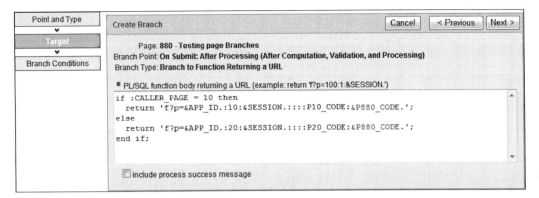

In the example, we are using an f?p URL that allows us to dynamically set a page item on the target page. In our example, P10_CODE or P20_CODE, depends on the target page.

Branch to PL/SQL procedure

This option allows us to use a PL/SQL stored procedure to implement the branch. The following screenshot shows an example of calling the BRANCH_TO_CALLER_PAGE procedure (stored in the BOOK package):

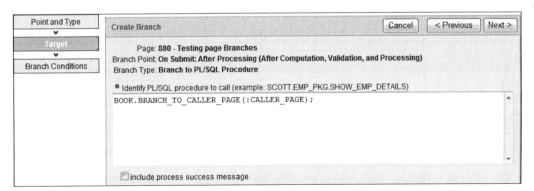

The BRANCH_TO_CALLER_PAGE procedure is defined as follows:

```
procedure branch_to_caller_page(p_caller_page in varchar2) is
  l_url varchar2(100);
begin

  -- Generate the basic syntax of the f?p URL
  l_url := 'f?p=' || v('APP_ID') || ':' ||
           p_caller_page || ':' || v('SESSION') || ':::::';

  -- Generate the part that set the page item value
  l_url := l_url||'P'||p_caller_page||'_CODE:'||v('P880_CODE');

  owa_util.redirect_url(l_url);

end branch_to_caller_page;
```

We are using the Oracle built-in packaged procedure owa_util.redirect_url()
to implement the actual branching.

> As we are using a stored procedure, we must use the APEX built-in
> v() function to retrieve the values of the APEX items.

Branch to page

This option allows us to simply note the page number that we want to branch to.
As can be seen in the following screenshot, this option includes a default option of
branch to page using redirect. This option allows us to declaratively define some of
the f?p URL segments while editing the branch. Leaving this option unchecked will
only allow us to set the target page number.

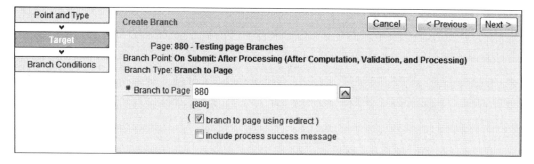

Branch to page accept processing (not common)

This option allows us to branch directly to the page ACCEPT phase of the branch target page. This means that we can take advantage of the entire page ACCEPT activities—Computations, Validations, Processing, and Branches—without rendering the page itself. As the option title implies, this option is not commonly used.

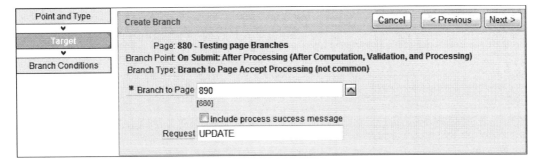

In the screenshot, we can see that we can set the **REQUEST** value to emulate a button press on the branch target page, e.g. we want to fire the **UPDATE** related activities in the target page.

Branch to Page Identified by Item (Use item name)

This option allows us to set the branch target page using an application or page item. This is a simple declarative option, yet it gives us some degree of flexibility, as we can use an item value—a page number or a page alias name—to set the branch target.

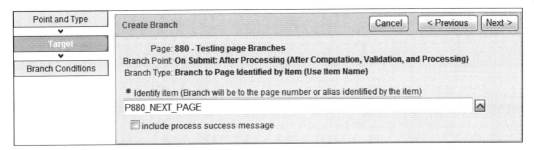

Branch to page or URL

This is the default option of the **Branch Type** field. It allows us to choose between using a direct page number or a URL within the same wizard screen.

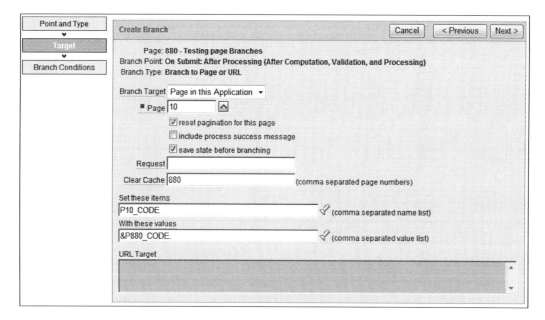

If we choose to use a **Branch Target** of **Page in this Application** then we'll be able to declaratively set some of the relevant branch parameters, such as the **Request** and **Clear Cache**, and also to set item values. In the screenshot, we can see an example of branching to page **10** while clearing the cache for page **880** (the current page), reset the pagination on the target page and set one of its items with a value from the current page.

> The **With this value** field should include a real value. As such, we can use a static (hardcoded) value or, like in the example, we can use a *Substitution String* notation so that the APEX engine will replace it with the value of an item at branch time.

If we choose to use a **URL** as the **Branch Target**, then all the declarative fields will be disabled, and we'll need to enter a valid URL as the next page target.

Why use the URL option if the wizard allows us simple declarative options? Well, think of a case where your next page is in a different APEX application using the first segment of the f?p URL syntax (and subject to security rules), or in cases where the next page is completely external to the APEX application. The URL option gives us more flexibility than the declarative option.

Save state before branching

In the previous screenshot, we can see that the option of **save state before branching** is checked. This option allows us to increase the security of our application by making it harder to tamper with the branch URL.

By default—this option is unchecked. Requests such as clear cache or setting the value of items in *Session State* are taking place after the branch. This means that the branch request URL will include the necessary information to perform these tasks. In our example, the APEX engine will generate a similar f?p URL to the following:

```
f?p=250:880:495596660586459::NO:880:P880_CODE:1374
```

You can see that some important information is exposed with this URL. We are asked to clear the cache on page 880 (segment 6 of the f?p syntax), and we are setting an item called P880_CODE with a value of 1347(segments 7 and 8 of the f?p syntax).

If we check the **save state before branching** option, then the *Session State* related action will take place before the branch while using the same database session. It means that less information needs to be passed in the open, especially with the branch request URL. Actually, the new f?p URL that the APEX engine will generate by using this option will not include any references to clear cache or setting a value of an item. The f?p URL will look similar to the following:

```
f?p=250:880:495596660586459::NO:::
```

Less information is exposed and tampering with the URL becomes slightly harder.

Branches URL and JavaScript

The previous screenshot is very similar to the **URL Optional Redirect** section on the **Edit Page Buttons** page. With buttons that implement a redirect without a submit functionality, we can also use a URL to set the target redirection of the button. This URL can include the **javascript:** keyword (the trailing colon is part of the syntax) followed by JavaScript code.

[Buttons that submit the page will create a separate branch process to implement redirection.]

What about the branch URL? Can this URL also include JavaScript? The answer is **No**. Unlike buttons, which are client-side components and can invoke JavaScript code, the branches are server-side components, and can't invoke JavaScript code.

Branch to URL identified by item (Use item name)

This option is similar to the **Branch to Page Identified by Item (Use item name)** option. However, with this option, the specified item should include a valid URL.

Sequence and branch conditioning

The next screen of the **Create Branch** wizard allows us to condition the branch, but first we need to set the **Sequence** of the branch. As usual, the **Sequence** determines the order in which branches are evaluated within their branch point. With branches, the pattern of behavior is that if the APEX engine finds a valid branch, then this branch will be fired, regardless of other possible branches with higher sequences. In this case, the branches with the higher sequences will not even be evaluated. It means that conditional branches should always be set with a lower sequence than the unconditional branch, which by this logic can only be one and always the last. A good practice would be to assign the unconditional branch a very high sequence, like 999, to ensure it will remain the last to be evaluated. We should choose the order of evaluation for both conditional and unconditional branches very carefully in order not to lose important application logic.

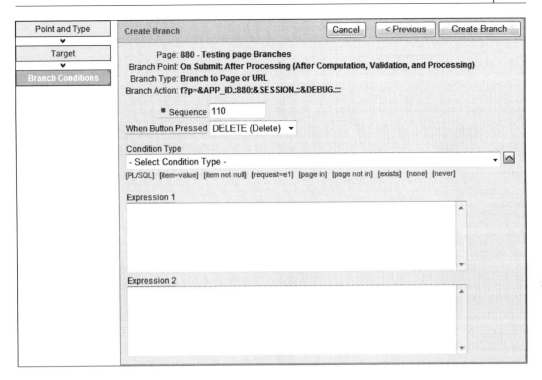

In the above screenshot, we can see an example of a branch being conditioned by the **DELETE** button. All the other pre-defined declarative conditions, supported by APEX, can also be used in here.

Bear in mind:

We can define multiple conditional branches, but it makes sense to only define one unconditional branch, as the first one will be fired and the others will not be evaluated. It's also important to remember that if a conditional branch has been fired, then all the following branches, including the unconditional one, will not be evaluated.

Edit branch

Every Branch can be edited using the **Branches** section on the *Page Definition* page. Besides all the options that were available to us through the **Create Branch** wizard, we can use the **Authorization** and **Configuration** sections to fine tune the access control and availability of the **Branches**, and the **Comments** section to document our actions.

Other ways to control the application flow

Branches are not the only means APEX provides us for controlling the application flow. We'll review some of these extra options in the following sections. As you'll see, APEX gives us a high degree of flexibility by supporting a large variety of application flow options and controls.

Branch with Buttons

As mentioned earlier in the chapter and was reviewed in Chapter 6, APEX Buttons, we can define branches as part of defining a button that implements a redirection without submit. The branch target can be defined declaratively or by using a URL, which is similar to what we have seen in this chapter.

Branch with PL/SQL

We can use the Oracle packaged procedure `owa_util.redirect_urt()` to define a branch target. We have seen a use of this procedure with the **Branch to PL/SQL Procedure** type. However, we can also use this procedure within a page process.

If we need to branch as part of the page SHOW phase, without actually rendering the page—e.g. we want to implement some logic that doesn't involve page display, such as manually generating a CSV file and saving it to the local file system—then we need to tell the APEX engine to stop the page rendering process. We can do that by using an APEX pre-defined special variable:

```
apex_application.g_unrecoverable_error := true;
owa_util.redirect_url('f?p=&APP_ID.:10:&SESSION.');
```

Setting the package variable `g_unrecoverable_error` to `true` instructs the APEX engine to stop the rest of the SHOW activities. As a result the next statement, which is a redirect instruction, will take place.

Branch with JavaScript

We can use the APEX built-in JavaScript function `redirect()` to branch from within a JavaScript code. This function accepts an `f?p` URL as its parameter.

Branch with an item

The **Select List** and **Radio** items include built-in options that allow us to define a branch as part of defining the item:

- Select list with Branch to page
- Select list with Redirect
- Radio group with Redirect

 These items also include a built-in submit page option. This option implements a page submit with self-branch.

Navigational aids

APEX supports several navigational aids, such as Tabs, Menus, Lists, Breadcrumbs, and a Navigational Bar, which allow us to branch to different pages on our application, implementing different types of logic and functionalities. For example, pressing a *Tab* will submit the current page and then branch to the new *Tab* page. Menus will redirect you to the target page, etc.

Summary

APEX branches allow us to implement and control the flow of our application. Branches can be defined declaratively or by PL/SQL code. We can set the branch target by directly noting the application page number or by using a URL with the f?p syntax.

Every application page must include at least one valid branch.

In the next chapter, we are going to review some APEX IDE built-in utilities that will help us to define our application database infrastructure, either declaratively or by using DDL commands and scripts.

11
APEX SQL Workshop

APEX is a data-centric application development environment. As such, the application data infrastructure, which consists of tables, views, indexes, sequences, triggers, etc., is very important.

When dealing with an application data infrastructure, we have two major initial phases—planning the data model and implementing it. APEX can help us a lot in the implementation phase by providing several user-friendly and declarative-based utilities that allow us to define (and maintain) the major database objects that we need for our application.

Many developers are not necessarily trained DBAs. Moreover, in the age of graphical integrated development environments, many developers, including the experienced ones, don't always remember all the syntaxes and options that are involved in manually creating database objects. Using declarative tools can make these tasks simpler and faster.

The APEX SQL workshop can also assist us when our data infrastructure is already defined. As we'll see in this chapter, some of the SQL workshop tools and options can alleviate some of the tedious tasks of manual coding, especially when large database tables are involved.

As the SQL workshop is run in an APEX context (after a successful login into the Application Builder), it is subject to the APEX security restrictions. As such, in this environment, it's easier to test SQL and PL/SQL snippets of code that are using (or protected by) internal APEX resources.

Advanced note:

When using the SQL workshop, as opposed to let's say, SQL*Plus, we don't have to manually set the security variable `security_group_id` (which identifies the APEX workspace), and we don't have to change the current schema. All the built-in APEX packages are available to us, and we can use our APEX developer credentials without being defined as database users, etc.

The concept of *data modeling* is not in the scope of this book. However, this is an important issue that can have a grave influence on the application performance. If you are not trained to do it, or don't have much experience in database schema design, then you are encouraged to ask for help on this issue from your trained or more experienced colleagues. It's important and can assist you in your development efforts.

The APEX SQL workshop includes four modules, which we'll review in this chapter:

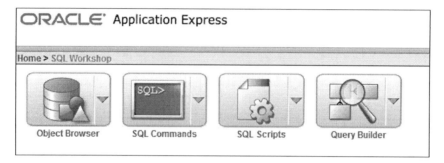

- **Object Browser**: This allows us to declaratively browse existing database objects and create new ones.
- **SQL Commands**: This allows us to run SQL and PL/SQL code within the APEX environment.
- **SQL Scripts**: This allows us to create and maintain a SQL and PL/SQL script repository.
- **Query Builder**: This allows us to create SQL queries declaratively while using graphical visual aids.

Navigating around the SQL workshop

Each SQL workshop module has its own graphical icon, as can be seen in the above screenshot. This graphical icon can act as a navigational aid in two ways. First, we can use the image part, or its title, to drill-down into the home page of the correlated module. The second option is to use the down-arrowhead part to open a drop-down menu for more specific functionalities in the module. The following screenshot displays the drop-down menu for the **Object Browser** module:

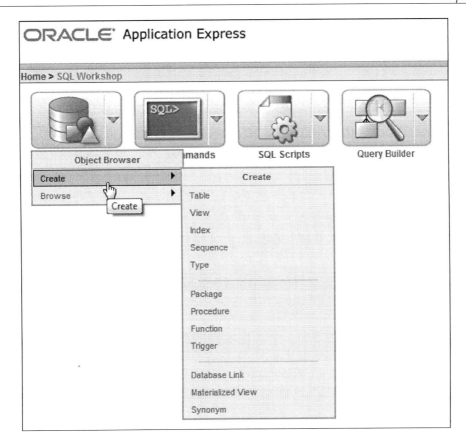

When you are inside a specific module (**SQL Script** excluded), you can also use the **Component** select list on the upper-right-hand of the screen, as can be seen in the next screenshot, to go directly to the selected module:

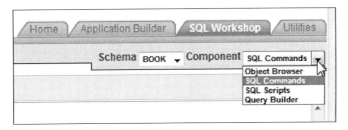

As we are dealing with database objects and other schema-related actions, we can also change the current schema we want to work in, as can be seen in the next screenshot:

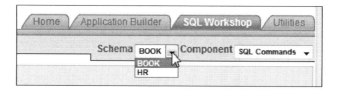

The **Schema** list includes the schema(s) associated with the APEX workspace.

Object Browser

The first module of the SQL workshop is the **Object Browser**. This module can be very useful and a productivity enhancer tool for both novice and experienced developers. It allows you to declaratively browse and manage the database objects within the schema(s) that is/are associated with the APEX workspace. In general, the *Object Browser* allows you to review and edit the structure of the database objects and their main features and attributes. It allows us to declaratively create new database objects, add new features to existing ones, and, of course, browse through stored data with the ability to *Insert*, *Update*, or *Delete* table records.

Exploring the database with the Object Browser

The following screenshot displays the upper-left-hand corner of the main **Object Browser** screen:

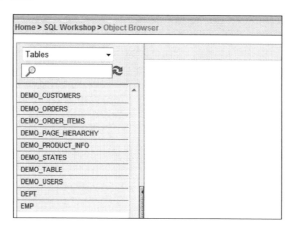

The select list field (displaying **Tables** in the example) allows us to choose the database object type we want to focus on. The Object Browser supports the following database objects: **Tables**, **Views**, **Indexes**, **Sequences**, **Types**, **Packages**, **Procedures**, **Functions**, **Triggers**, **Database Links**, **Materialized Views**, and **Synonyms**.

The text field below it (with the magnifying glass icon) allows us to filter the displayed objects by name. It implements a similar mechanism as the SQL LIKE operator—it will display any object that contains the filter string in any position. In the following screenshot, we entered the filter string **order**. As you can see, the object list—tables in this case—was reduced to only two. In both object names, the filter string has only a partial match with the object name and not from the beginning of it.

 The Object Browser uses AJAX technology extensively. In this context, the displayed list of objects will be modified in real-time as we type the filtering string.

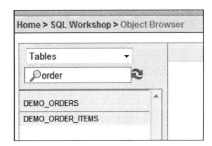

Choosing an object from the displayed list displays a specific, object-type dependent, main data screen. The following screenshot shows the main screen for tables:

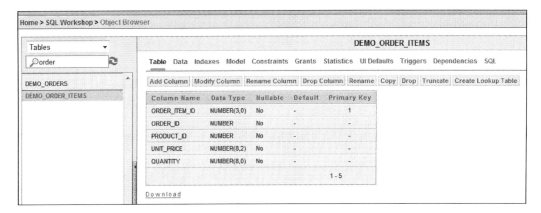

The main screen usually includes a series of tabs for various object-dependent categories (such as **Table**, **Data Indexes**, etc., in the example). Each tab includes a series of buttons, which represent various available, category-dependent options. In most cases, these options represent declarative actions on the object. In the screenshot, we can see the available actions for the **Table** tab—the **Add Column**, **Modify Column**, **Rename Column**, and more.

 I don't see much point in textual description of all the available options and actions, as there are many; just by reading, you probably won't remember much about them. The best way to get familiar with all the options is by hands-on explorations. I can assure you that this is time well spent. Mastering the *Object Browser* can make your life, as a developer, much easier.

Creating new database objects

In the upper-right-hand corner of the main *Object Browser* screen, we can find the **Create** button:

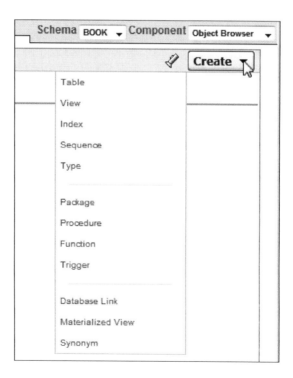

This is a dual behavior button. Pressing the down-arrowhead opens a drop-down menu that includes all the database objects we can create, using the *Object Browser*. Pressing the button itself displays a series of graphical icons with adjacent text links that represent the same database object list. Both menus lead us to a series of object-dependent wizards that allow us to create the database object we choose, declaratively.

> Note the **Schema** select list slightly to the left and above the **Create** button, which was mentioned earlier in the chapter. If more than one schema is associated with the current workspace, and as database objects must be defined within a specific schema, this select list allows us to choose the target schema for our newly created objects.

Now, let's use the *Object Browser* to create a new table for our application. After choosing **Table** from the **Create** menu we'll see the first page of the **Create Table** wizard, which allows us to name the new table and define its columns.

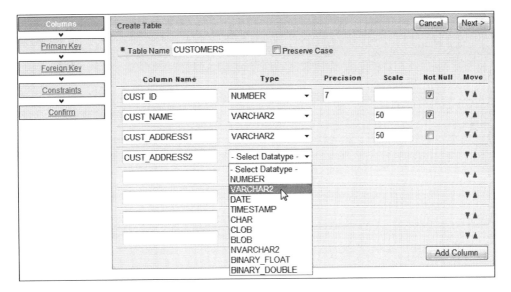

For each column we can define a **Column Name** and **Type**. According to the type, we can set the **Precision** and **Scale** column size attributes. Next, we can determine if the column is **Not Null** by checking the corresponding checkbox. At any point we can rearrange the order of the columns using the up and down arrowheads in the wizard's **Move** column. The wizard also allows us to add as many columns as we need using the **Add Column** button.

Pressing the **Next** button leads us to the next screen in the wizard, which allows us to define a **Primary Key** for the table. We have four options when setting the primary key:

- **No Primary Key**: The wizard will allow us to create the table without a primary key.

> This is not an advisable option. Each database table should have at least one column as a primary key. As we'll see later in the book, some of the APEX wizards create functionalities that rely on a primary key column. If you don't have a meaningful column to act as a primary key then you should define a non-meaningful one (e.g. based on a database sequence, as the next option allows).

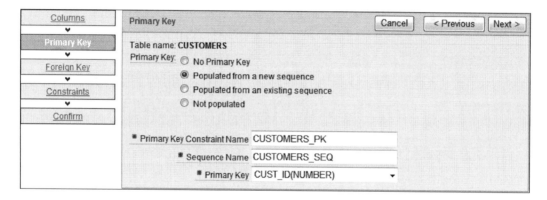

- **Populated from a new sequence**: This option allows us to create a new sequence to populate the primary key column. We must also select the **Primary Key** column, and the wizard will create the proper table trigger (i.e. a *before Insert for each row* trigger) that populates the primary key column, using the new sequence.

- **Populated from an existing sequence**: This option has a similar functionality to the previous one, but in this case, an existing sequence is used with the table trigger.

- **Not Populated**: With this option, we select the **Primary Key Constraint Name** and the **Primary Key** column(s). This option allows us to define a composite primary key (two segments only) without a way to auto-generate and populate it. This is useful, for example, when we want the user to supply the primary key value(s).

Pressing the **Next** button leads us to the next wizard screen, which allows us to define **Foreign Key** in the table. This is, of course, an optional step.

As can be seen in the following screenshot, we can select the column we want to define as the foreign key and then select the **References Table** and the **Referenced Column(s)**. In order to complete the definition of the foreign key we must press the **Add** button. Only the foreign keys in the upper list (**CUSTOMERS_FK** in the example) will be defined by the wizard at table creation time.

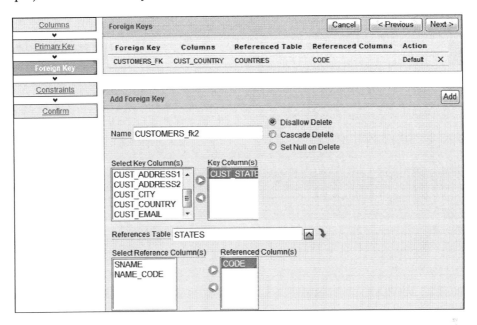

 The Object Browser view of an existing table includes a **Model** category that displays a graphical description of all the foreign key's relations that the current table has.

The next wizard screen—**Constraints**—is also optional, and it allows us to define extra constraints on the table columns:

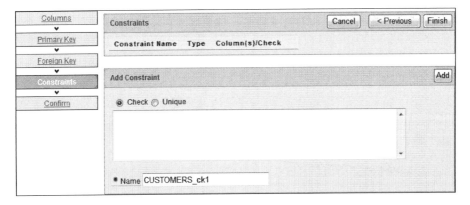

At this point we can press the **Finish** button and create the table. We can also choose to go to the last wizard screen by pressing the **Confirm** link.

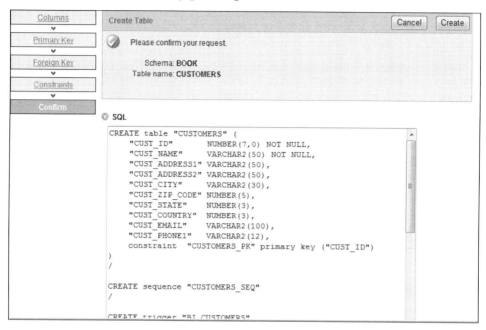

In this screen we can review the SQL script that will be used to create the table. If we approve the code, then we can press the **Create** button and the table will be created for us, with all of its supporting elements (e.g. indexes, constraints, sequence, and trigger). We didn't even need to write a single line of SQL or any DDL statement. The entire process was declarative.

UI defaults

This category , which is also part of the Object Browser table view, allows us to define default values to the User Interface-related parameters such as size, alignment, format, etc. When we are using APEX wizards to create a form or report based on the table, the APEX engine will use the **UI defaults** parameters while generating the form or report.

The **UI defaults** can be very helpful with formatted items such as dates, numbers, currencies, etc. The **UI defaults** can save us a lot of manual coding and ensure uniformity in the way the same item will be displayed throughout the application.

[The UI defaults (for all the tables in the workspace) are also accessible through the Shared Components module, under the **User Interface** section.]

Creating a package

I want to draw your attention to the option of using the *Object Browser* to create **Package with methods on database table(s)**.

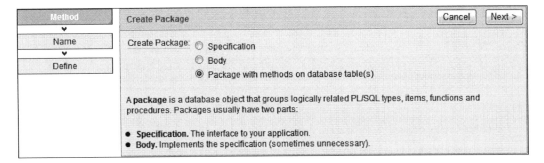

This wizard allows you to select a database table(s), and based on this selection, it will create all the necessary DML procedures for *Insert*, *Update*, *Delete*, and *Get* table(s) records.

The special benefit of using the Object Browser's **Create Package** wizard is that the *Update* related procedures, which are created by this wizard, are equipped with all the necessary *Optimistic Locking* capabilities. Dealing with the *Lost Updates* issue could be a complicated task, even for experienced developers, and it's not a trivial feature to implement.

This wizard can be of great assistance in cases where the built-in automatic DML processes can't be used (for example, because they don't support table attributes such as having a composite primary key with more than two segments), and for the manually constructed tabular forms (which we'll discuss later in the book, in Chapter 14).

You are strongly encouraged to create a sample package with the DML procedures and carefully review it. All the *Update* related procedures and functions could be a valuable learning source in order to understand how APEX implements *Optimistic Locking* and manages concurrency control in the Web environment.

SQL Commands

The next module of the SQL workshop is the **SQL Commands**. This module allows us to run SQL and PL/SQL code from within the APEX environment using the APEX context and the APEX developer privileges.

The **SQL Commands** screen is divided into two parts. The upper part is the code area (known as the *Command Editor* in the APEX documentation), where we can enter our SQL or PL/SQL code. The lower part is the results area (known as the *Display Pane* in the APEX documentation), where we can see the results of running the upper area code.

The SQL Commands code area

The following screenshot displays the upper left hand corner of the *Command Editor*:

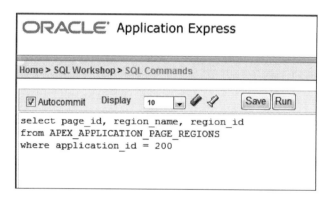

The default option of the *SQL Commands* is to perform an **Autocommit**, on the result (if applicable).

Bear in mind:
If you are working on real (production) data, working with the default setting of **Autocommit** means you can't roll back. Every change you make is for keeps.

The code area in the screenshot displays an example of a SELECT statement. In this case, it's a query to the APEX dictionary, bringing back all the names and IDs of page regions, in a specific application.

We can limit the returned number of records, using the **Display** select list. The next icon - - allows us to clear the working area from previous code. Its adjacent icon - - opens a popup window, which can be seen in the next screenshot. This popup window allows us to search for tables and views in the schema(s) associates with the APEX workspace. We can select a table or view, and see its structure. This utility also allows us to copy a SELECT statement, with all the table/view columns, back to the *SQL Commands* code area, by pressing the **Return Value** button. This option can be very useful with large tables/views, by saving us manual typing and possible syntax errors with the column names.

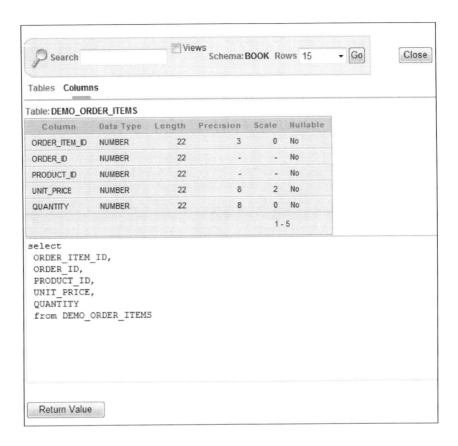

The *SQL Commands* code area also allows us to save the code we just built, in a named SQL and PL/SQL repository, using the **Save** button. It makes it very easy to save snippets of code for future reuse. Adjacent to the **Save** button is the **Run** button, which fires the code.

The SQL Commands results area (Display Pane)

The main functionality of the lower part of the SQL Commands screen is to display the results of running the code from the upper area. The following screenshot displays the results of the query to the APEX dictionary:

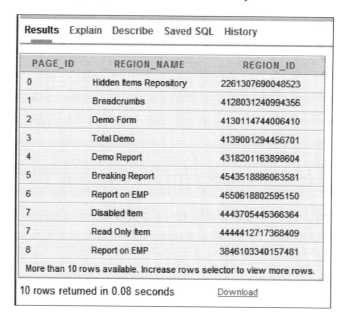

As can be seen in the above screenshot, our `select` statement returned more than the default 10 rows **Display** restriction, and a proper message is displayed to the user.

At the bottom of the screen, next to some statistics about the running code, we can see a **Download** link. This link allows us to download the results into a CSV file.

In cases where the database spotted an error, the *SQL Commands* engine will display a proper error message explaining how to fix it:

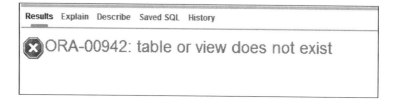

The results area also includes an **Explain** category. This category displays the execution plan for the running code. It can help us track bottlenecks in our code and ways to optimize it. In the following screenshot, we can see part of the **Explain** execution plan for the APEX dictionary query:

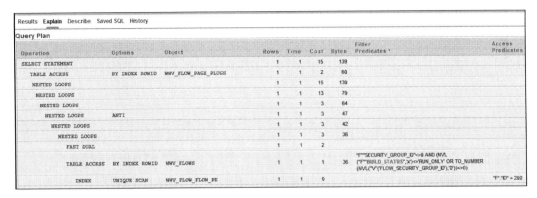

The results area also includes the **Saved SQL** category, which allows us to retrieve named SQL or PL/SQL code that we saved in the code area or queries that we constructed and saved using the **Query Builder** (which we'll review later in the chapter).

Another very useful category is **History**. The *SQL Commands* engine saves the last 200 snippets of code we have run, including the ones with errors. We can browse through this repository and reload any snippet of code we need.

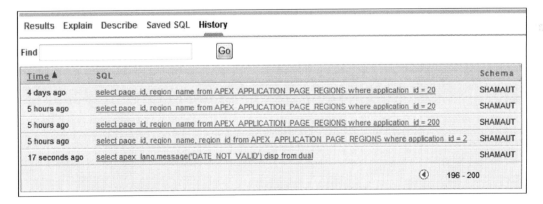

SQL Scripts

SQL Scripts is the third module of the *SQL workshop*. This module allows us to create and manage an independent repository of SQL and PL/SQL scripts. This repository is distinct from the **Saved SQL** or the **History** repository of the other modules (*SQL Commands, Query Builder*). We can create new scripts and save them into the repository, or we can upload external scripts into it. We can edit and run stored scripts, and we can also download them into our local filesystem. The following screenshot displays part of the *SQL Scripts* repository's main screen:

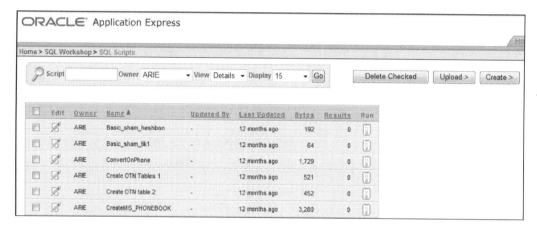

Pressing the **Edit** icon of a script leads us to the *SQL Scripts* **Script Editor**:

```
Home > SQL Workshop > SQL Scripts > Script Editor

Script Name Create OTN Tables 1          Cancel  Download  Delete  Save  Run

Undo  Redo  Find

1   CREATE TABLE  "RANDOMDATA"
2     (  "ID" NUMBER,
3        "NAME" VARCHAR2(30),
4        "RANDOM_DATA" VARCHAR2(255),
5        "RANDOM_DATA2" VARCHAR2(255),
6        "DESCRIPTION" VARCHAR2(4000),
7        CONSTRAINT "RANDOMDATA_PK" PRIMARY KEY ("ID") ENABLE
8     )
9   /
10
11
12  CREATE OR REPLACE TRIGGER  "bi_RANDOMDATA"
13     before insert on "RANDOMDATA"
14     for each row
15  begin
16     for c1 in (
```

This is a very simple editor; I wouldn't recommend it as your primary script editor, but it will do the job when you need it (and you don't have a better editor around).

Query Builder

The last *SQL workshop* module is the **Query Builder**. This module allows us to build a query on database table(s) using visual, graphical, and declarative means.

The *Query Builder*, like other similar tools, is often perceived as a tool for the novice user. This perception might be wrong. It's true that this tool can allow a complete novice to generate a fairly complicated query without much prior knowledge in SQL. However, an experienced user may also benefit greatly from this tool. Imagine you need to generate a SELECT statement on a 50 column table that includes several *Foreign Key* columns. Coding this statement manually can be very time consuming and tedious work, not to mention the possibility of irritable syntax errors and such. With the **Query Builder**, it can be a breeze.

The general layout of the *Query Builder* is similar to the *Object Browser*. On the left-hand side of the screen, we have a list of all the tables and views that are included in our APEX workspace schema(s). The remaining space is divided between an upper working area (known as the *Design Pane* in the APEX documentation), and a lower results area (known as the *Output Pane* in the APEX documentation). The principles of work are that we populate the working area with table(s)/view(s) from the list, and declaratively define the relationship between them. Every action we take in the working area is simultaneously reflected in the results area, which also gives us some fine-tuning options, (such as conditioning, sorting, and grouping) towards the final shape of the query.

The Query Builder working area (Design Pane)

Clicking on any entry from the list of available tables and views moves its element into the working area. We can populate the working area with as many elements (tables/views) as we need, and we can use the *drag & drop* feature of the working area to position them where it will be most visually clear and handy to us. In the following screenshot, we can see two tables that were moved into the working area—**CUSTOMERS** and **STATES**.

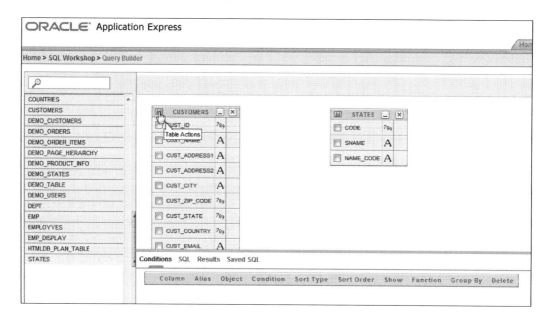

The *Query Builder* uses a dynamic tooltip system to help us locate and understand the options and functionalities that are available to us. The tooltip in the example points to **Table Actions**. It opens a context sensitive tasks box that allows us to check all the columns of the table or to add foreign key-related tables into the working area.

We can manually define relationships between tables/views in the working area, using visual and declarative means. In the row of the table column whose relationship we want to define, we can mark the (empty) cell in the outer-right-hand column. While hovering over the correct cell, the tooltip says **Click here to select column for join**. We should repeat this action with the related table/view. A graphical connection line will be drawn between the related elements.

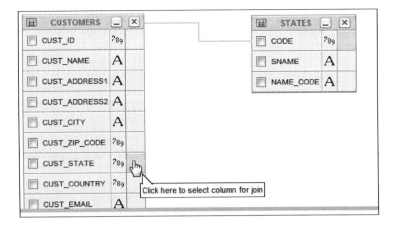

In this case, as the joined columns don't have the same name, a general connection line was drawn from the CUSTOMERS table to the CODE column in the STATES table. In other cases, where the joined columns share the same name, a direct connection line will be drawn between the columns.

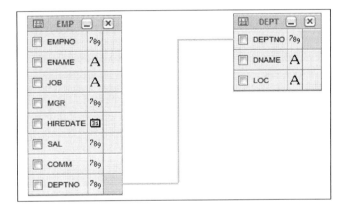

Hovering over the relationship line, a tooltip identifies the two parties in it. It can be very useful in a more crowded working area. Moreover, clicking this line opens a tasks box that allows us to delete the relationship or define a left/right outer join.

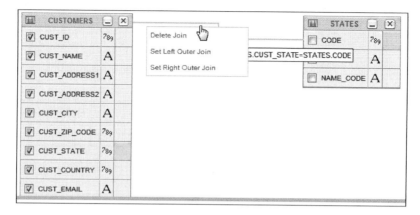

The Query Builder results area (Output Pane)

The *Query Builder* utilizes AJAX and DHTML technologies, which allows us to watch the effect of every action we take on in the working area, as it is immediately reflected in the results area. For example, for every table column we check on the working area, a corresponding line is generated in the results area **Conditions** tab. This tab allows us to declaratively filter the results of the query we are building or to define some group functions on the selected columns. The supported group functions include COUNT, COUNT DISTINCT, AVG, MAX, MIN, and SUM.

In the above screenshot we can see that a condition was set on the **CUST_CITY** column (we are looking for all our customers in London), and the results were ordered according to the **CUST_NAME** column.

The **SQL** tab displays the current SQL code, as it is constantly generated by the *Query Builder* engine and reflects the current status in both the working and results area (for the latter, it reflects the status of the **Conditions** tab).

```
Conditions  SQL  Results  Saved SQL

           "CUSTOMERS"."CUST_STATE" as "CUST_STATE",
           "CUSTOMERS"."CUST_COUNTRY" as "CUST_COUNTRY",
           "CUSTOMERS"."CUST_EMAIL" as "CUST_EMAIL",
           "CUSTOMERS"."CUST_PHONE1" as "CUST_PHONE1",
           "STATES"."CODE" as "CODE",
           "STATES"."SNAME" as "SNAME",
           "STATES"."NAME_CODE" as "NAME_CODE"
  from     "STATES" "STATES",
           "CUSTOMERS" "CUSTOMERS"
  where    "CUSTOMERS"."CUST_STATE"="STATES"."CODE"
   and     "CUSTOMERS"."CUST_CITY" = 'London'
order by CUSTOMERS.CUST_NAME ASC
```

In the **Results** tab, we can see the first 500 records that the current query fetched from the database. This max number cannot be changed. However, we can use the **Saved SQL** tab to name and save the newly constructed query, and we can reload it in the *SQL Commands* module where we can set the limit of fetched rows much higher.

Summary

In this chapter, we reviewed the APEX SQL workshop, a built-in supportive environment that helps us with the database objects we are using in our applications. Using declarative and visual means utilizing AJAX and DHTML technologies; this environment gives us (both novice and experienced developers) dynamic tools to easily create, manage, and browse our application data infrastructure.

With this chapter we have concluded the first part of our book, in which we reviewed the basic APEX concepts and elements. In the next chapter, we'll start learning how to utilize all that we learned so far to develop a simple APEX application.

12
APEX Forms

We have been hanging around the APEX kitchen for some time now, and so far we have learned about the ingredients that are available to us in it. Now it's time to take these ingredients—all the APEX concepts and components we reviewed thus far—and do some cooking. We'll start with a very basic dish—APEX **forms**.

As we have already mentioned several times before, APEX applications are data-centric. This means that entering data, and saving it into the database, is one of the most important and elementary actions that APEX should support. As we'll see in this chapter, APEX indeed does it very well with APEX forms.

Every form has two basic aspects that we, as developers, should address. The first one is the logic we want to implement with the form, and the second one is the form graphic and layout design. APEX helps us with both aspects.

Where design and layout are concerned, we made a major decision when we chose the application *Theme* (color coordination and the general look and feel of the application), and then some more layout and navigation decisions when we chose the *page template* to use (using tabs, menu, breadcrumbs, navigational bar etc.). The APEX form, implemented within its own region, is a natural extension of the application *Theme* and *page template*. It inherits their features while adding some of its own, which pertain to the form layout (e.g. items positioning), navigation, functionalities (e.g. the form's buttons) etc. The various APEX wizards we can use to create an APEX form consider all these aspects when they generate the code for the form.

In the logic aspect of the APEX form, which will be the focus of this chapter, we include the content of the form, i.e., what input resources it will include (mainly APEX items), and how to deal with that content, i.e. (in APEX terms) *Computations*, *Validations*, *Processes*, etc.

The *APEX IDE* includes several wizards that allow us to define most of the logic tasks we just mentioned while creating the APEX forms, based on a variety of sources.

In this chapter, we are going to review the following issues:

- The various sources we can use to create an APEX form
- How to use the APEX **Create Form** wizard to generate a new form
- A detailed example of how to use the APEX **Create Form** wizard to generate a new APEX form based on a table or view
- How to manually create an APEX form

Sources for creating a form

The input resources are usually the first form component we need to address, as the entire form revolves around them. As such, this is the main feature that differentiates between the various wizards that APEX provides us with to create our form. APEX supports the following options and sources to create a form:

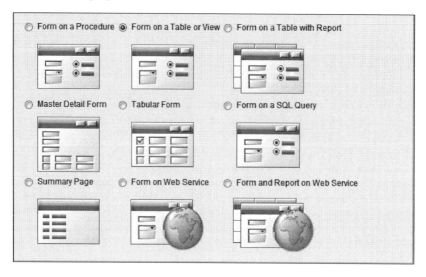

- **Form on a Table or View**: Database tables or views are the most logical resources for a form, as they allow us to populate it with their stored data. Alternatively, we can use the form to save new/updated data into them. The **Create Form** wizard generates the new form around the selected columns from the source table or view, while using **Database Column** as their **Source Type**. This wizard also allows us to select which DML processes (*Insert, Update, Delete*) will be created for the form. When the wizard runs its course, we get a fully-functional APEX form.

- **Form on a Table with Report**: This wizard actually creates two separate APEX regions—one for a report and the other for a form. These regions can be positioned on two different application pages or on the same one. The first region is a report region, which is based on a table or view (despite the title, this option also supports views). We'll review APEX reports in the next chapter. So for now, let's say that each row in the report has a link to a form that was created in the second region—The Form region—and this one contains all the report columns as the form items and allows us to edit them. This form is created with the same features as the **Form on a Table or View**.

- **Form on a Procedure**: A stored procedure can also be used as a form source. The **Create Form** wizard takes all the procedure parameters and allows us to select the ones that will be used as items on the form. The items are created as **Static Assignment** text items and are not associated with any database object. The wizard defines an *After Submit* process, which calls the stored procedure. Depending on the functionality of the source procedure, this is not always sensible (like if you are using a procedure with a fetch functionality). Therefore, you'll need to complete the data processing aspects of this type of form.

 This type of **Create Form** wizard allows us to utilize existing logic in our database. For example, in cases where we want to use some legacy code and logic in our new APEX application.

- **Tabular Form**: We'll devote an entire chapter to tabular forms (Chapter 14). However, I have already mentioned them in previous chapters. Tabular forms allow us to display and edit multiple records on a single form page, based on table(s) or view(s).

- **Form on a SQL Query**: This wizard takes the query columns and uses them as **Static Assignment** text items on the form. Although the source query includes at least one table (it can include more), the items on the form are not associated with any database object. Although this form includes proper buttons for DML processes, it doesn't include the DML processes themselves.

 This type of **Create Form** wizard allows us to create a form quickly and simply, based on an existing report (as every APEX report is based on a SQL query).

- **Master Detail Form**: This wizard offers us various options for defining and laying out a *Master Detail* form. It creates two form regions—for the master and detail tables—and has an option of also creating a *Report* region on the *Master* table (with a link/drill-down column to the correlated *Form* region). All these regions can be laid out on a single application page or on two or three separate ones. Each form is based on its own table, and we need to define the logical connection between them. The wizard creates the proper navigational links and buttons and the appropriate DML processes, so we are getting a fully functional **Master Detail Form**.

- **Summary Page**: This wizard allows us to create a display form based on a regular (input) form. After setting the form source page we can select the items to be displayed on the **Summary Page**. We can repeat this action for several source pages, thus displaying the summaries of multiple form pages, like in a typical confirm page of a wizard (APEX itself uses this option a lot in its own wizards).

- **Form on Web Service** and **Form and Report on Web Service**: Web services can include a lot of items, for both requesting and receiving information. The item names are pre-determined by the Web service. Therefore, a wizard that takes these items and embeds them on a form can be very useful, not to mention a serious time saver. These two wizards are doing just that.

Creating a new form

Let's create a new form on the CUSTOMERS table we created in the previous chapter.

If you haven't done so already, then now is a good time to create a new APEX application that will serve as your sandbox. You can find all the necessary information to do so in Chapter 4.

On the application IDE home page, press the **Create Page** button and choose to create a form page. From the list of available form types (like the screenshot in the 'Sources for creating a form' section) choose the **Form on a Table or View**.

In the first two screens of the **Create Form** wizard, we are asked to select the owner (database schema) of the source table/view we are going to use:

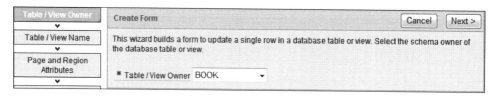

And the table/view name:

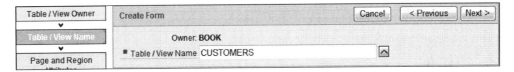

In the next wizard screen, we define the identification attributes of the application page—**Page Number** and **Page Name**—and for the *Form* region—**Region Title** and **Region Template**.

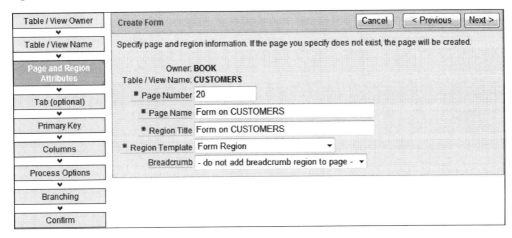

The next wizard screen, which is optional, allows us to associate the page with an existing *Tab* set.

The form primary key

In the next two screens of the **Create Form** wizard we need to define the **Primary Key** of the form table/view and how it's going to be populated. With the mandatory **Primary Key** select list item we can select a table/view column to be used as primary key, and if necessary, we can select a second segment (column) to that:

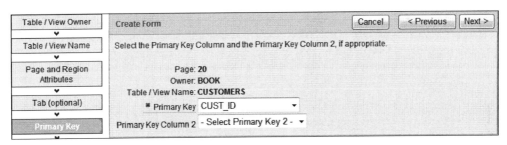

The **Create Form** wizard supports a compound *Primary Key* of up to two columns only. A higher number of the *Primary Key* columns will force us to manually enter code—either by defining our own DML processes (preferably by creating the proper DML package in the *Object Browser*) or by creating (or referencing) a new *Primary Key*. For example, we can create a view on a table with a *Primary Key* that contains more than two columns (or doesn't include a *Primary Key* at all for that matter) and use our own generated primary key column for the view. This will not get us off the hook completely as we still need to define INSTEAD OF triggers manually, but the wizard will still do most of the hard work for us.

Pressing the **Next** button leads us to the **Primary Key** source options screen:

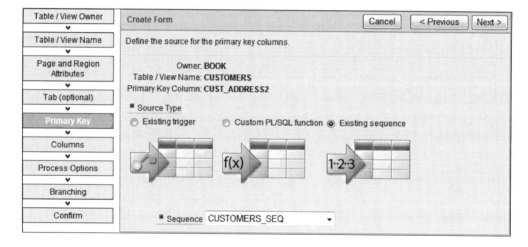

The **Create Form** wizard supports three source options:

- **Existing trigger**: With this option, the wizard relies on an existing table\view trigger, although it will not verify its existence. It's your responsibility, as a developer, to make sure an appropriate trigger exists.

- **Custom PL/SQL function**: With this option, we can use a PL/SQL function body to generate the *Primary Key*. This option is very useful in cases where the *Primary Key* value is derived from the table/view content or from other database resources. For example, we want to save several versions of the same file. In our tracking table, we can use a *Primary Key* column that comprises the filename and date of upload. We can use code similar to the following:

```
return :P20_FILE_NAME || '_' ||
    to_char('(systimestamp,'YYYYMMDDHH24MISS');
```

In this case, the wizard creates an *After Submit PL/SQL anonymous block* process (called, by default, Get PK) that fires the PL/SQL function we just defined and assigns its result to the *Primary Key* item on the *form*.

- **Existing sequence**: With this option, we are using an existing sequence to populate the *Primary Key* column. The wizard creates an *After Submit PL/SQL anonymous block* process (called, by default, Get PK), which queries the sequence we just noted for the next value and assigns it to the primary key item on the form.

> By default, the **Create Form** wizard doesn't support enterable (user populated) *Primary Key* items. The wizard creates the *Primary Key* item(s) as **Hidden and Protected** item(s). However, as we'll see in the next section, we can change that.

The form items

The next screen of the **Create Form** wizard—**Columns**—allows us to select the displayed items on the form, based on the columns of the table\view:

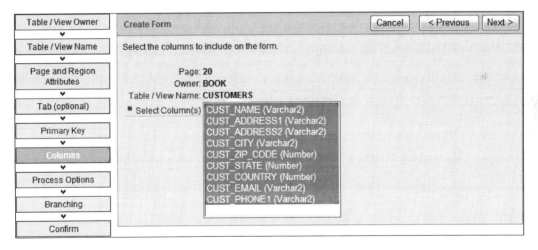

As can be seen in the above screenshot, the *Primary Key* item we selected in the previous wizard screen—CUST_ID—is not displayed for our selection. As was mentioned in the previous section, the wizard creates the *Primary Key* item(s) as **Hidden and Protected** item(s). However, we can change that while editing the form.

Sometimes we do want to display the *Primary Key* item that was generated by the database. In this case, we can change the *Primary Key* item **Display As** type to **Display As Text (saves state)**. In other cases, we might need to use enterable *Primary Key* item(s), allowing our users to populate them. In these cases, we can define the *Primary Key* item(s) as **Text** items. Of course, in these cases it will be our responsibility to make sure that the value(s) entered by the user is unique. Otherwise, we'll face a constraint violation database error.

The form DML options

The main process the **Create Form** wizard creates is an unconditioned **Automatic Row Processing (DML)** process that supports the DML operations of the form. Hence, the next wizard screen—**Process Options**—allows us to determine which DML operations will be available to us on the form. The available options are **Create** (Insert), **Save** (Update), and **Delete**. For each option that we select, a corresponding button will be created on the form, and the related DML operation in the **Automatic Row Processing (DML)** process will be enabled (the corresponding checkbox will be checked).

In some cases, additional *After Submit Processes* will be created to support specific aspects of the selected DML operations. For example, if you select the **Delete** option, a **Clear Cache for all Items on Pages (PageID,PageID,PageID)** process with a default name of `reset page` will be created and conditioned by the **Delete** button. Another example is a **PL/SQL anonymous block** process, with the default name of `Get_PK`, which will be created if we select the DML **Create** option and if we chose to populate our *Primary Key* item with an existing sequence. This process will be conditioned by the **Create** button.

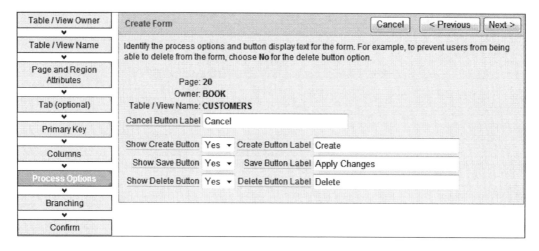

As can be seen in the previous screenshot, the first item on this wizard screen allows us to label the **Cancel** button. As we'll see in the next section, the wizard will create this button with a redirect functionality.

The form branches

As was mentioned in the *APEX Branches* chapter (see Chapter 10), every application page must include at least one valid branch. The *Create Form on a Table or View* wizard requires us to set two valid branches (which can have the same target).

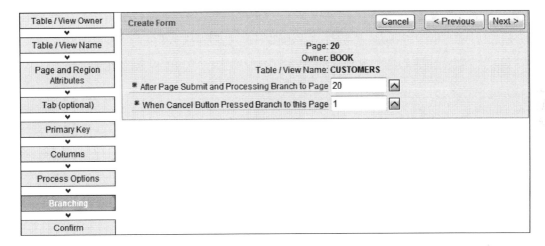

The first branch is an unconditional one that takes place after the *Page Processing* phase has run its course. The second branch is a page redirect that is conditioned by pressing the **Cancel** button.

In the previous screenshot, we can see an example where the natural flow of the page is to reload itself after a successful *Page Processing* phase (self-branch), and it redirects to page **1** in case of a cancel.

A new form has been created

After setting the branch target pages, the **Create Form** wizard displays a summary page of all our choices and allows us to **Finish**. The wizard creates a new, almost completely functional form.

I'm only using the word 'almost' because the wizard doesn't create *Form Validations* other than the NOT NULL validations on items that are defined as not nullable in the Oracle Data Dictionary. As *Validations* can be crucial to the health and integrity of our data, you are encouraged to check if the wizard has generated *Validations* (if any) and manually add the necessary and missing ones (if any).

In the next section, when we review the generated form, we'll see that in some cases we might also need to change the display type of some of the form items. However, the form will work just fine, even without these changes.

Now, let's examine the wizard-generated features and attributes of this newly created form.

The Page Rendering phase

The next page contains a screenshot of the **Page Rendering** column, taken from the *Page Definition* page of the new form.

As can be seen in this screenshot, the **Page** and **Regions** sections have been defined according to the details we supplied in the **Page and Region Attributes** wizard screen.

Next, in order, is the **Buttons** section. A button was created for each of the DML options we chose to include in the form (in this example, all four available options). The wizard automatically conditioned the buttons according to their functionality. The **Delete** and **Apply Changes** are conditioned by the built-in condition **Value of Item in Expression 1 Is NOT NULL**. The **Create** button is conditioned by the built-in condition **Value of Item in Expression 1 Is NULL**. In both cases, the item in expression 1 is the *Form Primary Key* item P20_CUST_ID. The **Cancel** button is not conditioned, and it is set to redirect to page **1**, as we defined it in the wizard.

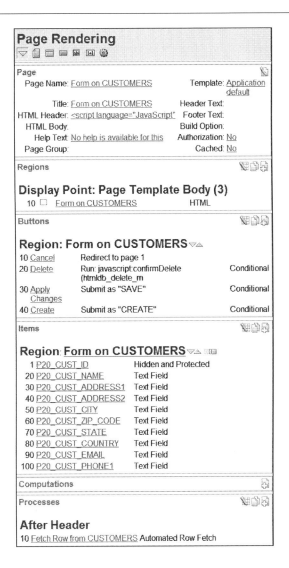

The items section

The wizard generated the item holding the *Form Primary Key*—P20_CUST_ID—as a **Hidden and Protected** item. All the other items were generated as **Text Field**.

In the case that the **Create Form** wizard identifies a table\view column of type DATE or TIMESTAMP, it will generate a **Date Picker** item. A column of type CLOB will be generated as a **Textarea** item, and for a BLOB column, a **File Browse** item will be generated.

As the customer ID might be the information we want to see on the form, let's change the display type of the P20_CUST_ID item to **Display as Text (saves state)**.

>
>
> **Note:**
>
> As P20_CUST_ID has been defined with a **Source Type** of **Database Column**, it's important to choose a **Display AS** option that saves state. Otherwise, the item, although displayed on the form, will not be submitted, and we'll lose the functionality of our *Primary Key*.

Next, we should deal with the items corresponding to **Foreign Keys** in the CUSTOMERS tables. We have the P20_CUST_STATE item, which relates to the STATES table, and the P20_CUST_COUNTRY, which relates to the COUNTRIES table. I chose to use a *Select List* item to display the available options for these items.

A *Select List* item needs a LOV to define its values. As we are referencing foreign key values, we need to define a dynamic LOV. In our example, we'll deal with the P20_CUST_STATE item, so the LOV should be based on the STATES table. The **List of Values** section of the item will appear, as shown in the following screenshot:

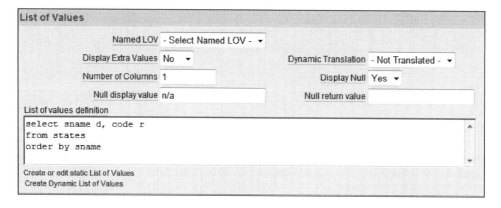

As you can see, I also chose to display a NULL value as part of the valid options and the displayed value in this case is **n/a**.

>
>
> If you anticipate using the COUNTRIES table in other forms of this application (for example, it might also be relevant to a SUPPLIERS file, etc.), you can define a **Named LOV** as part of the application *Shared Components* module and use it in all references to the COUNTRIES table.

After the displayed type changes we made to some of the form items, the revised **Items** section will look as follows:

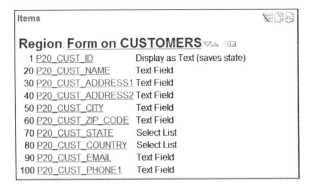

The Page Rendering Processes section

The **Create Form** wizard generated an *After Header* **Automated Row Fetch** process. This process will fetch the record whose *Primary Key* is the value of the P20_CUST_ID item. Although the wizard didn't condition the process, it will only be effective after a self branch, when the P20_CUST_ID holds a value. In order for that to happen, we'll need to edit the DML process that the wizard created for the *Page Processing* phase, and we'll discuss it in the corresponding section.

The Page Processing phase

The following is a screenshot of the **Page Processing** column:

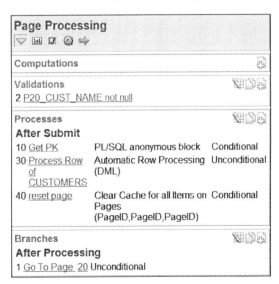

The Validations section

The **Create Form** wizard recognized (through the Oracle Data Dictionary) that the P20_CUST_NAME item is associated with a not null column. Hence it generated a **not null** *Validation* for it.

The Page Processing Processes section

The **Create Form** wizard generated an *After Submit* **Automatic Row Processing (DML)** process that implements the DML options we selected to include in the form. In our example, as we chose to include all the DML options, all of them will be supported by the process, as can be seen in the following screenshot taken from the **Edit Page Process** page of the form:

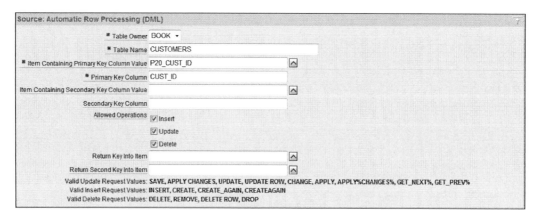

I want to draw your attention to the **Return Key Into Item** field. The wizard left this field empty in our example. In our specific example, it's okay as we chose to use an **Existing sequence** to populate our *Primary Key* item, and as we'll see next, a related process is taking care of that. However, for example, if we choose to use an **Existing trigger** as the source of our *Primary Key*, then we should populate this field with the *Form Primary Key* item. In our case it's the P20_CUST_ID item, so that the DML Insert operation will be able to populate it with the newly generated primary key. Otherwise, the **Automated Row Fetch** process will not operate properly after inserting a new record into the form table\view, as the P20_CUST_ID value will remain null (its initial value in a new form).

The second process the wizard created for us intends to support the DML Insert operation while using an **Existing sequence**, and as such, it will be created only when it is needed. The wizard named it Get PK by default, and as can be seen in the following screenshot, this is an *After Submit PL/SQL anonymous block* that retrieves the next value of the CUSTOMERS_SEQ sequence (our **Existing sequence**) and assigns its value to the *Form Primary Key* item P20_CUST_ID.

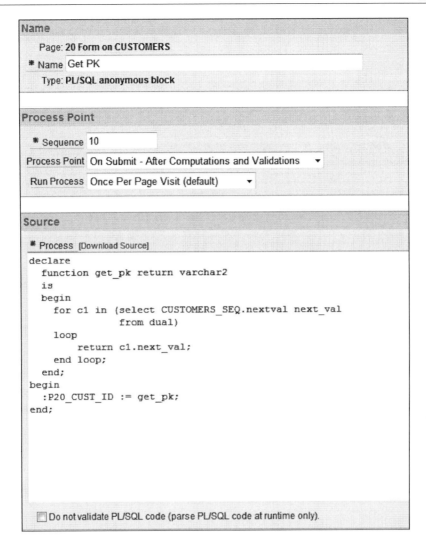

This process should be sequenced before the DML process, so the *Primary Key* value will be in place for the Insert operation, and as we can see, the wizard has done so.

The third process the wizard created for us—**reset page**—is of the type **Clear Cache for all Items on Pages (PageID, PageID, PageID)**, and it is conditioned by the **Delete** button. In this case, following the deletion of a record, all *Session State* values for the page will be cleared and we'll get a new (empty) form.

The Branches section

In the **Create Form** wizard we defined two branches, one for the natural flow of the page (after page submit, computation, validation, and processing) and one for the **Cancel** button. For the latter, we already saw the implementation of it as part of the **Cancel** button. For the first case, the wizard generated an unconditional *Branch*, and in our example, it's a self-branch.

That concludes the review of the new table\view based form we created. Although we made some manual changes to some features that were generated by the wizard, most of them were mainly to adjust the functionality of the form to our specific needs (like supporting foreign keys). The wizard did most of the hard work for us using declarative means, and we didn't have to write even a single line of code (HTML and PL/SQL alike).

Manually creating an APEX form

Using the APEX **Create Form** wizards to create the different types of forms we need, based on a variety of resources available to us, can save us a lot of time consuming manual work by not having to create these forms from scratch. However, as we saw, the APEX wizards don't always support all the options we need. It seems like the most common cases are the need to use a *Primary Key* that is more complex (compound) than the ones supported by the APEX wizards, or the need to use multiple database tables as the source of our tables.

We can manually create every *APEX Form* element we encountered so far while using the **Create Form** wizard, outside the wizard. We can create an *APEX Form*, starting from scratch, with only an empty application page. The first step will be to create a Form region, and then we can create our needed items and buttons in it. We follow this by creating the necessary rendering supported *Computations* and *Processes*. Next, just like in a wizard-generated form, we need to create proper *Validations* (unlike the wizard generated form, in a manually generated form we need to do that also for the *Primary Key* item(s)). Now it's time for the needed *After Submit Computations*, *Processes*, and *Branches*, and for that we can use all the wizards we already reviewed in the previous chapters of the book.

We can also use the **Create Form** wizard as a starting point to create the basic elements of the Form and then continue manually. This can be very useful if the main reason for not using the wizard is unsupported *Primary Key* or multiple tables we need to use on the form. In such cases, we can generate the Form skeleton, and then add/replace the components that don't meet our specific needs, like DML Processes (we can use the **Package with methods on database table(s)** that we discussed in the previous chapter) INSTEAD OF triggers (in case of using a view), and so on.

The point to remember is that the APEX **Create Form** wizard doesn't limit our Form options in the APEX environment. If our needs can't be met quickly, simply, and declaratively by the wizard itself, we can still use manual code to generate the exact Form we need.

Summary

In this chapter, we reviewed the options available to us for creating an *APEX Form*, which can be based on various resources, using the APEX **Create Form** wizards.

We specifically reviewed an example of creating a *Form* based on a table and examined the final result of the wizard—almost a fully functional *Form*, defined by declarative means.

The *Form* we created during this chapter appears in the demo application accompanying the book, and you are invited to check its final appearance and functionalities.

Bear in mind that this chapter only thoroughly covered the most basic APEX *Form* type—a *Form* based on table or view. Later in the book, we'll review a more complex and advanced option of the APEX *Form* (hint: the *Tabular Form*).

In the next chapter, we'll review the options for creating a simple APEX report.

13
APEX Reports

Reports are an essential component of any application as they provide a way to query and view data stored in our applications while providing the results in a meaningful format. In APEX, reports are defined using a report region. In the following chapter we will discuss how to build and modify a report region while exploring the reporting features APEX has to offer. Specifically, we shall be looking at:

- Creating a simple report using a wizard
- Modifying a report manually
- Building a parameterized report
- Creating charts

Report regions

As described earlier, regions are a container for content on an APEX page. A report region is used in APEX to display the results of a SQL Query in a formatted HTML table within a page. A page can contain multiple report regions and also co-exist with other region types, such as a chart or a form. Report regions offer many built-in functions that will be covered later in this chapter, such as column sorting, record pagination, templates, and printing.

As is common to most areas of APEX, a wizard is provided to help guide us through the creation of a report. The wizard ensures that we can rapidly add reporting functionality to our pages with minimal work. In APEX, the report region wizard provides four types of reports that we can add to a page, and they are:

- **SQL report**: This is where the report is based on a SQL query or a PL/SQL function that dynamically generates a SQL statement. A SQL query selects the columns we wish to display, together with the tables where the data is stored and any conditions used to filter the data, and defines how tables are related.

- **Interactive report**: This is similar to a SQL report in that it's based on a SQL query, but it provides many more features which can be applied at runtime by a user, such as customizing columns to display, applying data filters, conditional highlighting, sorting, and much more.

- **Report on a web service result**: This type of report is based on the results returned by a web service. The results of the web service are in XML format. APEX provides many features for using web services in your application, but they are beyond the scope of this book.

- **Wizard report**: This report type doesn't require any knowledge of SQL. The wizard will automatically build the SQL based report on the tables and columns selected to be displayed in the report. The wizard enables columns from multiple tables to be selected.

 Interactive reports were added in APEX version 3.1. All previous reports, such as the wizard report and SQL report, are referred to as **Classic** reports.

SQL reports and interactive reports are commonly used when building APEX applications. Although the wizard report makes it easy to create a report, they are limited in the complexity of the SQL that can be generated for the report. However, both SQL reports and interactive reports allow us to create more advanced queries by enabling custom SQL queries to be entered to control exactly how data is displayed in the report. In a later chapter we will explain interactive reports further, but for now we will take a look at how you go about creating a SQL report.

Creating a simple report using a wizard

In this section, we will walk through the process of creating a report region on an existing page. To demonstrate, we will create a report to list all employees stored in a database together with the department the employee belongs too. We will use the report region wizard to create a SQL report, which will generate our employee list.

The report region wizard can be started in a number of different ways:

- We can click the **Create Page** button from the Application Builder to create a brand new page with a report

- We can click the **Create** button from the Page Definition, which will prompt us to create a new page or a new region on the current page

- We can click the **Create Region** icon in the **Region** section of the Page Definition screen

There are certainly plenty of ways to get started. For our example, we will use the Create Region icon from the Page Definition screen. Now, let's walk through the steps to creating a report.

Start the report region wizard

In the screenshot, we see the Create Region icon. Click the icon (to the right of region) to start the wizard:

 Any attributes entered through the wizard can be modified after the wizard has been completed. The **previous** button can also be clicked to go back to previous steps and make changes.

Region type

The next step is to tell APEX that we wish to add a report region to our page. To do this, select the **Report** option and click **Next**:

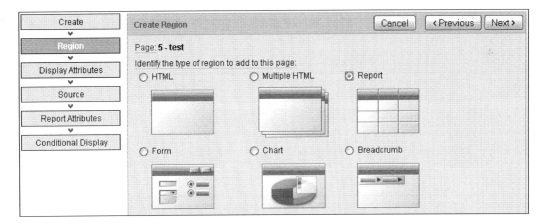

Report implementation

In the next step, we need to specify what type of report to create. Select the **SQL Report** option, and click **Next**:

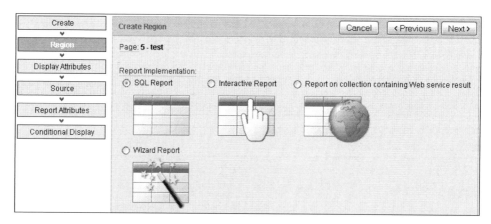

Display attributes

Once we have selected the SQL report wizard, the first thing we need to do is specify display attributes. Display attributes are used to control the look and positioning of the report region on the page. The **Title** is a mandatory attribute that is displayed as the title for the region, essentially a heading for your report. The **Region Template** attribute will control the overall look of the region. It can control things like borders, style, titles, button positions, and layout of the region.

In terms of the positioning of the region, the **Display Point** attribute tells us where in the page template the region will be displayed. We can use the flashlight icon next to the **Display Point** attribute to view the position of display points in a page and select the required display point. The mandatory **Sequence** attribute tells APEX the order in which the regions are displayed (i.e. if you have multiple regions). The **Column** attribute can be used to divide your page into columns and specify which column to display the region in.

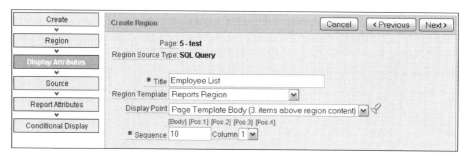

SQL source

The next step is the most important part of creating a report. It tells APEX what data needs to be displayed in the report. In the screenshot below, we have defined a SQL query to select columns from the employee and department tables. In this case, we have provided a SQL query, but we could also have entered a PL/SQL function that returns a SQL query as the source.

The PL/SQL method is a way of being able to define dynamic SQL. An example of when you may wish to use PL/SQL to generate a SQL query is if we need to build a matrix or pivot table report. In this case, we may not know the exact number of columns that will be displayed. We can use PL/SQL to determine the number of columns and build up a SQL query. In this case, we would tell APEX to use **Generic Columns**, as the number of columns is not known until runtime.

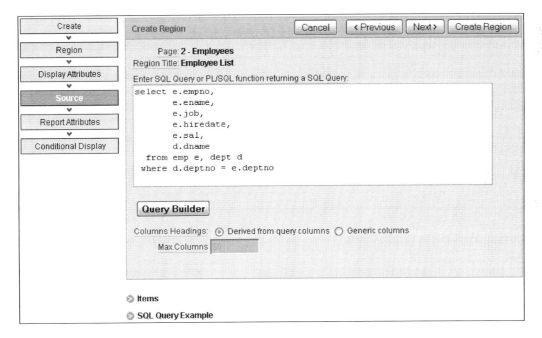

 After entering the SQL source, we have entered enough details for the wizard to create the report region. We can click **Create Region** to finish or continue to run through the wizard and set additional attributes.

Query Builder

You may remember the Query Builder from the SQL Workshop module of APEX. It can also be accessed via the create SQL report wizard by clicking the **Query Builder** button. The Query Builder is a great way to visually create SQL queries for reports, especially for developers who may not be familiar with SQL. When building a query in the Query Builder, click the **Return** button, and the query generated will be entered into the SQL source of the SQL report wizard.

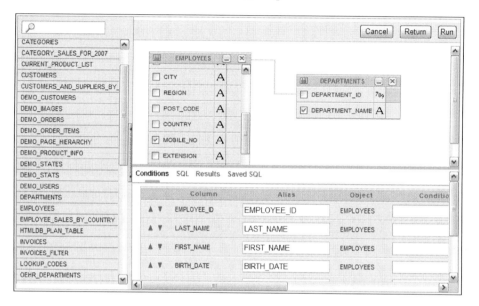

Report attributes

After defining our SQL source, the next step is to define the attributes that will control the look and feel of our report content. The **Report Template** attribute controls how the rows of our report are rendered, including layout and style. There are a number of templates to choose from that can alter the way report results are displayed.

The **break columns** attribute enables reports to have grouping on up to three columns. In our example, we could use breaking to group employees by each department or job position. The **rows per page** attribute enables us to control how many result rows are displayed on a page, and we can use record pagination to scroll between the rows.

The **Column Heading Sorting** attribute, when set to **Yes**, enables users to sort the results of a report by clicking on the report column headings. Clicking a column sorts the report in either ascending or descending order depending on the report column selected. The **Column Heading Sorting** attribute must be set to **No** if you intend to use a custom order in the report SQL.

The **CSV Output** attribute when set to **Yes**, will place a link in the report region that when clicked, enables all the report results to be exported into a comma separated file (CSV). This enables users to export CSV data into a spreadsheet or other application, where further analysis of the data can be performed. The link will only be displayed if the #CSV_LINK# substitution string is located in the report region template. The #CSV_LINK# substitution string also controls where in the report region the link will be positioned. The **Link Label** attribute will define the text to display for the link.

The **Report Printing** attribute provides us with a way of printing our reports into another **Output Format**, such as PDF, Word, Excel, or XML. This enables us to print reports with things like page breaks, headers, and footers, which are difficult to control using HTML. The **Link Label** attribute defines the text to display for the link.

The **Enable Search** attribute is used to add a search bar above the report region where search criteria and the number of records to display per page can be entered to filter the report. The search bar is only available for VARCHAR columns in the report SQL.

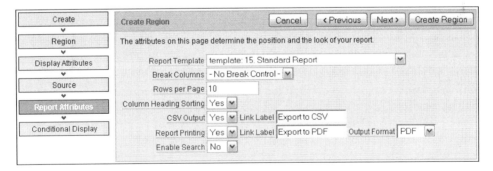

Conditional display

As described in previous chapters, APEX enables us to enter conditions to determine if the report region is displayed. In this example, we will not enter any display conditions.

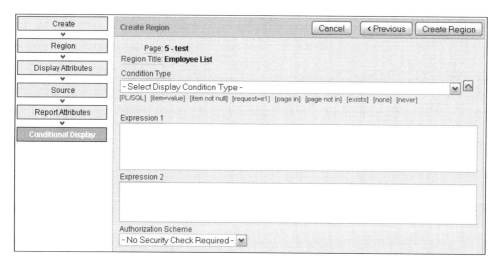

Wizard completion

The SQL report wizard has now gathered enough information to create our report. Clicking the **Create Region** button will add the report region to our page and then display the Page Definition screen. From here, we can click the **Run** button to view the report generated by the wizard, which can be seen in the following screenshot (the look and feel will vary depending on the theme you have selected for your application):

Employee List

EMPNO	EMPLOYEE_NAME	JOB	HIREDATE	SAL	DNAME
7369	SMITH	CLERK	17/DEC/80	800	RESEARCH
7499	ALLEN	SALESMAN	20/FEB/81	1600	SALES
7521	WARD	SALESMAN	22/FEB/81	1250	SALES
7566	JONES	MANAGER	02/APR/81	2975	RESEARCH
7654	MARTIN	SALESMAN	28/SEP/81	1250	SALES
7698	BLAKE	MANAGER	01/MAY/81	2850	SALES
7782	CLARK	MANAGER	09/JUN/81	2450	ACCOUNTING
7788	SCOTT	ANALYST	09/DEC/82	3000	RESEARCH
7839	KING	PRESIDENT	17/NOV/81	5000	ACCOUNTING
7844	TURNER	SALESMAN	08/SEP/81	1500	SALES

Export to CSV | Export to PDF

1 - 10 Next ⊘

In the screenshot, we can see that APEX has placed links on each of the columns; these links can be used to sort the report results on the selected column. APEX has also added record pagination where we can scroll through the records returned by the report. The report also has an Export to CSV link which will output all report results into a CSV file, while the Export to PDF link will open the report in a PDF file for printing.

As demonstrated, we can see that the report wizard is a very fast way to add report content to pages. In the next section, we'll discover how we can modify and enhance the report created by the wizard to take advantage of some of the built-in reporting functionality of APEX.

Modifying a report manually

A report region has many attributes that can be specified to help make it look, feel, and work exactly the way we would like. These attributes are divided into the following three main property pages:

- **Region Definition**: This controls the overall details about the report region, such as the SQL query source, display conditions, and report title.
- **Report Attributes**: This controls the appearance of the report, such as the layout, column headings, formatting, and pagination.
- **Print Attributes**: This controls the way the report region is displayed when printing, such as page sizes, headers, and footers.

These property pages can be accessed from the regions section of the Page Definition screen. In the following screenshot, you can see the Employee List report we just created listed with three hyperlinks. The **Employee List** link goes to the Region Definition property page, the **Report** link goes to the Report Attributes property page, and the **Print** link goes to the Print Attributes property page. Once in a property page, you can navigate between the property pages using the tabs displayed at the top of the page.

Regions
Display Point: Page Template Body (3)
10   Employee List   Report Print

Editing a Region Definition

The Region Definition property page enables us to modify details for the overall region. The property page is broken down into sections for identification, user interface, source, conditions, cache, header and footer, authorization, customization, configuration, and comments.

The identification section

The identification section enables us to specify overall details about our report region. The **Title** is a mandatory attribute that is used as our report heading, while the **Type** attribute tells APEX if we are using either a SQL query or PL/SQL that generates a SQL query for the SQL source of the report.

The **Static ID** attribute enables a name to be entered that can be used to identify the report region when using custom JavaScript. This can be referenced dynamically by using the `#REGION_STATIC_ID#` substitution string.

The **Region Attributes** field enables values to be substituted into the report region template, where the `#REGION_ATTRIBUTES#` substitution string is located.

The user interface section

The user interface section enables us to specify the overall look and position of the region in a page. The **Template** attribute defines the appearance of the region, such as borders, the report title, and the placement of buttons in the region. The **Mandatory** sequence attribute controls the ordering of regions in a page, together with the **Column** attribute that enables the page layout to be broken down into columns. The **Display Point** attribute can be used to place the report region in a specific position in the page template being used.

The **Region HTML table cell attributes** field is used when regions are displayed in multiple columns, and APEX renders each column in the page as HTML table cells. We can use the **Region HTML table cell attributes** to enter additional HTML settings for the region table cell, such as the vertical alignment. For example, specifying `valign="top"` would align the top of the region to the top of other columns should the other columns be greater in height.

The source section

The source section is used to control what data the report will display. This is defined by the **Region Source** attribute, which is used to specify the SQL query used for the report. If we need to add extra columns to our report or any other filtering, then we need to modify the SQL query with the changes. When using a normal SQL query the **Use Query Specific Column Names and Validate Query** option should be selected.

The **Region Source** attribute could also include PL/SQL code that returns a SQL statement. In this case, the **Use Generic Column Names (parse query at runtime only)** option would be selected to enable a SQL query to be generated dynamically, for example, adding where clauses or columns dynamically to a SQL query.

The **Region Error Message** attribute can be used to customize the error message displayed should there be any problems with the SQL source. The substation string `#SQLERRM#` can be used to display the error message raised from the Oracle database.

Source

Region Source

```
select e.empno,
       e.ename,
       e.job,
       e.hiredate,
       e.sal,
       d.dname
  from emp e, dept d
 where d.deptno = e.deptno
```

⊙ Use Query-Specific Column Names and Validate Query
○ Use Generic Column Names (parse query at runtime only)

Maximum number of generic report columns:

Region Error Message
`#SQLERRM#`

The caching section

The caching section is used to specify if a report region should be cached. Caching can help with the performance of a report, especially when the data being displayed is static and not likely to change. The **Caching** attribute determines if the region is to be cached and the **Timeout Cache After** attribute determines how long the report region will be cached for. Additionally, we can specify a condition to determine if the report region should be cached using the **Cache Condition Type** attribute, which works in a similar way to display conditions. This is useful should you not always want the report region to cache.

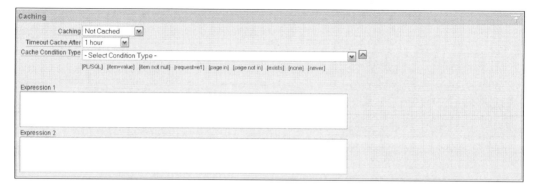

The header and footer section

The region header and footer section is used to enter custom HTML in the header and or footer of a region. These attributes are common to all types of regions in APEX, but there are some useful substitution strings we can use that are relevant to report regions:

- `&TOTAL_ROWS.`: The total rows returned by the report SQL query
- `&ROWS_FETCHED.`: The number of rows retrieved for the page
- `&FIRST_ROW_FETCHED.`: The position of the first row retrieved for the page
- `&LAST_ROW_FETCHED.`: The position of the last row retrieved for the page
- `&TIMING.`: The time it took to render the region

We can place these substitution strings together to show a message to display which records are being displayed in our report. For example, the following would be used to display "Rows 21-30 of 50" if our report returned 50 rows and we are displaying rows 21 to 30:

```
Rows &FIRST_ROW_FETCHED.-&LAST_ROW_FETCHED. of &TOTAL_ROWS.
```

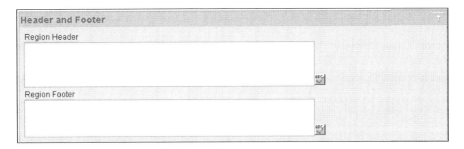

Editing Report Attributes

The Report Attributes property page is used to control the appearance of a report. The property page is broken down into sections for column attributes, layout and pagination, sorting, messages, report exports, break formatting, and external processing.

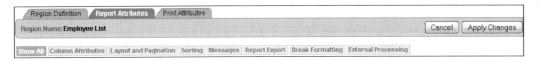

As for many property pages in APEX, a task list is displayed on the right-hand side that provides links to some useful functions. In the report attributes property page, the task list provides options to add a derived column or a column link to a report.

The column attributes section

The column attributes section is used to define details about the columns displayed in a report. Each column defined in the SQL query for the report is listed in a tabular form illustrated in the following screenshot. For each column, we can enter or view the following:

- Does the column display values as a link to another page? This is displayed in the **Link** attribute.

- Does the column display values as an editable item in the report, like a text box, select list, or calendar? This is displayed in the **Edit** attribute.

- The column heading text using the **Heading** attribute. Custom heading text can only be selected if the **Custom** option is selected from **Headings Type** attribute. By default, database column alias names are used for column headings. We can specify to have no column headings by selecting the **None** attribute or we could use the **PL/SQL** attribute to write code to determine column headings to display. This is useful when using dynamic SQL for the report and the number of columns are not known until running the report.

- The alignment of the column value using the **Column Alignment** attribute—left, center, and right.

- The alignment of the column heading using **Heading Alignment** attribute—left, center, and right.

- Is the column displayed in the report output? This is set using the **Show** attribute.

- Should a total be displayed for the column summing up all values? This is set using the **Sum** attribute.

- Should the column allow sorting, where by clicking the column heading, the report data is sorted by the column? This is set using the **Sort** attribute.

- Amend the default sort order of report results using the **Sort Sequence** attribute to define the sequence the columns will be ordered in.

If we are not happy with the order in which columns are displayed in the report, we don't need to re-adjust the SQL query. We simply use the up and down arrows to achieve the desired column order.

On this screen, we have seen the common attributes that can be set for each column, but there are additional attributes we can set by clicking the edit icon at the start of each report column listed. We will explore these properties later in the Column Attributes property page section.

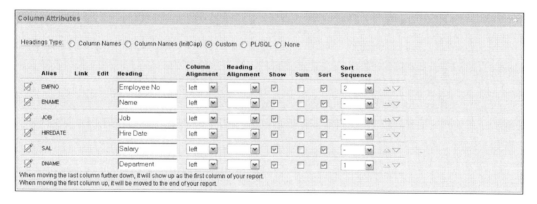

The layout and pagination section

The layout and pagination section controls not only the look and feel of how report rows are rendered, but also the number of records displayed and how we navigate between records. The **Report Template** attribute controls how the rows of our report are rendered including layout and style. We can use one of the many built-in templates or define our own row template to use.

The **Pagination Scheme** attribute controls how record pagination is displayed for a region. Record pagination is used to show next and previous links to navigate between records returned by a report. APEX has a number of predefined pagination schemes which can display row ranges to easily enable us to jump to a specific set of records and also display the total number of records. In the same way, APEX lets us control how record pagination is displayed. We can also choose where to display record pagination in the report region—top, bottom or top, and bottom, by setting the **Display Position** attribute.

> If a report SQL query returns many rows, use pagination as this will help make your pages generate and load faster as you are handling a smaller number of records in each page.
>
> Choosing a pagination scheme that does not show the total number of rows can help improve the performance of a report—such as the Row Ranges X to Y (with next and previous links) pagination scheme.

The **Number of Rows** attribute defines how many records to display on each page. It can be set dynamically through the **Number of Rows (item)** attribute that can reference a page or application item to determine the number of rows. We can also control the maximum number of rows that the report SQL query will return using the **Maximum Row Count** attribute. This can be used to help performance, as fewer rows need to be handled and counted when APEX is determining pagination for the report.

If a report region only contains a small number of rows, and we wish to display all the rows on page, we can choose to select no pagination and increase the **Number of Rows** attribute to be high enough to allow for all rows to be returned.

The **Enable Partial Page Refresh** attribute enables the report region to display the next or previous set of records without having to submit the entire page.

> This is useful if you have another region such as a form on the same page, data entry can continue in the form without needing to refresh the entire page to navigate records in the report region.

We can also control how null values are rendered by setting the **Show Null Values As** attribute. This enables us to specify a string to use if the column value has no value. If a column value contains HTML text, then we can set the **Strip HTML** attribute to determine if data values are rendered as HTML or as plain text. We can also use the **Sort Nulls** attribute to determine whether null values are included first or last when sorting query results.

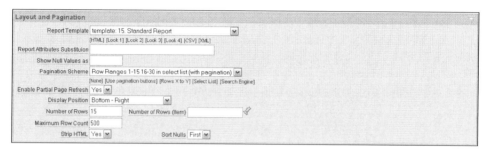

The messages section

The messages section is used to provide custom messages for a report region. The **When No Data Found Message** attribute is used to display a message when the report SQL query does not return any rows. The **When More Data Found Message** attribute is used to display a message to highlight if more rows exist after the **Maximum Row Count** attribute has been reached.

You can enter HTML text into these attributes together with the substitution strings specified earlier in the header and footer section to further customize these messages.

The report export section

The report export section adds functionality to reports to enable all report result data to be downloaded into a CSV file for use with spreadsheets and other applications. The **Enable CSV Output** attribute, when set to **Yes**, adds a link with the text specified in the **Link Label** attribute. The link will only be displayed if the `#CSV_LINK#` substitution string is located in the report region template. The `#CSV_LINK#` substitution string also controls where in the report region the link will be positioned.

The export file doesn't have to be comma delimited, it can use any delimiter specified in the **Separator** attribute. The default separator is a comma or semicolon depending on your current NLS settings. Data values are enclosed using the character in the **Enclosed** attribute. By default, the data values are enclosed with double quotes.

The **Filename** attribute is used for the filename of the export file. By default, the region name is used for the filename, followed by the extension `.csv`.

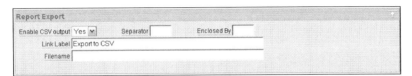

The break formatting section

The break formatting section enables reports to have grouping on up to three columns. The **Breaks** attribute determines which columns to group on. If we select to only break on the first column, we need to ensure that the first column in our report is the actual column we want to group on. The same also applies for the second and third columns.

The **Identify how you would like your breaks** to be **displayed** attribute enables column headings to be repeated for each break (or grouping), or only displayed once, which is the default. We can also specify how break totals, break rows, and break columns are displayed.

To demonstrate break formatting, in the following screenshot we have modified the Employee List to group employees by department. To do this, we have made the department name the first column in the report and specified the report to break on the first column. The sum column attribute has been set on the salary column that results in totals being displayed for each department and for the report overall.

Employee List

Department	Employee No	Name	Job	Hire Date	Salary
ACCOUNTING	7782	CLARK	MANAGER	09/JUN/81	2450
	7839	KING	PRESIDENT	17/NOV/81	5000
	7934	MILLER	CLERK	23/JAN/82	1300
Department Total:					**8750**
RESEARCH	7369	SMITH	CLERK	17/DEC/80	800
	7566	JONES	MANAGER	02/APR/81	2975
	7788	SCOTT	ANALYST	09/DEC/82	3000
	7876	ADAMS	CLERK	12/JAN/83	1100
	7902	FORD	ANALYST	03/DEC/81	3000
Department Total:					**10875**
SALES	7499	ALLEN	SALESMAN	20/FEB/81	1600
	7521	WARD	SALESMAN	22/FEB/81	1250

Export to CSV | Export to PDF

1 - 10 Next ⊚

The external processing section

The external processing section is used to define a server that will convert the results of a report region into another format, such as PDF. This allows the results of a report to be printed or saved in a nicer format, therefore avoiding many common problems of printing HTML from a web browser, such as headers, footers, page breaks, and repeating headings.

The URL attribute specifies an external server to call that is separate from APEX, and will convert the results of the report region, for example this might be Apache FOP or Cocoon. APEX will call the server and send the report region results in XML format. The XML is posted in the HTTP request as a form item named *vXML*. The **Link Label** attribute displays the text to be displayed for the link to call the external server.

External Processing

URL

Link Label

 The external processing section is separate to the built-in report region printing functionality provided by APEX. The built-in report region printing functionality will be covered later in the printing attributes section of this chapter.

Editing Column attributes

Column attributes is another property page, which is accessed via the column attributes section of the report attributes property page. It sounds confusing, but the report attributes property page only displays a small number of the actual properties that can be defined for a column. The column attributes property page enables more detailed attributes to be entered regarding the column. The property page is broken down into sections for column definition, column formatting, tabular form elements, a list of values, column link, authorization, conditional display, and comments.

The column definition section

The column definition section is used to define basic details about a column in a report. Attributes such as the column heading, alignment, compute sum, sort, and show can be defined via the report attributes property page for all columns in a report, but they can be edited here in the column attributes page for an individual column.

An attribute not included in the previous property page is the **Include In Export** attribute. This is used to determine whether a column is included in a CSV file export or when printing the report in PDF.

The column formatting section

The column formatting section is used to format the value of the column. The **Number / Date Format** attribute enables date values to be formatted with a particular date and number format mask—such as short date, long date, date with time, currency, percentages, and the like.

> The list of values icon next to the **Number / Date Format** field can be used to select a predefined date and number format mask. If the format mask you are after is not in the predefined list, select a similar format mask, and then modify it in the **Number / Date Format** field.

We can also apply a custom style sheet class to the column value using the **CSS Class** attribute to control the look and feel of the column value. Alternatively, we can define any style details in the **CSS Style** attribute.

The **Highlight Words** attribute can be used to physically highlight specific words if they exist in the column values of a report. This attribute can contain plain text or reference a page or application item to enable the highlighting to be more dynamic. This is useful on a search page, where we can highlight all occurrences of search criteria in the report results. In the screenshot, we can see an example where the word manager has been entered in the **Highlight Words** attribute for the job report column. When the report region is run, all occurrences of the word manager are highlighted.

Department	Employee No	Name	Job	Hire Date	Salary
ACCOUNTING	7782	CLARK	MANAGER	09-JUN-81	2450
ACCOUNTING	7934	MILLER	CLERK	23-JAN-82	1300
ACCOUNTING	7839	KING	PRESIDENT	17-NOV-81	5000
RESEARCH	7902	FORD	ANALYST	03-DEC-81	3000
RESEARCH	7788	SCOTT	ANALYST	09-DEC-82	3000
RESEARCH	7566	JONES	MANAGER	02-APR-81	2975
RESEARCH	7369	SMITH	CLERK	17-DEC-80	800
RESEARCH	7876	ADAMS	CLERK	12-JAN-83	1100
SALES	7521	WARD	SALESMAN	22-FEB-81	1250
SALES	7654	MARTIN	SALESMAN	28-SEP-81	1250
SALES	7844	TURNER	SALESMAN	08-SEP-81	1500
SALES	7900	JAMES	CLERK	03-DEC-81	950
SALES	7499	ALLEN	SALESMAN	20-FEB-81	1600
SALES	7698	BLAKE	MANAGER	01-MAY-81	2850

Employee List — 1 - 14

The **HTML Expression** attribute can be used to render HTML with data values for the column. You can reference the actual column value by using #COLUMN_NAME# syntax, where your database column name is surrounded by # symbols. The following example displays the EMP_NO column value wrapped with HTML bold tags:

```
<b>#EMP_NO#</b>
```

The tabular form element section

So far we have seen report attributes displayed as text. The tabular form element section enables a column to be displayed as a form element—like text boxes, and select lists rather than just text values. The **Display As** element is used to define the type of form element to show the column as, by default, columns are displayed as text. Currently, APEX report regions only support a small number of APEX item types.

As we can see, a report region can display each row as a form, making it into a grid or what is commonly referred to as a tabular form. Initially, it may seem confusing to see a report region being able to display as a form, but this provides the foundation for building tabular forms which will be explored further in the next chapter.

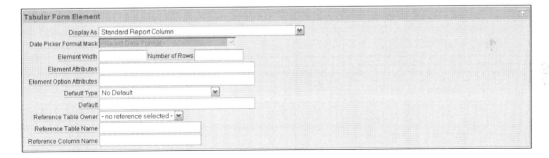

The column link section

Often in a report, we need to place hyperlinks on a report column to provide a drill down capability to an edit screen for a record, or even another report page. The column link section provides us with the ability to specify attributes about the link we wish to create.

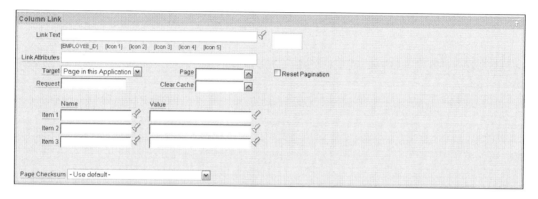

In the previous screenshot, we can see the attributes that can be set for a column link, including the **Link Text** to display the link and the **Page** to navigate to. We can also specify **Items** and the **Values** to populate the items with. This should be familiar from the Branching chapter, and you will notice that the attributes for both a column link and branch are identical.

> When building a drill down we need to pass the identifier of the report row to the page we are calling, so the page can be customized based on the record selected.

Conditional display

Conditional processing is built into many areas of APEX and is also available for report columns. We can enter conditions to determine if a report column is to be displayed or hidden.

Editing print attributes

So far, we have seen how report regions are displayed in a web browser in HTML format, but what if we need to print our reports? It can be very difficult to make HTML-based reports print nicely. Things like page sizes, headers, footers, and repeating table row headings are difficult to control in HTML. To get around HTML printing issues, APEX provides print attributes where we can export a report region into another format, such as PDF, and so these printing issues can be avoided.

The print attributes property page is used to control the appearance of report regions when we export them to files such as Adobe **Portable Document Format (PDF)**, **Microsoft Word Rich Text Format (RTF)**, **Microsoft Excel (XLS)**, or **Extensible Markup Language (XML)**. The property page is broken down into sections for printing, page attributes, page header, report column headings, report columns, and page footer.

The printing section

The printing section enables the report region to be exported to another file format to allow the report to be printed or saved. The **Enable Report Printing** attribute, when set to **Yes**, adds a link with the **Link Label** attribute used as the link text in the footer of the report (similar to CSV export). We can select the format that the report will be exported to, by setting the **Output Format** attribute—the options are PDF, RTF, XLS, HTML, and XML. This can also be dynamically set by using the **Item** attribute, which can reference a page or application item, to determine the format to use.

The **View File As** attribute can be set to *attachment* to be prompted to save/open the file or *inline* to view the file directly in the web browser.

The **Report Layout** attribute is similar to a report template. It determines how the report rows are rendered when printing and the look and feel used for the report. APEX provides a generic template by default, but you can create your own custom report printing templates using XSL-FO or Oracle BI Publisher Desktop with Microsoft Word when using Oracle BI Publisher as the print server.

The **Print URL** can be used to access the report; this is useful if you want to create your own print button where you can allow users to select an export format.

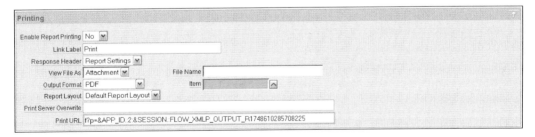

The page attributes section

The page attributes section enables basic details about the page—like paper size, page orientation, and borders to be defined for the report when printing.

The page header section

The page header section enables a custom header to be placed on report pages when printing. You can enter text that can include substitution strings, application items, and page items in the header. The header is useful for displaying things like any report parameters used for the report.

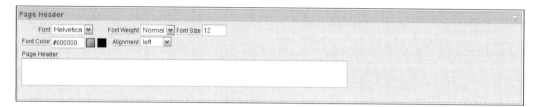

The column heading section

The column heading section controls the fonts and colors used for the column headings of the report when printing.

The report columns section

The report columns section controls how columns are displayed in a report when printing. We can specify fonts and colors to use for report columns, but we can also control the width of each column using the **Column Width** attribute. Widths can be entered in either pixels or as a percentage of the overall width of the table. The **Include in Export** attribute is used to specify whether the column is displayed or hidden in the export.

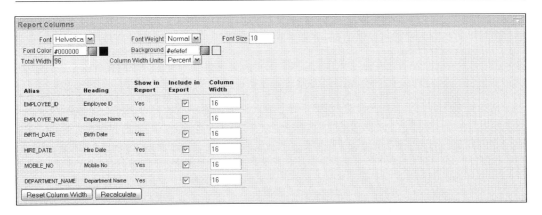

The page footer section

The page footer section is similar to the page header except in that it enables a custom footer to be placed on report pages when printing. You can again enter text that includes substitution strings, application items, and page items in the footer. The footer is useful for displaying things such as the date and the user who ran the report.

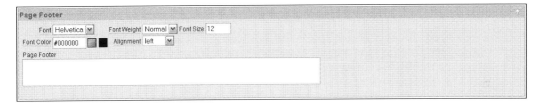

Enabling PDF printing

The print attributes property page for a report region shows how we can set attributes to control how a report can be exported to another format for printing. But this functionality requires an external report server, separate to APEX, for the export to work. The role of the external report server is to take the report data in XML format from APEX, together with the report template in XSL-FO or RTF, and transform it into the required output format. Oracle BI Publisher, Apache FOP, or equivalent XSL-FO processing engine can be used for the reporting server.

Setting up an external report server is outside the scope of this book, but once a report server is set up you need to register it in APEX. This can be entered by an APEX administrator in the Instance Settings of APEX. Once the report server is configured, APEX will take care of all the integration for us, so we don't need to worry about all the finer details. This means users will simply be able to click a print link and be able to view a report printed in PDF, while developers can simply set the enable **Report Printing** attribute to enable PDF printing for their report regions.

APEX offers additional reporting functionality in shared components under Report Queries and Report Layouts. This enables you to create custom templates for printing and also enables integration with the Oracle BI Publisher reporting tool.

Building a custom report row layout template

As we have seen already, APEX comes with a number of templates we can use to control how result rows are displayed in reports. But we can create our own templates if the built-in templates don't quite meet our requirements.

Report templates can be created from the Templates section under Shared Components. When creating a report template, we need to specify the HTML code for the layout we wish to achieve. The key thing we need to know is how to reference columns from our SQL query in the report template. APEX provides two ways in which we can reference query columns in report temples:

1. **Generic columns**: This is where SQL query columns are referenced in our report template by using the substitution string #1#, #2#, #3#, and so on. When we place #1# in our template, APEX will substitute it with the first column from our SQL query and so on. Using this approach is generic, and we can re-use the template in other report regions.

2. **Named columns**: This is where SQL query columns are referenced in our report template by using the actual column alias from the SQL query. In this method, we create substitution strings using the syntax #EMPNO#, #ENAME#, and so on. When we place #EMPNO# in our report template, APEX will substitute it with the matching column alias from the report SQL query. Using this method is not generic as it relies on having specific column names in your report SQL query. It has the advantage of making complicated report templates easier to follow and is not dependant on the order of columns in the report SQL query.

 Take a copy of an existing report template that is similar to the one you wish to create and modify it rather than starting from scratch.

Building a parameterized report

Parameterized reports enable users of our applications to enter values that can be used to filter the results displayed in a report. This makes our reports more interactive and makes it easier for users to find the records they are after. Parameterized reports serve many purposes in applications and can be used for building screens such as search pages, master detail pages, and other filtered listings.

To demonstrate a parameterized report, let's extend our Employee List report used earlier to include employee name and department as the parameters that will be used to filter the Employee List. To do this, we add an HTML region to our page, which will be used to hold the items used for the parameters. We then add a Text Field item for the Employee Name and a Select List item for the department to the HTML region. We also add a button to the HTML region which will be used to submit and refresh the page.

The magic of making this work lies in the SQL source for the report. In the SQL query, we can reference page items, application items, and substitution strings. This means we can create where clauses in the SQL query to restrict data based on the value of items stored in our page. Let's demonstrate this by modifying our report SQL query to include the Employee Name and Department parameters, the SQL query will look as follows:

```
select e.empno,
       e.ename,
       e.job,
       e.hiredate,
       e.sal,
       d.dname
  from emp e, dept d
  where d.deptno = e.deptno
   and (e.deptno = :P2_DEPARTMENT
    or  :P2_DEPARTMENT = 0)
   and (e.ename like '%'||:P2_NAME||'%'
    or  :P2_NAME is null)
```

In the query, we check whether our department item named P2_DEPARTMENT is equal to the department database column, or whether the department page item has not been entered. To determine if the department item has not been entered we check if its equal to zero as zero has been set as the **Null Return Value** in the **List Of Values** section for the item—the value when a department has not been selected. This ensures that the employee belongs to the department we selected or if the parameter is left empty (no value selected), that it will still display all employees regardless of their department.

For the Employee Name, this works in exactly the same way as the department parameter, with the exception that we are allowing a partial search to be done on the employee name. This means that we can enter part of the employee name and find any employees where the partial name is contained in the employee name. This is achieved by using the SQL like operator and the percent wildcard characters.

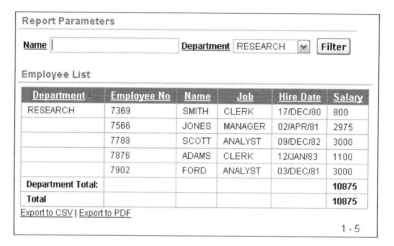

The screenshot above demonstrates our parameterized report example where a department has been selected, and the employee list has been filtered to only show employees for the selected department.

Charts

Often, data can be better represented visually instead of being listed in a table. APEX provides chart regions that can be used to render charts on a page. APEX provides many different chart types including pie, bar, and line types that can be displayed in 2D and 3D formats. Charts in APEX can also render a single or multiple series of data.

Charts have many similarities to report regions, in that multiple charts can be placed on a page, and a wizard can be used to guide us through the process of creating a chart. Charts can also be parameter driven and able to drill down to other pages. This makes them very useful for dashboards and other types of interactive pages.

A chart region can be added to a page by using the add region icon on the Page Definition screen. From here, we can create a chart region and specify the type of chart. When creating a chart, the SQL query is the most important property we need to define. The SQL query used for the chart needs to be in the following format:

```
select page_link,
       chart_label,
       chart_value
  from table_name
```

In the example query, page link is the APEX URL (e.g. `f?p=...`) used to navigate to when the value in the graph is clicked. The chart label and chart values provide the data we wish to plot on the chart. To demonstrate, we could build a pie chart to show how many employees belong to a department by using the following SQL:

```
select    2, d.dname, count(*)
    from emp e, dept d
   where e.deptno = d.deptno
group by d.dname
```

Using the preceding SQL query, the following screenshot shows the pie chart created by the chart region:

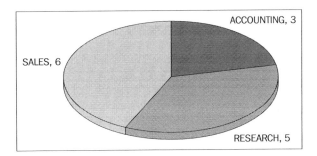

Summary

In this chapter, we have learned about report regions and how they can be created on pages using the SQL report wizard. We have also looked at how to modify a report region using the report definition, report attributes, printing attributes, and column attributes property pages. Report regions provide a number of built-in features that enable us to add report content to our pages very quickly and with very little coding required.

In the next chapter, we will look into the APEX Tabular Form concept and how we can use it in our applications.

14
Tabular Forms

When building applications, it's important to design screens that are user friendly and enable data to be displayed and manipulated easily. A **Tabular Form** is an APEX technique where multiple records can be displayed, created, updated, or deleted on a grid-like screen(s), where we can determine the amount of data displayed on each screen. It allows us to create a single unit of data manipulation, which includes all the DML actions we need, all under the same roof — a single APEX application page. In this chapter, we will discuss how to build a *Tabular Form* in APEX. Specifically, we shall be looking at:

- Creating a *Tabular Form* with a wizard
- Creating a *Tabular Form* manually
- Using the APEX provided APEX_ITEM API to create form items

What is a Tabular Form?

A common design approach when building web applications is to list records from a database table on one page, then link to another page where the particular record can be modified (also known as drill down). Using this approach means that in order to edit multiple records we need to navigate backwards and forwards between pages. From a user perspective, this can make the data manipulation process frustrating and more time consuming, especially if multiple records need to be manipulated at the same time.

Tabular Forms provide a way to help minimize the need to navigate to other pages by enabling multiple records to be manipulated on a single page. A *Tabular Form* can display both editable and non-editable fields in a grid-like format, allowing the user to see the "big picture", and by that, making its data manipulation task easier. *Tabular Forms* are not always going to be practical in all situations, but if we are only dealing with a small number of fields — the max limit is 50 editable columns — then they can be used to help simplify data entry in our applications.

In APEX, a wizard is provided to help us create *Tabular Forms*. The wizard generates a *Tabular Form* by using a specific report region—**SQL Query (updateable report)**— to render the form rows, essentially making each column (excluding the *Primary Key* column(s)) updateable. To start off, we will look at how we can create a *Tabular Form* in APEX using the form wizard.

Using a wizard to create a Tabular Form

In this section, we will walk through the process of creating a *Tabular Form* on an existing page. To demonstrate, we will create a *Tabular Form* to maintain all employees stored in a database table. In the *Tabular Form*, we will be able to add, update, and delete multiple employee records. We will use the form region wizard to create the *Tabular Form*. Now let's walk through the steps to create a *Tabular Form*.

Start the Report Region Wizard

In the following screenshot, we can see the Create Region icon; click the icon (to the right of region) to start the wizard:

Region type

The next step is to tell APEX that we wish to add a form region to our page. Select the **Form** option, and click **Next**:

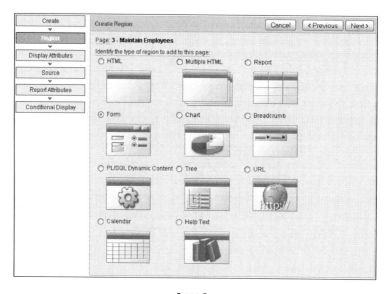

Form implementation

In the next step, we need to specify what type of form to create. Select the **Tabular Form** option, and click **Next**:

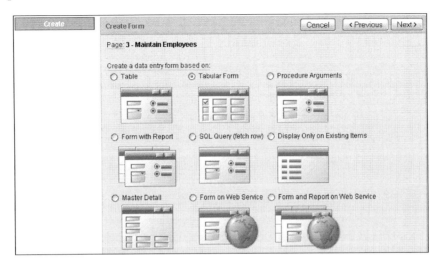

Identify Table/View Owner

Once we have selected the **Tabular Form** wizard, the first thing we need to do is specify the **Table/View Owner** attribute. This defines the database schema where the table or view we wish to base our *Tabular Form* on is located. We also define the data manipulation operations we wish to allow the *Tabular Form* to perform by using the **Allowed Operations** attribute. Using this attribute, we can control whether records can be inserted, updated, or deleted via the *Tabular Form*.

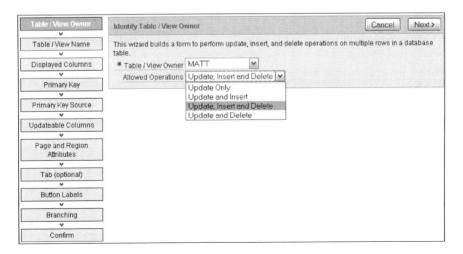

Identify Table/View Name

In the next step, we need to specify the database table or view that our *Tabular Form* will be based on. This is entered using the **Table/View Name** attribute. A lookup is displayed next to the **Table/View Name** attribute that can be used to search and display all tables and views that exist in the database schema specified in the previous **Table/View Owner** attribute. Selecting a table or view from the lookup will populate the **Table/View Name** attribute in the wizard.

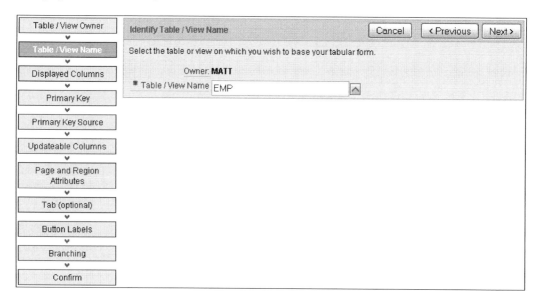

 A database view can enable details from multiple tables to be modified within a *Tabular Form*. To do this, create an `Instead Of` Trigger(s) for the view to control how records are inserted, updated, or deleted.

Identify columns to display

Now that we know the table or view to use for the *Tabular Form*, we need to specify which columns we want to display on the page. This is entered by using the **Select Column(s)** attribute. The columns we select can either be updateable or read-only, and we will select later in the wizard which fields will be updateable. For now, we need to select all columns that are to be displayed in the *Tabular Form*.

Bear in mind:

Although the used terminology is **Columns to Display**, we can still have an option of not displaying any of the selected column(s) in here, on the final version (or displayed version) of the *Tabular Form* by using the **Report Attributes** tab, and on the already wizard-generated *Tabular Form*. However, adding an updatable column that was not selected here, into an already generated *Tabular Form* might yield an application runtime error that will actually disable the *Tabular Form*. So when in doubt, you should select the column in here, and later, if needed, disable its display on the actual displayed *Tabular Form*.

If **User Interface Defaults** were defined to our target table, the **Use User Interface Defaults** attribute field will be displayed for us, to determine whether to apply these default attributes to the correlated *Tabular Form* elements. For the sake of demonstration, we have defined some UI default attributes on the EMP table, so the following screenshot of the wizard screen will include this option:

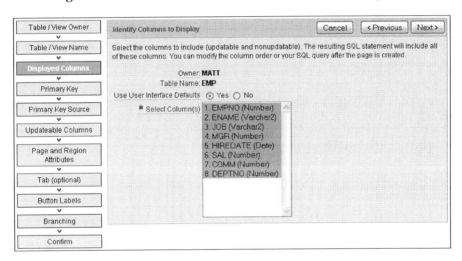

Identify Primary Key

In the next step, we need to define the *Primary Key* column which uniquely identifies records in the table or view selected. The column is selected using the **Primary Key Column 1** attribute. If the table or view requires a composite key, where there are multiple columns that uniquely identify the record, then the **Primary Key Column 2** attribute can be used to select an additional column.

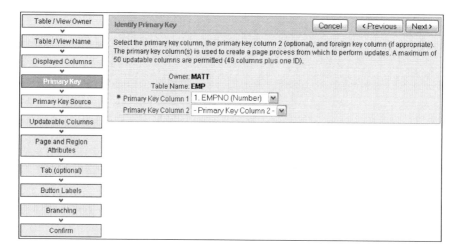

 The APEX wizard doesn't support the compound *Primary Key* with more than two segments. A *Primary Key* with more than two segments can be dealt with manually, as we'll see later in the chapter.

Primary key source

Once a *Primary Key* is selected, we need to tell APEX how the primary key gets populated when inserting records. This is defined by using the **Source Type** attribute. The following source types can be selected:

- **Existing Trigger**: This option tells APEX that the primary key is populated by a database trigger that already exists on the table.

Bear in mind:

The **Tabular Form** wizard doesn't ask you to name any existing trigger, nor does it verify the existence of such a trigger on the *Tabular Form* table. As such, this is a comfortable option to use if we don't want to deal with the issue of *Primary Key* population at this stage.

- **Custom PL/SQL function**: This option enables a PL/SQL function to be entered that will determine the value to use for the primary key.

- **Existing Sequence:** This option enables an existing database sequence to be selected that will be used to allocate the primary key.

The wizard's approach to building *Tabular Forms* does not support the entering of *Primary Key* values manually in the *Tabular Form*. The chosen *Primary Key* column(s) will be displayed on the *Tabular Form* as read-only columns.

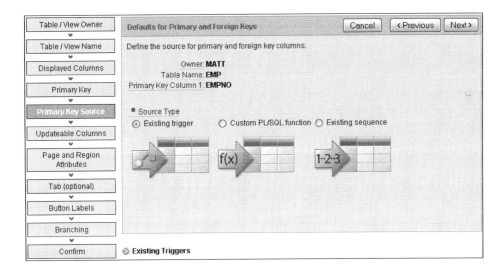

Updateable columns

Previously, we selected the columns to display in the *Tabular Form*. In this step, using the **Updatable Column** item, we select which of those columns are updateable (can be modified) in the *Tabular Form*.

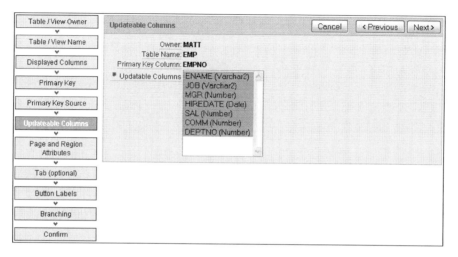

As you can see from the screenshot, the EMPNO column, which was selected as the *Primary Key*, is missing from the **Updatable Columns** list.

Page and region attributes

In the next step, we need to specify page and region attributes that will control the look and feel of the *Tabular Form* on the page. The **Page** attribute is used to define the page to add the *Tabular Form* to. This can be an existing page or a new page. While creating a new page, we can define the name of the page using the **Page Name** attribute. The **Region Title** attribute allows a heading to be defined for the *Tabular Form*.

> The APEX **Create Tabular Form** wizard supports only a single *Tabular Form* per page. If you need more than one *Tabular Form* on your page, then you should create the second one manually, as we'll describe later in the chapter.

The **Region Template** attribute will control the overall look of the region. It can control things like borders, styles, titles, button positions, and the layout of the region. The **Report Template** attribute controls how the rows of our *Tabular Form* are rendered, including layout and style. We can also use the **Breadcrumb** attribute to add breadcrumb navigation to our page.

You should avoid adding a breadcrumb region in each page. Instead, create the breadcrumb region in Page Zero, so it only needs to be defined once in the application, rather than on every individual page.

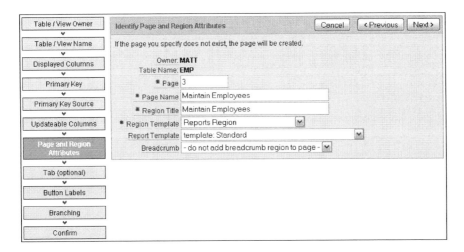

Button labels

Once page and region attributes have been entered, we can further control the look and feel of our *Tabular Form* by entering custom labels for the cancel, submit, delete, and add row buttons that will be generated. The button labels that we are prompted to enter will depend upon the **Allowed Operations** attribute entered earlier. If, for instance, we choose not to allow deletes in the *Tabular Form*, then we will not be prompted to enter a label for a delete button.

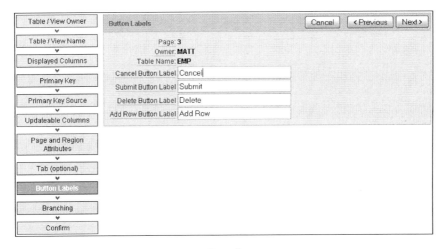

Branching

Once button labels have been defined, we need to tell APEX which pages to navigate to when buttons are pressed in the *Tabular Form*. The **After Page Submit and Processing Branch to Page** attribute is used to specify the page to display after the **Submit**, **Delete**, or **Add Row** button has been pressed. This will normally be the same page number as your *Tabular Form*. The **Tabular Form** wizard will use this attribute to add a branch in the page to handle the navigation.

The **When Cancel Button Pressed Branch to this Page** attribute is used to specify the page to display after the **Cancel** button has been pressed. The **Tabular Form** wizard will store this attribute in the **Optional URL Redirect** section of the **Cancel** button in the page.

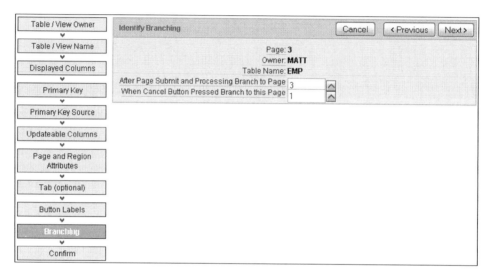

Confirmation

The **Tabular Form** wizard has now gathered enough information for APEX to create the region. A summary page is displayed showing the selections that have been entered via the wizard. If we wish to modify any details, the **Previous** button can be selected to go back to previous steps in the wizard. If we are happy with the selections, the **Finished** button can be selected to create the *Tabular Form*.

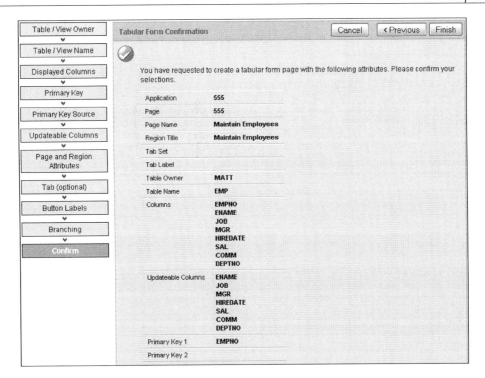

Wizard completion

The **Tabular Form** wizard now displays a confirmation that our *Tabular Form* has been created successfully. In this step, we can choose to run the *Tabular Form* generated by the wizard by using the **Run Page** icon. Alternatively, we can select the **Edit Page** icon to further refine the *Tabular Form* generated.

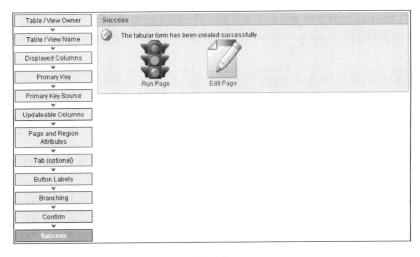

Show me the Tabular Form

In the following screenshot, we can see the actual *Tabular Form* generated by the wizard (the look and feel will vary depending on the theme you have selected for your application). We can see that the text fields have been displayed for report columns and there are buttons to save, add rows, delete, or cancel the page. Record pagination is also displayed to pass through all records stored in the table.

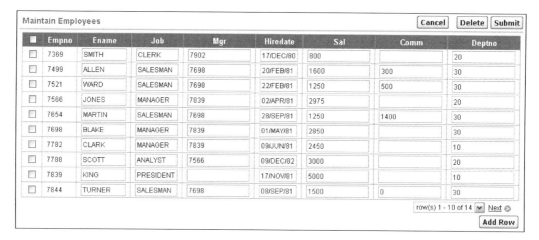

What does the Tabular Form wizard add to my page?

We have seen how to create a *Tabular Form* using the **Tabular Form** wizard, but what does the wizard create in our page to make the *Tabular Form* work? Firstly, the wizard generates a SQL query, based on the **Display Columns** we selected, and uses it as the **Region Source** for a report region it creates, as can be seen in the next screenshot:

```
Source

Region Source
select
"EMPNO",
"EMPNO" EMPNO_DISPLAY,
"ENAME",
"JOB",
"MGR",
"HIREDATE",
"SAL",
"COMM",
"DEPTNO",
from "#OWNER#"."EMP"
```

The report region is used to list rows from our table or view and display the columns we chose to be updatable as items (or form fields) rather than read-only text. As the *Tabular Form* is using a report region to render each of the form rows, we can use all the inbuilt functionality of a report region, such as record pagination and templates, also in our *Tabular Form*.

> If you have defined UI defaults for the *Tabular Form* table using the *Shared Component* module, attributes such as the region title and item types to display for each table column will be used by the wizard when creating the *Tabular Form*. This practice can save time, as you don't need to customize labels and items after the wizard has completed.

The next visible thing the wizard adds to our page is buttons. Buttons are used mainly to submit the *Tabular Form* and trigger its page level *Validations* and *Processes*. Depending on the **Allowed Operations** attribute selected earlier, the wizard will create buttons to add new records, update records that have been modified, delete any selected records, or cancel the changes made.

As part of implementing the **Delete** button functionality, the **Tabular Form** wizard adds a checkbox column as the first column of the *Tabular Form*. The column allows us to mark the candidate record(s) for deletion.

To enable the supported DML functionalities of the *Tabular Form*, we should allow the *Primary Key* column(s) to be updateable. Otherwise, the *Primary Key* column(s) will not be submitted, and the APEX engine will not be able to use it/them to identify existing records for *Update* or *Delete*. However, we already saw that the **Tabular Form** wizard, as a policy, doesn't support updatable *Primary Key* column(s). How to resolve this conflict of needs?

The **Tabular Form** wizard actually generates a duplicate set of column(s) for the *Primary Key*. In the first set, the column(s) is/are named by adding a suffix of '_ DISPLAY' to the *Primary Key* column(s) name. This set will be used for display purposes only, and will be rendered as a read-only column(s). In the second set, the *Primary Key* column(s) retains the original name(s), and will be rendered as hidden item(s) on the *Tabular Form*. Although not displayed, this/these hidden item(s) is/are a valid *Tabular Form* updatable item(s), which associate with the correlated database table *Primary Key* column(s), and as such, will be submitted and be available to the APEX engine. Alongside the buttons, the **Tabular Form** wizard also adds correlated *Branches*, as we discussed earlier in the chapter. The first *Branch* handles all the submit scenarios, and it is triggered by the **Add Row**, **Submit**, and **Delete** buttons, just after their correlated *Processes* ended running. This *Branch* is mostly a page self branch, and the new (refreshed) *Tabular Form* will immediately reflect the data changes we made. The second *Branch* is actually a page redirection that follows pressing the **Cancel** button.

Other APEX elements that the **Tabular Form** wizard adds to our page are *After Submit Processes*, which are correlated with the DML functionalities (buttons) we selected for our *Tabular Form*, and as such, are conditioned by them. These built-in declarative **Data Manipulation** *Processes* are used to perform DML actions in our page. The **Tabular Form** wizard can add the following **Data Manipulation** *Processes*:

- **Multi Row Update**: Two of these can be added to the Tabular Form; one to insert new records into our table or view (for the latter, pending the existence of proper `Instead Of` triggers, which we must define ourselves), and the other to update any changes made to existing records.

- **Multi Row Delete:** To delete any rows marked for deletion.

- **Add Rows to tabular form:** To create a blank row(s) in the *Tabular Form* to enable new records to be entered.

Bear in mind:

The **Add rows to tabular form** is an *After Submit Process*. This means that pressing the **Add Row** button will first submit the current screen of the *Tabular Form*, which will trigger its defined *DML Process*. Only after the existing changes, if any, are processed, will a page self-branch be performed. The blank added row(s) is/are rendered on the refreshed screen.

Advanced note on the Update process

One of the compelling reasons to use a wizard-created *Tabular Form* is the fact that its **Multi Row Update** processes were designed to handle the **Lost Updates** issue we might face while working in a multi-user environment.

While working on the Web, APEX must be very careful implementing its database resources locking policy. The APEX engine implements an algorithm called **Optimistic Locking**, which allows us to detect and prevent possible *Lost Updates*. In a nutshell, this algorithm is performed prior to updating the data in the database to check that no other concurrent users of the database (including users from other applications) have changed and committed the same data since it was initially fetched from the database into our *Tabular Form*. It does so by comparing the data we initially retrieved with the current database data at the time of the actual update. If these two sets—the initial fetched data and the current data—are identical, then the update action gets a "green light" and the database is updated. If some other database user beat us to it, it means that our initial retrieved data is no longer valid; the update action gets a "red light" and an error message issued to the user.

How does all that relate to our **Tabular Form** wizard? The APEX engine implements the *Optimistic Locking* algorithm by computing an MD5 value for each row on the current screen of the *Tabular Form*. This MD5 value is computed out of the content of all the updatable column(s) of the row and the updatable item(s) only.

The first MD5 computation takes place when the *Tabular Form* is first populated. In order to save this initial MD5 value, the **Tabular Form** wizard adds a hidden item to the last column of the *Tabular Form*, calling it fcs. As this is an HTML name, and not an HTML element ID, we can have as many items by that name as we need, and we need as many as the number of displayed rows on the current *Tabular Form* screen. The second MD5 computation takes place after the *Tabular Form* was submitted, and a **Multi Row Update** *Process* is triggered. All the fcs items were also submitted with the *Tabular Form*, and as such, are available to the APEX engine. While running the **Multi Row Update** *Process*, the APEX engine computes a new MD5 value(s), this time on the current stored data of the correlated (updatable) columns, for the row(s) that triggered the process. This newly computed MD5 value(s) will be compared with the initial MD5 value(s). Equal MD5 values means that no data changes have been made to the database table record, and it can be updated with the data from the *Tabular Form*; inequality means that the database table record has been changed since the *Tabular Form* was initially populated, and we can't update it as we might encounter a *lost update*.

Concurrency control issues are hard to implement in any working environment, more so in a Web environment, but they are crucial to our database integrity and consistency. If you thought that the description of what needs to be done is complicated, just think how complicated it can be to write the implementation code yourself. Using the *Tabular Form* wizard to generate the *Tabular Form* for you will take care of all these issues and will make your life a bit easier.

How does the Tabular Form wizard organize the data on a page?

We have already established that every updatable column in the *Tabular Form*, alongside the *row selector* column and the hidden *Primary Key* column(s) must be submitted to the APEX engine, which in turn, should provide us with a proper platform for doing so. Next, we'll review this platform and how we can utilize it to enhance the built-in functionality of the *Tabular Form*.

The APEX engine, or to be more precise, its `WWV_FLOW` package, which we can reference with the more meaningful synonym `APEX_APPLICATION`, includes 50 predefined PL/SQL arrays, starting with `G_F01`, ending with `G_F50`, and all the range in between. These are global packaged arrays, and we can reference them as `APEX_APPLICATION.G_F01` through `APEX_APPLICATION.G_F50`. As we are talking about arrays, each such array can hold multiple elements.

The **Tabular Form** wizard assigns a unique sequential ID number to every updatable column on the *Tabular Form*, in the range of 1-50, which corresponds with one of the `APEX_APPLICATION.G_Fxx` arrays—it's the `xx` part in the array's name. This unique ID that we'll refer to from now on, as the **column index ID**, is used to implement the *Tabular Form* functionality, on both the client side and server side.

The client side

On the client side, the *Tabular Form* is rendered as an HTML table. The **Tabular Form** wizard allocates a unique *column index ID* for every updateable column on the *Tabular Form*, starting with 1. The wizard adds an HTML `name` attribute—three characters long—to every updatable element in the column. This name starts with the letter `f` and the next two characters are a leading zero padded string representation of the *column index ID*. For example, we already mentioned that the **Tabular Form** wizard adds a first column of checkbox items (row selector) if the *Tabular Form* includes a delete functionality. Being the first column, the **Tabular Form** wizard will allocate it a *column index ID* of `1`. All the checkbox items in this column, which are implemented as a proper HTML `<input>` tag, will share an HTML `name` attribute of `f01`. The second updatable column, which in our *Tabular Form* example is a hidden column associated with the *Primary Key* column of the *Tabular Form*—`EMPNO`—will be assigned a *column index ID* of 2, and as such, all its updatable items will share an HTML `name` attribute of `f02`. The first visible updateable column in our *Tabular Form* example is the **Ename** column. This column will be assigned a *column index ID* of 3. Therefore, all its updateable items will share the same HTML `name` attribute of `f03`. The **Tabular Form** wizard will continue this routine for all the other updateable columns in the *Tabular Form*.

There isn't any necessary connection between the *column index ID* that was allocated by the **Tabular Form** wizard and the sequential location of the column in the *Tabular Form* source SQL query or its actual display location on screen. The best and probably the simplest and most reliable way to find out the *column index ID* of a specific column is by checking the HTML page code, which the APEX engine generated for the *Tabular Form*.

Having all the updateable items in a specific updateable *Tabular Form* column share the same HTML `name` attribute, making it very simple for us to collect all of them, using the DOM method `document.getElementsByName()`. This allows us to use JavaScript to manipulate the content or appearance of the column, on screen. For example, if we want to highlight all the items in the **Sal** column that are lower than 1500. Checking the page HTML code reveals that the *column index ID* of the column is 7. Please review the following (inline) JavaScript code:

```
<script type="text/javascript">
function colorSal(pCol) {
    var elms = document.getElementsByName(pCol);
    for (i=0; i< elms.length; i++) {
      if (elms[i].value < 1500) {
          elms[i].style.backgroundColor = 'yellow';
      }
    }
}
</script>
```

We can fire this function using the `onload` event:

```
onload="colorSal('f07');"
```

The following screenshot is the result:

	Empno	Name	Job	Mgr	Hiredate	Sal	Comm	Deptno
Maintain Employees						Cancel	Delete	Submit
☐	7369	SMITH	CLERK	7902	12/17/1980	800		20
☐	7499	ALLEN	SALESMAN	7698	02/20/1981	1600	300	30
☐	7521	WARD	SALESMAN	7698	02/22/1981	1250	500	30
☐	7566	JONES	MANAGER	7839	04/02/1981	2976		20
☐	7654	MARTIN	SALESMAN	7698	09/28/1981	1250	1400	
☐	7698	BLAKE	MANAGER	7839	05/01/1981	3001		30
☐	7782	CLARK	MANAGER	7839	06/09/1981	2450		10
☐	7788	SCOTT,T	ANALYST	7566	04/19/1987	3000		20
☐	7839	KING	PRESIDENT		11/17/1981	5000		
☐	7844	TURNER	SALESMAN	7698	09/08/1981	1500	0	30

row(s) 1 - 10 of 14 ▼ Next ⊗

Add Row

Advanced note:

In order for this technique to work with the pagination option, you should set the **Enable Partial Page Refresh** field (on the **Report Attributes** tab) to **No**. Otherwise, the onload event will fire the JavaScript function only once for the first screen of the *Tabular Form*. If you want to apply this technique to partial page refresh *Tabular Form* (where the onload event is fired only once, when the first screen of the *Tabular Form* is populated), you must also fire the JavaScript function from the pagination link. This will require you to define a specific report template with a proper **Pagination Subtemplate** code. A full example is out of the scope of this chapter, but will be included in the demo application accompanying this book. For now, I'll just give you a hint:

```
<a href="#LINK# colorSal('f07');" class="t1pagination">
#PAGINATION_NEXT#<img src="#IMAGE_PREFIX#themes/theme_
1/paginate_next.gif" alt="Next"></a>
```

So, we can collect and manipulate the items of an entire updateable column on our *Tabular Form*, but can we target a specific single item on it? The **Tabular Form** wizard also helps us with that by attaching a unique HTML element ID to every updatable item in the *Tabular Form*. This element ID is comprised from the HTML name of the item, followed by an underscore (_) and a four character string, which is a leading zero padded string representation of the serial number of the item's row on the current *Tabular Form* screen.

For example, the **Tabular Form** wizard will assign the item on the second row of the f03 updatable column the HTML element ID 'f03_0002'. In order to reference this specific item, we can use the built-in JavaScript function $x('f03_0002'), which is based on the DOM method document.getElementById(). For example, the following JavaScript code:

```
if ($v('f15_0010') < 0) {
$x('f15_0010').style.color = 'red';
}
```

will write the value of the tenth row item, in the fifteenth updatable column, in red, if it's a negative number.

The server side

On the server side, we are dealing with the submitted data from the *Tabular Form*. As we discussed before, each updatable column is assigned a unique *column index ID*, and when submitted, the APEX engine uses this ID to populate the column's items into the correlated APPLICATION_ITEM.G_Fxx array, where the xx is the *column index*

ID of the submitted column. As such, the items of the first updatable column—f01—will be pushed into APEX_APPLICATION.G_F01, the items of the second updatable column—f02—will be pushed into APEX_APPLICATION.G_F02, and so on.

> At the beginning of this chapter, we mentioned that *Tabular Forms* support up to 50 updateable columns. Now you can understand why. For each updateable column, we need a correlated APEX_APPLICATION.G_Fxx array, and there are only 50 of those.
>
> The limit of 50 updateable columns was set by the APEX development team and it can't be changed by developers. Personally, I don't see it as a real limit because 50 consecutive columns can display a lot of information, they will most likely require horizontal screen scroll and will be hard to manage as it is. If you think you need to display more than 50 columns to your end user, I believe you should seriously reconsider the functionality and efficiency of your *Tabular Form*. After all, we are trying to ease the burden of the end user where data manipulation is the concern, and not drown them in it.

On the client side, we had to use a DOM method to collect all the elements of an updateable column. On the server side, all these elements are already available to us in a specific APEX_APPLICATION.G_Fxx array, and we can loop through them. For example, the following snippet of code loops through all the items of the updateable column f05:

```
for i in 1..APEX_APPLICATION.G_F05.count loop
   ... APEX_APPLICATION.G_F05(i) ...
end loop;
```

In the following sections, we'll see more specific examples of how we can utilize these APEX_APPLICATION.G_Fxx arrays to expand and enhance the *Tabular Form* functionality on the server side.

Report regions revisited

In the previous chapter, we looked at report regions and saw how they are used to help make a *Tabular Form*. By using report regions, we can take advantage of many of their built-in features, such as record pagination and templates. Moreover, we can make our *Tabular Forms* parameterized in the same way we did for report regions. We can add column links in our *Tabular Form* to enable navigation to other pages, for example, a more detailed edit page for the *Tabular Form* row. By using the built-in features, we can help make our *Tabular Form* more interactive and functional.

In the previous chapter, we also looked at the **Report Attributes** property page. The first section of this page—**Column Attributes**—allows us to define specific attributes for a specific report column. For each report column, we can drill down to its **Column Attributes** page. This page is very important in the context of building *Tabular Forms* as it includes a special section called **Tabular Form Element**, which can be seen in the following screenshot:

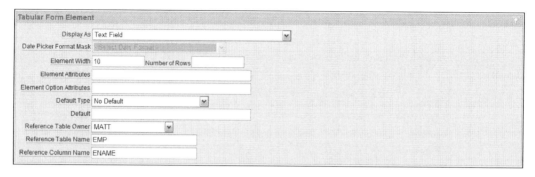

In this section, we can tell the APEX engine to render the report column as a form item (that is, a updatable item) of various types. This means that we can turn over every classic report into a *Tabular Form*, and by that, gain more flexibility in our application design.

The **Display As** attribute is used to define the type of form item to display for the column, such as the text field, date picker, or select list. If we are displaying a date picker, the **Date Picker Format Mask** attribute can be used to define the format we wish to display the date in.

The **Element Width** attribute controls the width of an item, while the **Number of Rows** attribute controls the height of a text area item. If we need to enter any JavaScript events, custom styles, or other HTML properties, then this can be entered using the **Element Attributes** property. The **Element Option Attributes** property allows additional HTML properties to be entered for items in a radio group or checkbox.

The **Reference Table Owner, Reference Table Name**, and **Reference Column Name** attributes are used to compare column references across applications to User Interface Defaults. We can also default form items by using the **Default Type** attribute. We can define either an item name or PL/SQL expression or function using the **Default** attribute, which will provide a default value for a form item.

Validating the Tabular Form

Once we have finished dealing with the rendering aspects of the *Tabular Form*, we now need a way to validate any data entered, just as we are doing with a regular form. Examples of validations that we could apply to a *Tabular Form* include checking whether mandatory fields have been entered or values are entered in the correct date or number format. Unfortunately, the **Tabular Form** wizard doesn't support out-of-the-box *Tabular Form Validations*, and it doesn't generate any *Validations* for us. However, we can generate our own *Validations* using the **Page level validation** option.

Tabular Form Validations will mostly include a column level validation, and we can implement them by looping through the relevant APLICATION_ITEM.G_Fxx array, validating its members. To demonstrate, we'll create a *Validation* on the Sal column, checking that the value of the employee's salary is not less than 900.

To create a validation for our *Tabular Form*, we create a page level validation with **PL/SQL** as the **Validation Method** and **Function Returning Error Text** as the **Validation Type.** This means we will be writing PL/SQL code to return an error message.

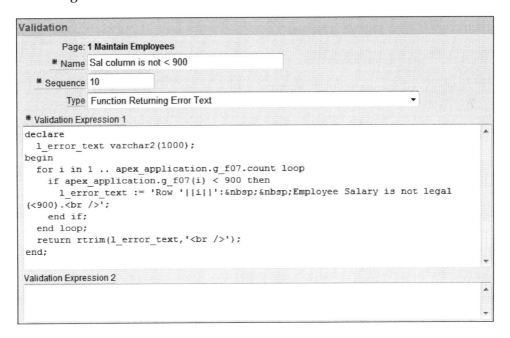

In our PL/SQL validation, we use the following code:

```
DECLARE
  l_error_text varchar2(1000);
BEGIN
  for i in 1 .. apex_application.g_f07.count loop
    if apex_application.g_f07(i) < 900 then
      l_error_text := 'Row '||i||':  Employee Salary
      is not legal (<900).<br />';
    end if;
  end loop;
  return rtrim(l_error_text,'<br />');
END;
```

In the code, we iterate through each row in our *Tabular Form*. We count how many rows are in the *Tabular Form* by counting the number of elements in the APEX_APPLICATION.G_F07 array, which associates with the employee salary column.

Bear in mind:

We'll discuss checkboxes later in this chapter, but for now, just remember that you can't use a column of checkboxes to count the *Tabular Form* rows.

Next in the code, for each row, we check if the employee salary column array — APEX_APPLICATION.G_F07 — is less than 900. If it is, we issue an error message.

We use the XHTML <br /> tag to place each error message on a new row. Once we have processed all rows, the error message is returned and displayed on our page.

Now let's run our *Tabular Form* and try to update the salary of Smith from **900** to only **800**. As this is not a legal salary according to our defined *Validation*, an error notification should be displayed, as the following screenshot shows:

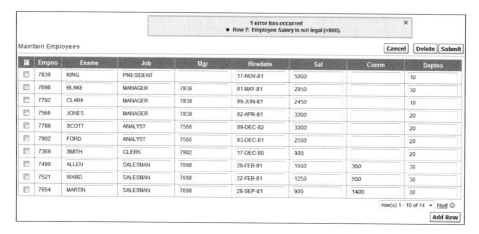

This screenshot exposes us to some major cons for using *Tabular Forms*. Firstly, there isn't any visual connection between the error message in the notification area and the specific cell it points to. Unlike a regular *Form*, where you can display the *Validation* error message both in the notification area and in the item's label cell, with *Tabular Forms*, the out-of-the-box *Validation* error message can only be displayed in the notification area.

Moreover, the second con reason points to a much more problematic behavior of *Tabular Forms*. If you look carefully into the **Sal** cell of row 7, you'll see the value of 900. This value is not the value that caused the *Validation* error—we tried to update it to 800. The displayed value is actually the original, prior to update, value of this cell. Unfortunately, this is the default behavior of the APEX *Tabular Form*. Upon *Validation* error, the APEX engine renders the *Tabular Form* in a *Validation* error mode, which means that the *Computations* and *Processes* of both *Page Processing* and *Page Rendering* phases will not be run. However, the *Tabular Form* is rendered with its original populated data (**900** in our example) and not with the *Session State* data (**800** in our example). This means that all the changes made by the user, including cell changes that passed *Validation*, will not be retained, and will not be reflected in the *Tabular Form* in its *Validation* error state.

> This is an ironic situation. One of the major pros to using *Tabular Forms* is the comfortable and simple option of reviewing and editing a large amount of data. However, the way the *Tabular Form* deals with *Validation* errors sterilizes this advantage a bit, as every *Validation* error resets all the updated cells to their original (prior to update) values, without any simple, out-of-the-box ways/means for tracking these changes. As a result, it seems that without extra measures taken by us as developers to change this default behavior, it would be prudent to edit (or add) only one *Tabular Form* row at a time.

Enhancing Validation Errors Messages

We can take several actions, some of them are very simple, to increase the friendliness of the *Validation* error messages, make it easier to treat them, and enhance their overall efficiency. We'll review some of them in the next sections.

Changing the default error message phrase

By default, the APEX engine counts the number of *Validation* error(s) it finds and specifies the number as part of the error message. As can be seen in the previous screenshot, the error message starts with **1 error has occurred**, followed by the error details.

However, the APEX engine is only aware of the errors on the *Validation* component level. We are returning a single error message, but this message can include several *Validation* errors that occurred on the same column. In this case, the APEX engine will count them as only a single error. That can lead to the following:

1 error has occurred	×
● Row 3: The employee Salary is not legal (<900).	
● Row 5: The employee Salary is not legal (<900).	

This error message is clearly wrong. In order to fix it, and overcome this problem, we need to replace the built-in error message prefix with a more general phrasing that doesn't include the number of errors.

We define an **On Load-After Header** process that is conditioned by **Inline Validation Errors Displayed** and includes the following code:

```
DECLARE
    j1  pls_integer;
    j2  pls_integer;

    l_err_msg  varchar2(2000);

BEGIN
    j1 := instr(apex_application.g_notification_message,'/>');
    j2 := instr(apex_application.g_notification_message,'occurred');
    l_err_msg := substr(apex_application.g_notification_message,
        1,j1+1) || 'Please check the following Validation error(s):'
        || substr(apex_application.g_notification_message,j2+8);

    apex_application.g_notification_message := l_err_msg;

END;
```

This code extracts the original error message prefix, which includes a reference to the number of errors, and replaces it with our own general prefix **Please check the following Validation error(s):**. The result can be seen in here:

Please check the following Validation error(s):	×
● Row 3: The employee Salary is not legal (<900).	
● Row 5: The employee Salary is not legal (<900).	

Bear in Mind:

The notification area is *Theme* dependent. As such, the error message HTML code can vary, which makes this code example specific to our current *Theme* (Theme 1). The code should be changed according to the *Theme* in use.

Add row number column

We have built our *Validation* error message to include the row number in which the *Validation* error occurred. However, our *Tabular Form* doesn't include a column that specifies the row's number. Such a column can make it easier to locate the specific cell that caused the *Validation* error.

In adding such a column, we can use the APEX built-in *Substitution String* #ROWNUM# . While rendering the current page view of the *Tabular Form* according to its pagination scheme, the APEX report engine replaces the #ROWNUM# with the current serial number of the row within the current page view. This means that the serial number of the first row in every page view of the *Tabular Form* will always be 1, regardless of the pagination scheme in use (unlike the database pseudo-column rownum, which is unique to every row in the entire fetched data-set of the *Tabular Form* and will not repeat itself)As we are talking about a non-editable column, it will not disrupt the columns' ID numbers, as they were originally assigned by the *Tabular Form* wizard. As such, no *Validation* code changes are required.

In our example, the *Tabular Form* source query will look similar to the following:

```
select
'#ROWNUM#' as Sno,
"EMPNO",
"EMPNO" EMPNO_DISPLAY,
"ENAME",
.  .  .
"DEPTNO"
from "#OWNER#"."EMP"
```

As the APEX report engine substitutes #ROWNUM# with a string representing the current row serial number, it should be wrapped with single quote characters.

Using Page Error for the Validation error message(s)

Instead of using an inline error messages display, we can use the option of **On Error Page** as the display location. On one hand, the *Error Page* is completely separate from the *Tabular Form* screen, as can be seen on the next screenshot, which makes it a bit harder to follow (especially if there is more than one error). On the other hand, when returning to the *Tabular Form* screen, all the changes made to it, including those that caused the *Validation* error(s), are retained and displayed on the screen.

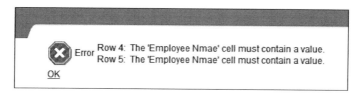

Unlike the inline *Validation* error messages display, which uses the notification area to display all the *Validation* error messages found at once, when we choose to use *Error Page*, each defined *Validation* component displays its error messages on a separate *Error Page*, so correcting all the errors will be sequential (one *Validation* component at a time).

Now you should decide, based on the nature and features of the underlying *Tabular Form* and your target user audience, which will be the best error handling policy. On one hand, going back and forth between the *Tabular Form* screen and the *Error Page(s)* retains, out-of-the-box, all the changes made by the user. On the other hand, inline error message display where all the *Validation* errors are displayed at once, and as we'll see in the next section, can be marked more clearly. But, there is a risk of losing track after changes made by the user pass *Validation* and still reset to their original (prior to update) value.

Bear in mind:

When returning from the *Error Page*, although the *Tabular Form* retains all the changes made by the user, it still renders in a *Validation* error mode (*Computations* and *Processes* are not fired). However, the condition of **Inline Validation Errors Displayed** is not set to `true`.

Using JavaScript and AJAX

In Chapter 8, which deals with APEX *Validations*, we discussed the merits of client-side validations. In the context of *Tabular Forms*, client-side validations, based on JavaScript, can help us overcome (or at least considerably reduce) the issue of losing cell value updates due to a server-side *Validation* error.

First, we need to define the appropriate event on the updatable column we want to validate. We are going to use an `onblur` event to fire a validation JavaScript function every time the user shifts focus from the corresponding *Tabular Form* cell.

We are not using the `onchange` event on purpose. Think of a situation where you are changing a cell value and move on. The `onchange` event triggers the validation function and as it happens, validation fails. You receive a proper error message and focus is set back to the offending cell. Now you are using the mouse to shift focus to a different cell. An `onchange` event will not trigger the validation function for the second time, as you didn't make any change to the cell. However, the cell value still won't pass validation. With the `onblur` event triggering the validation function, this scenario can't happen.

In the following screenshot, you can see the **Tabular Form Element** section of the SAL column (as part of the **Column Attributes** page). We are using the **Element Attributes** field to define the `onblur` event. In the example, this event fires a JavaScript function called `checkSal()`.

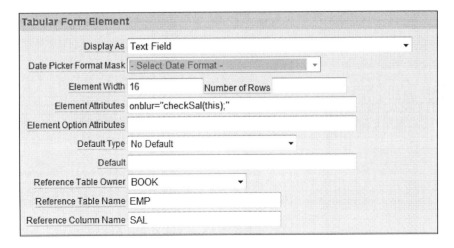

We are using the JavaScript keyword `this` to pass an object reference of the current cell. The JavaScript code is as follows:

```
function checkSal(pThis) {
    if ($v(pThis) < 900) {
        pThis.style.backgroundColor = 'lightblue';
        alert('The value in the colored cell must be higher than 900');
        var str1 = 'resetFocus(\''+pThis.id+'\')';
```

```
        setTimeout(str1,5);     }
    else {
        pThis.style.backgroundColor = '';
    }
}

function resetFocus(pId){
    $x(pId).focus();
}
```

The validation function checks the value of the cell, using the APEX built-in JavaScript library function $v(). If the value is lower than 900, the background color of the cell is set to lightblue, a proper error message is displayed to the user, and the cursor focus is set back to the cell. In case the value is legal, the background color of the cell is cleared (the browser sets it back to the default background color) to ensure that the cell will not remain colored after the user fixed its value.

> HTML doesn't allow us to immediately set the focus back on the changed object field, using the same function that was triggered by an event on this field. In our example, we are using a simple hack to bypass this. We first generate a string — str1 — which forms a call to a function called resetFocus(), with a parameter of the current cell ID. Then we are using this string as a parameter to the JavaScript built-in function setTimeout(), using a delay of five milliseconds.

As we can see in the following screenshot, trying to set one of the **Salary** cells to 800 yields a colored cell and an alert with the appropriate error message:

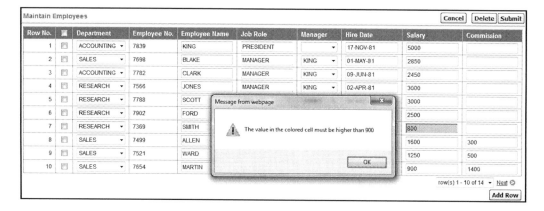

The APEX built-in JavaScript library includes the $v_IsEmpty(pThis) function, which can be very useful in client-side validation. The function returns true if the DOM node value (like item name) is empty. The function considers space and whitespace characters, like tab, form-feed, and so on, to be empty.

Smart use of client-side validations can catch most, if not all, of the validation errors prior to submitting the *Tabular Form*, and by doing that, save us the need to deal with the issues that accompany the *Tabular Forms* server-side *Validations*.

However, as we stated in Chapter 8, client-side validations should never replace server-side *Validations*. So we still need to define those, and JavaScript can also help us with them.

In order to use APEX *Validations* effectively, while displaying inline validation error messages, we need to overcome the issue of resetting all the changes made to the *Tabular Form* upon *Validation* error. The technique we've chosen to use is to capture the current *Tabular Form* view just before submitting it, by storing its innerHTML tag content in a built-in APEX collection that includes a CLOB column (a large enough space to hold a fairly long and complex HTML code of a large *Tabular Form*). We are doing that by calling a JavaScript function called clipReport() with every button that submits the *Tabular Form* (e.g. **Submit** and **Add Row**). For example, with the **Submit** button, we are using the following in the **URL Target** field:

```
javascript: clipReport('SUBMIT');
```

The clipReport() function uses the APEX AJAX framework to store the content of the *Tabular Form* innerHTML tag and then submit the page with the pressed button REQUEST value. We are going to discuss AJAX in Chapter 17 so a full description of the function and its derivatives at this point is premature. The demo application accompanying the book includes a full example of the technique we are using, and you are encouraged, after reading Chapter 17, to study it more carefully.

A few words about using the innerHTML tag: Using the innerHTML tag in this solution is not straightforward, as this tag is implemented differently by Microsoft IE and Mozilla Firefox (the two most common Web browsers in the market today).

When a user updates a value of a DOM node, MS IE updates, in real-time, the corresponding innerHTML tag to reflect the new value. Firefox, on the other hand, does not. It retains the original value of the innerHTML tag. This means that while in MS IE, the innerHTML tag reflects the current view of our *Tabular Form*. In Firefox, it reflects the view of the *Tabular Form* at population time. This behavior conflicts with our need to store the *Tabular Form* view with all the changes made by the user.

To overcome Firefox behavior, we must specifically update the DOM node value with the DOM method setAttribute(). This method causes the innerHTML tag to be updated even in Firefox; ergo it will also reflect the current view of the *Tabular Form*, just as we need. The following is the JavaScript function we are using:

```
function set_innerHTML(pThis) {
    pThis.setAttribute('value',pThis.value);
}
```

The set_innerHTML() function can be used as part of the client-side JavaScript validation function or as a standalone function in the updatable column **Element Attributes** field.

 It's important to use the set_innerHTML() function with every updatable column in our *Tabular Form* if we want the innerHTML tag to correctly reflect the *Tabular Form* view, prior to submit.

Now that we have the *Tabular Form* view stored for us, we can define the *Validations*. On top of the validation functionality, each *Validation* component will also save the HTML cell ID in which a *Validation* error has occurred. Later on, we'll use these IDs to color the offending *Tabular Form* cells. We are going to use an application item—TF_CELL_ID—to hold a colon-delimited string of all the cell IDs. As we are using an application item that is persistence by nature, we should initialize it in our first *Validation* component. In our last *Validation* component, we'll trim its last colon (:) character. The following is an example of two *Validation* components we defined:

First *Validation* component—**Ename not null**:

```
DECLARE
   l_error_text varchar2(1000) := '';
BEGIN
    :TF_CELL_ID := '';

    for i in 1 .. apex_application.g_f03.count loop
      if apex_application.g_f03(i) is null then
        l_error_text := l_error_text ||
          'Row '||i||':  Ename must contain
           a value.<br /><li>';
        :TF_CELL_ID := :TF_CELL_ID||'f03_'||lpad(i,4,0)||':';
      end if;
    end loop;
    return rtrim(l_error_text,'<br /><li>');
END;
```

Last *Validation* component—**Sal column is not < 900**:

```
DECLARE
  l_error_text varchar2(1000) := '';
BEGIN
  for i in 1 .. apex_application.g_f07.count loop
    if apex_application.g_f07(i) < 900 then
      l_error_text := l_error_text ||
        'Row '||i||':  Employee Salary is not
        legal (<900).<br /><li>';
      :TF_CELL_ID := :TF_CELL_ID||'f07_'||lpad(i,4,0)||':';
    end if;
  end loop;
  :TF_CELL_ID := rtrim(:TF_CELL_ID,':');
  return rtrim(l_error_text,'<br /><li>');
END;
```

As you can see, these *Validation* components are not generic. Each of them includes specific information regarding the APEX_APPLICATION.G_Fxx array the updateable column is using. This information is used both to scan the array and to construct the cell ID in case of *Validation* failure.

Next, we should define the *Processes* that handle *Validation* error(s) when they occur. As we are using inline *Validation* error messages, we should first define the *Process* that displays the appropriate error message in the notification area, just as we described it earlier in the chapter. Next, we should define an **On Load – After Regions** Process of type **PL/SQL anonymous block**, conditioned by **Inline Validation Errors Displayed**, which will be fired only when such errors were discovered. The source code of such a Process should be similar to the following:

```
DECLARE
  l_tf_cell_id  apex_application_global.vc_arr2;

BEGIN
  l_tf_cell_id := apex_util.string_to_table(:TF_CELL_ID);

  htp.p('<script type="text/javascript">');
  htp.p('getClob();');

  -- whait for readyState = 4 and check the DOM
  -- availability of the last offended cell
  htp.p('var pnt = setInterval(function() {');
  htp.p('if (DOM_flag == 0) {return;}');
  htp.p('else {');
  htp.p('if ($x('''||l_tf_cell_id(l_tf_cell_id.count)||
```

```
            ''') == false) {return;}');
    htp.p('else {clearInterval(pnt); }}');

    for i in 1..l_tf_cell_id.count loop
        htp.p('$x(''' || l_tf_cell_id(i) ||
            ''').style.backgroundColor="lightblue";');
    end loop;
    htp.p('},250);');

    htp.p('</script>');
  END;
```

At the beginning of the code, we are using the APEX built-in API function `apex_util.string_to_table()` to slice the colon delimited value of our `TF_CELL_ID` application item into a matching array. Each array member includes the ID of a *Tabular Form* cell that failed *Validation*.

Next, we are constructing a JavaScript `<script>` tag that will be added to the page rendering code and will be fired at the page rendering time on the Web browser (as we already discussed in earlier chapters, we can't fire JavaScript—a client-side resource—from a PL/SQL Process, which is a server-side resource).

The JavaScript calls the `getClob()` function, which fires an asynchronized AJAX call, which then restores the `innerHTML` tag we saved prior to submit. This tag will overwrite the current (*Validation* error mode) *Tabular Form* view, which doesn't include any changed cell values, with a view that reflects all the changes made by the user prior to submitting the form. As we are using an asynchronized process, the next segment of the JavaScript initiates a repeated interval (every 250 milliseconds) that checks if the replacement of the `innerHTML` tag was completed and the relevant DOM node(s) is available for further manipulations. When the DOM is ready, all that is left for us is to color the offending cells, so it will be easier for the user to locate and fix them. The final result, including some rearrangement made to some of the columns, which also demonstrate the power of the APEX engine report, can be seen in the following screenshot:

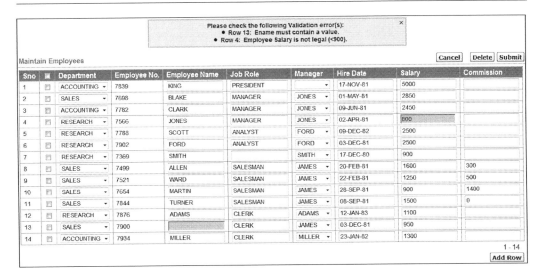

Please check the following Validation error(s):
- Row 13: Ename must contain a value.
- Row 4: Employee Salary is not legal (<900).

Maintain Employees

Sno	☐	Department	Employee No.	Employee Name	Job Role	Manager	Hire Date	Salary	Commission
1		ACCOUNTING ▾	7839	KING	PRESIDENT	▾	17-NOV-81	5000	
2		SALES ▾	7698	BLAKE	MANAGER	JONES ▾	01-MAY-81	2850	
3		ACCOUNTING ▾	7782	CLARK	MANAGER	JONES ▾	09-JUN-81	2450	
4		RESEARCH ▾	7566	JONES	MANAGER	JONES ▾	02-APR-81	800	
5		RESEARCH ▾	7788	SCOTT	ANALYST	FORD ▾	09-DEC-82	2500	
6		RESEARCH ▾	7902	FORD	ANALYST	FORD ▾	03-DEC-81	2500	
7		RESEARCH ▾	7369	SMITH		SMITH ▾	17-DEC-80	900	
8		SALES ▾	7499	ALLEN	SALESMAN	JAMES ▾	20-FEB-81	1600	300
9		SALES ▾	7521	WARD	SALESMAN	JAMES ▾	22-FEB-81	1250	500
10		SALES ▾	7654	MARTIN	SALESMAN	JAMES ▾	28-SEP-81	900	1400
11		SALES ▾	7844	TURNER	SALESMAN	JAMES ▾	08-SEP-81	1500	0
12		RESEARCH ▾	7876	ADAMS	CLERK	ADAMS ▾	12-JAN-83	1100	
13		SALES ▾	7900		CLERK	JAMES ▾	03-DEC-81	950	
14		ACCOUNTING ▾	7934	MILLER	CLERK	MILLER ▾	23-JAN-82	1300	

Cancel Delete Submit

1 - 14

Add Row

Without the proper background in AJAX, this solution might seem cryptic and very complex. As I recommended at the beginning of this example discussion, you are encouraged to return to this section after reading Chapter 17. I'm sure things will look much simpler and much clearer then.

The next version of APEX, version 4.0, will introduce enhanced and much improved ways to handle Tabular Form Validations, including the ability to use some pre-defined, specially designed Validations for the Tabular Form and an out-of-the-box solution for saving all the changes made by the user, even if Validation error(s) occurred. Still, the technique we just described for coloring the offending cells in the Tabular Form can be very useful in the next version of APEX also, as it will allow you to display the error messages from your own constructed Validations in the same manner that they will be displayed by the pre-built APEX Validations.

Manually building a Tabular Form

What happens if our needs demand features and attributes that the *Tabular Form* wizard does not support? Things like the need to have more than one *Tabular Form* on the page, using *Primary Key* with more than just two segments, or using item types that are not supported by the wizard, such as checkboxes, prevent us from generating our *Tabular Form* using the APEX wizard.

In this section, we will look at how to build a *Tabular Form* manually to overcome some of the limitations we've encountered using the wizard and also enable the *Tabular Form* to meet our exact requirements. Specifically, we will see how to render a *Tabular Form* on a page, validate any data entered, and then save any changes to the database.

Displaying the Tabular Form

The first step to creating a *Tabular Form* manually is to render the form rows on a page. To do this, there are a number of options we can use:

- *Changing Standard (classic) report into Tabular Form*: Like the **Tabular Form** wizard, we can use a report region to render a *Tabular Form*. In the **Tabular Form Element** section of the **Report Attributes** property page, we can specify the item type to display for the column. Changing it from **Standard Report Column** to any of the other input supported types will convert the standard display of only a column into an updateable one. This option is best used with already existing reports, when we need to equip them with an updatable functionality.

- *Report Region using SQL to generate form fields*: In this approach, which is the most common, we still use a report region and with its source SQL query, we are generating an HTML code for the updatable items. We can do that using the APEX_ITEM API, which was designed specifically for that. By using a report region, we can still take advantage of report region features like record pagination.

- *PL/SQL Region*: In this option, we code PL/SQL to output our *Tabular Form*. This offers great flexibility, but requires more code to be created to render the *Tabular Form* and also handle things like record pagination. We can use the database supplied HTP.prn procedure to output HTML source to the browser. We can also use the APEX_ITEM API to generate the HTML for form items.

We have used the database-supplied procedures HTP.PRN and HTP.P several times before. In the context of generating an HTML code, it's useful to clarify the difference between the two. The HTP.P procedure will automatically add a new-line character at the end of the code it's generating. This means that any code that will follow the newly generated one will start on a new line. The HTP.PRN procedure will generate the HTML code without any supplements, and by that, it allows us to use several HTP.PRN calls to generate a single (possibly long) line of HTML code. Bear in mind, these procedures don't affect the output of the generated code, just how this code will look on the page HTML source code.

APEX_ITEM API

APEX_ITEM is a synonym to an APEX PL/SQL package—HTMLDB_ITEM, in the APEX owner schema (for APEX 3.2.x, it's the APEX_030200 schema). This package provides functions that can be used to dynamically generate form items on a page. This makes it simple to add items such as text fields, text areas, select lists, checkboxes, date pickers, hidden fields, popup LOVs, and radio groups, without the need to write any HTML code.

To demonstrate the APEX_ITEM API, let's look at the function to generate an HTML select list based on an SQL query. The following is the corresponding API function signature to generate a select list based on a SQL query:

```
APEX_ITEM.SELECT_LIST_FROM_QUERY(
    p_idx           IN      NUMBER,
    p_value         IN      VARCHAR2 DEFAULT NULL,
    p_query         IN      VARCHAR2,
    p_attributes    IN      VARCHAR2 DEFAULT NULL,
    p_show_null     IN      VARCHAR2 DEFAULT 'YEs'
    p_null_value    IN      VARCHAR2 DEFAULT '%NULL%',
    p_null_text     IN      VARCHAR2 DEFAULT '%',
    p_item_id       IN      VARCHAR2 DEFAULT NULL,
    p_item_label    IN      VARCHAR2 DEFAULT NULL,
    p_show_extra    IN      VARCHAR2 DEFAULT 'YES')
RETURN VARCHAR2;
```

The APEX documentation (currently on http://download.oracle.com/docs/cd/E14373_01/apirefs.32/e13369/toc.htm) and the *Application Builder* help system, under **API Reference**, includes a full description of all the procedures included in the APEX_ITEM API and detailed description of the parameters every procedure can use. Most of the procedures include the following parameters:

- p_idx: This parameter sets the value of the *column index ID*, and as such, determines the APEX_APPLICATION.G_Fxx array that will be populated with the values from the column of this item. For example, if we are using 5 as the p_idx parameter, the HTML name of all the cells in the created column will be 'f05', and after submit, they will be stored in the APEX_APPLICATION.G_F05 array.

  This parameter must be unique within the application page it was defined on. For example, using the APEX_ITEM API, we can define more than one *Tabular Form* on our application page—two (or more) report regions, each with its own SELECT statement. The p_idx must be unique across all the *Tabular Forms* on the page, and because each p_idx is related to a specific G_Fxx array, and we only have 50 of them available per page, the total number of columns in all the *Tabular Forms* on a page can't exceed 50.

- p_value: This parameter sets the value source of the column. Usually it's a table column.

- p_attribute: This parameter allows us to define any valid HTML attribute that the generated item supports. It can be used to attach a DOM event to the item, style it, disable it, check it (if applicable), etc.

- p_item_id: This parameter allows us to attach an HTML ID to every cell of the column, just like the *Tabular Form* wizard is doing. It is our duty to use a mechanism (expression) that will create a unique ID to every cell.

Now let's go back to our APEX_ITEM API example. The following code illustrates how to create a select list to show departments:

```
SELECT . . .,
APEX_ITEM.SELECT_LIST_FROM_QUERY(11, deptno,
    'select dname, deptno from dept order by 1',
    null, 'YES', 0, '--Please Select--','f11_#ROWNUM#') dept,
. . .
From TABLE1
```

We chose 11 as the p_idx parameter; ergo the HTML column name will be set to f11. Next, we are using the table column deptno as the source of the column (and it means that TABLE1 must include a deptno column). The following is the p_query parameter, and we are using a SELECT statement to retrieve the department names (to be displayed on the select list) and department numbers (to be returned, upon selecting an option). The next parameter is p_attributes. We don't have any HTML attributes to define, but as we must use positional notation with the parameters list, we can't just skip a parameter, and we are using null as a place holder. The next three parameters deal with the if/how to treat the null option in the select list. The last parameter, p_item_id, allows us to set the HTML ID attribute for each cell in the column. To maintain simplicity, we are going to use a very similar ID convention as the *Tabular Form* wizard. The p_idx determines the first segment of the ID, in our example, f11_. Adjacent is the serial number of the row, and for that we are using, the built-in *substitution string* #ROWNUM#.

> The naming convention we are using for the HTML ID of the cells is very similar to the naming convention of the *Tabular Form* wizard, but not identical. We are using the #ROWNUM# *substitution string* without padding the serial row number with 0 (we can't properly use the lpad() function with a *substitution string* as a parameter). You should remember that when you construct *Validations* to the manually built *Tabular Form*.

Finally, we are using dept as the column alias. We must use column aliases with all the created columns with the APEX_ITEM API functions. Otherwise, the APEX report engine will issue an error message.

The following HTML is generated for our department select list (for the fourth row):

```
<select name="f11" id="f11_4" >
  <option value="0">--Please Select--</option>
  <option value="10" >ACCOUNTING</option>
  <option value="40" >OPERATIONS</option>
  <option value="20" selected="selected">RESEARCH</option>
  <option value="30" >SALES</option>
</select>
```

Rendering the Tabular Form

To demonstrate building a *Tabular Form* manually, we will create a *Tabular Form* using a SQL report region that uses a SQL query to generate the updatable columns in our *Tabular Form*. In the example, we will use various functions from the APEX_ITEM API.

```
select '#ROWNUM#' sno,
    apex_item.checkbox(01, empno) del,
    empno || apex_item.hidden(02,empno) empno,
    apex_item.text(04, ename, 10, 10,
        'onchange="set_innerHTML(this);"', 'f04_' ||
        '#ROWNUM#') ename,
    apex_item.text(05, job, 9, 9, null, 'f05_' ||
        '#ROWNUM#') job,
    apex_item.date_popup(06, null, hiredate,
        'MM/DD/YYYY', 11, 11, null, 'f06_' ||
        '#ROWNUM#') hiredate,
    apex_item.text(07, sal, 10, 10,
        'onblur="checkSal(this)"', 'f07_' || '#ROWNUM#') sal,
    apex_item.select_list_from_query(08, deptno,
        'select dname, deptno from dept order by 1',null,
        'NO', null, null, 'f08_'||'#ROWNUM#') ||
    apex_item.md5_checksum(ename, job, hiredate, sal,
        deptno) deptno
  from emp
union all
select '#ROWNUM#' sno,
    apex_item.checkbox(01, null) del,
    null || apex_item.hidden(2,null) empno,
    apex_item.text(04, null, 10, 10,
```

```
         'onchange="set_innerHTML(this);"', 'f04_' ||
         '#ROWNUM#') ename,
   apex_item.text(05, null, 9, 9, null, 'f05_' ||
      '#ROWNUM#') job,
   apex_item.date_popup(06, null, null,
      'MM/DD/YYYY', 10, 10, null, 'f06_' ||
      '#ROWNUM#') hiredate,
   apex_item.text(07, null, 10, 10,
      'onblur="checkSal(this)"', 'f07_'||'#ROWNUM#') sal,
   apex_item.select_list_from_query(08, null,
      'select dname, deptno from dept order by 1', null,
      'NO', null, null, 'f08_'||'#ROWNUM#') ||
   apex_item.md5_checksum() deptno
from dual
where :REQUEST = 'ADD_ROW'
```

In the example, the SQL query shows a UNION ALL query, where the first query is used to generate the *Tabular Form* rows for each record in the employee table. The second half of the query is used to display a blank row for inserting new records only when the **Add Row** button has been clicked :REQUEST = 'ADD_ROW'.

As we are dealing with a manually built *Tabular Form*, we also need to create manually all the buttons we need on the form. The **Add Row** button is one of them. With this specific button, we need to set the REQUEST value specifically in the corresponding Branch, as this value condition is the second part of our UNION ALL SQL query.

As we can see, a number of the APEX_ITEM API functions have been used to generate hidden fields, text fields, select lists, and date pickers for each record displayed in our *Tabular Form*. Each form field has been allocated a unique number, with 01 used for the **Delete** checkbox through to 08 for the department select list. Moreover, to allow us to utilize the *Optimistic Locking* algorithm also in our manually created *Tabular Form*, we also use the APEX_ITEM.MD5_CHECKSUM() function. More about this specific function further down the chapter.

The allocation of the p_idx parameters in our example was sparse—we skipped the number 3. This is perfectly legitimate. The p_idx values don't have to be sequential. We have used the p_item_id parameter to attach a unique HTML ID to every updateable cell on the *Tabular Form*. This allows us to use the *Validation* techniques we discussed earlier in the chapter and also with the manually constructed *Tabular Form*. For simplicity, we didn't add a client-side validation to all the updatable columns. However, with column f07 (**Salary**) we did use the p_attributes parameter to add an onblur event for client-side validation, and with column f04 (**Employee Name**), we added an onchange event for updating the innerHTML tag in Firefox.

Bear in mind:

As you can see from the example code, using the p_attributes parameter can make the SQL query a bit crowded. Another option is to use the **Element Attributes** field in the **Tabular Form Element** section of the updatable column, just as we did with the wizard-generated *Tabular Form*.

In the following screenshot, we can see the resulting *Tabular Form* created using our example code:

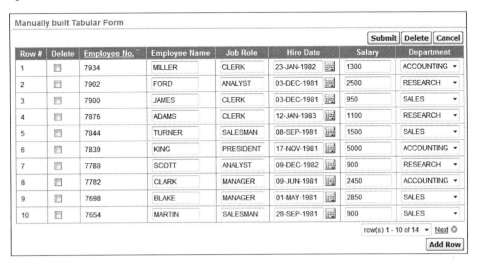

It seems that without the title (and possibly the order of the top buttons), you can't really tell the difference between this Tabular Form and a wizard-generated one.

Referencing and validating Tabular Form items

Using the p_item_id parameter with all the APEX_ITEM API functions, in the manner we have described—e.g. 'f01_#ROWNUM#'—creates a *Tabular Form* HTML code that is very similar to the code created for the wizard-generated *Tabular Form*. It allows us to reference specifically every updateable cell on our manually generated *Tabular Form*, using the same techniques we described for the wizard-generated *Tabular Form*. Still, we need to remember that the serial row number segment in the manual version of the cell ID is not a four characters, leading zeros padded string, but the serial number only. Hence, we need to make a minor adaptation to our *Validation* code. The following is a *Validation* code we can use on the Ename column:

```
DECLARE
   l_error_text varchar2(1000) := '';
BEGIN
   :TF_CELL_ID := '';
```

```
for i in 1 .. apex_application.g_f04.count loop
  if apex_application.g_f04(i) is null then
    l_error_text := l_error_text ||
      'Row '||i||':  Ename must contain
      a value.<br /><li>';
    :TF_CELL_ID := :TF_CELL_ID||'f04_'||i||':';
  end if;
end loop;
:TF_CELL_ID := rtrim(:TF_CELL_ID,':');
return rtrim(l_error_text,'<br /><li>');
END;
```

As you can see in the bold row, we are only using the serial row number, without having padded it with leading zeros.

Using checkboxes

The traditional use for a checkbox column in *Tabular Forms* is to mark candidate records for deletion. In our example code, we are also using the first column—f01—for that purpose.

We have already mentioned before that checkbox items behave differently than the other HTML items at submit time. Non-checked checkbox items are not submitted to the server. Hence, the checkbox column corresponding G_Fxx array will contain the values of the checked items only. If you look back at the previous screenshot, you'll see that the current view of the *Tabular Form* displays ten records. Let's say we marked two of them to be deleted. After submitting the page, the APEX_APPLICATION.G_F01 array will include only two members, while all the other G_Fxx arrays will include ten members.

As we used the empno column as the returned value of the checkbox—apex_item. checkbox(01, empno) del—the G_F01 array will include two empno values, which happens to be the *Primary Key* of our table. As we are using this column for deletion purposes, we can use the following code:

```
for i in 1 .. apex_application.g_f01.count loop
  delete from emp
  where empno = apex_application.g_f01(i);
end loop;
```

However, what will happen if, for example, we need to use a compound *Primary Key* with more than two segments? Or what will happen if we want to use a checkbox as an informative item and not just as a row selector? After all, these requirements are not supported by the **Tabular Form** wizard, so we are compelled to use a manually built one.

The problem with the checkboxes sparse G_Fxx array is that it contains only the values of the checked items, and we can't directly connect these value with the actual rows (records) they represent. Let's say that the second row we marked for deletion in our *Tabular Form* is number 8. Its value will be stored as the second member of G_F01, and we can't tell that it belongs to row number 8.

The **Tabular Form** wizard uses the row serial number as the returned value of the row selector checkbox. In turn, we can use this value as the index on the other G_Fxx arrays in the *Tabular Form*, to retrieve the array members corresponding to the row number.

The other option, which is most suited for informative checkbox columns, is to define an adjacent hidden column that will be populated each time the checkbox is clicked.

We've added a new column to the EMP table, called TENURE, and we want to display it in our *Tabular Form*. Please study the following snippet of code:

```
select '#ROWNUM#' sno,
   apex_item.checkbox(01, empno) del,
   empno || apex_item.hidden(2,empno) empno,
   apex_item.checkbox(12, tenure,
      'onclick="f=$x(''f13_'||'#ROWNUM#'||''');
      (this.checked == true) ? f.value = ''Y'' : '||
      'f.value = ''N'';"','Y')||
   apex_item.hidden(13, tenure, null, 'f13_'||
      '#ROWNUM#') tenure,
   apex_item.text(04, ename, 10, 10,
      'onchange="set_innerHTML(this);"', 'f04_'||
      '#ROWNUM#') ename,

   . . .

UNION ALL
select '#ROWNUM#' sno,
   apex_item.checkbox(01, null) del,
   null,
   apex_item.checkbox(12, null,
      'onclick="f=$x(''f13_'||'#ROWNUM#'||''');
      (this.checked == true) ? f.value = ''Y'' : '||
      'f.value = ''N'';"')||
   apex_item.hidden(13, null, null, 'f03_'||
      '#ROWNUM#') tenure,
   apex_item.text(04, null, 10, 10,
      'onchange="set_innerHTML(this);"', 'f04_'||
      '#ROWNUM#') ename,

   . . .
```

As you can see, the 'f12' column is a checkbox column with a returned value from the `tenure` column. It has an `onclick` event, which fired for every click on the checkbox. If the click checks the checkbox, the value of the adjacent column—f13—is set to 'Y', else it set to 'N'.

The adjacent column is defined as a hidden item, also with the value of the `tenure` column. A standalone column, generated with the `APEX_ITEM.HIDDEN()` function, will create a visible (with header) but empty column. This is not what we want. We want this column to be completely invisible. The technique is to concatenate the hidden column with a visible one. In this case, the two HTML `<input>` tags will occupy the same table cell (a single `<td>` tag) but only one of the `<input>` tags—in the example, it's the checkbox type—will be visible.

> We already saw a similar use of this technique by the **Tabular Form** wizard. The wizard doesn't support an updateable *Primary Key* column, but we still need one to be submitted with the form. The **Tabular Form** wizard creates an updateable yet hidden *Primary Key* column and concatenates it to one of the visible columns, just as we did with the `empno` column. Now you know how to do the same with your manually built *Tabular Form*.

The following screenshot shows how this *Tabular Form* might look to the end user:

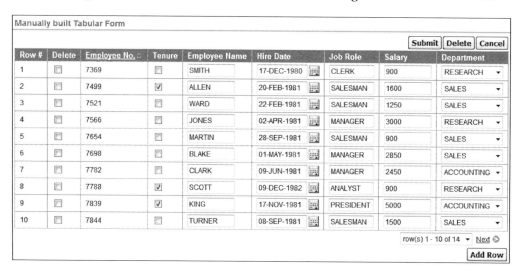

DML on the Tabular Form

After *Validation*, it's time to implement the DML actions associated with our manually created *Tabular Form*. As with the wizard generated *Tabular Form*, we need to support Insert, Update, and Delete. In the following sections, we will review each of these DML actions.

Delete

We support the DELETE action with a PL/SQL *Process*, which should be conditioned by pressing the **Delete** button. We are dealing with the DELETE action separately as it is a good practice to ask the user for confirmation prior to actually deleting records from the database. Based on our example code, the following is a possible code for the delete *Process*:

```
-- Initialise the counter for deleted row(s)
:P160_ROWS_DELETED := 0;

for i in 1..apex_application.g_f01.count loop
  delete from emp
  where empno = apex_application.g_f01(i);
  :P160_ROWS_DELETED := :P160_ROWS_DELETED + 1;
end loop;
```

We are looping through G_F01, which holds the empno value(s) of the checked record(s), using it in the WHERE clause of our DELETE statement. For each deleted record, we are incrementing a counter — :P160_ROWS_DELETED in our example. It's a hidden page item that we have defined, and we can use it in the **Process Success Message** field of the *Process*:

```
&P160_ROWS_DELETED. row(s) were deleted
```

Last, but not least, we can use the APEX built-in JavaScript function confirmDelete(pMessage, pRequest) to alert the end user about the upcoming delete action. The function receives two parameters: the first is the text message to be used in the alert box, and the second is the REQUEST value to be set. In the following example, which should be used as the **Delete** button **URL Target**, we are using a predefined message:

```
javascript:confirmDelete(htmldb_delete_message,'DELETE');
```

Update

As we mentioned at the beginning of this chapter, one of the compelling reasons to use the **Tabular Form** wizard is that it is implementing the *Optimistic Locking* algorithm out-of-the-box. When we are creating the *Tabular Form* manually, we should take care of it ourselves.

Another issue is how to perform the actual table updates. The simplest option is to loop through all the *Tabular Form* rows and update all of them, regardless of if they were really changed by the user. As we are going through all the rows, all the changes made by the user will be registered into the table. This method is very simple, but it can be a bit problematic if we are auditing changes in our table. In this case, we'll be registered as the last user to make a change on the record, even if we didn't make one. The other option, which the wizard-generated *Tabular Form* implements, is to update only the rows that were actually changed. In our example, we'll implement this method.

So, what we need is a method to record the status of each row on our *Tabular Form* at population time (our baseline), after submitting the page (to check if it was updated) and just before updating the database, as part of the *Optimistic Locking* algorithm. We are going to use the MD5 Hash algorithm to record the checksum value of each row, at various points in time.

In order to compute and save the MD5 values for the records we are populating into our manual *Tabular Form*, we are using the APEX_ITEM.MD5_CHECKSUM() function. This function accepts as parameters a list of columns we want to include in our MD5 computation. This list should include all the updateable columns in the *Tabular Form*. The function creates a hidden column, with the HTML name of 'fcs'. As a hidden column, it is concatenated to its last adjacent visible column. At submit time, the values of this column are populated into a dedicated array—APEX_APPLICATION.G_FCS.

After submit, we need to loop through all the *Tabular Form* rows and compute a new MD5 value for each row that comprises the submitted values. If this MD5 value is different from the corresponding value in the G_FCS array, it means that this row was changed by the user. For doing so, we need to build our own MD5 computation function that uses the same algorithm as the built-in MD5_CHECKSUM() function. The following is the code we should use:

```
create or replace function build_md5 (
    p_value01    in varchar2 default null,
    p_value02    in varchar2 default null,
    p_value03    in varchar2 default null,

    . . .
```

```
    p_value49     in varchar2 default null,
    p_value50     in varchar2 default null,
    p_col_sep     in varchar2 default '|')
    return varchar2
is
begin
   return
 utl_raw.cast_to_raw(dbms_obfuscation_toolkit.md5(
    input_string=>
          p_value01||p_col_sep||
          p_value02||p_col_sep||
          p_value03||p_col_sep||


  . . .


          p_value48||p_col_sep||
          p_value49||p_col_sep||
          p_value50
           ));

end build_md5;
```

> **Important:**
> The real code of this function must include definitions of all 50 possible
> parameters, both in the function signature and as parameters to the
> database `utl_raw.cast_to_raw()` functions. As you can see, even
> null parameters are separated with the function delimited character, so
> they are affecting the final result of the MD5 computation. Moreover, to
> maintain compatibility with the `MD5_CHECKSUM()` function, you should
> not change the default delimited character. The function we built is
> actually identical to an undocumented function called `wwv_flow_item.`
> `md5()`. If you don't have a problem using undocumented features, you
> can use it instead of defining your own.

The second time we need to use this function is if we have determined whether
a specific row has been changed. In this case, according to the *Optimistic Locking*
algorithm, we need to fetch the current record from the database and compare it with
the original record that was fetched to populate the *Tabular Form*. If both records are
the same, we can update the database table; if not, then we should issue a proper
message to the end user, telling him/her that the database table has been changed
since it was first fetched, and he/she needs to refresh the *Tabular Form*. The following
is an example code of a possible update *Process*:

```
DECLARE
   l_md5    varchar2(32767) := null;
BEGIN
   -- initialize page items to be used in the
```

```
-- process success message
:P160_ROWS_UPDATED := 0;
:P160_ROWS_INSERTED := 0;

for i in 1..apex_application.g_f04.count loop

    -- Update

    if apex_application.g_f02(i) is not null then
      -- Compute MD5 for the after submit row values
      l_md5 := build_md5(
        apex_application.g_f04(i),
        apex_application.g_f05(i),
        to_date(apex_application.g_f06(i),'MM/DD/YYYY'),
        to_number(apex_application.g_f07(i)),
        to_number(apex_application.g_f08(i))
      );

      -- if the row has been changed
      if l_md5 != apex_application.g_fcs(i) then
        -- check to see if database record has changed
        for c1 in (
          select * from emp
          where empno = to_number(apex_application.g_f02(i))
          FOR UPDATE) loop
            l_md5 := build_md5(c1.ename, c1.job, c1.hiredate,
                             c1.sal, c1.deptno);
        end loop;

        if l_md5 = apex_application.g_fcs(i) then
          update emp
          set     ename = apex_application.g_f04(i),
                  job   = apex_application.g_f05(i),
                  hiredate = to_date(apex_application.g_f06(i),
                    'MM/DD/YYYY'),
                  sal   = to_number(apex_application.g_f07(i)),
                  deptno = to_number(apex_application.g_f08(i))
          where empno = to_number(apex_application.g_f02(i));

          :P160_ROWS_UPDATED := :P160_ROWS_UPDATED + 1;
        else
          raise_application_error (-20001,'The database record
            for Employee no. '|| apex_application.g_f02(i) ||
            ' has been changeed since you fetched it. Please
```

```
          refresh your page');
     end if;

   end if;

else . . .
```

> This is only the first part of the code, which should also include code for dealing with Insert new records. We'll complete the code in the next section.

The first time we are using our `build_md5()` function is with the submitted values from our *Tabular Forms*. Hence, we are using the members of the corresponding `G_Fxx` arrays as input parameters. In order to maintain compatibility with the `MD5_CHECKSUM()` computation, it is important to cast the array members into the appropriate corresponding data types.

The `raise_application_error()` function creates an error page. Hence, it's important to provide the user with some information that will help him to easily identify the record that caused the problem. In our example, we used the **Employee No.** value for that.

> **Bear in Mind:**
>
> Implementing the *Optimistic Locking* algorithm is crucial in a multi-user environment. If concurrency control is not an issue with your application, you can use a much simpler code that will directly update your table, without all the preliminary checks.

Insert

As we are using the **Empno** column—which populates the hidden column `'f02'`—as a *Primary Key*, we can safely assume that if a member of the `G_F02` array is `null`, then we are dealing with a new record that we need to insert into our table. The `INSERT` statement is very straightforward and can be looked at as the following complementing code:

```
else
    -- Insert
    insert into emp (empno, ename, job, hiredate,
                     sal, deptno)
    values (
       null,
       apex_application.g_f04(i),
```

```
          apex_application.g_f05(i),
          to_date(apex_application.g_f06(i),'MM/DD/YYYY'),
          to_number(apex_application.g_f07(i)),
          to_number(apex_application.g_f08(i))
      );

      :P160_ROWS_INSERTED := :P160_ROWS_INSERTED + 1;
    end if;
  end loop;
end;
```

 The opening else here is the same as the closing else in the first segment of the code (the UPDATE part).

We can combine the UPDATE part and the INSERT part into a single *Process*, which should be conditioned by the REQUEST values of both the **Submit** and **Add Row** buttons. We can use the following code as the *Process* success message:

```
&P160_ROWS_INSERTED. row(s) inserted, &P160_ROWS_UPDATED. row(s)
updated
```

The following screenshot shows an example of our manually created *Tabular Form* after adding a new line and updating another:

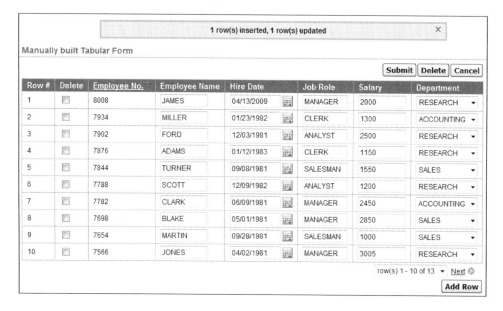

Summary

In this chapter, we have learned about APEX *Tabular Form* and how it can be created on a page using the **Tabular Form** wizard. We have also seen some of their limitations and how we can overcome them, including by creating *Tabular Forms* manually. While manually creating *Tabular Forms*, we have learned how to utilize the APEX_ITEM API to generate the updateable columns, apply validations to rows, and create processes to save newly changed records.

In the next chapter, we will look at how we can use calendar components in our applications.

15
Calendars

Calendars are very useful in our day-to-day lives. They help us to record and display dates such as birthdays, anniversaries, and other important events. They also enable us to visually see important dates for a month, which can help us to better plan our time. While calendars are useful in our day-to-day lives, they can also be very useful in our applications. APEX provides a calendar region which can be used to render dates stored in a database table onto a calendar. In this chapter, we will discuss how to build a calendar in our application. Specifically we shall be looking at:

- Creating a calendar with a wizard
- Modifying calendar attributes

Calendar region

So far in this book we have seen how calendars are used by the Date Picker item type to enter dates in forms. But how can we display date entries in a calendar format? To do this, APEX provides a calendar region, which enables date information from a database table to be rendered in a calendar format. In the calendar region, we specify both a date and description column from a database table. This determines what is displayed in the calendar, and where. For each entry in the calendar, we can create a link to other pages in our application. By adding links, we can create a drill down capability to view additional information for the entry.

By default, a calendar region can be rendered in different views, including monthly, weekly, and daily. The monthly view displays a calendar entry for each day in a month. We can also display a weekly or daily view of the calendar, where entries can be displayed against each hour of the day for an entire week or an individual day.

The calendar region certainly provides a user friendly interface and makes it easy for us to add date and time scheduling functionality into our applications. To create a calendar region in a page, APEX provides a wizard to help guide us through the process. To start, we will look at how to create a calendar in APEX using the calendar wizard.

 APEX only allows one calendar region to be created per page.

Using a wizard to create a calendar

In this section, we will walk through the process of creating a calendar region on an existing page. To demonstrate, we will create a calendar region to display events stored in a database table. In the calendar, we will be able to move between monthly, weekly, and daily views. Now, lets walk through the steps to creating a calendar region.

Start the calendar region wizard

In the following screenshot, we can see the Create Region icon. Click the icon (to the right of **Regions**) to start the wizard:

Region type

The next step is to tell APEX that we wish to add a calendar region to our page. Select the **Calendar** option, and click **Next**:

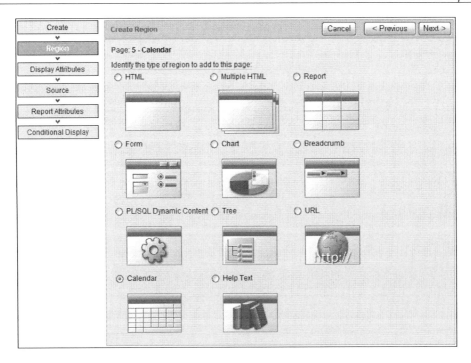

Calendar implementation

In the next step, we need to specify what type of calendar region to create. The **Easy Calendar** option creates a calendar based on a single database table, while the **SQL Calendar** option creates a calendar based on a custom SQL query. In our example, we will select the **SQL Calendar** option and click **Next**.

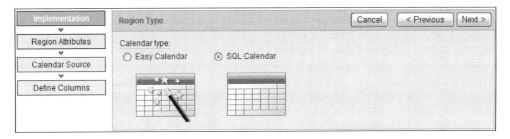

Region attributes

In the next step, we need to specify the page and region attributes that will control the look and feel of the calendar region in the page. The **Title** attribute allows a heading to be defined for the calendar. The **Region Template** attribute will control the overall look of the calendar region, including borders, the style, titles, button positions, and the layout of the region.

The **Display Point** attribute tells us where in the page template or page body to display the calendar. We can then use the **Sequence** attribute to control the order in which the region is displayed within the display point in the page. To divide the page into columns, we can use the **Column** attribute to specify which column the region is displayed in.

We can also control how the calendar is refreshed to display different months, weeks, or days by using the **Display Type** attribute. Selecting the **Standard** type will submit the entire page to refresh the calendar, while selecting the **Partial Page Refresh** type uses AJAX to only refresh the calendar region and not the entire page.

> The **Display Type** attribute cannot be changed once a calendar is created in a page. To modify the **Display Type** attribute, the calendar region needs to be deleted and re-created. The **Display Type** attribute was introduced in APEX version 3.1

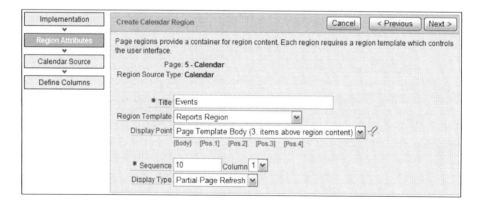

Calendar source

The calendar source step is the most important part of creating a calendar region as it defines the calendar entries to display. A SQL query needs to be defined with the following columns:

- **Date column**: This determines where in the calendar the entry is displayed. The date column can also include timestamps.

- **Description column**: This defines the text description used in the calendar entry.

The calendar source can also contain additional columns such as a unique identifier or further description, which can be used when customizing how the calendar entry is displayed or for links. In the screenshot, we can see that the date and description columns are being selected from the events database table:

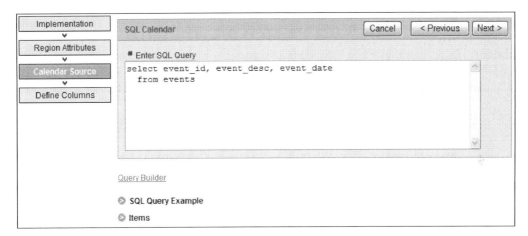

A link to the Query Builder is displayed in the wizard, which can be used to visually create the query without needing to know how to write SQL queries.

A more complicated description for the calendar entry can be created by concatenating multiple columns in the calendar SQL query. The following example will display an event description column together with a location column in italics:

```
SELECT EVENT_DATE, EVENT_DESC||'-<i>'||LOCATION||'</i>' EVENT_DESC
  FROM EVENTS
```

Define columns

Once we have defined the SQL query for the calendar, we need to specify which table columns in the query contain the date and description for calendar entries. The **Date Column** attribute is used to define the actual date to display in the calendar, while the **Display Column** attribute defines the description text to display for the calendar entry.

At this point, the calendar wizard has now gathered enough information for APEX to create the region on our page. Clicking the **Create Region** button will add the calendar to our page:

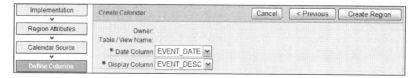

Viewing the calendar

Now that the Calendar Wizard has been completed we can run our page. The wizard has added a calendar displaying day entries from our events database table. The wizard has also added buttons to display the calendar in **Monthly**, **Weekly**, or **Daily** views. Buttons have also been added to jump to today's date and browse the previous and next months. The current date is highlighted with a red border; this will vary depending on the calendar template you are using. In the following screenshot we can see the calendar region created by the wizard:

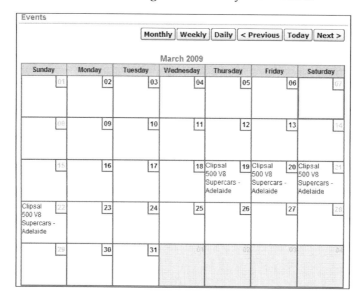

The weekly view enables us to show calendar entries for every hour in a day for an entire week. The **Next** and **Previous** buttons will navigate between weeks. In the next screenshot we can see the weekly view of the calendar:

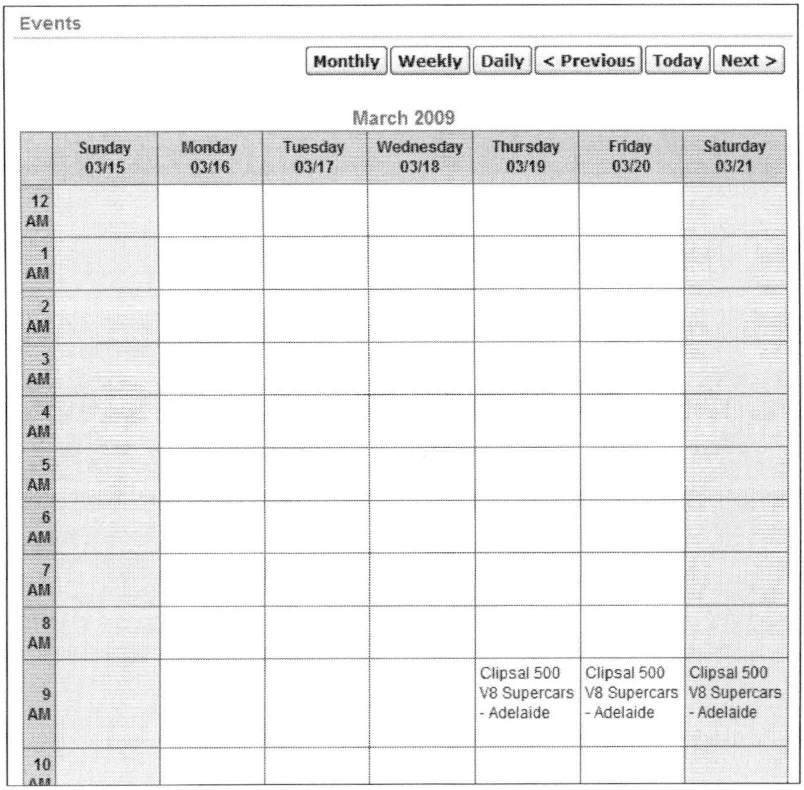

Events						

Monthly | Weekly | Daily | < Previous | Today | Next >

March 2009

	Sunday 03/15	Monday 03/16	Tuesday 03/17	Wednesday 03/18	Thursday 03/19	Friday 03/20	Saturday 03/21
12 AM							
1 AM							
2 AM							
3 AM							
4 AM							
5 AM							
6 AM							
7 AM							
8 AM							
9 AM						Clipsal 500 V8 Supercars - Adelaide	Clipsal 500 V8 Supercars - Adelaide	Clipsal 500 V8 Supercars - Adelaide
10 AM							

Modifying a calendar manually

A calendar region has a number of attributes that can be specified to help make it look, feel, and work exactly the way we would like. These attributes are divided into the following property pages:

- **Region definition:** This controls overall details about the calendar region, such as the SQL query source, display conditions, and calendar title.

- **Calendar attributes:** This controls the appearance of the calendar, such as templates, date format, and links.

Region Definition

The **Region Definition** property page enables us to modify details for the overall calendar region. The property page is broken down into sections for identification, user interface, source, conditions, cache, header and footer, authorization, customization, configuration, and comments.

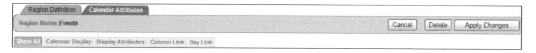

 Calendar regions can also take advantage of many common region features including conditional processing and caching.

Region Source

The most important section of the **Region Definition** property page is the **Region Source** section. This defines the SQL query used to retrieve the calendar information that we wish to display in the calendar region. The SQL query is entered using the **Region Source** attribute. As we saw when using the calendar wizard, the SQL query must contain at least a date column and description column.

 We can refer to page and application items in the **Region Source**, which can be used to filter the calendar to show only relevant entries.

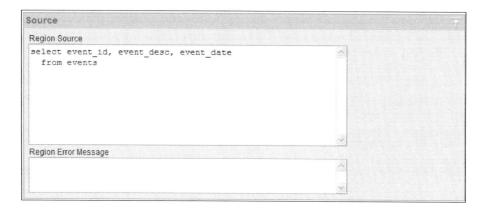

Calendar Attributes

The **Calendar Attributes** property page is used to control the appearance of entries in the calendar. The property page is broken down into sections for calendar display, display attributes, column link, and day link.

The Calendar Display section

The **Calendar Display** section is used to define how the calendar will be rendered in the page. The **Calendar Template** attribute controls how the overall calendar will be rendered, including layout, styles, and size. APEX provides a number of built-in templates by default, but we can always create our own calendar template to control exactly how the calendar is displayed.

The **Date Column** attribute is used to define which column in our SQL query stores the date to be displayed in the calendar. When using the calendar, we can specify a page item to store the date currently selected in the calendar by using the **Date Item** attribute. We can also specify a page item in the **Calendar Type** attribute to store the current calendar view. The item will automatically store one of the following values depending on the current calendar view:

- M = **monthly view**
- W = **weekly view**
- D = **daily view**

 Hidden items for both the **Date Item** and **Calendar Type** attributes are automatically created by the calendar region wizard with the names Pn_CALENDAR_DATE and Pn_CALENDAR_TYPE (where n is the current page number).

We can also control how the description for each calendar entry is displayed using the **Display Type** attribute. The following display types are available:

- **Column:** This enables a column from the calendar SQL query to be used as the description for the calendar entry. The column name is selected using the **Display Column** attribute.

- **Custom**: This enables custom HTML text and multiple columns to be used as the description for the calendar entry. This is entered by using the **Column Format** attribute. Custom descriptions can include values from the calendar SQL query by using #COLUMN_NAME# substitution syntax. The following example will display an event description column together with a location column in italics:

  ```
  #EVENT_DESC#-<i>#LOCATION#</i>
  ```

- **No Display Value**: No description is displayed for the calendar entry.

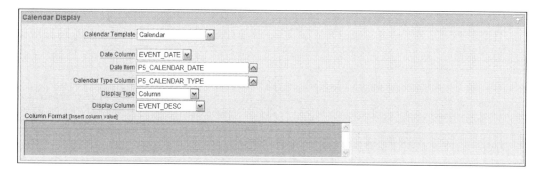

The Display Attributes section

The display attributes section is used to control how days and times are rendered in the calendar. We can use the **Begin at Start of Interval** attribute to determine whether the calendar starts from the first day of the month or from the current day in the month. The **Item Containing Start Date** and **Item Containing End Date** attributes are used to refer to items that define the start and end date of the calendar. The values of dates stored in these items need to be in the format YYYYMMDD.

The starting day of the week in a monthly calendar can be specified by entering the **Start of Week for Monthly Calendar** attribute. We can also specify the start and end day for a weekly calendar by using the **Start Day for Weekly Calendar** and **End Day for Weekly Calendar** attributes.

The **Time Format** attribute is used to determine if time in the weekly, or daily, calendar is displayed in 24-hour or 12-hour formats. In the weekly or daily calendar, we can also control which time hours to display by using the **Start Time** and **End Time** attributes. This is useful should we only want to show the calendar, for example, from 9 a.m. to 5 p.m., all other hours will not be displayed. The **Start Time** and **End Time** attributes are hardcoded and cannot refer to a page or application item.

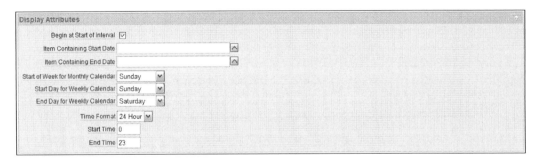

The Column Link section

The **Column Link** section is used to enter a page or URL to link to when an entry in the calendar is clicked. This can be used to navigate to another page where additional information regarding the calendar entry can be viewed.

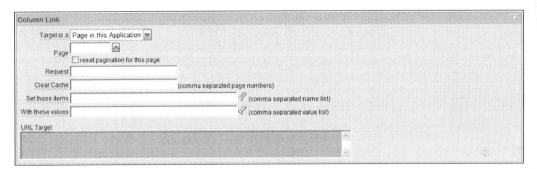

The Day Link section

The **Day Link** section is used to enter a page or URL to link to when the day number in the calendar is clicked. This can be used to navigate to another page where new calendar entries can be created for the day number clicked.

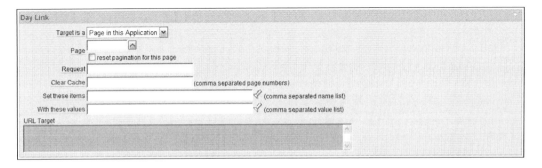

Summary

In this chapter, we have seen how calendars can be added quickly and easily to our pages using the calendar region wizard. We have also seen how calendar attributes can be modified to add links and control how the calendar is rendered. The calendar region is a very useful way to display date and time information from a database table and to add scheduling functionality to our applications.

In the next chapter, we will look at how we can use Interactive Reports in our applications.

16
Interactive Reports

In an earlier chapter, we looked at how report content can be added to pages using a Classic Report Region. Classic Report Regions offer a number of built-in functions out of the box, but this has been taken to a whole new level with the introduction of Interactive Report Regions in APEX. Interactive Report Regions enable users to customize reports dynamically at runtime. Users can add or remove columns, apply conditional highlighting, filter report data, and apply many other useful customizations. This enables us to make our reports more interactive and functional with no additional coding required. In this chapter, we will discuss how to use Interactive Reports in our applications. Specifically, we shall be looking at:

- Interactive Report Region features
- Creating an Interactive Report
- Modifying an Interactive Report

Interactive Report Regions

Interactive Report Regions are a new feature in APEX 3.1 and provide many new features over Classic Report Regions. Interactive Reports provide users with the ability to customize reports at runtime, ensuring that they can tailor a report to suit their own needs. Users can add or remove columns, apply sorting, perform conditional highlighting, and filter report results. Users can also add calculated columns, control breaks, and even generate charts based on report data. Once a report has been customized, the display changes can be saved and re-applied again at a later stage. Interactive Report results can also be exported to other formats for printing or viewing.

In the following screenshot, we can see an example of an Interactive Report Region:

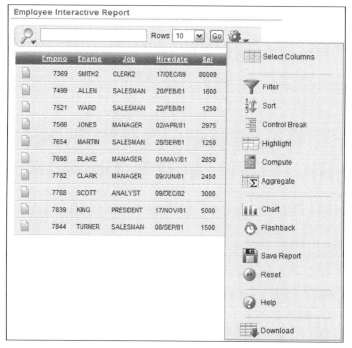

You will start to notice a number of differences compared to a Classic Report Region. The main difference is the Search Bar at the top of the report results. The Search Bar enables us to enter search criteria to filter the report results. We can click the Search Button (or magnifying glass icon) in the Search Bar to select specific columns to search within. The Action Menu (or cog icon) in the Search Bar displays options we can apply to customize the Interactive Report. Through the Search Bar, we can also control how many records are displayed on a page.

By default, only one Interactive Report Region can be added per page, although it is possible to display more through the use of HTML iframes. HTML iframes enable another page to be displayed within an inline frame on a page. This makes it possible for us to display another page containing an Interactive Report in our page. The following is an example of an HTML iframe:

```
<iframe src="f?p=123:1" width="100%" height="300"></
iframe>
```

Let's now explore the built-in features provided by Interactive Reports by using the Action Menu (or cog icon) in the Search Bar, and see how they can be used in our applications.

Select Columns

The Select Columns function enables users to choose which columns are displayed in a report. Columns can be added or removed from the report by using the less-than and greater-than icons. The display order of columns can also be modified by using the up and down arrows.

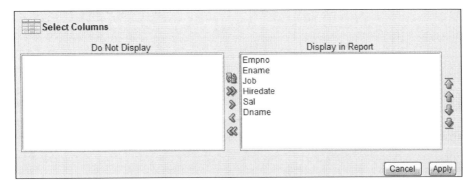

Filter

The filter feature enables users to define one or more conditions (or filters) to restrict the results displayed in a report. This is equivalent to applying a `Where` clause to a SQL query for the report. To add a filter, we select a report column in the **Column** attribute, a comparison type from the **Operator** attribute, and value to compare the column to in the **Expression** attribute. The LOV icon next to the **Expression** attribute displays a list of common values for the column that can be selected to populate the expression. In the following screenshot, we have entered a filter to only show records where `empno = 7654`. Once the filter is created, it is displayed below the Search Bar with a link to edit the filter, a checkbox to enable or disable the filter, and an icon that can be used to delete the filter.

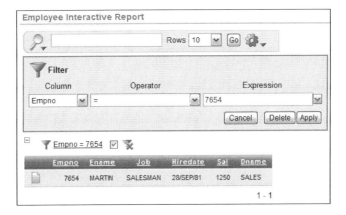

Interactive Reports also enable data to be filtered by clicking on a report column heading. In the following screenshot, we can see a menu that is displayed when a column heading is selected. In the menu, we can filter data by selecting one of the common values listed for the column or by entering specific search text. The menu also displays icons to adjust the sort order for the column, hide the column, or add the column as a break column.

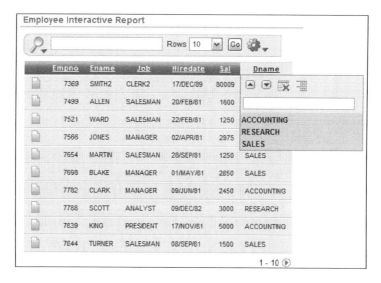

In the following screenshot, we can see that when an Interactive Report contains a date column, selecting the column heading displays special filtering options for a date, such as like only showing dates within the last year.

Sort

The Sort feature enables a custom sort order to be applied to the results of a report. We can select which report columns to sort by using the **Column** attribute. The **Direction** attribute will determine if the column is sorted in ascending or descending order. The **Null Sorting** attribute controls whether null values in the column are displayed first or last. Report results can also be sorted by clicking individual report column headings when viewing the report.

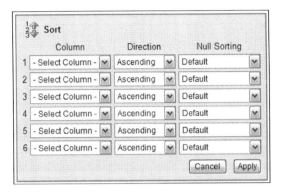

Control break

The control break feature enables grouping to be added to our report on one or more columns. The **Column** attribute defines which column to group on and the **Status** attribute determines whether the control break is active or not.

In the screenshot, we can see that report results are grouped by the Department Name column. The Control Break column created is listed below the Search Bar. A checkbox is displayed next to the control break column and is used to turn the control break on or off. The control break can be deleted from the report by clicking the delete icon.

Highlight

Have you ever wanted to apply conditional highlighting to clearly flag important data? Interactive Reports provide a highlight feature that enables users to display data in different colors based on a condition. In the following screenshot, we can see that when the Salary column is greater than two thousand, the background will be displayed in red. Multiple highlights can be defined for a report.

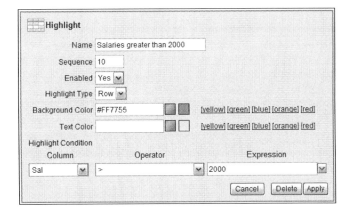

Compute

The compute feature enables calculated columns to be added to an Interactive Report. A computation can include other columns from the report and use standard Oracle database functions. To add the calculated column to the report, we also define a column heading and format masks for the value. In the following screenshot, a new column will be added to the report which increases the salary column by ten percent:

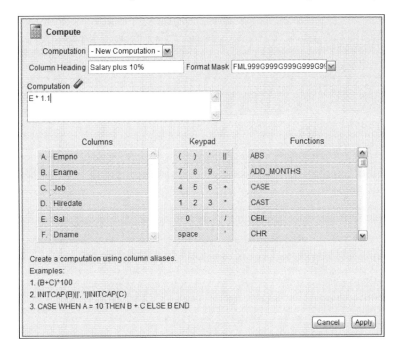

Aggregate

The Aggregate feature enables an aggregate total to be performed for a column. We can use this to sum, count, or average data in the column. If the Interactive Report contains a control break, then the aggregate total is displayed for each break group and the report overall. In the following screenshot, an aggregate will be created to sum the salary column and display the total at the end of the report:

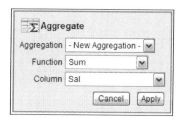

Chart

Interactive Reports also enable charts to be generated based on the results of the report. We can specify the type of chart together with the data in the report we wish to chart. In the following screenshot, a vertical bar chart will be created using the department name for the chart labels and a sum of the salary column for the chart values:

In the next screenshot, we can see an example of the vertical bar chart. The chart displays a sum of employee salaries for each department. A link is displayed to edit the chart or view the report results.

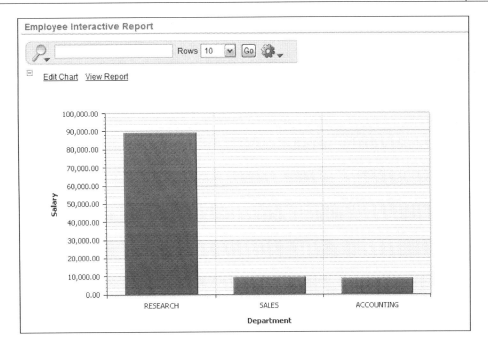

Flashback

Have you ever modified data by mistake in a production system and wondered what data existed before the change? The Flashback feature can help us answer this question. The Flashback feature enables us to view the data that existed in a database at a particular point in time. This enables us to see the exact data in the database before any data changes were made.

 To use Flashback in an Interactive Report, the Oracle database being used must support flashback and have it enabled. The length of time that we can go back using flashback to see the exact state of a table will depend on your database configuration.

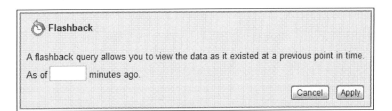

Save report

As we have seen, there are a number of filters, highlights, and other customizations that we can apply to our reports. Rather than having to re-enter these customizations each time we run the report, we can tell APEX to remember these customizations so they can be re-applied next time we run the report. Each user can save multiple reports of their own by assigning them a report **Name**. The names of each saved report are displayed as tabs above the Interactive Report Region. Selecting a tab will re-apply the saved customizations to the report.

The Save Report feature also provides a way for developers to define default Interactive Report settings that will be applied to all users. This is entered via the **Save** attribute, which is only displayed for developers. In the **Save** attribute, the value **As Default Report Settings** can be selected to create defaults for the Interactive Report.

Reset

The Reset feature enables the report to be reset to its original default settings. This clears any filters, highlights, or other customizations that have been added to the report.

Download

Once we have added columns, sort orders, filters, and calculations, we can use the download feature to save the report results or analyze the data further in another application. Report results can be downloaded in CSV, Microsoft Excel, Adobe PDF, or RTF formats. The available formats will depend on whether a print server has been configured in the APEX Instance Settings by your APEX administrator.

Converting an Existing Report Region

As we have seen, Interactive Report Regions provide many great features that can be used in our applications. You may start to wonder, can Classic Report Regions be converted into Interactive Report Regions in APEX? Luckily for us, APEX provides an easy way to migrate our Classic Report Regions to Interactive Report Regions. The migration feature is accessed from the Region Definition property page of a Classic Report Region. In the following screenshot, a task menu is displayed on the right-hand side of the screen with a **Migrate to Interactive Report** link, clicking the link will start the migration:

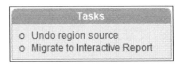

When a Classic Report Region is migrated to an Interactive Report Region, the SQL query source for the report may need to be altered. This is relevant when a Where clause in the report SQL query references page or application items from the session to filter data in the report. These Where clauses may need to be removed, as Interactive Reports have their own mechanism for filtering data from the Search Bar. Once a Classic Report Region is migrated, a copy is kept in the page with a display condition set to never. This means that we still have a copy of the old Classic Report Region, but it will never be displayed when running the page.

 Once a Classic Report Region has been converted to an Interactive Report Region, it is worth deleting the old Classic Report Region when you are happy with the page. APEX does not enable an Interactive Report Region to be converted back to a Classic Report Region.

Create an Interactive Report using a wizard

We have seen how existing Classic Report Regions can be migrated to Interactive Reports, but in this section, we will walk through the process of creating a brand new Interactive Report on our page. To demonstrate, we will repeat the same employee list example from the Classic Report Region chapter. This report will list all the employees stored in a database together with the department the employee belongs to. We will use the Interactive Report Region Wizard to create the report. Now, let's walk through the steps to create an Interactive Report Region.

Start the Interactive Report Region Wizard

In the screenshot, we can see the Create Region icon, click the icon (to the right of region) to start the wizard:

Region Type

The next step is to tell APEX that we wish to add a report to our page; select the **Report** option, and click **Next**:

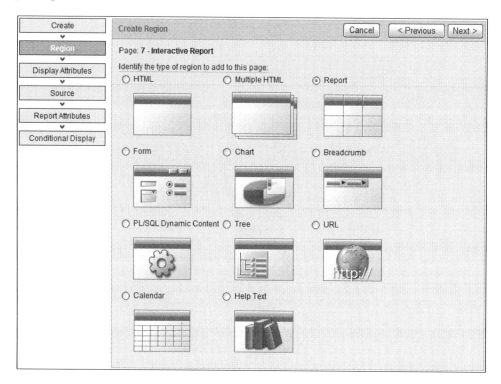

Report Implementation

In the next step, we need to specify what type of report to create; select the **Interactive Report** option, and click **Next**:

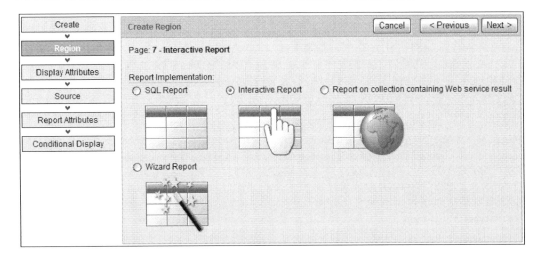

Display attributes

Once we have selected the Interactive Report wizard, the first thing we need to do is specify display attributes. Display attributes are used to control the look and positioning of the report region on a page. The **Title** attribute allows a heading to be defined for the report. The **Region Template** attribute will control the overall look of the region. It can control things such as the borders, style, titles, button positions, and layout of the region.

The **Display Point** attribute tells us where in the page template or page body to display the region. We can then use the **Sequence** attribute to control the order in which the region is displayed on the page. To divide the page into columns, we can use the **Column** attribute to specify which column the region is displayed in.

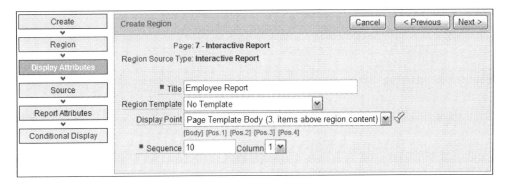

Source

The next step is the most important part of creating an Interactive Report. It tells APEX what data needs to be displayed in the report. In the screenshot, we have defined a SQL query in the **Enter a SQL Select Statement** attribute to select columns from the employee and department tables.

We then specify how the Interactive Report uniquely identifies rows by using the **Uniquely Identify Rows By** attribute. By default, the **ROWID** is used to identify rows, but we can also specify a **Unique Column** from our SQL query to identify rows. This column name is entered using the **Unique Column** attribute.

Interactive Reports also provide an option where a single record can be selected and viewed separately. This is set using the **Link to Single Row View** attribute. When set to Yes, a view icon is placed at the start of each record to enable the record to be selected.

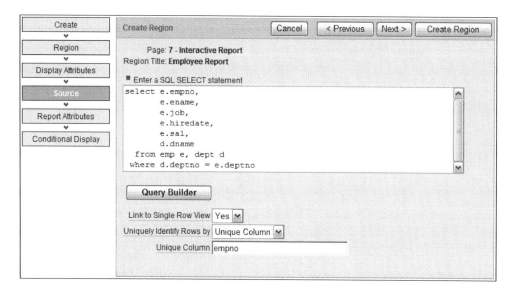

 A link to the **Query Builder** is displayed in the wizard, which can be used to help visually create queries without needing to know how to write SQL queries.

Conditional Display

As described in earlier chapters, APEX enables us to enter conditions to determine whether the Interactive Report Region is displayed. In this example, we will not enter any display conditions:

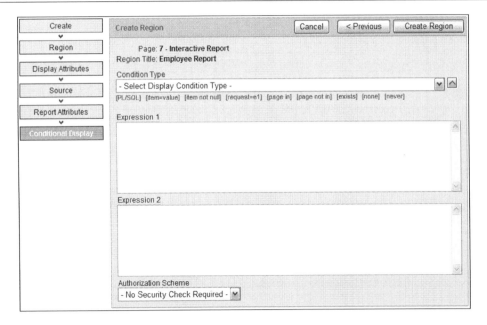

Wizard completion

The Interactive Report wizard has now gathered enough information to create our report. Clicking the **Create Region** button will add the Interactive Report Region to our page and then display the Page Definition screen. From here, we can click the **Run** button to view the interactive report generated by the wizard.

Manually modifying an Interactive Report

Once an Interactive Report Region has been created there are many attributes that can be specified to help make it look, feel, and work exactly the way we would like. Interactive Report Regions share a number of attributes that we have seen previously in the *Classic Report Regions* chapter. Interactive Report Regions, like Classic Report Regions, are divided into the following three main property pages:

- **Region Definition**: This controls the overall details about the region, such as the SQL query source, display conditions, and report title.

- **Report Attributes**: This controls the appearance of the report, such as the layout, column headings, formatting, and pagination.

- **Print Attributes**: This controls the way the report region is displayed when printing such as page sizes, headers, and footers.

These property pages can be accessed from the regions section of the Page Definition screen.

> The Region Definition and Page Attributes are very similar to those covered earlier in the Classic Report Region chapter. In this section, we will explore **Report Attributes** and **Column Attributes** that are specific to Interactive Reports.

Report Attributes

The Report Attributes property page is used to control the appearance of an Interactive Report. The property page is broken down into sections for Column Attributes, Groups, Default Report, Pagination, Sorting, Search Bar, Download, Link Column, Advanced, and Description.

Column Attributes

The Column Attributes section provides the ability to view and set basic details about each column in our report. The **Heading** attribute is used to define custom headings for each column in our report. The **Type** attribute specifies whether the column is a number, a string, or a date, while the **Link** attribute specifies whether the column contains a link. We can use the **Display Text As** attribute to determine how the column is rendered in the report. We can set the default sequence order of columns in the report by using the up and down arrows. Further column attributes can be modified by clicking the edit icon next to each column name.

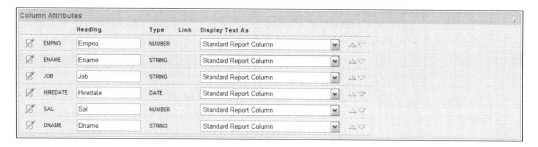

Column Groups

The Column Groups section enables report columns to be grouped into sections when the record is displayed in a single row view. Once a group is created, individual columns in the report can be assigned to the group. The group name assigned is shown as a header with any columns in the group displayed below the heading, which can be expanded or collapsed. This provides a neat way to group and associate like fields together when the report contains many columns and the record is viewed in the single row view mode.

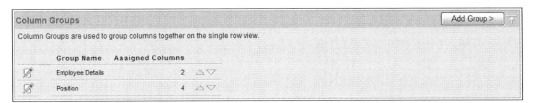

Default Report Settings

The Default Report Settings section provides an easy way for us to see if any default settings such as filters and highlights have been saved for the Interactive Report. These defaults are initially displayed for all users when the Interactive Report is run. The section lists columns selected in the report, data filters, sort columns, control breaks, highlight conditions, compute columns, aggregate columns, and charts that have been saved as default. We saw earlier in this chapter that default settings can be saved for an Interactive Report by selecting Save Report from the action menu. From the Save Report screen, we can select **save As Default Report Settings**:

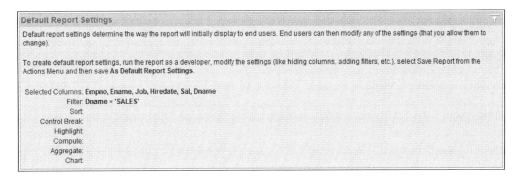

Pagination

The Pagination section controls the number of records displayed in an Interactive Report and how we navigate between records. The **Pagination Type** attribute controls how record pagination is displayed for a report. Record pagination is used to show next and previous links to navigate between records returned by a report. We can also choose where to display record pagination in the report region—top, bottom, or top and bottom, by setting the **Display Position** attribute.

The **Maximum Row Count** attribute defines the maximum number of records that will be displayed in the Interactive Report. This attribute may affect the performance of the Interactive Report. If the report returns more rows than the Maximum Row Count, then we can define a warning message in the **When more than maximum row data found message** attribute. In the event that the report query returns no records, we can define a message in the **When No Data Found Message** attribute.

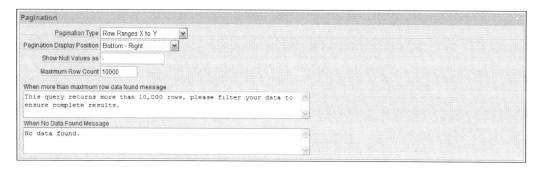

Search Bar

The Search Bar section is used to control whether the Search Bar is displayed in the report and what options are available when the Interactive Report is run. The **Include Search Bar** attribute determines whether the search bar is displayed. We can then customize the Search Bar using the following options:

- **Search Field**: This determines whether a text field in the search bar is displayed where the user can enter search criteria

- **Finder Drop Down**: This determines whether the user can search on a selected column or all columns in the report

- **Rows Per Page Selector**: This determines whether the user can select the number of records displayed per page

- **Actions Menu**: This determines whether the action menu is displayed where a user can select options to customize the report

We can further customize the actions menu by specifying which features we would like to be available in the Interactive Report. Options include Select Column, Filter, Sort, Control Break, Highlight, Compute, Aggregate, Chart, Flashback, Save Report, Reset, Help, and Download.

The Search Bar section also lets us control how buttons are rendered in the Interactive Report by selecting a template from the **Button Template** attribute. The actions menu icon can also be changed from the default cog icon; we can specify an alternative image in the **Action Menu Image** attribute. The label for the search button (or magnifying glass icon) can be set using the **Search Button Label** attribute.

The **Maximum Rows Per Page** attribute can be used to specify how many records are displayed per page. Alternatively, we can allow users to select how many rows to display per page by checking the **Rows Per Page Indicator** attribute.

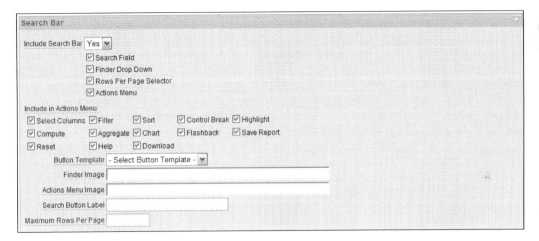

Download

The Download section enables details to be specified about the file formats that the report can be exported to for viewing or printing. The **Download Formats** attribute enables us to select which formats the report can be exported to including CSV, Microsoft Excel, Adobe PDF, and Microsoft Word (RTF).

For CSV files, we can specify a delimiting character using the **CSV Separator** attribute. The default separator is a comma or semicolon depending on your current NLS settings. Data values are enclosed using the character in the **Enclosed** attribute. By default, the data values are enclosed with double quotes.

The **Filename** attribute is used for the filename of the export file. By default, the region name is used for the filename, followed by the file extension.

Link Column

The Link Column section enables link details to be provided for the view icon at the start of each record (or link column). The link column can display the single row view for a selected record, it can link to a custom target (page or URL), or not be displayed at all. This is specified using the **Link Column** attribute. If **link to a custom target** is selected, then we need to specify a page number and other attributes that would normally be set when creating a branch or button.

In the **Link Column** section, we can also specify how the Interactive Report uniquely identifies rows by using the **Uniquely Identify Rows By** attribute. By default, the **ROWID** is used to identify rows, but we can also specify a **Unique Column**. If **Unique Column** is selected, we need to enter a column from our SQL query that uniquely identifies a row in the **Unique Column** attribute.

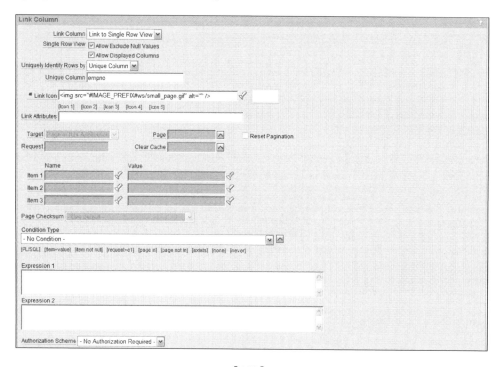

Advanced Attributes

The Advanced Attributes section provides some useful settings that can be used when programmatically controlling the Interactive Report. The **Report Alias** attribute enables an alias to be assigned that can be used to reference an Interactive Report via code. The **Report Alias** assigned must be unique in your application.

The **Report ID Item** attribute is used to store a page item containing the Report ID for a specific saved version of the Interactive Report. This enables a specific saved version of the Interactive Report to be displayed to the user instead of the default view. The Report ID of an Interactive Report can be found by using the APEX view named APEX_WORKSHEET_RPTS. The torch icon enables a page item containing the Report ID to be selected.

The **Show Saved Reports as Tabs** attribute determines whether saved versions of the Interactive Report are displayed as tabs in the page. Set the **Show Saved Reports as Tabs** attribute to **No** if you wish to create your own page or menu of saved Interactive Report versions.

The **Page Items to Submit** attribute enables multiple page items to be saved in a user's session state when the **Go** button is clicked in the Search Bar. This is useful as an Interactive Report does not physically submit the entire page, therefore page items will not automatically be saved into session state when the **Go** button is clicked. Multiple page items can be defined by entering a comma separated list of page items.

Column attributes

The column attributes property page enables more detailed attributes to be entered for a column. The property page is broken down into sections for column definition, list of values, link, authorization, conditions, help, and comments.

Column Definition

The Column Definition section is used to define basic details about a column in an Interactive Report. The column can be assigned into a logical group when displayed in the single row view mode by using the **Group** attribute. The **Display Text As** attribute determines how the column is rendered in the report, while the **Column Heading** attribute is used to define a custom heading for the column. The **Row View Label** attribute can be used to assign a different label for the column when it's displayed in the single row view mode. The **Number/Date Format** attribute is used to apply formatting masks for dates and numbers in the column. We can also control heading and column alignment, and specify whether the column can be used in actions such as sort, filter, control break, aggregate, compute, or chart.

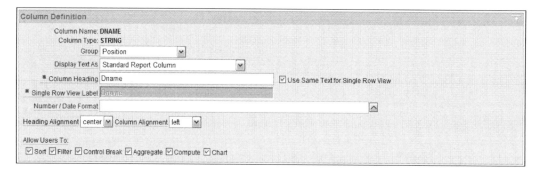

List of Values

The List of Values section provides a way to determine what values are displayed for the column in the **Filters** action. This is determined by the **Column Filter List of Values** attribute, which can contain the following values:

- **None**: No list of values are displayed.

- **Default Based on Column Type**: A list of values will be based on distinct values for the column.

- **User defined List of Values**: A SQL query is defined in the **List of values definition** attribute to determine the list of values to use. The SQL query must only return one column.

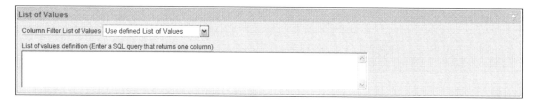

Column Link

The Column Link section is used to define links on columns in an Interactive Report.
Column link attributes are set the same way as we would for branches or buttons.
Column links can be useful for creating drill down capability in our reports or for
linking to other pages to view more detailed information.

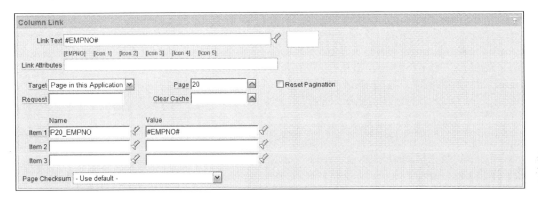

Linking to Interactive Reports

Interactive Reports also provide a feature where, as developers, we can automatically
add filters to the Interactive Report when the page is first displayed. This is useful if
we need to link to an Interactive Report from another page and dynamically filter the
results to only show relevant records. To add a filter via a link, we first need to define
the filter operation and column in the item names section of the APEX URL. This is
entered in the following format:

```
IR<operator>_<column alias>:<value>
```

In the filter format, `<column alias>` is the column in our report SQL statement that
we wish to place the condition on. The `<operator>` defines the type of condition we
wish to apply for the filter. The following operators can be used:

- EQ: Equals (this is used by default if no operator is specified)
- LT: Less Than
- LTE: Less Than or Equal To
- GT: Greater Than
- GTE: Greater Than or Equal To
- LIKE: SQL Like Operator
- N: Null
- NN: Not Null

Now that the column and operator have been defined, we then pass a condition value in the item values section of an APEX URL. To demonstrate, let's add a filter in an APEX URL, so when we navigate to the Interactive Report, a filter is automatically applied to only show department names that equal sales.

```
f?p=101:6:1234567890::::IREQ_DNAME:SALES
```

To restore an Interactive Report to its default settings via a link, we can pass the string RIR in the clear cache section of the APEX URL. This is the same as selecting reset from the actions menu. We can also go a step further and clear all settings from the Interactive Report, including default settings, by passing the string CIR in the clear cache section of the APEX URL. To demonstrate, the following URL is used to reset the Interactive Report to its default settings:

```
f?p=101:6:1234567890:::RIR
```

Summary

In this chapter, we have learned about Interactive Report Regions and how users can customize reports by using built-in actions such as filters, highlights, and many others. We have also seen how Classic Reports can be migrated and how Interactive Reports can be created on pages using the Interactive Report wizard. We have also seen how Interactive Report Region properties can be modified and how we can link to them from other pages. Interactive Report Regions provide many great features, which can be added to pages quickly and easily to help make our applications more functional and interactive.

In the next chapter, we will look at how we can use JavaScript and the APEX AJAX framework in our applications.

17
AJAX with APEX

AJAX (Asynchronous JavaScript and XML) is a collection of technologies that were in use separately for a long time in the Web environment. Putting them to work together, with some new APIs, gives us something new — the ability of the client side to trigger server-side activities without relinquishing full control. With AJAX, the client side can initiate an HTTP communication with the server using a local scripting language and requests for server-side information. This request can trigger any action we need on the server side, and in our context, any allowed database activity. The new benefit of AJAX is that this type of client-server dialog can happen without the need to submit the page, and re-render it from scratch upon receiving the server response, as was the case prior to AJAX.

APEX has a dedicated AJAX framework, which allows us to utilize this important technology both on the client side (using the APEX built-in JavaScript library), and on the server side (mainly using PL/SQL code). Although this framework is not fully declarative, it can still shield us from some of the more complex aspects of implementing AJAX, especially in a cross-browser environment.

In this chapter, we'll review the AJAX technology; how it's implemented in the APEX environment, and how we can use it in our APEX applications, mainly to optimize and enrich our user's experience.

Personal Note:

This chapter includes many details and snippets of code. You might find it difficult at first, and I'm sorry for that, but I did it intentionally. AJAX is not the purpose here. It's only a means. A means to achieve what we need in our APEX applications. I believe it's important to understand the principles of the AJAX technology, but more important, in our context, is to understand how they can be used in the APEX environment. If you feel that you didn't get it all in your first reading, then please don't despair. You are encouraged to try again. I can tell you from my own experience, that eventually it all makes sense, and it will definitely be worth your while.

The AJAX technology

As we'll see in this chapter, the name—AJAX—can be a bit misleading. Every component mentioned in the name—Asynchronous communication, JavaScript, and XML—is not used exclusively in the technology. We can also use synchronous forms of communication, data formats other than XML, and even use scripting languages other than JavaScript (although the APEX built-in AJAX framework supports only JavaScript).

In the following sub-sections, we'll briefly review some major AJAX concepts that I believe are important to know and understand, in order to better utilize the technology better.

The XMLHttpRequest object

AJAX is based on an HTTP communication between the client side and the server side. The go between is a DOM object called **XMLHttpRequest**. The object API—a series of built-in object methods—allows us to generate and use it in a client-side scripting language (in our case JavaScript) in order to send a request to the server and in turn, process the server response and use it on the client side.

Microsoft first introduced a client-side support for the *XMLHttpRequest* concept in IE5.0 with its own implementation—an ActiveX control called *XMLHTTP*. In IE7 Microsoft added a configuration option to natively support *XMLHttpRequest* in a similar fashion to the other major Web browsers in the market. This means that as long as we want to support IE versions earlier than IE7, implementing AJAX is a cross-browser issue and must be implemented accordingly. It also means that IE versions that don't support *XMLHttpRequest* natively can't use AJAX if their *ActivX* support is disabled.

 The APEX AJAX implementation supports cross-browser platforms and it generates the *XMLHttpRequest* object according to the Web browser support in it.

Communication

Although the A in the AJAX acronym stands for asynchronous (communication), the AJAX implementation allows us to use either asynchronous or synchronous communication between the client and the server. A synchronous AJAX request means that the Web browser will wait for the server response before it continues executing the rest of its code. An asynchronous AJAX request means that the Web browser will not wait for the server response, and will continue with its code.

It's up to us, as developers, to track the response status and when the response transmit is complete, to process it as we need. Of course, the *XMLHttpRequest* API supplies us with the proper means to do that.

Why make the client side wait for the server response instead of always using asynchronous communication?

It should depend on the nature of the AJAX request. Often we are using an AJAX request to determine our next step, e.g. the options of a select list item that are based on a previous user input or an auto-complete mechanism, which retrieves possible values based on the last user keyboard input. There is no sense in letting the Web browser continue with its code flow, as this flow depends on the server response. In other cases, where the AJAX response doesn't affect the immediate next step of the client-side flow, asynchronous communication can be chosen. Further in the chapter, we'll see APEX AJAX examples of both options.

Data format

Although the X in the AJAX acronym stands for XML it is not the only supported format for the server response. The AJAX server response can be formatted as a valid XML fragment or as a simple text string, which can be assigned to a `String` JavaScript variable. Another option for formatting the simple text response is to use **JSON (JavaScript Object Notation)**. The *JSON* format allows us to serialize more complex data structures and still use fairly simple and readable text format. JSON objects can be easily parsed in JavaScript, without necessarily resorting to dedicated parsers, as in the case of XML. Another advantage of using JSON is that its format is more compact than XML, which can be an important advantage where Web applications are concerned.

Parsing *JSON*, especially using the built-in JavaScript `eval()` function, can have security implications. As *JSON* is out of the scope of this book, you are encouraged to explore this issue further, prior to using it with your applications.

AJAX implementation in APEX

APEX introduced AJAX supports in version 2.0 (the product was called HTML DB back then). The support includes a dedicated AJAX framework that allows us to use AJAX in our APEX applications, and it covers both the client and the server sides.

AJAX support on the client side

The APEX built-in JavaScript library includes a special JavaScript file with the implementation of the AJAX client-side components. In earlier versions this file was called `htmldb_get.js`, and in APEX 3.1, it was changed to `apex_get_3_1.js`.

In version 3.1, APEX also started to implement JavaScript namespace in the `apex_ns_3_1.js` file. Within the file, there is a definition to an `apex.ajax` namespace.

 I'm not mentioning the names of these files just for the sake of it. As the AJAX framework is not officially documented within the APEX documentation, these files can be very important and a useful source of information.

By default, these files are automatically loaded into every application page as part of the `#HEAD#` substitution string in the **Header** section of the page template. This means that, by default, AJAX functionality is available to us on every page of our application, without taking any extra measures.

The htmldb_Get object

The APEX implementation of AJAX is based on the `htmldb_Get` object and as we'll see, creating a new instance of `htmldb_Get` is always the first step in performing an AJAX request.

The `htmldb_Get` constructor function has seven parameters:

```
function htmldb_Get(obj,flow,req,page,instance,proc,queryString)
```

1—obj

The first parameter is a `String` that can be set to `null`, a name of a page item (DOM element), or an element ID.

- Setting this parameter to `null` will cause the result of the AJAX request to be assigned in a JavaScript variable. We should use this value every time we need to process the AJAX returned result, like in the cases where we return XML or JSON formatted data, or when we are relaying on the returned result, further in our JavaScript code flow.

The APEX built-in JavaScript library defines, in the `apex_builder.js` file, (which is also loaded into every application page, just like `apex_get_3_1.js`), a JavaScript global variable called `gReturn`. You can use this variable and assign it the AJAX returned result.

- Setting this parameter to the name (ID) of a page item will set the item `value` property with the result of the AJAX call. You should make sure that the result of the AJAX call matches the nature of the item `value` property. For example, if you are returning a text string into a text item it will work just fine. However, if you are returning an HTML snippet of code into the same item, you'll most likely not get the result you wanted.

- Setting this parameter to a DOM element ID, which is not an input item on the page, will set its `innerHTML` property to the result of the AJAX call.

Injecting HTML code, using the `innerHTML` property, is a cross-browser issue. Moreover, we can't always set `innerHTML` along the DOM tree. To avoid potential problems, I strongly recommend that you use this option with `<div>` elements only. Later in the chapter we'll see an example of that.

2—flow

This parameter represents the application ID.

If we are calling `htmldb_Get()` from an external JavaScript file, this parameter should be set to `$v('pFlowId')` or its equivalent in version 3.1 or before (`$x('pFlowId').value` or `html_GetElement('pFlowId').value`). This is also the default value, in case this parameter is left `null`.

If we are calling `htmldb_Get()` as part of an inline JavaScript code we can use the *Substitution String* notation `&APP_ID.` (just to remind you that the trailing period is part of the syntax).

Less common, but if you are using *Oracle Web Toolkit* to generate dynamic code (for dynamic content) that includes AJAX, you can also use the bind variable notation `:APP_ID.` (In this case, the period is just a punctuation mark.)

3—req

This `String` parameter stands for the REQUEST value. Using the keyword **APPLICATION_PROCESS** with this parameter allows us to name an application level *On Demand – PL/SQL Anonymous Block* process that will be fired as part of the AJAX server-side processing. For example: `'APPLICATION_PROCESS=demo_code'`. This parameter is case sensitive, and as a `String`, should be enclosed with quotes.

If, as part of the AJAX call, we are not invoking an on-demand process, this parameter should be set to `null` (which is its default value).

4—page

This parameter represents an application page ID.

As we'll see later in the chapter, the APEX AJAX process allows us to invoke any application page, to run it in the background, on the server side, and then clip portions of the generated HTML code for this page into the AJAX calling page. In these cases, we should set this parameter to the page ID that we want to pull from.

The default value of this parameter is 0 (this stands for page 0). However, this value can be problematic at times, especially when page 0 has not been defined on the application, or when there are inconsistencies between the Authorization scheme, or the page Authentication (such as *Public* and *Required Authentication*) of page 0 and the AJAX calling page. These inconsistencies can fail the execution of the AJAX process.

In cases where you are not pulling information from another page, the safe bet is to set this parameter to the page ID of the AJAX calling page, using `$v('pFlowStepId')` or its equivalent for versions earlier than 3.1. In the case of an inline code, the `&APP_PAGE_ID.` *Substitution String* can also be used.

> Using the calling page ID as the default value for this parameter can be considered a "good practice" even for upcoming APEX versions, where implementation of page level on-demand process will probably be introduced. I hope you remember that as of version 3.2, we can only define on-demand processes on the application level.

5—instance

This parameter represents the APEX session ID, and should almost always be left `null` (personally, I never encountered the need to set it otherwise). In this case, it will be populated with the result of `$v('pInstance')` or its earliest versions.

6—proc

This *String* parameter allows us to invoke a stored or packaged procedure on the database as part of the AJAX process.

The common behavior of the APEX AJAX framework is to use the application level *On Demand PL/SQL Anonymous Block* process as the logic of the AJAX server-side component. In this case, the on-demand process is named through the third parameter—`req`—using the keyword **APPLICATION_PROCESS**, and this parameter—`proc`—should be left `null`. The parameter will be populated with its default value of `'wwv_flow.show'`(the single quotes are part of the syntax, as this is a *String* parameter).

However, the APEX AJAX framework also allows us to invoke an external (to APEX) stored (or packaged) procedure as the logic of the AJAX server side. In this case, we can utilize an already existing logic in the database. Moreover, we can benefit from the "regular" advantages of stored procedures, such as a pre-complied code, for better performance, or the option to use wrapped PL/SQL packages, which can protect our business logic better (the APEX on-demand PL/SQL process can be accessed on the database level as clear text).

The parameter should be formatted as a URL and can be in the form of a relative URL. In this case, the system will complete the relative URL into a full path URL based on the current `window.location.href` property.

 As with all stored or packaged procedures that we wish to use in our APEX application, the user (and in the case of using DAD, the APEX public user) should have the proper privileges on the stored procedure.

In case the stored procedure, or the packaged procedure, doesn't have a public synonym defined for it then the procedure name should be qualified with the owner schema. For example, with inline code we can use:

```
'#OWNER#.my_package.my_proc'
```

For external code, you should retrieve the owner and make it available on the page (e.g. assign it to a JavaScript global variable) or define a public synonym for the owner schema and package.

7—queryString

This parameter allows us to add parameters to the stored (packaged) procedure that we named in the previous parameter—proc. As we are ultimately dealing with constructing a URL, that will be POSTed to the server, this parameter should take the form of POST parameters in a query string—pairs of **name=value**, delimited by ampersand (&).

Let's assume that my_proc has two parameters: p_arg1 and p_arg2. In this case, the queryString parameter should be set similar to the following:

```
'p_arg1=Hello&p_arg2=World'
```

As we are talking about components of a URL, the values should be escaped so their code will be a legal URL. You can use the APEX built-in JavaScript function htmldb_Get_escape() to do that.

If you are using the req parameter to invoke an APEX on-demand process with your AJAX call, the proc and queryString parameters should be left null. In this case, you can close the htmldb_Get() syntax right after the page parameter. If, on the other hand, you are invoking a stored (packaged) procedure, the req parameter should be set to null.

Code examples

Let's see some examples of how to use the htmldb_Get class with various scenarios:

```
var ajaxReq = new htmldb_Get(null, $v('pFlowId'),
        'APPLICATION_PROCESS=demo_code',0);
```

- With this code, we create a new object instance of htmldb_Get and assign it to ajaxReq.

- The first parameter is null, and that means that the returned AJAX response should be assigned to a JavaScript variable.

- Next we set the Application ID using the $v('pFlowId') function. Using this version of the function means that we are on APEX 3.1 or higher instance, and that this code fits either inline code or external JavaScript file.

- We set the third parameter—req—to point to an application level *On Demand PL/SQL Anonymous Block* process, called demo_code, as the logic of the AJAX server-side component.

- We specifically set the `page` parameter to a value of `0` (zero).

- As we don't need any of the following parameters, we just closed the parameter list.

Although setting the `page` parameter to `0` is a very common practice, I mentioned earlier that this is not the best choice, as it can be problematic at times. I consider the following code, with the same functionality, to be the "**best practice**":

```
var ajaxReq = new htmldb_Get(null, $v('pFlowId'),
             'APPLICATION_PROCESS=demo_code', $v('pFlowStepId'));
```

Let's review the following code:

```
var ajaxReq = new htmldb_Get('P10_COMMENTS', $v('pFlowId'),
             'APPLICATION_PROCESS=demo_code', $v('pFlowStepId'));
```

With this code, we set the first parameter to `'P10_COMMENTS'`, which is a page text item. This means that the returned AJAX response will be assigned directly to the `P10_COMMENTS` text item. It is our responsibility, as developers, to make sure that the returned response is a simple text.

The following code looks almost the same as the previous one:

```
var ajaxReq = new htmldb_Get('call', $v('pFlowId'),
             'APPLICATION_PROCESS=demo_code', $v('pFlowStepId'));
```

However, in this case we set the first parameter to `'call'`, which is the ID of a `<div>` tag on the application page. This means that the returned AJAX response will be set as the value of the `innerHTML` attribute of this `<div>`. It is our responsibility, as developers, to make sure that the returned response is a valid HTML code that can fit the `<div>` innerHTML.

In the following example we are invoking a packaged procedure as part of the AJAX process:

```
function formatItem(pThis) {

  var params = 'p_arg1=' + htmldb_Get_escape($v(pThis));
  var get = new htmldb_Get(null, null, null, &APP_PAGE_ID.,
      null, '#OWNER#.my_package.my_proc', params);

  . . .

}
```

- The JavaScript function takes `pThis` as a parameter, and later we are passing it into the packaged procedure as its parameter.

- The use of `#OWNER#` and `&APP_PAGE_ID.` implies that this snippet of code is part of an inline JavaScript code.

- We are invoking the my_proc procedure stored in the my_package package. In the example, we are using a full-qualified name of the procedure.

- The my_proc procedure accepts one parameter—p_arg1. The first line in our code retrieves the value of a DOM node based on the pThis parameter of the formatItem() function—$v(pThis). As we are going to use this value in a URL, we are escaping it—htmldb_Get_escape($v(pThis)). Now, we can complete the build of the quertString parameter for the htmldb_Get as a valid pair of an item name and a value, and assign it to the JavaScript variable params. We are using this variable as the last parameter of our call to a new htmldb_Get instance.

 If the system doesn't find a complete match between the parameters of the stored (packaged) procedure we are invoking and the value of the queryString parameter, it will produce a 404 HTML error message telling us that the procedure we are calling for is not found on the server. As you know, this is not the case, and you should check the arguments list first.

- As we are using the sixth parameter—proc—to call our packaged procedure, the third parameter—req—is set to null.

The htmldb_Get methods

The htmldb_Get object has several built-in methods that help us to utilize its functionality, and perform the actual AJAX call. In the following sub-sections, we'll review the more public ones; those we most likely need to use ourselves.

.Add(name,val)

If we are invoking a stored (packaged) procedure we can use the queryString parameter to pass the necessary parameters to the procedure. But what about the on-demand PL/SQL process? It's an anonymous PL/SQL block without parameters. How can we pass necessary data from the JavaScript on the client side to the PL/SQL anonymous block on the server side? In general, the answer is *Session State*. We can use the add() method to set the *Session State* of application or page items, and those will be available to us in the PL/SQL code.

The add() method accepts two parameters; the first is a String parameter, representing a name of an application or page item, and the second is its value.

As we are dealing with a method, it should be associated with an object. We are going to use the ajaxReq object we created in our previous examples:

```
ajaxReq.add('TEMP1',$v('P10_SEARCH'));
```

In this example, we are using an application item called TEMP1 and we are setting its value with the value of a page item called P10_SEARCH. The value of TEMP1 will be set in *Session State*, and will be available for us to use in any PL/SQL code in the on-demand PL/SQL process we are invoking as part of the AJAX call. We can reference TEMP1 by using a bind variable notation— :TEMP1 —or by using the APEX built-in v('TEMP1') function.

According to our needs, we don't have to only use (temporary) application items. We can also use page items, as used below:

```
ajaxReq.add('P10_SEARCH',$v('P10_SEARCH'));
```

In this case, the *Session State* value of the page item P10_SEARCH will be set according to its current DOM value, i.e. the value of the item that is being displayed on screen.

Setting *Session State* with the add() method does not depend on actually invoking an on-demand PL/SQL process. We can use the AJAX framework to just set *Session State* from JavaScript code without any other server-side activity. We'll see an example of that later in the chapter. This can be used as the client-side equivalent to the APEX API procedure APEX_UTIL.SET_SESSION_STATE(p_name, p_value). We have mentioned both the add() and APEX_UTIL.SET_SESSION_STATE options in our Chapter 3 discussion about *Session State*.

.AddParam(name,val)

APEX 3.1 introduced 10 new pre-defined global package variables, which we can use with our AJAX calls without the need to define specific, temporary by nature, application items. In the client side we can reference them as x01 to x10, and in the server side, within the on-demand PL/SQL process we are invoking in the AJAX call, we should use apex_application.g_x01 to apex_application.g_x10.

In some code examples out there, you might see a reference of wwv_flow.g_x01 to wwv_flow.g_x10. That means these new variables are actually global variables in the wwv_flow package, which has a public synonym of apex_application. You can use both references as you see fit.

Now it's also easier to explain the difference between client-side and server-side references. In the client side, we are actually setting wwv_flow.show parameters, x01 to x10, while on the server side, in the PL/SQL code, we reference the actual package global variables, g_x01 to g_x10.

APEX 3.1 also exposed the `addParam()` method, which we can use to set the values of these new variables so that they will be available to us in the on-demand PL/SQL process that we are invoking in the AJAX process. We are invoking the `addParam()` method in a similar manner to the `add()` method, although it's important to remember that they don't have the same functionality. With `addParam()`, instead of defining a special application item—`TEMP1`—which we'll only use with the AJAX processes, we can use the following:

```
ajaxReq.addParam('x01',$v('P10_SEARCH'));
```

Now we can use this variable in the on-demand PL/SQL process, for example, as part of a WHERE clause:

```
select col1, . . .
from my_table
where col1 = apex_application.g_x01;
```

> `addParam()` is not setting *Session State*. As such, the `g_x01` to `g_x10` variables have no persistence features. As we are talking about package variables, their scope is only the on-demand PL/SQL process that we are invoking with the AJAX call. After the on-demand PL/SQL anonymous block has run its course, these variables will be initialized, just like any other package variable, upon new database session.

General remarks

The following are some general remarks about the functionality and relationship of `add()` and `addParam()`:

- Both `add()` and `addParam()` are actually creating a single string, ampersand (&) delimited, which comprised of *name=value* pairs. Ultimately, this string acts as a parameter in one of the methods that initiates the AJAX process (the *XMLHttpRequest* `send()` method).

  As such, we can call these methods as many times as we need in order to set all the variables we need. For example:

  ```
  var ajaxReq = new htmldb_Get(null, $v('pFlowId'),
              'APPLICATION_PROCESS=demo_code', $v('pFlowStepId'));

  ajaxReq.addParam('x01',$v('P10_SEARCH'));
  ajaxReq.addParam('x02',$v('P10_MAX_ROWS'));
  . . .
  ```

- The `addParam()` method is not replacing the `add()` method. Each has its own unique role in the APEX AJAX framework.

  We should use the `add()` method when we want to set the values of application or page items and save these values in *Session State*.

   We can't use `add()` to set the APEX 3.1 and above `x01` to `x10` parameters. Doing so will ultimately lead to an error message.

  In version 3.1 and above we should use the `addParam()` methods to set the values of the `x01` to `x10` parameters.

   We can't use `addParam()` to set the values of the application or page items to be used in the AJAX call. Doing so will ultimately lead to an error message.

- We can't use `add()` or `addParam()` to set the parameters of a stored (package) procedure that we want to invoke with AJAX. For that, we must use the `queryString` parameter of `htmldb_Get()`.

  If we set the `queryString` parameter of `htmldb_Get()`, the system will ignore any `add()` or `addParam()` calls, and their values will not be set.

- There are several more global variables, just like the `g_x01` to `g_x10`, that are already defined in the `wwv_flow` package. It is not advisable at this point (APEX 3.1/3.2) to use these global variables as temporary variables in the AJAX related on-demand PL/SQL processes. Although it will not break anything in these versions, the APEX development team is going to use them in future versions for some other purposes. Using them now could expose your application to upgrade risks in future APEX versions.

.get(mode, startTag, endTag)

The `get()` method is the method that implements the AJAX call itself by generating the *XMLHttpRequest* object, and using its methods with the proper parameters that were constructed with the `htmldb_Get` object and its `add()` or `addParam()` methods.

The `get()` method implements a synchronize POST AJAX request. Until APEX 3.1, a synchronized AJAX call was the only mode that APEX supported. This means that the JavaScript code always waits for the server-side AJAX response before it continues with the JavaScript code flow.

A synchronized AJAX call, as APEX is using, can cause the Web browser to freeze for a moment while it waits for the server-side response. In most cases, it probably will not be noticeable, but it really depends on the complexity of the server-side logic, the amount of the AJAX-returned data, and the quality and bandwidth of the communication lines.

The mode parameter

The first parameter of `get()` is a `String` one, and it can be set to `null` or to `'XML'`. This parameter determines the data format of the AJAX response. If set to `null`, then the returned data will be a `String` JavaScript object, which should be assigned to a JavaScript variable.

JSON, in this context, is considered a JavaScript String object, so the `mode` parameter should be set to `null`.

If this parameter is set to `'XML'`, then the returned AJAX response must be formatted as a valid XML fragment. It's our responsibility, as developers, to make sure that the returned data that we are generating on the server side, as part of an on-demand PL/SQL process or a stored (packaged) procedure, is formatted properly. Failing to do so will also fail the AJAX process.

The startTag and endTag parameters

The second and third parameters are only relevant when we are pulling a clip of content from an application page using AJAX. In this case, the first parameter should be set to `null` and the `startTag` parameter should be set to a `String` that marks the starting point of the clipping; the `endTag` parameter should be set to a `String` that marks the ending point of the clipping.

Although the `startTag` and `endTag` parameters can be set to any string text on the pulled page, they should be unique so that the clipped area will be well-defined. As the clipped code is going to be injected into the AJAX caller page, using an `innerHTML` property, it's best to start the clipping with an HTML tag and end it with its closing tag. As HTML tags are usually not unique, it's best for us to embed our own unique tags to designate the starting and ending points of the clipping.

Code examples

Now, we can see a complete AJAX call:

```
var ajaxReq = new htmldb_Get(null, $v('pFlowId'),
           'APPLICATION_PROCESS=demo_code', $v('pFlowStepId'));

ajaxReq.addParam('x01',$v('P10_SEARCH'));
ajaxReq.addParam('x02',$v('P10_MAX_ROWS'));
gReturn = ajaxReq.get();
ajaxReq = null;
```

The AJAX cycle starts by creating a new instance of `htmldb_Get` and assigning it to `ajaxReq`. While doing so, we are setting the `req` parameter to be `'APPLICATION_PROCESS=demo_code'`, which means that in this AJAX call we want to invoke an on-demand PL/SQL process called `demo_code`.

Next, we set two "temporary" variables — `x01` and `x02` — with values from the AJAX calling page. The `apex_application.g_x01` and `apex_application.g_x02` will be available to us within the `demo_code` on-demand PL/SQL process.

We are firing the AJAX process by using the `get()` method. In this case, we are using `get()` without any parameters, which means that the AJAX returned response will be formatted as a JavaScript `String` object, hence we are assigning it into the `gReturn` variable, which I hope you remember is a global JavaScript variable, defined as part of the APEX supplied JavaScript library.

It's considered a "good practice" to set the pointer to the AJAX object to `null` when it ran its course. That allows the web browser engine to collect its memory and avoids memory leaks. In our example, we assign `null` to `ajaxReq`.

Let's review the following code:

```
var ajaxReq = new htmldb_Get(null, $v('pFlowId'),
           'APPLICATION_PROCESS=filter_options', $v('pFlowStepId'));
ajaxReq.add('P10_SEARCH',$v('P10_SEARCH'));
gReturn = ajaxReq.get('XML');
ajaxReq = null;
```

In this example, we are calling an on-demand PL/SQL process called `filter_options`. We are setting the value of the page item `P10_SEARCH` using the `add()` method, so it will be available to the `filter_options` on-demand process.

We are firing the AJAX process by using `get('XML')`. This means that the AJAX server response, which will be assigned to `gReturn`, must be formatted as a valid XML fragment. It is our responsibility, as developers, to make sure that the returned information will be formatted properly within the `filetr_options` on-demand process. Otherwise, the AJAX process will fail.

In the following example, we are using AJAX to clip content from one of our application pages:

```
var ajaxReq = new htmldb_Get('prev_cal',$v('pFlowId'),null,20);
ajaxReq.add('P20_CALENDAR_DATE',$v('P40_PREV_MONTH'));
ajaxReq.get(null,'<cal:clip>','</cal:clip>');
ajaxReq = null;
```

In this case, we are using the first parameter of `htmldb_Get` to determine that the AJAX returned data will be injected into a `<div id="prev_cal">` element, using its `innerHTML` property. The third parameter—`req`—is set to `null`, as we are not invoking any on-demand PL/SQL process. The fourth parameter—`page`—is set to 20. This is the page ID that we want to pull.

In the next line of code, we are using the `add()` method to set the value of the page item `P20_CALENDAR_DATE` (on the pulled page) to the value of the page item `P40_PREV_MONTH` (on the AJAX calling page).

Next, we fire the AJAX process using the `get()` methods. The first parameter is set to `null` as it's not relevant in this case. The second parameter is set to `'<cal:clip>'` and the AJAX process will start clipping the HTML code of page 404 from this tag. The clipping will end with the `</cal:clip>` tag, the value of the third parameter.

Restrictions with AJAX pulling content

When using AJAX to pull content from another application page, we should avoid clipping code that defines active page elements such as page items, buttons, or pagination components (which I'll address separately, as we can overcome this restriction).

When we create a page element on an application page, this element associates specifically with the page it was created on. This element can't be activated—i.e. submitted or `POST`ed—on any other page other than the one it was created on, unless we take special measures to allow it.

While clipping the HTML page code, the AJAX process includes **all** the code between the start and the end tags in the second and third parameters of the `get()` methods. The clipping process can't differentiate between a code that renders data and code that renders active page elements. The clipped code is injected into the calling AJAX page, using the `innerHTML` property of one of its DOM elements. If we are not careful enough it can include code to active page element(s). This/these element(s) will be rendered on the AJAX calling page. However they can't be used on their new location, as I mentioned before. If such an element is referenced on the AJAX calling page it will produce an error message saying that this element can't be found on the current page (as in the APEX metadata tables, it's associates with a different page, the one it was created on).

However, sometimes we do need to use page items on the pulled page to use them with the page logic, for example in a `WHERE` clause or as a starting date to a calendar. One such way of using these page items is to make sure that they are laid out outside the content area we are going to clip. Another option is to not render them on the page. We can do that by conditioning their display to `Never`. The APEX engine allocates a proper variable for the page item, which can be referenced in the page logic. However, the page item itself will never be rendered on the page, hence its code can't be clipped as part of the AJAX call.

Pulling report with pagination

One of the more common uses of the AJAX capability to pull content from another application page is to pull the content of a report, for example, displaying a filtered report, based on a search term, without submitting the page.

This use of AJAX requires special attention as APEX reports may include, by default, some active elements that need to be taken care of. One element is the option to highlight rows in the report. Another is the report pagination element. Both of these elements include JavaScript functions that use the report region ID (the APEX engine internal number, not the one represented by `#REGION_STATIC_ID#`). Unfortunately for us, the APEX engine hardcode the region ID into the HTML code of the application page. Moreover, the pagination element also uses the page hidden item `pFlowStepId`, which holds the application page ID. This value, naturally, is not the same on the AJAX calling page, which runs the pagination element, after it was pulled, and on the original report page, which holds the report query, in which the pagination parameters has a meaning.

A very simple solution to these problems will be to avoid the elements that cause them. Just don't use the report highlight feature and avoid pagination.

Further in the chapter, in the *Examples of using AJAX in APEX* section, we'll review an example of using AJAX to pull a report content and see how we can overcome the restrictions we just described.

.GetAsync(pVar)

The getAsync() method, introduced in APEX 3.1, extends the htmldb_Get functionality to also include an asynchronous AJAX request. An asynchronous AJAX request means that the client side initiates an AJAX request and sends it to the server. The JavaScript code flow continues without waiting for the server-side response. It's up to us, as developers, to monitor the status of the server response and act accordingly.

GetAsync() accepts a single parameter, which represents a function that will be fired each time the server-side response status changes. This is not a regular JavaScript function. It's actually a value of a property—onreadystatechange—of the *XMLHttpRequest* object that was created by GetAsync() and was assigned to a JavaScript global variable called p. We can use this p variable each time we need to reference the *XMLHttpRequest* object or one of its properties.

One of the *XMLHttpRequest* object properties we need to reference, while using asynchronous AJAX request, is the readyState property. This property reflects the status of the server-side response. It can have five different values, starting with 0, and sequentially growing to 4, which state that the server-side response has been completely accepted by the client side. In most cases, this is the status that interests us. However, each time the value of readyState changes, the function stored in onreadystatechange—the function that we used as the parameter of GetAsync()—is fired. Hence, this function should include a code that can handle all the readyState status values and take the proper action for each of them (or as it may be the case for a status other than 4, doing nothing).

Another *XMLHttpRequest* object property we can use is the responseText. In APEX context, p.responseText holds the server-side AJAX response and we can use it on the client side, just like we are using the synchronous AJAX response.

The pVar function

The function that we are using as the `pVar` parameter of `GetAsync()` can be defined as inline code or as an external (to the `getAsync()` method) function.

The following is an example of using inline code:

```
ajaxReq.GetAsync(function(){return;});
```

In this case, the function doesn't do anything, regardless of the `readyState` value.

In the following example, we are using an external function:

```
ajaxReq.GetAsync(checkAll);

function checkAll() {
  switch (p.readyState) {
    case 1:  /* The AJAX request has been set up */
      setStatusBar();
      break;
    case 2:  /* The AJAX request has been sent */
    case 3:  /* The AJAX request is in process */
      break;
    case 4:  /* The AJAX request is complete */
      clearStatusBar();
      gReturn = p.responseText;
      . . .
      break;
  }
}
```

In this example, the `checkAll` function treats the various values of `readyState` differently. At the beginning of the AJAX process, when `readyState` is changed to 1, it calls a function called `setStatusBar()`. It actually ignores the `readyState` changes to 2 and 3, and when `readyState` is changed to 4, which is the state that the AJAX request was completed, it calls the `clearStatusBar()` function and assigns the server-side response to the global `gReturn` variable. The rest of the code can be of any logic you need to implement using the AJAX request result.

The function we are using as the `pVar` parameter is not a regular JavaScript function and it can't accept parameters. However, it can call a second JavaScript function, this time a regular JavaScript function, which can accept parameters. For example:

```
ajaxReq.GetAsync(checkAll);

function checkAll() {
  if (p.readyState == 4) {
    var p_page = $v('pFlowStepId');
```

```
    checkOnPage(p_page);
  }
}

function checkOnPage(p_page) {
      . . .
}
```

 Always remember that the checkAll function will be fired for every status change of readyStatus. This means that if the logic of the function is meant to be run only after the AJAX request is completed, it should be conditioned, as in the above example.

 It's important to understand the principles and the reasoning behind the processes we are dealing with here. Please don't try to find any real logic in the above specific code. The *checkAll*, *setStatusBar*, *clearStatusBar*, and *checkOnPage* functions are all figments of my imagination, and I'm only using them to make a point.

Namespace for the APEX AJAX framework

In version 3.1, APEX started to implement a namespace strategy with its supplied JavaScript library to ensure smooth operation with other external JavaScript libraries. The apex_ns_3_1.js file contains the current APEX JavaScript namespace definitions, and it includes a namespace definition for some APEX AJAX elements – apex.ajax.

In some demo code out there, you can see a reference to apex.ajax.ondemand(). This method is a wrapper to an APEX asynchronous AJAX call. The method accepts two parameters. The first is a string parameter that includes the name of the *on-demand PL/SQL process* we wish to invoke in the AJAX process. As we are dealing with an asynchronous AJAX call, the second parameter points to the onreadystatechange function—this function is fired each time the readyStatus value changes. Usually this function processes the server-side response.

 You are encouraged to review the apex.ajax namespace in the apex_ns_3_1.js file to learn more about it.

AJAX support on the server side

So far, we covered the client-side aspects of the AJAX call. Now it's time to review the options available to us on the server side. These options should implement the logic we are seeking in the AJAX call.

Application on-demand PL/SQL process

The `htmldb_Get` third parameter—`req`—allows us to define the server-side PL/SQL process we want to invoke as part of the AJAX call. This process must be an application level **On Demand: Run this application process when requested by a page process** type of process. For short, we'll just call it *on-demand PL/SQL process*.

In future versions of APEX a full page level on-demand PL/SQL process might be implemented, but for now (APEX 3.2 and earlier), on-demand processes are available to us only on the application level, although we can call them from the page level.

The *on-demand PL/SQL process* is a regular PL/SQL anonymous block, and it can contain any valid PL/SQL code we need to implement the logic of the server-side AJAX call.

The following is a simple example of an *on-demand PL/SQL process* code:

```
declare
  l_status  varchar2(10);
begin
  begin
    select 'non-unique' into l_status
    from my_table
    where col1 = apex_application.g_x01;
  exception
    when NO_DATA_FOUND then
      l_status := 'unique';
  end;

  htp.prn(l_status);
end;
```

This process returns the value 'unique' if the value of `apex_application.g_x01` is not found in `col1` of the `my_table` table; it returns 'non-unique' if the value already exists in the table.

In the addParam section of this chapter (page 395), we mentioned the 10 pre-defined, AJAX related, global package variables that we can use with the AJAX process. At the client side, we reference them by x01 to x10. At the server side, as we are in a PL/SQL anonymous block, we must use a proper syntax for these AJAX related global package variables and properly qualify them. We have two options to do that. The first is to use the real name of the package in which they were defined — wwv_flow. In this case, we can reference wwv_flow.g_x01 to wwv_flow.g_x10. The second option is to use a pre-defined synonym of the wwv_flow package — apex_application. In this case, we'll reference apex_application.g_x01 (as in the example code) to apex_application.g_x10.

The *on-demand PL/SQL process* must be able to return the AJAX server-side response — the result of the PL/SQL logic — to the JavaScript function that initiated the AJAX call. We can do this by using the Oracle supplied procedure htp.prn. In this context, you can treat the htp.prn procedure as the return statement of the *on-demand PL/SQL process*.

Unlike the return statement of a function, you can call the htp.prn procedure as many times as you need, and the AJAX server-side response will be compiled from all the htp.prn calls (the response will be a concatenation of all the htp.prn calls).

Stored (packaged) procedure

Although using an application level *on-demand PL/SQL process* is the most common way to implement the AJAX server-side component, the htmldb_Get() constructor also allows us to invoke stored (packaged) procedures, which were defined outside the APEX environment, as part of the AJAX server-side logic. We can use the htmldb_Get() sixth parameter — proc — to name the stored (packaged) procedure we want to invoke, and the seventh parameter — queryString — to pass the needed parameters to the procedure (as we described in the htmldb_Get section).

As with all the stored (packaged) procedures we want to invoke, from within our APEX application, the AJAX invoked procedures should also be "APEX compatible", i.e. they should use bind variables and the v() / nv() functions to access APEX items and *Session State* values.

Handling errors in the AJAX process

The APEX AJAX framework doesn't excel in error handling. The AJAX process doesn't generate an error report on the APEX level. That means that the APEX application is not stopped due to an error in the AJAX process. It is up to us, as developers, to inspect the server-side response and determine if the AJAX process was successful.

One indication of a failed AJAX process is a server-side response of `null`. This will happen if the APEX engine was not able to run the server-side logic, such as in the case of security or privileges issues (including APEX authentication, authorization, and page access control failures), or any other error that the APEX engine found in the PL/SQL code that doesn't generate a specific database error. In cases where database or Web server (`mod_plsql`) errors were generated, the server-side response will include them but no other error message will be issued.

Debugging a failed AJAX process

Debugging a failed AJAX process should include several stages. The first one is to use the JavaScript `alert()` function to display the server-side returned value. If we are lucky, and the returned value includes an error message, we should resolve this first. If, however, the returned response is empty we should move to the next step.

We should determine if the communication between the client side — the specific AJAX calling page — and the server side is working properly. We can do that by setting the *on-demand PL/SQL process* to a very minimal and simple code. For example:

```
htp.prn('Hello from the server side');
```

If the returned value includes this message, the AJAX communication is working fine. If, however, the returned response is still empty it probably means that you have a security issue. The most common error in this category is to initiate an AJAX call from a public page alongside using page 0, which *Require Authentication*, as the `page` parameter in `htmldb_Get()`. The solution in this case is very simple. Replace page 0 with `$v('pFlowStepId')`.

 Using `$v('pFlowStepId')` as the default `page` parameter for `htmldb_Get()`, as we recommend, will prevent this type of error.

If the AJAX communication is working fine, and no specific error message is returned from the server, but we are still not getting the AJAX server-side response we expect, it usually means that the PL/SQL code is not working properly. One of the common problems in this case is a syntax error with a bind variable—the code contains a bind variable name that doesn't exist. No error message is generated, but the PL/SQL code doesn't work. In these cases, I recommend that you copy the PL/SQL code to the APEX *SQL Commands* utility and try to debug it in there. This is also what you need to do if the AJAX process returns a wrong response from the application logic point of view.

Examples of using AJAX in APEX

The Internet, in general, and the APEX forum on OTN, in particular, (http://forums.oracle.com/forums/forum.jspa?forumID=137) are filled with AJAX examples for the more common tasks, such as cascading items (the value of one item depends on the value of another), querying the database, etc. The APEX development team has also released a white paper—Using AJAX in your Application (http://www.oracle.com/technology/obe/hol08/apexweb20/ajax_otn.htm), which also includes some AJAX examples for APEX. So, in this section, I'll try to bring examples, which adds more value, especially to the APEX environment.

In the demo application that accompanies this book you can find examples of using AJAX to enhance the functionality of APEX, and overcome some "out-of-the-box" limitations. In the following sections, we'll review two of them.

Multiple calendars on a single application page

The **Create Calendar** wizard supports only a single calendar per application page. The application page **Multi Calendars on a single page**, from the demo application demonstrates how we can use AJAX to display three related calendars on the same application page. The idea is to have a "regular" main calendar, which will be in the center of the page functionality, and two smaller calendars at its side, which will display the previous and next months, relative to the displayed month of the main calendar This is shown in the following screenshot:

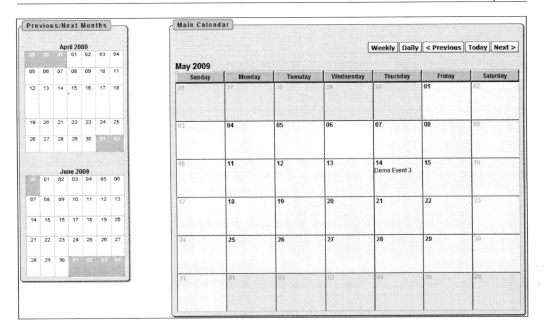

We are going to use a separate page to create the smaller calendars, and from the main page, use AJAX to clip and inject them into it.

The calendar main page (page xx)

On the main page there are two regions. The first holds the smaller calendars and the second holds the main calendar.

The 'Previous/Next Month' region

The **Region Source** section of this region includes the following code:

```
<div id="prev_cal">
</div>
 <br />
 <br />
<div id="next_cal">
</div>
```

We are using two, uniquely identified, `<div>` tags as placeholders for the small calendars. The AJAX process will inject the clipped calendars into these `<div>` tags.

The 'Main Calendar' region

This is the main region on page and it includes a wizard created, SQL based, calendar. The SQL query I've used is very simple and basic:

```
select edate, description
from events
```

On top of the standard hidden items created by the **Create Calendar** wizard — Pxx_CALENDAR_DATE and Pxx_CALENDAR_TYPE, I've added two **Hidden and Protected** items — Pxx_NEXT_MONTH and Pxx_PREV_MONTH. We are going to use these items as the base date for the smaller calendars. As their value should be relative to the main calendar displayed month, I'm using the following **After Header PL/SQL Anonymous Block** process to compute them:

```
-- For the first page load
if v('Pxx_CALENDAR_DATE') is null then
  :Pxx_CALENDAR_DATE := to_char(sysdate,'YYYYMMDD');
end if;

-- For the others
:Pxx_NEXT_MONTH := to_char(to_date(add_months(to_char(to_date(:Pxx_
  CALENDAR_DATE,'YYYYMMDD')),1)),'YYYYMMDD');

:Pxx_PREV_MONTH := to_char(to_date(add_months(to_char(to_date(:Pxx_
  CALENDAR_DATE,'YYYYMMDD')),-1)),'YYYYMMDD');
```

Now, we are ready for the AJAX call, which I placed in the **Region Footer**:

```
<script type="text/javascript">

var ajaxReq = new htmldb_Get('prev_cal', $v('pFlowId'),
    null,yy);
ajaxReq.add('Pyy_CALENDAR_DATE',$v('Pxx_PREV_MONTH'));
ajaxReq.get(null,'<cal:clip>','</cal:clip>');

ajaxReq = null;

var ajaxReq = new htmldb_Get('next_cal', $v('pFlowId'),
    null,yy);
ajaxReq.add('Pyy_CALENDAR_DATE',$v('Pxx_NEXT_MONTH'));
ajaxReq.get(null,'<cal:clip>','</cal:clip>');

ajaxReq = null;

</script>
```

We are using two separate AJAX calls, one for each small calendar we want to pull. As these calls are synchronous calls (we are using the get() method), it's not a problem.

The first htmldb_Get parameter—obj—is set to 'prev_cal' in the first AJAX call and to 'next_cal' in the second one. Hence, the clipped small calendar code will be injected into the corresponding <div> tags using their innerHTML property.

The page parameter in both calls, are set to yy—the page ID we are going to pull.

The Pyy_CALENDAR_DATE is the base date item for the small calendar. In the next line of code, after creating a new instance of htmldb_Get, we are setting its value, in *Session State*, using the add() method (as we are setting the value of a page item, we are not using addParam()). On the first AJAX call, we are setting its value using the Pxx_PREV_MONTH item, and in the next call we are using the Pxx_NEXT_MONTH item. This technique allows us to use a single page to create the small calendars, but to receive different result each time it's pulled.

Now, we are ready to fire the AJAX call itself using the get() method. As we are using the AJAX call to pull content from another page, the first get() parameter is set to null, as the result is formatted as a String. The next parameter is set to '<cal:clip>', and the third one to '</cal:clip>'. These parameters represent unique tags on the pulled page, and mark the boundaries of the clipped content. We'll return to these tags shortly.

This concludes our AJAX related actions on the main page, and we can start reviewing the page we are pulling the content from.

The small calendars page (page yy)

Before creating this page we already know that we want to use the APEX **Small Calendar** template as the base template of the clipped calendar, so we need to modify it to answer the AJAX clipping needs, mainly to include start and end tags and to mark the boundaries of the content we want to clip. As a "best practice" I always try not to change APEX pre-defined templates. As such, in the **Template** section of the *Shared Components* module, I've created a copy of the **Small Calendar** template and named it **Small Calendar—AJAX**.

I've chosen to edit the newly created template, and in the **Monthly Calendar** tab under the **Month Format** section, I've added the `<cal:clip>` tag as the first line in the **Month Title Format** field, as can be seen in the following screenshot:

```
Month Formats

Month Title Format
<cal:clip>
<table cellspacing="0" cellpadding="0" border="0" summary=""
class="t10SmallCalendarHolder">
  <tr>
    <td class="t10MonthTitle">#IMONTH# #YYYY#</td>
  </tr>
```

Next, I added the closing tag `</cal:clip>`, as the last line in the **Month Close Format** field, as can be seen in the next screenshot:

```
Month Close Format
</table></td>
</tr>
</table>
</cal:clip>
```

Saving these changes ended my work on the template. Now, we are ready to create the page that contains the small calendar we want to clip.

This page was created with the **Create Calendar** wizard using the following SQL query:

```
select edate, '*' description
from events
```

Every day in the calendar which holds information will be marked by an asterisk (*).

In the **Calendar Attributes** tab I chose **Small Calendar – AJAX** as the **Calendar Template**. Next, and as we don't want to clip any active elements from this page, I've deleted all the buttons that were created by the **Create Calendar** wizard. Moreover, as we are not going to submit the page – it will only run in the server background as part of the AJAX process, I also deleted all the processes the wizard created since we don't need them either.

This concludes the work on this page, and now it's ready to be pulled by the AJAX process.

Remember:

In real life, you should replace the xx and yy with actual page numbers in your application.

As you can see, a pretty simple AJAX process, with a bit of preparation (mainly minor changes to a pre-defined template, and very simple HTML code for a region source) allows us to overcome the APEX "out-of-the-box" limitation of supporting single calendar per page. The example we reviewed here is very simple and very basic. Taking all you have learned in the Calendar chapter, it can be expanded to include other, more complex functionalities. The lesson should be that if you understand the technology and how to utilize it, you can set the bar very high.

In the next section, we'll review another example that will help us overcome one of APEX limitations, this time using asynchronous AJAX request.

Checkbox persistence in Tabular Forms (Reports)

One of the problems we are facing with *Tabular Forms* is that pagination doesn't submit the current view of the *Tabular Form (Report)* page, and if we are using *Partial Page Refresh* (PPR), it doesn't even reload the entire page. As such, *Session State* is not saved prior to us moving to the next/previous view. Without saving *Session State*, all the changes that we might have made to the current form view will be lost upon using pagination. This problematic behavior is most notable when we are using a checkboxes column in our *Tabular Form (Report)*. We can mark specific checkboxes in the current *Tabular Form (Report)* view, but if we paginate to another view, and then return, the marked checkboxes will be cleared (no *Session State*, no history to rely on).

In some cases, it can be very useful to save the marked checkboxes while paginating through the *Tabular Form (Report)*. Joel Kallman, from the APEX development team, blogged about this issue (`http://joelkallman.blogspot.com/2008/03/preserving-checked-checkboxes-in-report.html`) and offered a simple solution, which uses AJAX and APEX collections. Using APEX collections means that the marked checkboxes will be preserved for the duration of a specific user's current APEX session. If that's what you need, Joel's solution is very good as it utilizes built-in APEX resources in an optimal way. However, sometimes the current APEX session is not persistent enough. In one of my applications I needed more lasting persistence, which can be used crossed APEX users and sessions. So, I took Joel's idea and modified it a bit. Instead of using APEX collections, I've decided to save the checked checkboxes into a database table. The database table, of course, can support unlimited persistence across users.

My original implementation (multiple mailing lists functionality) is too long and complicated to be used in a book, so the following example is a simplified version of it, however it includes all the elements and principles I want to demonstrate. You can see it in work as part of the demo application accompanying this book.

Report on CUSTOMERS

We are going to use a simple report on the CUSTOMERS table, where the first column is a checkboxes column. The following is a screenshot of the report region:

Report on CUSTOMERS

	Full Name	Address (line 1)	Address (line 2)	City	Zip (postal) Code	State	Country
☐	Andrew Dolbert	34 Willow Road		Birmingham	B30 2AS		United Kingdom
☐	Carol Fisher	550 Main Street		Oneonta	13820	New York	U.S.A
☐	Chrles Hansly	81 Lily Road		Birmingham	B26 1TE		United Kingdom
☐	Danis Silver	Burkoff	132 Nassau St.	New York	10038	New York	U.S.A
☐	David Fish	50 S 3rd Ave.	Point Varnon	New York	10550	New York	U.S.A
☐	Jacob Hamish	99 Mandeville Court		London	E4 4ED		United Kingdom
☐	James Robson	55 Buckland Road		London	E10 6Qs		United Kingdom
☐	Joel Robinson	2370 E Main Street	#103	Columbus	43209	Ohio	U.S.A
☐	Jully Ackerman	1000 east Street		Ohio	61349	Illinois	U.S.A
☐	Keren Kelly	155 Cromwell Road		Manchester			United Kingdom

row(s) 1 - 10 of 19   ▾   Next ▷

We are going to use AJAX to preserve the status of the checkboxes in the following scenarios:

- Using the checkbox in the header of the first column to check or clear all the checkboxes in the first column of the current report view

- Individual row check or clearing of a checkbox

The first column—the checkboxes column—represents the CUST_ID column of the CUSTOMERS table, and we are going to implement persistence by saving the values of this column, for all the checked rows, in a table called CUSTOMERS_VIP. This table includes only one column:

```
CREATE TABLE  "CUSTOMERS_VIP" (
  "CUST_ID" NUMBER(7,0) NOT NULL ENABLE,
   CONSTRAINT "CUSTOMERS_VIP_PK" PRIMARY KEY ("CUST_ID") ENABLE
)
```

Bear in mind:

In this particular example we are talking about crossed APEX users and sessions persistence. If, however, you need to maintain a specific user-level persistence, as it happens natively when using APEX collections, you can add a second column to the table that can hold the APP_USER of the user. In this case, you'll need to amend the appropriate WHERE clauses and the INSERT statements, to include and reflect the second column.

The report SQL query

The following is the SQL code used for the report:

```
SELECT
   apex_item.checkbox(10,l.cust_id,'onclick=updateCB(this);',
      r.cust_id) as cust_id,
   l.cust_name, l.cust_address1, l.cust_address2,
   l.cust_city, l.cust_zip_code,
   (select r1.sname
    from states r1
    where l.cust_state = r1.code) state,
   (select r2.cname
    from countries r2
    where l.cust_country = r2.code) country
FROM customers l,
      customers_vip r
WHERE r.cust_id (+) = l.cust_id
ORDER BY cust_name
```

The Bold segments of the SELECT statement are the ones we are most interested in.

The APEX_ITEM.CHECKBOX function creates a checkboxes column in the report. Its third parameter—p_attributes—allows us to define HTML attributes within the checkbox <input> tag. We are using this parameter to attach an onclick event to every checkbox in the column. The event fires a JavaScript function—updateCB(this)—which takes the current checkbox object as a parameter and initiates an AJAX process.

The fourth parameter of the APEX_ITEM.CHECKBOX function—p_checked_values—allows us to determine the initial status of the checkbox. If the value of this parameter is equal to the value of the checkbox (determined by the second parameter—p_value) the checkbox will be checked. This parameter is the heart of the solution. Its value is taken from the CUSTOMERS_VIP table using outer join with the value of the checkbox. The outcome is that every time the CUSTOMER_VIP table contains a CUST_ID value equal to the current checkbox value, this checkbox will be checked.

The report headers

In the **Report Attributes** tab we can set the report headers using the **Custom** option. We are going to use this option to set friendlier report headers, but mostly to define the first column header—a checkbox that allows us to toggle the status of all the column checkboxes.

The full HTML code we are using for the header of the first column is:

```
<input type="checkbox" id = "CB" onclick="toggleAll(this,10);"
title="Mark/Clear All">
```

We are actually creating a checkbox, with an ID of CB and an onclick event that fires the JavaScript function toggleAll(this,10). The first parameter of this function is a reference to the checkbox object, and the second one is the first parameter—p_idx—of the APEX_ITEM.CHECKBOX function we are using to create the checkbox column.

The AJAX client-side JavaScript functions

So far, we have mentioned two JavaScript functions that initiate an AJAX call. The first—updateCB()—initiates an AJAX call that updates the CUSTOMERS_VIP file according to the status of a single (row) checkbox. The second one—toggleAll()—initiates an AJAX call that updates the CUSTOMERS_VIP file according to the status of the entire checkboxes column. Let's review these functions.

The updateCB() JavaScript function

The following is the code of this function:

```
function updateCB(pItem){
  var get = new htmldb_Get(null, $v('pFlowId'),
      'APPLICATION_PROCESS=update_CB',$v('pFlowStepId'));

  get.addParam('x01',pItem.value);
  get.addParam('x02',pItem.checked);

  get.GetAsync(function(){return;});

  get = null;
}
```

The function accepts, as a parameter, a reference to an object—this—that points
to the checkbox we just clicked. We are using this reference to set the temporary
item x01 to the value of the checkbox and x02 to its status (checked/unchecked).
As we are using the AJAX related temporary items, we are using the addParam()
method to do so. These items will be available to us in the *on-demand PL/SQL process*
update_CD, which implements the server-side logic of this AJAX call. We stated
this process in the third parameter of the htmldb_Get constructor function—
'APPLICATION_PROCESS=update_CB'.

> In this example, we are using the name 'get' for the variable referencing
> the new instance of htmldb_Get object. The use of this name is very
> common in many AJAX examples, especially on the OTN APEX forum,
> and its related examples.

As we'll see when we review the server-side logic of this AJAX call, all it does is
update—insert or delete—the content of the CUSTOMERS_VIP table. As such, it doesn't
have an immediate effect on the client side, and we don't need to wait for its result.
This is a classic case for us to use an *asynchronous* AJAX call. We do so by using the
GetAsync() method. In this specific case, as the client side doesn't need to process
any server response, we can use an empty function as the GetAsync() parameter.

The toggleAllCB() JavaScript function

The following is the related code for this function:

```
function toggleAll(pItem,pIdx){
  var l_fname;

  if (pIdx < 10) {
    l_fname = 'f0' + pIdx;
  }
  else {
    l_fname = 'f' + pIdx;
  }

  var elm = document.getElementsByName(l_fname);
  var status = pItem.checked;
  for (i=0; i < elm.length; i++) {
    elm[i].checked = status;
  }

  var get = new htmldb_Get(null, $v('pFlowId'),
      'APPLICATION_PROCESS=updateCB_all',$v('pFlowStepId'));

  get.addParam('x01',array_to_string(elm));
  get.addParam('x02',pItem.checked);

  get.GetAsync(function(){return;});

  get = null;
}

function array_to_string(pArr) {
  var str = '';

  for (i=0; i< pArr.length; i++) {
    str = str + pArr[i].value + ':'
  }
  str = str.substr(0,str.length-1);
  return (str);
}
```

In the first step of the function, it uses the second parameter—pIdx—to construct the HTML name of the checkboxes column. Using that name, the function collects all the column elements into an array called elm.

Using the first parameter—pItem—the function determines the status of the column header checkbox and uses this status to check/clear all the elements in the elm array.

In the next step, we are passing the `elm` array, as a parameter, to another JavaScript function—`array_to_string()`. This function takes the `elm` elements and generates a single colon-delimited string out of them. We are using this string as the value of `x01`, setting it with the `addParam()` method. Using the same method, we are setting `x02` to the status of the column header checkbox.

As usual, the `x01` and `x02` will be available to us inside the on-demand PL/SQL process `updateCB_all`, which is the server-side logic in this AJAX call, as it was defined while generating a new instance of the `htmld_Get` object.

All the reasons that led us to use asynchronous AJAX call in the `updateCB()` function are still valid for the `toggleAll()` function so the AJAX request is fired using the `GetAsync()` method. As we still don't need to process any server response, the parameter of `GetAsync()` is an empty function in this case.

The header_CB_Status() JavaScript function

This function doesn't fire any AJAX process. However it helps us to maintain the proper functionality and status of the column header checkbox. Just as we need special processes to preserve the status of the "regular" column checkboxes (because of the absence of *Session State*), we need special process to preserve, or in this case to compute, the proper status of the column header checkbox. This checkbox should be checked if all the checkboxes in the column are checked.

```
function header_CB_Status(pItem, pIdx){
  var status = true;
  var l_name;

  if (pIdx < 10) {
    l_fname = 'f0' + pIdx;
  }
  else {
    l_fname = 'f' + pIdx;
  }

  elms = document.getElementsByName(l_fname);
  for (i=0; i < elms.length; i++) {

    if (!elms[i].checked){
      status = false;
    }
  }
  $x(pItem).checked = status;
}
```

This function accepts the same parameters as the `toggleAll()` function, and it also uses them in a similar manner. At first, `header_CB_Status()` generates the proper HTML name for the checkboxes column, and with this name, it collects all the column checkbox elements into the `elm` array. Next, it passes through all the elements in the array and determines if all the checkboxes in the column are checked. If they are, the function checks the column header checkbox.

As our example deals with a cross APEX session persistence situation, a case where the first view of the report includes a full checked first column, is possible and valid (for example, a different user, or even you in a previous APEX session, checked all the entries of the report first view). Hence, the `header_CB_status()` function should be fired the first time the report is loaded and after that, every time pagination is used. Locating a call to `header_CB_status()` in the report **Region Footer** will fire the function for the first view of the report, and if we are **not** using the *PPR* option (*Partial Page Refresh*) it will also be fired for every pagination action.

```
Region Footer
<script type="text/javascript">
header_CB_Status('CB',10);
</script>
```

Using the *PPR* option makes things a bit more complicated, as the page is not reloaded upon pagination, so the JavaScript function located at the **Region Footer** will not be fired. In this case, we must involve the pagination code itself.

The pagination code is generated based on the **Pagination Subtemplate** section of the report template. As report templates are accessible to us, this is a good place to add a call to the `header_CB_status()` function. I created a copy of the report **Standard** template, and because the JavaScript function includes very specific parameters, I named it '**Standard—page xx**'.

The following is a screenshot of the **Next Page Template** section of the report template, **prior** to any changes:

```
Next Page Template
<a href="#LINK#" class="t10pagination">#PAGINATION_NEXT#<img
src="#IMAGE_PREFIX#themes/theme_10/paginate_next.gif" alt="Next"></a>
```

The active pagination code, as the APEX engine generates it, is "hiding" under the #LINK# *Substitution String*. As this code includes specific, hardcoded details pertaining to the report region, we don't want to change or tamper with it. It will stay as is. In addition, and as we want header_CB_status() to be fired after the pagination action, we'll add it just after the #LINK#. The new template code should look similar to the following:

```
Next Page Template
<a href="#LINK# header_CB_Status('CB',10);" class="t10pagination">#PAGINATION_NEXT#<img
src="#IMAGE_PREFIX#themes/theme_10/paginate_next.gif" alt="Next"></a>
```

At runtime, after the APEX engine replaced #LINK# with its code, we are getting a similar code to the following:

```
<a href="javascript:$a_report('6076516344846584',
   '11','10','10'); header_CB_Status('CB',10);" class=
"t10pagination">Next
<img  src="/i/themes/theme_10/paginate_next.gif"
 alt="Next"></a>
```

This is exactly the code we need. The header_CB_Status() function will be fired as part of the pagination action, but only after the pagination process itself (which also uses AJAX) has finished and a new report view has been injected into place.

After duplicating this action to all the other pagination templates in the **Pagination Subtemplate** section, our column header checkbox status will be updated with every pagination action.

This concludes our work on the client side.

The AJAX server-side processes

There are two **On Demand PL/SQL Anonymous Block** processes involved in this AJAX example server side.

update_CB

This process, which is called from the JavaScript function updateCB(), updates the CUSTOMERS_VIP table with the status of a specific row checkbox in the report view.

```
declare
  l_code    number;
  l_status varchar2(10);
```

```
begin

  l_status := wwv_flow.g_x02;
  l_code := to_number(wwv_flow.g_x01);

  if l_status = 'true' then
     insert into customers_vip
     values(l_code);
  else
     delete from customers_vip
     where cust_id = l_code;
  end if;
end;
```

As we are in a PL/SQL anonymous block, we must use a proper syntax for the global package variables. In this example, we are qualifying the variable by using the original name of the package—wwv_flow.g_x01, which stands for the x01 in the client-side JavaScript code, and wwv_flow.g_x02, which stands for x02.

updateCB_all

This process, which is called from the JavaScript function toggleAll(), updates the CUSTOMERS_VIP table with the status of the entire column checkboxes for the current report view.

```
declare
  l_vc_arr2 APEX_APPLICATION_GLOBAL.VC_ARR2;
begin
  l_vc_arr2 := APEX_UTIL.STRING_TO_TABLE(apex_application.g_x01);

  if apex_application.g_x02 = 'true' then
    FOR i IN 1..l_vc_arr2.count LOOP
       begin
         insert into customers_vip
         values(l_vc_arr2(i));
       exception
         when others then null;
       end;
    end loop;
  else
    FOR i IN 1..l_vc_arr2.count LOOP
      delete from customers_vip
      where cust_id = l_vc_arr2(i);
    end loop;
  end if;
end;
```

In this example, we are qualifying the global package variable by using the wwv_flow package synonym apex_application. So first, we are using apex_application. g_x01—a colon delimited string that was generated by the JavaScript array_to_ string() function and includes all the column checkboxes values—as a parameter to the APEX built-in apex_util.string_to_table() function. The result is a PL/SQL array—l_vc_arr2 that holds all the values we need to insert into, or delete from, the CUSTOMERS_VIP table. The exact nature of the DML operation—insert or delete—is determined by the value of apex_application.g_x02, which holds the status of the column header checkbox.

As can be seen in the code of both these on-demand PL/SQL processes, it doesn't generate any server-side response. Hence, the client side doesn't have to wait for the server side, we can use an asynchronous AJAX call and we don't have to define a function to deal with the server response.

This concludes our discussion on the AJAX server-side aspects, and by that we have finished reviewing all the relevant AJAX aspects of this example.

Bear in mind:

For simplicity sake, we ignored concurrency control in a multi-user environment. As the persistence we are using is crossed APEX users, all the users access the same table and the same records. We should ensure that only one user at a time will use the report and change its checked records. Otherwise, the final result will be a mess.

Summary

In this chapter, we reviewed the AJAX framework within APEX. We learned about the basic principles of the AJAX technology and how APEX implements them using both synchronous and asynchronous mode of communication. Finally, we reviewed an example(s) of how we can use AJAX to enrich our application UI and user experience and how we can use AJAX to overcome some APEX "out-of-the-box" limitations.

In the next chapter, we are going to deal with the APEX translation mechanism and see how we can develop multi-lingual APEX applications.

18
Globalization and Localization With APEX Applications

APEX, with its **IDE (Integrated Development Environment)** and its generated product, the developed APEX applications, was designed to support **Globalization** and **Localization**.

APEX supports *Globalization* by including several built-in mechanisms and wizards that allow us to implement the *Localization* we need, separately from the application logic. One of these mechanisms is the APEX built-in text translation mechanism, which uses the **XLIFF (XML Localization Interchange File Format)** standard.

In this chapter, we'll try to understand what *Globalization* and *Localization* support means and how APEX achieves it. We'll review the following APEX features and capabilities:

- **Native IDE support of multiple languages**: The APEX IDE can be run under 10 different User Interface languages—English and nine more.

- **Multi language support**: APEX applications currently support 132 languages, dialects, and territories (locales) as the APEX application primary language. We can develop applications for these languages under each of the 10 languages supported by the APEX IDE.

- **Developing multi-lingual applications**: The same APEX application logic can be run under several UI languages. As we'll see, APEX gives us several options to derive and set the UI language.

We'll pay special attention to the APEX built-in translation mechanism and how we can use it to develop APEX applications that support a variety of languages. It also includes those languages written from Right-To-Left (e.g. Arabic and Hebrew), which will be reviewed in The next chapter.

So let's start by clarifying what we are talking about.

A brief introduction to Globalization and Localization

If we are going to deal with *Globalization* and *Localization*, it only makes sense that we'll define them first, so we are all speaking the same language.

Globalization

Globalization support, in the context of a RAD tool, is the ability of the development environment to support developing applications that perform well and correctly in a multiple languages and locales environment, regardless of the core application logic.

APEX was designed with *Globalization* in mind. It includes several wizards and mechanisms that allow us to implement the *Localization* we need and operate in a multi-lingual environment.

APEX includes options for setting the primary application language (which can be different from the language of the APEX IDE) and how it should be derived. Its *Import/Export* mechanism allows us to import external files in various languages and encodings and to export CSV files that match the application language and encoding, as well as the local desktop NLS (*National Language Support*) parameters. Moreover, APEX includes several built-in features that support the implementation of the *Localization* features we need, including text translation, date format, local currency support, decimal and group separator characters, and more. The APEX engine supports *Globalization* by automatically performing some pre-defined *Localization* related statements that adjust the **database** session NLS parameters, according to the APEX application *Globalization* parameters. As we are talking about adjusting the database session, and not the APEX session, the APEX engine runs these statements at the beginning of every SHOW and ACCEPT procedure.

 You can follow these *Localization* related statements while running the APEX application page in a *debug* mode.

The APEX *Globalization* support can be used regardless of the core application logic. The *Localization* features of the APEX application can be implemented in any phase of the application development cycle without the need to change this core logic. However, as we'll see later in the chapter, if you know you'll need to implement *Globalization*, it's better to plan ahead.

Localization

Localization is the process of using the *Globalization* support to adapt the application to support a specific language and locale.

APEX has several built-in mechanisms and wizards that allow us to take advantage of the APEX *Globalization* support and implement *Localization* for 132 different languages, dialects, and locales. All of that is done without any direct interference with, or any need to change, the core APEX application logic. Moreover, APEX allows us to use the same core application logic with different *Localization* implementations—a single APEX application that can simultaneously run under multilingual *User Interface*, with several options on how to derive/set the desired UI language.

Although localized support can be added to the APEX application at any point in the development cycle, we'll see that planning ahead can make *Localization* easier and optimal. If there is any chance that your application will need to be localized, it is prudent to consider it from the beginning and plan it properly (e.g. proper character set support in the database using translatable components, etc.). More specific details will follow later.

Native IDE support of multiple languages

The primary language of the APEX IDE is English, and the initial APEX instance is installed in that language. However, the APEX IDE also supports a *User Interface* that has been translated into nine more languages—German, Spanish, French, Italian, Japanese, Korean, Brazilian Portuguese, Simplified Chinese, and Traditional Chinese. Each of these languages can be loaded into the APEX IDE to transform the entire development environment—mainly the UI, the internal messages of the APEX engine, and error messages—to be displayed in the loaded languages. If more than one language has been loaded, then the language setting of the local browser will determine the language of the APEX IDE.

Multiple APEX IDE languages don't mean multiple APEX instances. As we'll see in the APEX installation appendix, each database can only hold a single APEX instance. This rule still applies. We are talking about a single APEX instance that supports multiple APEX IDE languages.

Loading another language into APEX IDE

All the necessary files to load the supported languages into the APEX IDE are distributed with the standard APEX distribution file. In the directory where you have unzipped the APEX distribution file (as part of the installation process), under the `apex\builder` directory, you'll find nine more directories, each named according to the language code it holds. For example, the directory `apex\builder\fr` holds all the necessary script files to load French into the APEX IDE.

> The *Managing Application Globalization* chapter, in the APEX documentation, includes a table of all the languages that APEX supports. From this table you can learn the language code and the associated NLS_LANGUAGE and `NLS_TERRITORY` parameters of each supported language.

Prior to installing another language into the APEX IDE we should check that the database character set supports that language. Otherwise, the operation will not be a success. The **AL32UTF8** character set supports all the languages that can be loaded into the APEX IDE. In fact, this character set supports all the languages that we can use as our APEX application primary or translated language, so it will be a good choice to make.

We should set the value of the environment variable `NLS_LANG` regardless of the database character set or the language we are going to load. We must set the character set segment of this variable to *AL32UTF8*. For example, if we are in a Windows environment, and we want to load French into the APEX IDE, then we should set `NLS_LANG` similar to the following:

```
set NLS_LANG=FRENCH_FRANCE.AL32UTF8
```

We can use *SQL*Plus*, connected as *SYS* with the *SYSDBA* role, to run the language loading script. In each of the supported language directories you can find a specific language loading script named according to the pattern `load_<lang>.sql`. For example, in the `apex/builder/fr` directory, it will be named `load_fr.sql`.

Although the use of this script is very well documented in the *Oracle Application Express Installation Guide*, I recommend that you use another script—`load_trans.sql`. This is a generic script that requires less manual coding and can be found in the root of the APEX distribution files in the `apex` directory, where all the other 'regular' installation scripts are found.

The `load_trans.sql` accepts the name of the language we wish to load into the APEX IDE as the parameter, using all capital letters. Hence, the legal parameter values are:

Language name	Language code
BRAZILIAN PORTUGUESE	pt-br
FRENCH	fr
GERMAN	de
ITALIAN	it
JAPANESE	ja
KOREAN	ko
SIMPLIFIED CHINESE	zh-cn
SPANISH	es
TRADITIONAL CHINESE	zh-tw

If no parameter is given, then the default installation language is German.

 We can use SQL*Plus, connected as SYS with the SYSDBA role, to also run the `load_trans.sql` script.

The translated language of the APEX IDE UI does not necessarily determine the primary language of the developed APEX application. As we have already mentioned, APEX can support 132 different languages, dialects, and locales, and each of them can be used under each of the APEX IDE supported languages. This means that we can, for example, develop an English APEX application using French translated APEX IDE UI.

Unloading the APEX IDE translated language

Loading another language into the APEX IDE is a reversible operation. In each of the supported language directories you can find a specific language unloading script, named according to the pattern `unload_<lang>.sql`. For example, to unload the Italian language from the APEX IDE, you should go to the `apex/builder/it` directory and run the `unload_it.sql` script using *SQL*Plus*.

> You should run the unloaded language script, while connected as the APEX owner user. For APEX 3.2, it's *APEX_030200*. For previous versions, the format of the APEX owner name is FLOWS_xxxxxx, where xxxxxx stands for the version number, like 030100 or 020200.
>
> If you choose to connect as *SYS* (with the *SYSDBA* role), you should set the current schema to the APEX owner schema, e.g. ALTER SESSION SET CURRENT_SCHEMA = FLOWS_030100.

Bear in mind that unloading a language from the APEX IDE will immediately affect the application that was developed under this language. For example, if we use the translated Italian UI to develop an APEX application with Italian as its primary language, then all the internal report engine messages (e.g. page 1 of 10) would be displayed in Italian, as all these messages that were translated into Italian, were added to the APEX messages repository when loading the language. Unloading the language will also unload all these translated messages, and all the internal APEX engine messages will be displayed in English.

Loading another language into APEX Runtime Environment

APEX also supports loading all the native supported languages into the APEX Runtime Environment. All the setup preparations that were discussed for loading supported languages into the APEX ID also apply to the Runtime Environment.

For loading the supported languages into the Runtime Environment, we should assume the role of the APEX owner (as explained in the previous section). For the Runtime Environment we don't have a generic script to load the supported languages, so we need to use a specific script for each language. The script can be found in the correlated language directories under the name pattern of rt_<lang>.sql. Hence, if we want to load the French language into our APEX Runtime Environment, we should go to the apex/builder/fr directory and run the rt_fr.sql script.

Multi-language support

It's only natural that we'll be able to develop applications that support the APEX IDE language we've used during development. However, APEX allows us to develop applications in various other languages that are not natively supported by the APEX IDE UI. In these cases, translation starts playing its role, as we need to translate the internal messages that the APEX engine is using in its user dialogs.

First, we need to define the primary language of the application and how we want to derive it. The APEX IDE will allow us to define all we need to implement the *Localization* that fits the chosen language and locale.

How do we start Globalization support?

While creating a new application, we can define the most basic parameters to start *Globalization* support. The following screenshot is taken from the **Create Application** wizard, under the **Attributes** tab:

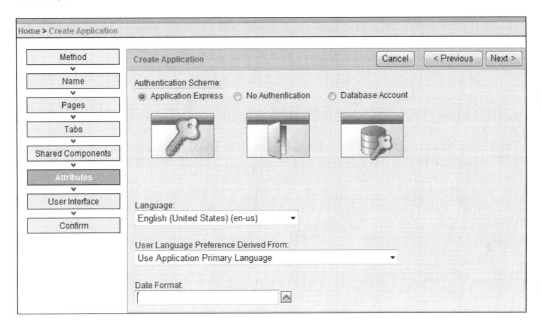

Setting the APEX application language

First, we need to choose the primary language of the application. The default language is the language of the APEX IDE. However, we can choose any language we need out of the 132 supported languages in the select list.

Next, we need to determine how to derive the end user UI language. We have the following five options:

- **No NLS (Application not translated)**: This option should be chosen if no translation is taking place in the developed APEX application. This can happen only if the developed application language matches the APEX IDE language.

- **Use Application Primary Language**: This option should be chosen if we always want to use the APEX application's primary language (regardless of any local settings), and this language is different from the language of the APEX IDE. In this case, as we'll see further in the chapter, we need to use the APEX translation mechanism.

- **Browser (use browser language preference)**: This option is effective only if the APEX application has been translated into more than one language, and it should be chosen if we want to derive the APEX application language from the local Web browser configuration. The APEX application language will be set according to the Web browser language if a matching language has been used to translate the APEX application. Otherwise, the application primary language will be used.

 This option allows us to set the APEX application language per user, per APEX login.

- **Application Preference (use FSP_LANGUAGE_PREFERENCE)**: This option allows us to set the APEX application language according to the application preference FSP_LANGUAGE_PREFERENCE. The preference can be set using the APEX_UTIL.SET_PREFERENCE procedure (included in the documented APEX APIs).

 As application preferences are persistent, this option allows us to set the APEX application language across users and their logins.

- **Item Preference (use item containing preference)**: This option allows us to derive the APEX application language from an application item called FSP_LANGUAGE_PREFERENCE, which we should define ourselves. This option allows us full and dynamic control over the APEX application language.

This option allows us to set the APEX application language per user, per APEX login, but also allows us to develop a mechanism that can change the APEX application language at runtime, per user request.

Date format

One of the major *Localization* aspects is the date format. Different locales often use different date formats. The last item on the **Create Application** wizard screen, which the previous screenshot displays, is **Date Format**. This item allows us to define, on the application level, the date format we want to use, and, if necessary, set it to be different from the default date format of the database. The content of this field can be any valid Oracle date format or application *Substitution String* (the &ITEM. notation) that we can define, which will also represent a valid Oracle date format. Leave it blank and the default application date format will be derived from the database parameter NLS_DATE_FORMAT. If filled, the value will be used to alter the database session value of NLS_DATE_FORMAT. Do you remember that we mentioned some *Localization* related operations that the APEX engine performs at the beginning of any SHOW and ACCEPT? Altering the database session value for NLS_DATE_FORMAT is one of them.

Using the APEX Date Picker

The APEX built-in *Date Picker* item was pre-designed to support *Globalization*. When we define a *Date Picker* item we are provided with a list of 30 predefined dates and dates with time formats. I believe that this list covers the most common date (and time) formats. However, if the necessary date (and time) format we need for our application is not included in this list, we have three more options to define exactly what we need:

- **Date Picker (use application Date Format)**: This option uses the application **Date Format** to format the *Date Picker* entry. The application **Date Format** can take the form of any valid Oracle date/time format. (This option was introduced in APEX 3.1.)

- **Date Picker (use application format mask)**: This option uses an application item, or an application *Substitution String* called PICK_DATE_FORMAT_MASK, to format the *Date Picker* entry. We need to define the *Substitution String* or the application item ourselves. In the case of the latter, we also need to populate the application item with the appropriate date/time format.

- **Date Picker (use item format mask)**: This option uses the **Format Mask** field in the item **Source** section to format the Date Picker entry. Usually, this field is only applied to items with a **Source Type** of **Database Column**, but this *Date Picker* option can also use it. (This option was introduced in APEX 3.0.)

As we can see, we can control the format of every date (date and time) item in the application using an application level format or per item format. The demo application that accompanies this book includes a page that demonstrates the use of each of these *Date Picker* options, as can be seen in the next screenshot:

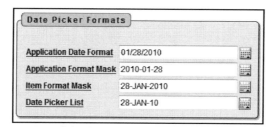

 The default date format of the APEX application is determined by the database NLS_DATE_FORMAT parameter. Defining the application **Date Format** will suppress that. Using the **application format mask** will take precedence over the application format. Using the **item format mask** or any of the predefined *Date Picker* options will take precedence over all the other options.

Adding or editing Globalization

As we have already mentioned, *Globalization* support can be added at any phase of the APEX application development cycle. Hence, the *Shared Components* module includes a section on **Globalization** that allows us to add or edit *Globalization* and *Localization* related parameters and functionalities.

The **Edit Attributes** option leads us to the following screen:

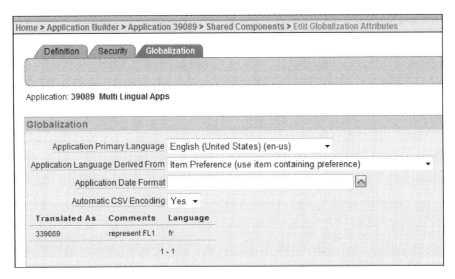

We are already familiar with the first three parameters. The fourth is a new one and is explained as follows:

- **Automatic CSV Encoding**: The default setting of this parameter is **Yes**. It means that the APEX engine will encode the exported CSV file using a (local) character set that matches the APEX application language. Our client side doesn't always support a multi-language character set like UTF-8 (especially when older versions or legacy software is involved). In these cases, especially if the CSV file contains multi-byte language characters and the local desktop only supports single-byte encoding, the exported CSV file might appear corrupt. The default option — using a local matching encoding — should ensure that the desktop client will be able to correctly read the exported CSV file. Setting this option to **No** will cause the APEX engine to export the CSV file using the character set defined in the APEX DAD file. As we'll see in the APEX installation appendix, this character set must be set to AL32UTF8. Hence, using the **No** option will export the CSV file encoded with UTF-8.

Finally, at the bottom of the screen, you can see a list of all the translated versions of the application, if any exist. Discussion on this is continued later in the chapter.

Load Data—Localization

The **Automatic CSV Encoding** parameter allows us to export CSV files with matching encoding to the client local desktop, but what happens when we want to import a local encoded file from the client? The APEX **Data Load/Unload** wizard, which can be seen in the next screenshot, allows us to set all the necessary parameters for a successful load of a text file that was encoded using a local character set, and includes some typical characteristics to a specific locale.

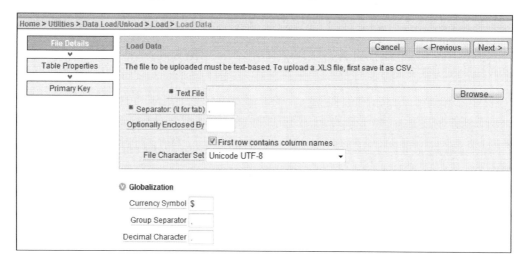

After you choose the **Text File** to be uploaded, set its **Separator** and **Optionally Enclosed By** characters, note whether the **First row contains column names**, and finally, select the **File Character Set**. We can select a matching character set to the uploaded file from a list of 30 supported character sets. This list contains some very common character sets, such as **Unicode UTF-8**, **US-ASCII**, **Western European ISO-8859-1,** and **Western European Windows 1252**, and some that might be considered less common like **Arabic ISO-8859-9**, **Hebrew ISO-8859-8-i**, or **Vietnamese Windows 1258**. Among all these 30 supported character sets, we should be able to upload most (if not all) of the local encoded files that we'll encounter.

Next, we can expand the **Globalization** section. Although the title of this section is *Globalization*, its content actually allows us to implement *Localization*. We can set the **Currency Symbol, Group Separator**, and the **Decimal Character** fields to match the locale properties of the local character set used to encode the uploaded file. The previous screenshot shows us the default values of these fields: a dollar sign ($), a comma (,) and a period (.).

Translating Text Messages

The APEX engine uses a built-in repository of predefined *Text Messages*. It uses these *Text Messages* in a variety of cases, mainly to generate UI components that convey useful/important information to the end user. Notable examples are error messages (e.g. **1 error has occurred**); *Date Picker* related text messages (e.g. **OK** and **Close** for the *Date Picker* buttons); and a range of reports and pagination related messages (e.g. **report total** or **row(s)%0 - %1 of %2**). Another major feature of APEX that massively uses the *Text Messages* repository is the **Interactive Reports**.

The language of the *Text Messages* in the repository is English, since it is the primary language of the APEX IDE. Each time we load an extra language to the APEX IDE, the matching *Text Messages*, translated into the loaded language, are added to the *Text Messages* repository. This is great if we are developing an application in a language that matches one of the loaded APEX IDE language(s). However, what if we want to develop an application that supports a language that the APEX IDE doesn't support natively? Moreover, what if we just don't want to load another language to the APEX IDE? For example, many developers prefer to always develop in English, no matter what the language of the developed application is. In these cases, we need to translate all the internal *Text Messages* into the language of the developed application. The APEX IDE allows us to do just that.

> The APEX documentation includes a list of a large number of the exposed *Text Messages* that developers can translate using the APEX translation mechanism. For the latest version—3.2.1—it can be found in tables 16-3 and 16-4 at the following URL: `http://download. oracle.com/docs/cd/E14373_01/appdev.32/e11838/ global.htm#BABHCAAH`.

The Text Messages translation wizard

From the *Shared Component* **Globalization** section, we can open the **Text Messages** translation wizard. The basic screen can look similar to the following screenshot:

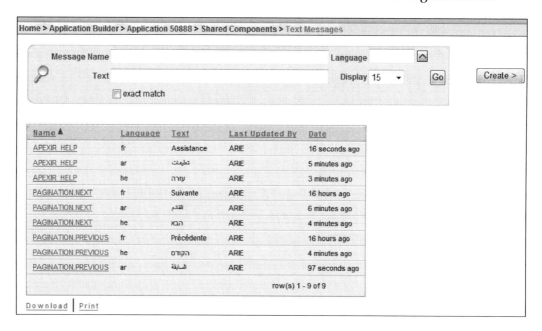

This screen displays all the translated *Text Messages* that were entered manually, if any exist. It will not display any of the APEX predefined *Text Messages* in the repository.

The screen also allows us to filter the displayed messages. As can be seen in the previous screenshot, we can filter the translated *Text Messages* by their **Message Name**, which is also the identification key of the message, and by their **Language** or **Text**, which is the actual content of the message. We can also use combinations of these fields to narrow down the search.

The **Print** option at the bottom of the *Text Messages* list will appear only if a valid print server was defined for the APEX instance.

The **Create** button leads us to the **Create/Edit Text Message** wizard, which can be seen in the following screenshot:

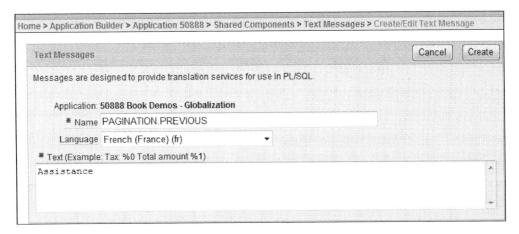

This wizard includes the following fields:

- **Name**: This field contains the name of the *Text Message* and identifies it. If we are dealing with an APEX predefined *Text Message*, the name should be taken from the APEX documentation (which we referenced on page 437). We can also define our own *Text Messages* and name them as we wish. In this case, we should use an all uppercase name.

- **Language**: This field associates the *Text Message* with a specific language or locale. In the following screenshot, we can see several options for the French language—**French (Belgium) (fr-be)**, **French (Canada) (fr-ca)**, **French (Luxembourg) (fr-lu)**, and so on. If we choose a specific language locale, for example **French (Monaco) (fr-mc)**, the APEX translation mechanism will use it only if the application language, as it was derived from the application *Globalization* parameters and is set specifically to this language and locale. However, if we choose to use the generic language option, French (France) (fr) in our example, the APEX translation mechanism will use it for every locale of French that was set as the APEX application language.

Additional notable generic language options include **English (en)**, **German (Germany) (de)**, **Spanish (Traditional Sort) (es)**, **Chinese (zh)**, and **Arabic (ar)**.

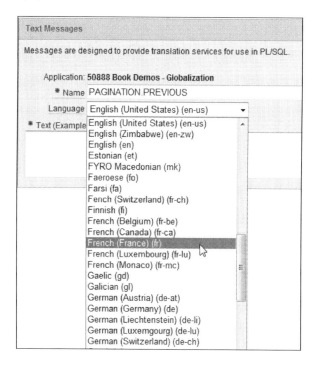

- **Text**: The last field includes the translated text of the message, and it should match the language we chose in the previous field. The APEX APIs for the translation mechanism, which we'll review in the next section, allows us to use up to 10 parameters that will be included in the content of the translated *Text Message*. An example of that can be seen in the full title of this field: **Text (Example: Tax: %0 Total amount %1)**.

Manage the Text Messages repository

The first option of the *Shared Components* **Globalization** section (as can be seen in the screenshot on page 434) is **Translate Application**, which leads us to the APEX translation mechanism home page. We are going to review this mechanism in a short while, but for now, I want to draw your attention to two windows on the *Assistance Column* of the home page on its right-hand side. They can be seen in the following screenshot:

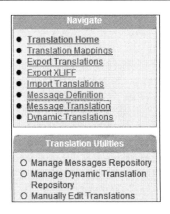

The **Message Translation** option in the **Navigate** window, just like the **Manage Messages Repository** option in the **Translation Utilities** window, leads us to the **Translate Messages** screen, which can be seen in the next screenshot. From the **Edit** column, we can drill down to the **Create/Edit Text Message** wizard screen, in which we can edit the correlated *Text Message*. A drill down from the **Translate** column will also lead us to the **Create/Edit Text Message** wizard, only this time it allows us to create a new translated version of the correlated *Text Message*. The **Translate Messages** screen also includes a **Create** button (which isn't shown on the screenshot) that allows us to create a complete new *Text Message*. It means that this screen actually includes all the management options we need for the *Text Messages* repository.

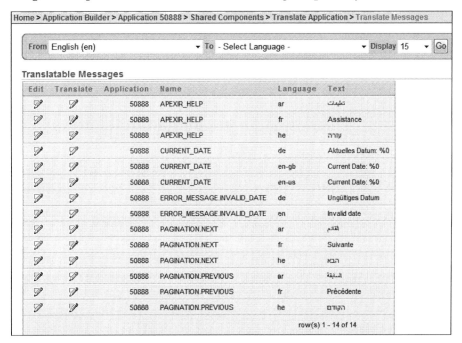

Using APEX Shortcut with Text Messages

In Chapter 3 of this book we discussed the APEX *Shortcuts*. There are two types of *Shortcuts* that can interact directly with the *Text Messages* repository: **Message** and **Message with JavaScript Escaped Single Quotes**. In both cases, if we want the *Shortcut* to take its value from the *Text Messages* repository, the **Name** of the *Shortcut* must be identical to an existing *Text Message* in the repository.

For example, in the following screenshot, you can see two text messages by the name of **ERROR_MESSAGE.INVALID_DATE**, one for English (**en**) and another for German (**de**):

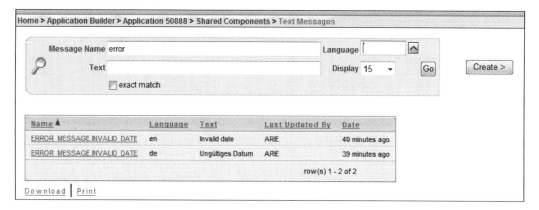

In the next screenshot, you can see a *Shortcut* that was defined using an identical name to the previously defined *Text Messages*. Its **Shortcut** field remains empty, as the content will be taken from the Text Messages repository according to the current application language/locale.

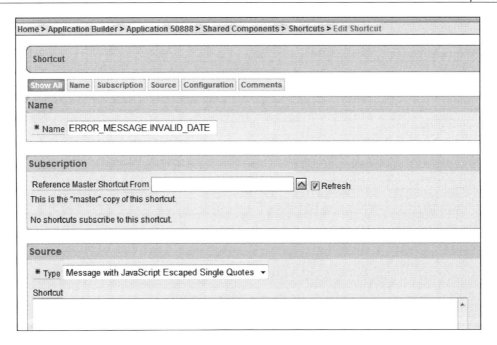

Now we are ready to use this *Shortcut*. The following snippet of JavaScript code can be placed in the **HTML Header** section of an application page:

```
<script type="text/javascript">
function is_Date_Valid(pThis){
   . . .

   if (err){
     alert('"ERROR_MESSAGE.INVALID_DATE"');
   }
}
</script>
```

In the `alert` statement, we first use a single quote character to wrap the string we want to display (according with the syntax rules of JavaScript), and then a double quote character that denotes the use of a *Shortcut*. The real content of the alert message will be determined at runtime, according to the application language/locale at the time.

Bear in mind:

Shortcuts are only available to us in certain contexts within the APEX Application Builder. External JavaScript files are not one of them. As such, our example is only valid for inline JavaScript code.

Dynamic Translations

So far, we have been restricted to translating specific *Text Messages* in a specific repository. Can we also use the APEX translation mechanism to translate data in our database tables? Can we retrieve some translated data as part of a query? The answer is yes. APEX provides us with a **Dynamic Translations** repository that can hold translations to data retrieved by a query.

The principle of the *Dynamic Translations* repository is that it contains strings of text that (might) appear in our database tables. For each such string, we can attach a translation in any of the 132 APEX supported languages.

From the home page of the translation mechanism, choosing the option of **Dynamic Translations** from the **Navigate** window or the option of **Manage Dynamic Translation Repository** in the **Translation Utilities** window leads us to the *Dynamic Translations* wizard, which can be seen in the following screenshot:

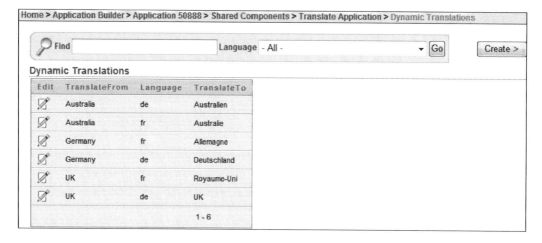

As with similar wizards that we have encountered before, this screen also displays the existing content of the repository, and the *Search Bar* allows us to filter it and display more targeted translations. The **Edit** column allows us to drill down to an edit screen of the correlated entry, and the **Create** button leads us to a similar screen that allows us to create a new **Dynamic Translations** entry, as can be seen in the next screenshot:

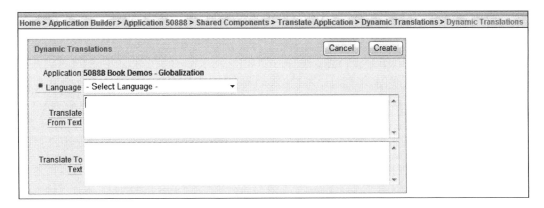

The wizard includes the following fields:

- **Language**: This is the language of the translation. The text string retrieved from the database will be translated into this language.

- **Translate From Text**: This is the source text string for translation. The APEX engine will compare the retrieved text string to this text string in order to find a match. If there is a match then a translation will be performed.

> The **Translate From Text** is not attached to a specific language. The content of this field should match the content we expect to retrieve from our database tables and can be in any language that our data is in.

- **Translate To Text**: This is the translated text string. The language of this string should match the **Language** field.

Using the Dynamic Translations repository

The most common use of this functionality is to dynamically translate, at runtime, the content of LOV items that derive their values by querying the database. We can reference the **Dynamic Translations** repository using the built-in `APEX_LANG.LANG` function, which we'll review in the next section, along with an example.

Using the APEX_LANG APIs

The APEX engine includes two documented APIs that allow us to utilize its translation functionalities while coding in PL/SQL.

APEX_LANG.MESSAGE

The APEX_LANG.MESSAGE function allows us to use the translated *Text Messages* as part of any PL/SQL code including external (to APEX) code such as stored/packaged procedures/functions, triggers, and so on. The function signature is as follows:

```
APEX_LANG.MESSAGE (
  p_name IN VARCHAR2 DEFAULT NULL,
  p0 IN VARCHAR2 DEFAULT NULL,
  p1 IN VARCHAR2 DEFAULT NULL,
  p2 IN VARCHAR2 DEFAULT NULL,
  ...
  p9 IN VARCHAR2 DEFAULT NULL,
  p_lang IN VARCHAR2 DEFAULT NULL)
RETURN VARCHAR2;
```

Here we have the following:

- p_name— this is the name of the *Text Message*, as it was defined in the *Text Messages* repository. We can use either a predefined APEX *Text Message* or one we created ourselves.

- p0...p9— these are ten optional string parameters. While defining the *Text Message*, we can reference them by %0 … %9, respectively. At runtime, the APEX engine will dynamically replace them with their values.

- p_lang— this is the language/locale code to use for retrieving the corresponding translated message. This is also an optional parameter, and if left blank, the current APEX application language, as it was derived from the application *Globalization* parameters, will be used.

Let's see an example of how to use `APEX_LANG.MESSAGE` to display a proper date format according to the application language/locale. The following figure represents three snapshots of the same application page, each under a different locale:

First, we set the application *Globalization* parameter **Application Language Derived From** to be **Item Preference (Use item containing preference)** and define the application item `FSP_LANGUAGE_PREFERENCE` to complement the mechanism we'll use to determine the current application language/locale. We also defined an *After Submit Computation* on page 101 of the application—the login page—that sets the default value of `FSP_LANGUAGE_PREFERENCE` to **en-us**. It means that the default application language and locale will be set to **English (United States) (en-us).**

Another application item we defined is `LOCAL_DATE`, and we'll use it to hold the local current date in its matching format to the application language and locale.

Next, we defined an **On Load: Before Header (page template header)** *Application Process* with the following PL/SQL code:

```
CASE :FSP_LANGUAGE_PREFERENCE
   WHEN 'en-gb' THEN
      EXECUTE IMMEDIATE 'alter session set TIME_ZONE=''0:0''';
      :LOCAL_DATE := to_char(current_date,'DD/MM/YYYY HH24:MI:SS');
   WHEN 'de' THEN
      EXECUTE IMMEDIATE 'alter session set TIME_ZONE=''1:0''';
      :LOCAL_DATE := to_char(current_date,'DD-MM-YYYY HH24:MI:SS');
   ELSE
      EXECUTE IMMEDIATE 'alter session set TIME_ZONE=''-7:0''';
      :LOCAL_DATE := to_char(current_date,'MM/DD/YYYY HH24:MI:SS');
END CASE;
```

We are using the PL/SQL built-in function `current_date` to retrieve the database date and time, subject to the current database session time zone parameters. The last step in creating the infrastructure we need for our example application page is to define the *Text Messages* we'll use. We need to define three *Text Messages*, one for each language/locale we are going to use. The following screenshot shows the *Text Messages* repository, after we used the string **tz** to filter it, in order to display only the *Text Messages* relevant to our example:

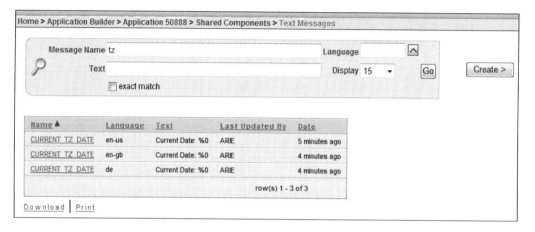

Now we are ready to define the example application page. The following is a screenshot of the **Regions** section in the *Page Definition* of the example page:

The first region—**Locale Dependent Date**—is of type **PL/SQL Dynamic Content**, and its **Region Source** contains the following PL/SQL code:

```
htp.p(apex_lang.message('CURRENT_TZ_DATE',:local_date));
```

We are invoking the `APEX_LANG.MESSAGE` API to retrieve the `CURRENT_TZ_DATE` *Text Message*, with a bind variable notation of the application item `LOCAL_DATE`, as its first parameter.

The proper translated message, according to the current application language/locale, which includes the matching date/time format, will be displayed on the region using the Oracle supplied package function `htp.p()`.

The second region, without a visible title, includes two APEX page elements:

The first element is a **Select List** item (P10_LOCALE), based on a static LOV that includes 3 pairs of values and is defined as:

```
STATIC2:USA;en-us,UK;en-gb,Germany;de
```

The second element is an HTML button (P10_REFRESH) that we defined using the **Create a button displayed among this region's items** option. The button, with a **Refresh** title, submits the page.

The last component on the example page is an *After Submit* **Computation**.

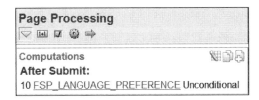

The computation assigns the value of the *Select List* item P10_LOCALE into the application item FSP_LANGUAGE_PREFERENCE. This is the item from which the APEX engine derived the current language/locale of the application. Cycle complete.

 The entire underlying infrastructure for the **Locale Dependent Date** page, with the page itself, can be seen in the demo application accompanying this book.

APEX_LANG.LANG

The APEX_LANG.LANG function allows us to use the *Dynamic Translations* repository to translate text we retrieved by a query. Mostly, we use it to translate LOV items that are based on a query. The function signature is as follows:

```
APEX_LANG.LANG (
    p_primary_text_string IN VARCHAR2 DEFAULT NULL,
    p0 IN VARCHAR2 DEFAULT NULL,
    p1 IN VARCHAR2 DEFAULT NULL,
```

```
    p2 IN VARCHAR2 DEFAULT NULL,
    ...
    p9 IN VARCHAR2 DEFAULT NULL,
    p_primary_language IN VARCHAR2 DEFAULT NULL)
RETURN VARCHAR2;
```

Here we have the following:

- `p_primary_text_string`— this is the text to be translated. We should enter the column name that holds the data we want to translate. The APEX engine compares the content of the column, record by record, to the *Dynamic Translations* repository. Each time it finds a match, the returned value will be the translated text. If no match is found then the original content is returned.

- `p0...p9`— these are the ten optional string parameters that we can reference in the translated text using the notation `%0...%9` respectively.

- `p_primary_language`— this is the translation language. If we don't specify a translation language, the APEX engine uses the current application language/locale, as derived from the application *Globalization* parameters.

Let's see an example of how to use `APEX_LANG.LANG` by adding a *Select List* item, based on LOV, to the **Locale Dependent Date** demo page. The item should display a list of countries from a table in the following format:

```
CREATE TABLE  "COUNTRIES"
   ("CODE" NUMBER(3,0) NOT NULL ENABLE,
    "COUNTRY" VARCHAR2(50) NOT NULL ENABLE,
     CONSTRAINT "COUNTRIES_PK" PRIMARY KEY ("CODE") ENABLE
   )
```

This table holds the name of three countries in plain English, as can be seen in the following screenshot of the *Object Browser*:

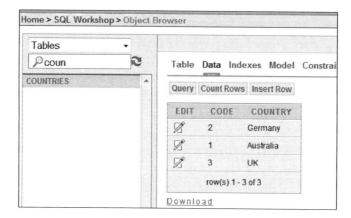

[The list of **Tables** is filtered using the string **coun**.]

A non-translatable *Select List* item would include the following LOV source:

```
select   country d, code r
from countries
```

However, in our case we want the displayed values of the `country` column to be language-dependent. The `APEX_LANG.LANG` API can help us do just that. The translatable LOV source in our example looks like the following:

```
select apex_lang.lang(country) d, code r
from countries
```

For each fetched value in the `country` column that the APEX engine will find a matching *Dynamic Translation* to the current application language/locale, the translated content will be displayed. I ran the demo page while setting the **Locale** item to **Germany**. The result — the **Country** *Select List* item displays the country names, translated into German — can be seen in the following screenshot:

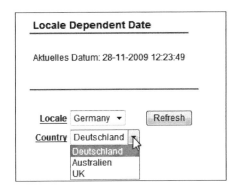

Multi-lingual applications

So far, we have built an APEX application with a specific (single) primary language that can be any one of the supported languages by APEX (or actually by the Oracle database, for that matter). We learned how to translate the internal APEX engine *Text Messages*, how to define our own translatable *Text Messages*, how to use them within PL/SQL code, and how to dynamically translate data retrieved from database tables. But what about translating the entire APEX application UI to multiple languages? Can we run the same APEX application logic under different UI languages? As we already hinted at the beginning of this chapter, this is not only possible, but it's also fully supported by APEX.

All the translation related actions we have taken so far, mainly the translation of the APEX engine's internal messages, are also needed for the next stage of translating the entire application UI. So, the next step is actually an extension of all the previous actions we have taken.

The translation mechanism home page

I have already mentioned the translation mechanism home page, or to be more exact, its right-hand side with the assistance column. Its left-hand side, which can be seen in the next screenshot, is what interests us now. It lists, in a menu-like manner, six steps we need to take in order to fully translate an APEX application. The first four steps are mandatory for translating the application UI, and they should be performed in the order of the list.

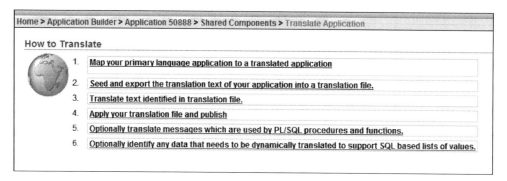

1—Application Language Mapping

Every application has its primary language. This is the first language the application supports, and as mentioned before, it doesn't have to match the language of the APEX IDE. This language is the anchor for all the other translated versions of the application.

The first step in the **How to Translate** list—**Map your primary language application to a translated application**—leads us to the **Application Language Mappings** screen. This screen lists the already existing language mappings, if any, and its **Create** button leads us to the **Create/Edit Application Language Mapping** wizard, which can be seen in the next screenshot:

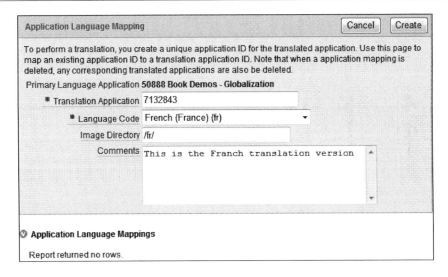

The **Create/Edit Application Language Mapping** wizard includes the
following fields:

- **Translation Application:** This is a mandatory field that holds the *Application
  ID* of the translated application. As with all the other *Application IDs*, it
  must be unique within the entire APEX instance (and not only within the
  application *Workspace*). Unlike the *Application ID* of a "regular" application (in
  the current context, the *Application ID* of the primary language application),
  the *Application ID* of a translated application **can't be changed** when
  deploying the application into other APEX instances. It means that this
  Application ID should be chosen to be unique, not only within the APEX
  instance we are using for development, but all around. Unfortunately, there
  isn't any global registration that can help us maintain unique *Application IDs*
  for our translated application versions, so we should try and come up with a
  random number, hoping it will be unique in all the APEX instances that we
  are going to deploy our applications to. Personally, I'm using a 7 or 8 digit
  number without any noticeable digit pattern.

  The end user of the application will only see the *Application ID* of the primary
  language application, and this is the only number that should be referenced.
  Therefore, you should not worry about the translated *Application ID* not being
  'user-friendly'.

> The *Application ID* number of a translated application must
> not end with zero (0). An error message will be produced if
> it does.

- **Language Code**: This is also a mandatory field and it holds the language/locale code of the translated application. Each time the APEX engine derives the application language/locale to match this code, the associated translated version of the application will be used. This is why we should always reference the *Application ID* of the primary language. The APEX engine derives the desired application/locale from the *Globalization* parameters of the application and acts accordingly. Referencing any of the translated *application IDs* will most likely yield an error message.

- **Image Directory**: A translated version of the application can have its own `images` directory, which can hold specific files and images that pertain to this specific language/locale. The value of the field should match an alias we defined in the APEX instance DAD file, which points to the actual `images` directory.

  The following is an example of possible code in a DAD file:

  ```
  Alias /i/ "C:\product\10.1.3\OracleAS_1\Apache\Apache\images/"
  ```

  ```
  Alias /fr/ "C:\product\10.1.3\OracleAS_1\Apache\Apache\images_fr/"
  ```

  The first alias — /i/ — points to the "regular" `images` directory. The second alias — /fr/ — points to a new directory that we have created, called `images_fr`, which includes specific files and images for the French translated version of the application, on top of the original `images` directory content.

   In order for the translated version specific `images` directory alias to be effective, all the references to the `images` directory in the primary language application should be done using the APEX built-in *Substitution String* `#IMAGE_PREFIX#`. A good practice (in any case, not just for translated applications) is to not hardcode the alias path to the `images` directory.

- **Comments**: This field can hold any comments and documentation that you find helpful.

Pressing the **Create** button will create a new language mapping, as can be seen in the following screenshot:

It's important to understand that although the translated application has its own Application ID, it is not really a standalone application, and it will not appear in the list of available applications on the *Application Builder* home page. We should never directly reference a translated Application ID. Instead, we should always directly reference the primary language Application ID. We also never directly edit the translated application. Every change in the application logic or the application UI should be performed on the primary application. From there it can be synchronized with the translated versions as part of the seeding and publishing process, which we'll discuss next.

2—Seed and export

The second step on the **How to Translate** list—**Seed and export the translation text of your application into a translation file**—starts with the **seeding** process. This process collects all the translatable components in the application and populates the **Translation Text** repository. This repository is the source for creating the **XLIFF** file, which we are using to actually translate the text that we want translated. There will be more about that in a moment.

The seeding process is responsible for more than just preparing the infrastructure for the XLIFF file. It's actually responsible for synchronizing the primary language application with its associated translated versions. The metadata of the primary language application is synchronized with the metadata of the translated applications, including everything related to the application logic. This means that every change we make in the primary language application, regardless of its nature—it doesn't have to be related to new/changed translated components—should lead to performing a new seed process.

The following screenshot is from the **Seed Translatable Text** wizard. In this stage we should choose the **Language Mapping** that we want the seed process to run for:

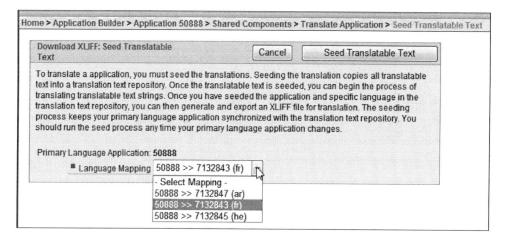

Clicking on the **Seed Translatable Text** button leads us to the next wizard screen, **XLIFF Export**, which allows us to export an XLIFF file, either for the entire application or just for a specific page (that we have changed in the primary language application).

XLIFF (XML Localization Interchange File Format) is a standard of **OASIS (Organization for the Advancement of Structured Information Standards)**. An XML-based format standardizes the implementation of *Localization*. An XLIFF file includes translatable units — text related components that might need translation. Each translatable unit includes a pair of `<source>` and `<target>` attributes — the `<source>` attribute includes the text (candidate) to be translated, and the `<target>` attribute includes the translated text. In case we choose not to translate a translatable unit, its `<source>` and `<target>` content will be the same.

APEX supports the XLIFF standard by both generating and exporting XLIFF files, and importing them.

At the top of the **XLIFF Exports** wizard screen, as can be seen in the next screenshot, the APEX engine summarizes for us the seeding process XLIFF-wise — new, updated, purged, and the total number of attributes that might need translation in this language mapping XLIFF file.

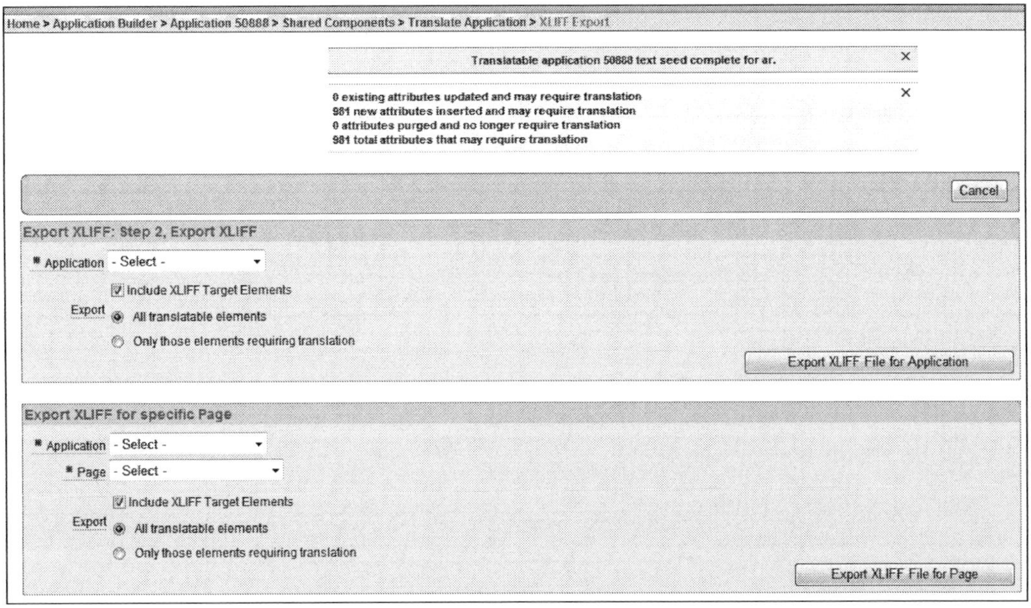

Now we are ready to define the general parameters for generating the XLIFF file. As you can see from the above screenshot, the **XLIFF Export** wizard allows us to generate an XLIFF file for the entire application or just for a specific page. If your application includes many pages, then this option can be a time saver. Moreover, the generated XLIFF file will be much smaller and targeted, so it will be easier to locate the translatable units that need our attention.

First, we need to choose the source **Application** for the XLIFF file. We need to choose the language mapping we want the XLIFF file to be associated with. If we select the **Application** field of the **Export XLIFF for specific Page** section, the **Page** select list field will be populated with all the pages of the selected application, allowing us to choose the source page for the XLIFF file.

Next, there is a checkbox item titled **Include XLIFF Target Elements** that is checked by default. Unchecking this option will generate an XLIFF file with only the `<source>` attributes. Originally, this option was added for internal use with some Oracle in-house XLIFF-related translation tools. If your XLIFF parser/editor requires an XLIFF file that includes both `<source>` and `<target>` attributes, then you should just ignore this option and leave it checked.

Lastly, we need to choose the **Export** scope. The first option—**All translatable elements**—will include all the translatable elements of the application/page in the generated XLIFF file. The second option—**Only those elements requiring translation**—will include only the new or updated translatable elements of the application/page in the XLIFF file (an incremental process, relative to the last XLIFF export).

Pressing the **Export XLIFF File for Application / Export XLIFF File for Page** button leads the APEX engine to generate the corresponding XLIFF file, and the client browser will display a dialog box, similar to the following screenshot, giving us the option to save the file:

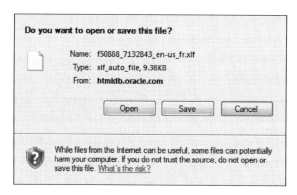

 Please pay attention to the name of the XLIFF file, as it was generated by the APEX engine. It includes the primary language *Application ID*, the translated *Application ID*, the primary language code, and the translated language code. This is all the information we need to easily identify the content of the file.

3—Translating the text

The third step in the **How to Translate** list—**Translate text identified in translation file**—is the heart of the APEX translation mechanism, although we are performing it outside of APEX.

We should carefully scan the XLIFF file and translate every bit of text that needs to be displayed in the translated language. An XLIFF file, as you can see from the following snippet of the XLIFF file we generated in Step 2, is actually a legal (well-formed) XML file. There are some commercial XLIFF editors out there, but if your XLIFF file is relatively simple (or you just don't want to spend any money on a professional XLIFF parser/editor), then any text editor will do.

```
<?xml version="1.0" encoding="UTF-8"?>
<!--
    ********************
    ** Source     :   50888
    ** Source Lang:   en-us
    ** Target     :   7132843
    ** Target Lang:   fr
    ** Filename:      f50888_7132843_en-us_fr.xlf
    ** Generated By: ARIE
    ** Date:          07-DEC-2009 14:04:05
    ********************
  -->
<xliff version="1.0">
<file original="f50888_7132843_en-us_fr.xlf" source-language="en-us"
target-language="fr" datatype="html">
<header></header>
<body>
<trans-unit id="S-2-5631463302105424927-50888">
<source>Logout</source>
<target> Déconnexion</target>
</trans-unit>
<trans-unit id="S-2.1-5631463302105424927-50888">
<source>Logout</source>
<target> Déconnexion</target>
</trans-unit>
<trans-unit id="S-3-7830898624816108954-50888">
<source>Error setting current date</source>
<target> Erreur lors de la définition de la date actuelle</target>
</trans-unit>


  . . .


</body>
</file>
</xliff>
```

The first XLIFF copy that will be generated by the APEX engine includes identical `<source>` and `<target>` attributes. For every translatable unit we want to translate, the text translation should be entered to the `<target>` attribute. After importing the translated XLIFF file back to APEX, as we'll do in the next step, the APEX engine will 'remember' the translatable units for us in the *Translation Text* repository. The next time we generate an XLIFF file for this mapping language, the XLIFF file will include the already translated `<target>` attributes, so we will not have to repeat the translation process from scratch.

4—Import and publish the translation

The fourth step in the **How to Translate** list—**Apply your translation file and publish**—is the last mandatory step in translating the application UI (assuming you already translated the APEX engine internal messages as part of the *Text Messages* repository).

This option leads us to the **XLIFF Translation Files** wizard, which can be seen in the following screenshot:

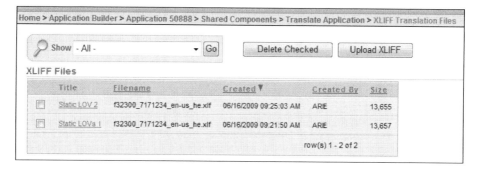

The screen displays the current **XLIFF repository** and allows us to delete the previously loaded XLIFF files by checking them and clicking the **Delete Checked** button. Clicking on the **Upload XLIFF** button leads us to the next wizard screen— **XLIFF Upload**—which can be seen in the following screenshot:

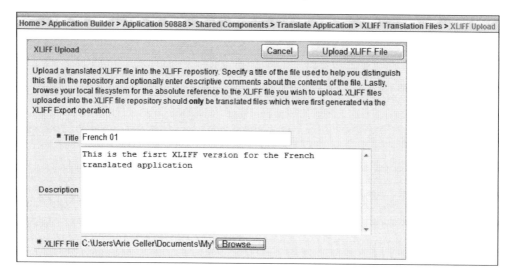

This wizard screen allows us to give a **Title** to the uploaded XLIFF file, to enter an optional **Description**, and with a *File Browse* item to populate the **XLIFF File** field that points to the XLIFF file on our filesystem.

Clicking on the **Upload XLIFF File** button will upload the chosen XLIFF file into the XLIFF repository and will take us back to the repository screen.

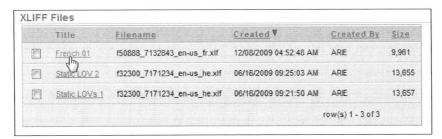

This time, we can see the newly uploaded file—**French 01**. Clicking on this file leads us to the next wizard screen—**XLIFF File Details**—that can be seen next:

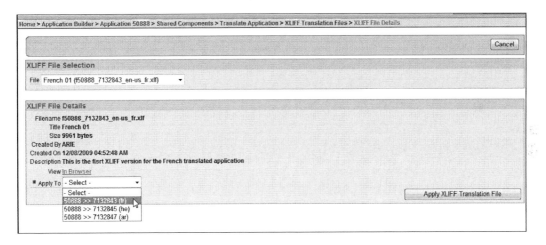

The **File** field in the **XLIFF File Selection** section will be set to the XLIFF file we just uploaded, although you have the option of choosing to deal with a previously loaded XLIFF file. Next, we should choose the language mapping we want the XLIFF file to **Apply To**. In our example, as the loaded XLIFF file includes French translation, we chose the **50888>>7132843 (fr)** language mapping.

Clicking on the **Apply XLIFF Translation File** button leads us to the last wizard screen—**Create Translation Application**—as can be seen in the following screenshot:

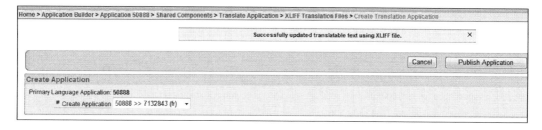

The **Create Application** field will be populated, by default, with the language mapping we chose on the previous screen, although we have an option of changing that. Clicking on the **Publish Application** button is the last action in creating the translated application. The APEX engine will create/update the translated application details with all the translatable components in the XLIFF file and populate or synchronize the translated metadata with the metadata of the primary language application.

If the publishing process was successful we'll be returned to the translation mechanism home page, with a success message similar to the following:

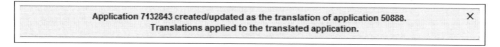

Editing the Translatable Text repository

The APEX translation mechanism home page includes an option for editing the **Translatable Text** repository (the third option in the `Translation Utilities` box on the right-hand side of the home page). As can be seen in the following screenshot, the wizard displays the language and the source and target content of the translatable units as they appear in the XLIFF file of all the translatable units in the application, while allowing us to narrow down the scope of the displayed strings.

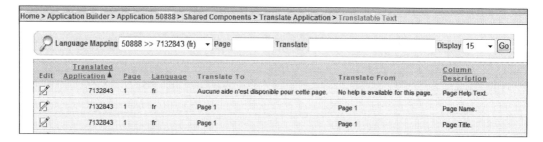

This is a very easy and quick way of correcting any translation linguistic errors or for just editing the translated content in a specific translatable string(s) without involving the entire XLIFF file. After editing the repository we need to republishing the translated application.

Running translated applications

As was mentioned before, we should only reference the primary language *Application ID*. In our example, it should be a URL that includes the following:

```
f?p=50888: ...
```

If we want to run a translated version of the application, we should set the application *Globalization* parameter **Application Language Derived From** to yield the language/locale code we want to use. When the APEX engine identifies a language/locale code that matches one of the defined language mappings, it will automatically invoke the corresponding translated version of the application.

Deploying translated applications

The only time we can, and should, treat a translated application as an independent entity is while preparing to deploy the primary language application with all its translated versions.

The **Export Application** wizard lists the translated applications as a viable export option, as can be seen in the following screenshot:

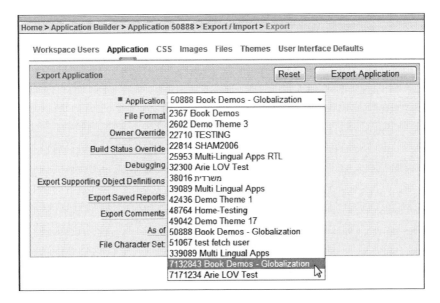

First, we should export the primary language application. This exported file will include the *Text Messages* and the *Dynamic Translations* repositories, alongside proper instructions to create the language mapping(s) that is(are) associated with the primary language application. Next, we should export every translated application we wish to deploy.

In the target deployment APEX Instance, we should first import the primary language application while using the option of **Reuse Application ID xxxx From Export File** (the **xxxx** will be replaced with the original *Application ID*). Using the same option, we should import every translated application we wish to deploy on this instance.

The scenario we just reviewed is the simplest and most straightforward for deploying translated applications. However, sometimes we'll need to change the *Application ID* of the primary language application. We have already established that the *Application ID* of the translated application(s) can't be changed.

Attention:

The following scenario involves changing the original exported files of the APEX applications. **This scenario IS NOT supported by Oracle**. Although the scenario doesn't change the original APEX instance and can't harm the original applications, you should use it at your own discretion.

As before, you should export the primary language application and then all the translated application versions you wish to deploy. Next, you should determine the new *Application ID* you are going to use on the deployment instance. Carefully scan the exported file of the primary language application and replace every reference to the original *Application ID* with the new one. Personally, I'm using the **replace** option of my editor to do that. Perform the replacement one string at a time, while making sure you only replace references to the *Application ID*. Repeat this process for every translated, application-exported file.

Now you can import the primary language application using the **Reuse Application ID xxxx From Export File** option. The primary language will be installed using the new *Application ID*, and a proper language mapping(s) will also be created. Next, import the translated Application(s).

There are also options for hacking the XLIFF file itself. However, the `<trans-unit>` ID attribute comprises the primary language *Application ID*, which is the easy part, and forms an internal APEX Primary Key number that uniquely identifies the APEX component in the APEX metadata tables. This number can be changed when deploying the application into a new APEX workspace. Changing these numbers can be very difficult (it's not practical in my humble opinion).

Hacking the XLIFF file is highly **NOT** recommended.

Summary

In this chapter, we reviewed the *Globalization* and *Localization* that APEX provides us.

We saw that the APEX IDE can run in 10 different UI languages. It allows us to develop applications that support 132 different languages and locales, while allowing us to translate the internal APEX engine *Text Messages*, define our own *Text Messages* to be used in a PL/SQL code, and define *Dynamic Translations* to dynamically translate data from database tables, mainly to be used in LOV-based items.

We also reviewed the full APEX translation mechanism, which allows us to run the same APEX application under multilingual UI.

The next chapter will discuss Right-To-Left support for APEX applications.

19

Right-To-Left Support in APEX

In the previous chapter, we reviewed the *Globalization* and *Localization* support mechanisms APEX provides us, which allow us to develop and translate applications in 132 different languages and locales. Some of these languages are written from right-to-left; the most notable are Arabic and Hebrew. These languages need our special attention.

In this chapter, we'll review the APEX support of Right-To-Left oriented applications and how to implement it in respect to the following:

- Why Right-To-Left support needs special care and attention
- Using CSS and JavaScript to implement Right-To-Left support
- Specific APEX issues concerning Right-To-Left support

Why we need special Right-To-Left support

Arabic, which is actually a generic name for several languages and dialects supported in the Oracle database environment, alongside the **Hebrew** language, are Right-To-Left oriented languages. This means that text in these languages is written from right-to-left, while numbers and some date formats are written in the "regular" direction of left-to-right. Hence, these languages are, in fact, bi-directional. A proper Right-To-Left support means that the client Web browser will display content in these languages properly, i.e., in the correct order and direction, as well as allowing us to feed data into our application in a natural way to these languages – text from right-to-left and numbers or dates from left-to-right.

Reversing the application page orientation from the natively supported Left-To-Right to the desired Right-To-Left might seem very simple at first glance. CSS provides us with an attribute called `direction`, which can be assigned the values `LTR` or `RTL`, and it determines the general direction orientation of the HTML page. Using an external CSS file, or as inline code in the application *page templates*, we can take advantage of the CSS cascading effect and define the following CSS selector:

```
body { direction: rtl }
```

We are using the `body` selector to widen the scope and effect of the `direction` attribute to a maximum, while relying on the inheritance feature of CSS. If we position the external CSS load file statement properly, or the inline CSS code, the new `direction` attribute will have precedence over the default `direction` and our page will be Right-To-Left oriented. Simple right?

Well, unfortunately things are a bit more complicated than that. The CSS `direction` attribute does indeed change the orientation of the application page to Right-To-Left, making the Web browser to reverse the page layout and the positioning of all the page elements on it. However, while doing so, the internal content of the objects is not changed or reversed, as might be expected.

The top half of the next screenshot displays the upper-left corner of a Left-To-Right oriented page. It includes three rows of text—in English, Arabic, and Hebrew—and an image of a right arrow pointing towards a computer image. We changed the orientation of this page to be Right-To-Left, and the result can be seen in the bottom half of the following screenshot:

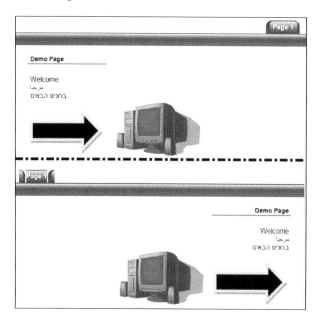

As the screenshot shows, changing the orientation of the application page didn't change the content of any of the page objects (elements). However, their position on the page has been horizontally reversed.

Pay attention:

This is NOT a mirror image of the Left-To-Right screen, as the internal direction of the objects' content has not changed. For example, the right arrow is still pointing to the right. It didn't become a left arrow when we changed the page orientation.

The effect of the page orientation change can be problematic from both the visual / graphical and the functional aspects. From the visual aspect, look at what happened to the shape of the page TAB headline. In the original Left-To-Right page it looks like a one well formed shape; in the Right-To-Left page it looks like three separate components that don't form a cohesive shape — the original left border image became the right border image, and vice versa. We'll experience similar effects with template-based *APEX Buttons*, table corners, navigational bars, and so on.

From the functional aspect, let's go back to the right arrow. On the Left-To-Right application page, it points toward the computer image. However, on the Right-To-Left oriented page, this arrow points away from the computer image. With the Left-To-Right page, this combination of images can be interpreted, for example, as representing input or import action. With the Right-To-Left page, the reordered combination might be interpreted as representing the exact opposite, an output or export action. Later in the chapter, we'll see that something similar is happening with the *APEX Shuttle* item. This behavior might impair functionality.

The problematic behavior and potential problems we just reviewed compel us to allocate special care and attention to the correct implementation of the APEX Right-To-Left support.

Basic Right-To-Left scenarios

As we reviewed in the previous chapter, there can be two scenarios for Right-To-Left support. The first is when a Right-To-Left language is acting as the primary and only language of the application. The second scenario is when a Right-To-Left language is acting as the language of a translated application. If this scenario includes a case where one language (primary or translated) is a Left-To-Right language and the other is Right-To-Left language, e.g. English and Arabic or Hebrew, the complexity rate is even higher.

Right-To-Left as a single language

With this scenario, all the changes we need to make in order to implement Right-To-Left support (as we'll review them throughout this chapter) should be done directly on the relevant APEX components, such as *Templates* and graphical icons.

The "best practice", in this case, will be to duplicate the *Theme* we chose to use in the application and make all the changes on this *Theme*. First, it will allow us to use the original *APEX Theme* with other applications that don't need Right-To-Left support. Second, it will be easier for us to track the duplicated *Theme* after upgrading our APEX instance to a newer version. The upgrade will not change the duplicated *Theme*, and it will continue to support Right-To-Left. Of course, if the new version of the *Theme* offers new features that we want to adopt, we will have to re-duplicate the newer version and manually adapt it, one more time, to Right-To-Left support. That is why it will be wise of you to document all the changes you perform as part of the Right-To-Left implementation.

> You can duplicate an existing *Theme* by choosing the **Themes** option under the **User Interface** section in the *Shared Components* module. On the **Themes** home page, you should choose the **Copy Theme** option from the **Tasks** window.

On top of all the changes to the application *templates*, we might need to create some new graphical icons or (horizontally) reverse some of the icons provided by APEX, especially if we are going to use image-based *APEX Buttons* or *APEX List*.

Right-To-Left as a translation language

With this scenario, we should define all the templates we are using as translatable, and most of the changes we need to make to the APEX elements (mainly *Templates*) will be carried out in the corresponding XLIFF file.

With this scenario, we might also need to create some new graphical icons that support the Right-To-Left orientation.

> **Bear in mind:**
>
> When defining a new language mapping, we have the option of defining a new images directory that will be associated with the translated language. We can use this images directory to store our specific language related icons. However, it will require manually creating and defining this directory, which might be a cumbersome (even complex) action to the end user, when deploying the application.

APEX templates with Right-To-Left support

Right-To-Left orientation is part of the look and feel of the application page, and in the APEX environment, it's mainly controlled by the *Theme's* relevant *Templates*. In the next sub-sections, we'll review the most common templates we need to adapt as part of the Right-To-Left support implementation.

Templates, by default, are not included in the translatable elements of the application, mainly because they can seriously crowd the XLIFF file, which, even without them, can be quite packed with complicated (and baffling) strings of text and code.

If our Right-To-Left language is the only language of the application, we can make all the changes we need for the Right-To-Left support directly on the *Templates*. Otherwise, we need to include the *Template* in the XLIFF file generated by the APEX translation mechanism. We can do that by checking the **Translatable** checkbox in the appropriate *Template*, as can be seen in the next screenshot of a *Page Template*:

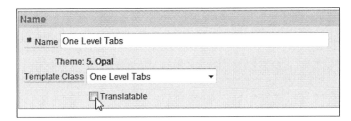

Page templates

The *Page templates* include very basic and important code we need to change or translate as part of the Right-To-Left support implementation.

The Header section

The **Header** section of a *Page Template* includes the statements for loading our external CSS or JavaScript files (if we are using any), whether they are part of the `images` directory or they were uploaded into the database (using the **Files** section in the *Shared Component* module).

Right-To-Left as a single language

In this case, we can work directly on the *Page Template*, using the following for example:

```
<link rel="stylesheet" href="#WORKSPACE_IMAGES#My_RTL_CSS.css"
    type="text/css" />
<script src="#IMAGE_PREFIX#javascript/MyScripts.js"
    type="text/javascript"></script>
```

The first statement loads a CSS file that was uploaded into the database. Uploaded CSS files are available to us on the workspace level. Therefore, we are using the *substitution string* #WORKSPACE_IMAGES# as a prefix to the filename.

The second statement loads a JavaScript file that was stored as part of the images directory. Hence, we are using the *substitution string* #IMAGE_PREFIX#, which points to the images directory as a prefix to the filename.

> Usually, our external CSS and JavaScript files will be stored on the same type of location—as part of the images directory or as uploaded files in the database. Our example code uses both just for demonstration purposes.

Right-To-Left as a translation language

In this scenario, we should define a language mapping to a Right-To-Left language. An example of such a definition can be seen in the following screenshot:

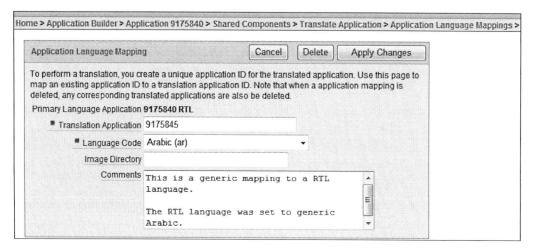

In our example, we'll assume a scenario of mixed orientation—the application primary language is a Left-To-Right language, and the translated language is a Right-To-Left language.

The **Header** of the *Page Template*, which we marked as a **Translatable**, includes the following statements for loading our external CSS and JavaScript files:

```
<link rel="stylesheet" href="#WORKSPACE_IMAGES#My_LTR_CSS.css"
    type="text/css" />
<script src="#IMAGE_PREFIX#javascript/My_LTR_Scripts.js"
    type="text/javascript"></script>
```

In this context, the `My_LTR_CSS.css` file can be empty, as no actions need to be taken for the Left-To-Right support.

Our JavaScript file can include text messages to the end user (e.g. using the `alert()` function) and as such, can be considered language dependent. We can deal with the language factor within a single JavaScript file by using `IF` or `SWITCH` statements to classify the text message according to the current application language, or we can maintain separate language-dependent JavaScript files, similar to our CSS files. In this case, we need to use the appropriate filenames for each language or orientation (like in our example).

Using the APEX translation mechanism, we can export the XLIFF file, and now we need to locate the relevant *Page Template* `<trans-unit>`, which includes the code we are dealing with. The correlated snippet of code from the `<source>` tag should look similar to the following:

```
. . .
#HEAD#
&lt;link rel="stylesheet" href="#IMAGE_PREFIX#themes/theme_5/My_LTR_
CSS.css" type="text/css" />
&lt;script src="#IMAGE_PREFIX#javascript/My_LTR_Scripts.js"
    type="text/javascript">&lt;/script>
. . .
```

In the `<target>` tag, we need to make the following "translation":

```
. . .
#HEAD#
&lt;link rel="stylesheet" href="#IMAGE_PREFIX#themes/theme_5/My_RTL_
CSS.css" type="text/css" />
&lt;script src="#IMAGE_PREFIX#javascript/My_RTL_Scripts.js"
    type="text/javascript">&lt;/script>
. . .
```

We should repeat this action for all the `<trans-unit>` of all the *page templates* we are using in the application.

 We should have all the referenced files in the *Page Templates* and the XLIFF file in their correct location.

In case of the `My_RTL_CSS.css` file, it should include the CSS attribute `direction` as we described it at the beginning of this chapter. In case of the JavaScript file, it should include text messages in the correlated language.

The Body and Footer sections

These sections usually include references to graphical images that build some of the page *Theme* graphical elements, such as the navigational bar or other graphical page decoration elements. For example, the **Footer** section of *Theme* 1 includes the following code:

```
<tr>
<td><img src="#IMAGE_PREFIX#themes/theme_1/bot_bar_left.png"
    alt="" /></td>
<td class="t1BotbarMiddle">
<div id="t1user">&APP_USER.</div></td>
<td class="t1BotbarMiddle">
<div id="t1copy"><!-- Copyright Here -->
<span class="t1Customize"> #CUSTOMIZE#</span></div></td>
<td><img src="#IMAGE_PREFIX#themes/theme_1/bot_bar_right.png"
    alt="" /></td>
</tr>
```

We have already seen what happens when we are changing the page orientation to Right-To-Left—the left border becomes the right one and vice versa. Hence, if we are working on the template itself, we need to change the order in which the borders are rendered—instead of rendering the left border first, we'll render the right one. The matching Right-To-Left code should look similar to the following snippet of code:

```
<tr>
<td><img src="#IMAGE_PREFIX#themes/theme_1/bot_bar_right.png"
    alt="" /></td>
<td class="t1BotbarMiddle">
<div id="t1user">&APP_USER.</div></td>
<td class="t1BotbarMiddle">
<div id="t1copy"><!-- Copyright Here -->
<span class="t1Customize"> #CUSTOMIZE#</span></div></td>
<td><img src="#IMAGE_PREFIX#themes/theme_1/bot_bar_left.png"
    alt="" /></td>
</tr>
```

In case we are working with an XLIFF file, we should locate the corresponding `<target>` tag and make the same changes in it.

 The **Header** and **Footer** sections can also include some general text-based elements, which also need our attention. For example, in the example code we can see a placeholder for a copyright message. Other elements can include text logo, date, and time displayed on every application page, etc.

Tab attributes sections

Page templates that support TABs include special sections for the current / noncurrent TABs. In the first screenshot of this chapter, we already saw the effect of Right-To-Left orientation on non-treated TABs. We should apply the same Right-To-Left support principles we have described for the page decoration elements to the TABs elements.

Button templates

The next major templates section we need to deal with is the *Button templates*.

The following is an example code from a template button:

```
<td class="t5R"><a href="#LINK#">
  <img src="#IMAGE_PREFIX#themes/theme_5/button_left.png"
    alt="" /></a></td>
<td class="t5C"><a href="#LINK#">#LABEL#</a></td>
<td class="t5L"><a href="#LINK#">
  <img src="#IMAGE_PREFIX#themes/theme_5/button_right.png"
    alt="" /></a></td>
```

We need to change the order in which the border of the template-based *Button* will be rendered one more time. The following is the corresponding snippet of code from the XLIFF <target> tag:

```
&lt;td class="t5R">&lt;a href="#LINK#">
&lt;img src="#IMAGE_PREFIX#themes/theme_5/button_right.png"
  alt="" />&lt;/a>&lt;/td>
&lt;td class="t5C">&lt;a href="#LINK#">#LABEL#&lt;/a>&lt;/td>
&lt;td class="t5L">&lt;a href="#LINK#">
&lt;img src="#IMAGE_PREFIX#themes/theme_5/button_left.png"
  alt="" />&lt;/a>&lt;/td>
```

> **Bear in mind:**
>
>
>
> With the last code, we only dealt with the Right-To-Left appearance of our template-base *Buttons*. We didn't translate the label of the button. The label, represented in this *Template* by the *substitution string* #LABEL#, will appear as a separate <trans-unit> in the XLIFF file. A dedicated <trans-unit> will be created for every template-based Button in our application.

Popup List of Values Template

The last *Template* we'll review here is the **Popup List of Values** *Template*. Every application can have only one template of this type, and it includes sections that deal with all the aspects of displaying this pop-up window.

As before, if we are working with the APEX translation mechanism, we need to mark this template as **Translatable**, so it will be included in our XLIFF file. Otherwise, we can make the necessary Right-To-Left support changes directly in the *Template*.

The first section that needs our attention is the **Buttons** section, which can be seen in the following screenshot:

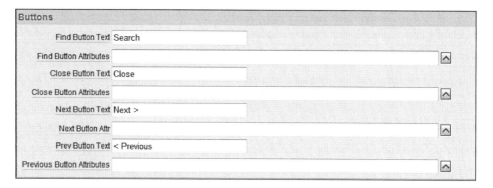

This *Template* allows us to directly define the labels of all the *Buttons* that appear in the pop up LOV window. We can translate the labels directly in the *Template*, or if we are working with an XLIFF file, search the correlated <trans-unit> tags, and translate the content of the <target> tags, as we can see in the following snippet of code:

```
<trans-unit id="S-72-2269119571085387-9175840">
<source>Search</source>
<target>البحث</target>
</trans-unit>
```

```
<trans-unit id="S-73-2269119571085387-9175840">
<source>Close</source>
<target>قم بإغلاق</target>
</trans-unit>
<trans-unit id="S-74-2269119571085387-9175840">
<source>Next ></source>
<target>הבא ></target>
</trans-unit>
<trans-unit id="S-75-2269119571085387-9175840">
<source>&lt; Previous</source>
<target>&lt; הקודם</target>
</trans-unit>
```

In this last example, some of the strings were translated into Arabic and some into Hebrew. We'll continue to mix these two Right-To-Left languages in the following examples.

The next field we should translate is the **Result Row X Of Y** under the **Pagination** section. The following is an example for it:

```
<trans-unit id="S-112-2269119571085387-9175840">
<source>&lt;br />&lt;div style="padding:2px;
    font-size:8pt;">Row(s) #FIRST_ROW# -
    #LAST_ROW#&lt;/div></source>
<target>&lt;br />&lt;div style="padding:2px;
    font-size:8pt;">שורות #LAST_ROW# - #FIRST_ROW#
    &lt;/div></target>
</trans-unit>
```

On top of translating the text string 'Row(s)' (into Hebrew in this case), we also reversed the order of the *substitution strings* #FIRST_ROW# and #LAST_ROW# so that they will be displayed in the correct order with a Right-To-Left application.

Lastly, we need to deal with the **Page Attributes** section, which allows us to set the **Page Title** of the pop up LOV window:

```
<trans-unit id="S-63-2269119571085387-9175840">
<source>Search Dialog</source>
<target>إطار البحث</target>
</trans-unit>
```

Also, there are the **Page Body Attributes**, which we'll use to add the CSS `direction` attribute, as we can see in the following snippet:

```
<trans-unit id="S-65-2269119571085387-9175840">
<source>onload="first_field()" style="margin:0;"</source>
<target>onload="first_field()" style="margin:0;
    direction: rtl"
</target>
</trans-unit>
```

The final Right-To-Left result can be seen in the following screenshot:

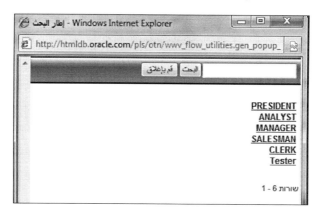

All the other template types

By now, the main principles of applying Right-To-Left support to the *APEX Templates* should be clear to you—translating relevant text messages and reversing the rendering order of graphical elements. If the Right-To-Left language is the only language of the application, then we can apply the necessary changes directly to the template. Otherwise, we should use the relevant `<target>` tags in the XLIFF file. As mentioned before, APEX allows us to mark every *Template* as **Translatable**, and as such, the relevant sections of the *Template* will be included in the XLIFF file.

The APEX Shuttle item

The *APEX Shuttle* item has some prominent features that are direction-oriented. As such, it needs special attention so its functionality will not be impaired.

Every *APEX Shuttle* item is built from two major columns—source and destination, and in between, some graphical control icons that allow us to move its members from one column to the other. The top half of the next screenshot displays the *APEX Shuttle* item in a (native) Left-To-Right page. The left column includes all the options we can select from in the item. The right column includes all the options that were selected. In between, there are five graphical controls. For example, the third one from the top is a right arrowhead, pointing from the available options column to the already selected options one. This control **Move** our selection from the left (source) column to the right (destination) column.

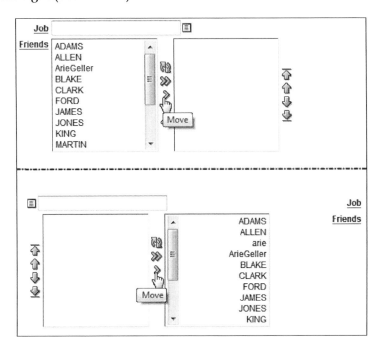

The bottom half of the previous screenshot shows how the *APEX Shuttle* item will be rendered on a Right-To-Left oriented page, without further treatment. As was expected, the source column is now the right column and our selections will appear in the left column. No noticeable changes have been made to the graphical controls (and by now, that also should be expected). However, although its functionality didn't change, the right arrowhead points now from the selected options column to the available options column. If you highlight a selected option and click the right arrowhead control, nothing will happen. If you highlight an available option on the right column and click this control, it will move the option from the right column to the left one, in the opposite direction it points to. This behavior can be very confusing to the end user, and might seriously impair the *Shuttle* item functionality. To preserve the correct and intuitive behavior of the Shuttle item, we need to reverse the orientation of the four arrowhead controls. Luckily for us, the *APEX Shuttle* item includes both the right and left, single and double arrowheads, so we only need to render them on page in the correct order.

The *APEX Shuttle* item is a compound item that is generated internally by the APEX engine. As such, we don't have any built-in measures to control the appearance of its graphical controls. In this case, JavaScript is the answer.

The following JavaScript function—shuttleRTL()—will render the graphical controls of the *APEX Shuttle* in the correct order, while translating their tooltip. In our example, we are using a mix of Arabic and Hebrew. In the real world, you'll probably use a single language of your choice:

```
function shuttleRTL(){
    var imgs = document.getElementsByTagName('IMG');

    for (i=0; i < imgs.length; i++) {
        if (imgs[i].src.indexOf('shuttle_right') > -1) {
            imgs[i].src = imgs[i].src.replace(/right/,'left');
            imgs[i].title = 'نقل';
            continue;
        }
        if (imgs[i].src.indexOf('shuttle_left') > -1) {
            imgs[i].src = imgs[i].src.replace(/left/,'right');
            imgs[i].title = 'قم بإزالة';
            continue;
        }
        if (imgs[i].src.indexOf('shuttle_first') > -1) {
            imgs[i].src = imgs[i].src.replace(/first/,'last');
            imgs[i].title = 'החזר הכל';
            continue;
        }
        if (imgs[i].src.indexOf('shuttle_last') > -1) {
            imgs[i].src = imgs[i].src.replace(/last/,'first');
            imgs[i].title = 'העבר הכל';
            continue;
        }
        if (imgs[i].src.indexOf('shuttle_reload') > -1) {
            imgs[i].title = 'טען מחדש';
        }
    }
}
```

The filenames of the relevant *Shuttle* control images include specific strings: right, left, first, and last. The function collects all the images on the page and search, by name, for the specific *Shuttle* item images. When it finds a relevant image it changes right to left and first to last, and vice versa. While doing so, it also attaches the correct tooltip to the control. As a result, the *Shuttle* controls appear in the correct order, pointing to the correct direction and having the correct translated tooltip.

The calling code for the function was entered into the **Region Footer** field of the region holding the *Shuttle* item:

```
<script type="text/javascript">
shuttleRTL();
</script>
```

If we are working with the APEX translation mechanism, and our primary language is a Left-To-Right one, we should comment the function call (as we don't need it in a Left-To-Right page) and enable it in the XLIFF file.

 You shouldn't delete the function call, just comment it so it will be easier for you to locate the corresponding `<trans-unit>` for it in the XLIFF file.

The following is the corresponding snippet of code from the XLIFF file:

```
<trans-unit id="S-27-12870008625537973001-9175840">
<source>&lt;script type="text/javascript">
/*
shuttleRTL();
*/
&lt;/script></source>
<target>&lt;script type="text/javascript">
shuttleRTL();
&lt;/script></target>
</trans-unit>
```

The final result can be seen in the following screenshot:

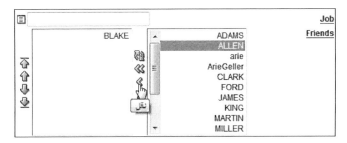

Labels and input fields alignment

By default, in a Left-To-Right *Form*, the label—located on the left-hand side—is aligned to the right and the input field—located to the right of the label—is aligned to the left. That makes the content of them adjacent, as they are both aligned to the same internal cell border. When we reverse the page to be a Right-To-Left *Form*, the label—now on the right side, is still aligned to the right and the input field—now located to the left of the label—is also still aligned to the left. That makes their content aligned apart from each other, as they are aligned to the (separate) external cell borders.

You can see a hint to this behaviour with the **Job** item in the last screenshot. The label is aligned to the right border of the item labels' column, while the input field is aligned to the far-left border of the input fields' column, which was determined by the *Shuttle* item as the widest element on this column.

The following JavaScript function—`alignRight()`, which we can invoke in exactly the same manner as the `shuttleRTL()`, is a very generic solution to this behaviour:

```
function alignRight () {
  var TDs = document.getElementsByTagName('td');
  for (i=0; i < TDs.length; i++){
    if (TDs[i].align == 'left'){
      TDs[i].align = 'right';
    }
  }
}
```

The function collects **all** the TDs on our Right-To-Left page and checks their alignment. In the case of a left alignment, the function changes it to a right alignment. With this JavaScript function, our Right-To-Left items will look like the following:

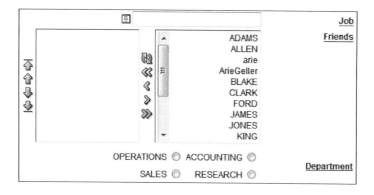

Bear in mind:

This is a very generic solution as the function changes the left alignment of all the TDs on the page. Some of these left alignments might be the correct alignment. You should check the effect of the `alignRight()` function on every page you choose to use it on, and see if the result meets your demands.

Date and time

In the previous chapter, we already reviewed the *Globalization* support that APEX provides us with to deal with date and time. However, in a Right-To-Left environment, displaying adjacent date and time needs our special attention.

In Right-To-Left environment, certain dates and time formats are displayed from left-to-right, e.g. **10/03/2010 21:30:23**. However, on a page, the Web browser sees two different elements—the date and the time. While reversing the page orientation to Right-To-Left the Web browser will reverse the rendering order of these two elements and on the page we'll see **21:30:23 10/03/2010**. To avoid this effect, we need to reverse the order of the date and time prior to it being reversed by the Right-To-Left orientation.

The following is an example of populating a **Display as Text (does not save state)** field with the database timestamp:

```
if :FSP_LANGUAGE_PREFERENCE = 'en' then
  return to_char(systimestamp,'MM-DD-YYYY HH24:MI:SS');
else
  return to_char(systimestamp,'HH24:MI:SS DD/MM/YYYY');
end if;
```

We should apply the same principle when working with an XLIFF file.

Summary

In this chapter, we complemented the discussion about APEX support of *Globalization* by reviewing the special measures we need to take to implement a Right-To-Left environment in our APEX applications.

We learned how to adapt APEX *templates* to support the Right-To-Left environment, how to use the XLIFF file for the same purpose, how we can harness CSS and JavaScript to achieve Right-To-Left orientation, and how to "fix" some of its side effects.

In the next chapter we'll deal with the options APEX provides us to deploy our developed application into other APEX instances.

20
Deploying APEX Applications

Being able to deploy applications between environments is an important aspect of application development. Often, we may need to deploy applications from a development environment to an acceptance test or production environment. We may also need to build applications that anyone can install and run in their own APEX environment. In this chapter, we will learn how to deploy our APEX applications to another APEX environment. Specifically, we shall be looking at:

- Supporting objects
- Exporting an application
- Importing an application

What do we need to deploy?

To deploy an application to another APEX environment, there are a number of items that need to be included in the deployment to ensure that the application will run. These items include the following:

- Application Source: This includes all the pages, templates, and shared components that make up our application
- Database Changes: This includes all database objects required for our application to work, such as tables, views, and stored procedures
- Data Load Scripts: This populates database tables to ensure that the application has all the necessary data to work
- Cascading Style Sheets (CSS)
- Images
- Static Files
- Theme Files

In this chapter, we will explore how these components can be deployed to another APEX environment. To start off, we will look at how database changes and data load scripts can be deployed using Supporting Objects.

Supporting Objects

When deploying an application we may often need to create or modify data, tables, stored procedures, and other database objects necessary for our application to run correctly. One way to deploy database changes is through SQL script files. In the SQL script files we enter DML and DDL statements for all required database changes. These scripts can then be run against the destination database schema to make the required changes. The SQL script files are separate to our application and means that there is an additional step on top of deploying the application source.

Supporting Objects is a function in APEX that can be used to create a single file for deployment. This file includes the application source together with any database changes, data load scripts, or static files. This means that we have a single file to deploy in our entire application. Using this approach is similar to having an installer for our application and is referred to as a **Packaged Application** in APEX. The Supporting Objects function simplifies the deployment of our APEX applications and gives us greater control in how the changes are deployed.

To view Supporting Objects in APEX we can access them from the main toolbar in the Application Builder.

In the following screenshot, we can see the Supporting Objects page:

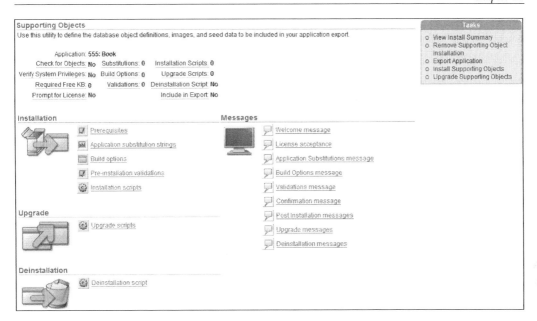

In the Supporting Objects page we can define scripts to be run when we install, upgrade, or deinstall our application. The scripts can contain not only SQL, DML, and DDL statements, but also CSS, images, and static files required for our application. We can also define messages and other checks to customize the installation of Supporting Objects, but also ensure our deployment goes smoothly without errors. Supporting Objects, once defined, will be included in the export of our application, which we will see later in this chapter. Specifically, in the Supporting Objects page, we can define the following:

- **Messages:** This enables custom text messages to be defined for the application install screens. Examples of messages we can define include the welcome message, license agreement, and post installation messages.

- **Prerequisites**: This enables checks to be defined to determine if the application can be installed. We can check if the database schema has enough free space, the required database privileges, and that specific database objects do not already exist.

- **Substitutions**: This enables values of Application Substitution Strings to be set for the destination APEX instance.

- **Build Options**: This provides the ability to enable or disable functionality if build options have been defined.

- **Validations**: This enables multiple checks to be defined to ensure that we can deploy database changes and load data scripts successfully.

- **Install Scripts**: This enables SQL scripts containing the database changes required for our application to be entered or uploaded. Multiple SQL scripts can be defined, and we can control the order in which they are run.

- **Upgrade Scripts**: Like Install Scripts, we can define SQL scripts to run when upgrading to a newer version of the application. With Upgrade Scripts, we only need to include new database objects that have been created since the last version of the application.

- **Uninstall Scripts**: Like Install Scripts, we can define SQL scripts to run when the application is deleted or uninstalled from the APEX workspace.

- **Export Options**: This is used to define if Supporting Object definitions are included in the export of the application. If Supporting Object definitions are not included in the export, then they will not be installed.

To define Supporting Object definitions we simply click the links in the Supporting Objects page in the appropriate section. A property page is then displayed where further details can be entered. We will begin by looking at the definition of Messages.

Messages

Using Messages we can tailor install screens to display custom text messages and descriptions that are specific to the deployment of our application. Messages can be accessed by the **Messages** tab or by the individual message type on the main Supporting Objects screen. In the following screenshot, we can see the text edit fields for the welcome and license messages:

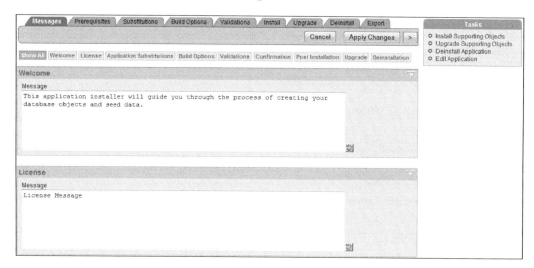

The Supporting Objects function enables us to define the following types of messages:

Message Type		Description
Welcome		Welcome is the first message to be displayed when installing Supporting Objects and is used to provide an overview of the installation process and any related information.
License		License can be used to define a license agreement that needs to be accepted by the user before Supporting Objects can be installed. This message is only displayed if the license message contains text, and when installing or upgrading Supporting Objects.
Application Substitutions		This enables a custom message to be displayed when prompted for the value of Application Substitution Strings. This message is displayed when installing or upgrading Supporting Objects.
Build Options		This enables a custom message to be displayed when prompted for Build Options. This message is displayed when installing or upgrading Supporting Objects.
Validations		This enables a custom message to be displayed when listing the validation checks to be performed. This message is displayed when installing or upgrading Supporting Objects.
Confirmation		This enables a custom message to be displayed after all validations have been checked, to confirm if the user wishes to proceed with running the installation scripts.
Post Installation	Install Success	This enables a custom message to be displayed when the installation scripts have run successfully without errors.
	Install Failure	This enables a custom message to be displayed when the installation scripts have finished running and errors have been encountered.

Message Type		Description
Upgrade	**Welcome**	Welcome is the first message to be displayed when upgrading Supporting Objects and is used to provide an overview of the upgrade process and any related information.
	Confirmation	This enables a custom message to be displayed after all validations have been checked, to confirm if the user wishes to proceed with running the upgraded scripts.
	Success	This enables a custom message to be displayed when the upgrade scripts have run successfully without errors.
	Failure	This enables a custom message to be displayed when the upgrade scripts have finished running and errors have been encountered.
Deinstallation	**Deinstall**	This enables a custom message to be displayed when confirming the deinstallation of the application.
	Post-Deinstall	This enables a custom message to be displayed when the deinstallation scripts have finished running.

 When defining messages, the following HTML tags can be used: bold `<b>`, italics `<i>`, underline `<u>`, paragraph `<p>`, line break `<br>`, horizontal rule `<hr>`, unordered list `<ul>`, ordered list `<ol>`, list `<li>`, and pre-formatted text `<pre>`.

Prerequisites

The **Prerequisites** property page enables checks to be defined to determine if the application can be installed in the destination database. This helps avoid errors in the installation due to missing system privileges or database objects that already exist in the database schema. The prerequisite checks are the first operation performed when installing Supporting Objects.

The **Required Free Space in KB** attribute is used to define how much free space is required for the application. The default tablespace in the parsing database schema will be checked for the required free space when the application is installed.

The **Required System Privileges** attribute checks if the database schema where the database objects will be created have the appropriate system privileges. Using this attribute we can check if we have system privileges to create tables, views, procedures, and other database objects. This helps prevent any issues where we may try to create a database object like a table, but do not have the required system privilege to create a table. This would result in a privilege error, and the database object would not be created.

We can also avoid errors where database objects that are to be created in our installation scripts already exist in the destination database, by using the **Objects that will be installed** section. The **Object Names** attribute can be used to enter the name of the database object that we wish to check does not already exist. The list of values icon next to the attribute can be used to select database object names that already exist. Clicking the **Add** button will add the database object to the list of database objects to check. We can remove a database object by selecting an item from the list and clicking the **Remove** button. If any of the database objects exist, then the installation will not proceed and details of the error will be displayed to the user.

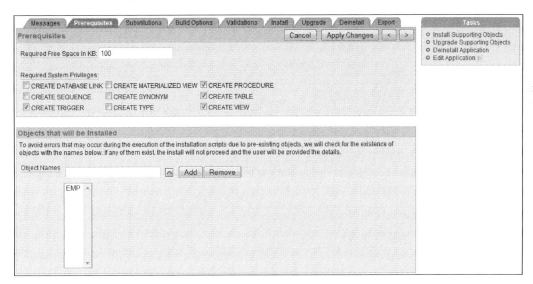

Substitutions

The **Substitutions** property page is used to select the Application Substitution Strings a user can change when installing Supporting Objects. All Substitution Strings defined for the application are listed on the page, with the **Prompt?** attribute determining if the user can change the Substitution String during the installation. The page also displays the name and existing value of the Substitution String in the **Substitution String** and **Current Value** attributes. The **Prompt Text** attribute allows custom text or a prompt to be entered to describe the Substitution String during the installation.

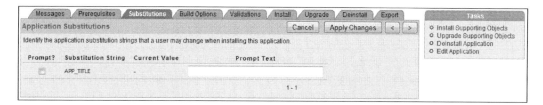

Build Options

The **Build Options** property page is used to identify the Build Options a user can select when installing Supporting Objects. This will allow a user to enable or disable functionality in the application during the installation. The **Prompt for Build Options** attribute lists each Build Option defined in the application. Selecting the checkbox next to the **Build Option** name will enable the Build Option to be selected during the installation.

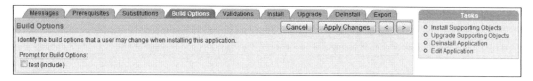

Validations

The **Validations** property page enables multiple checks to be defined to ensure the installation scripts will run successfully with no errors in our destination database. Validations are useful to ensure that we won't encounter errors due to database objects already existing, or other some condition that will cause an error in our installation scripts.

The page displays the order the validation will be performed in, a name for the validation, and details of the condition to apply for the validation using the **Sequence, Name, Validation Type**, and **Condition** attributes. We can add a new validation by clicking the **Create** button and modify an existing validation by clicking the edit icon next to each validation.

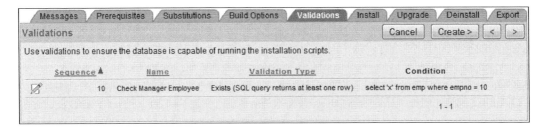

Create/Update a Validation

The following screenshot is displayed if we have selected to create or modify a validation from the **Validations** property page:

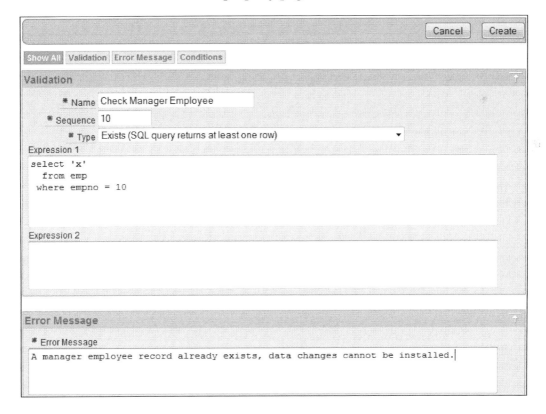

In the previous screenshot, we use the **Name** and **Sequence** attributes to define a unique name to identify the validation and determine the order in which the validation will be run. The **Type**, **Expression 1**, and **Expression 2** attributes are used to specify details about the condition to apply for the validation, for example, a SQL or PL/SQL expression. The **Error Message** attribute defines an error message that will be displayed if the validation fails during the installation of Supporting Objects.

Install

The **Install** property page is used to add SQL scripts containing DDL and DML statements that are used to install the database objects required for the application. The page displays the name, the sequence order the scripts will be run in, and the source code for installing scripts using the **Name**, **Sequence**, and **Script** attributes. We can add a new script by clicking the **Create** button and modify an existing script by clicking the edit icon next to each script.

 The task menu on the page provides useful links we can use to install, upgrade, or deinstall the Supporting Objects definitions we have defined. The **Display Single Script** link is also useful to view all scripts defined in a single merged script. You will see this task menu displayed throughout many of the Supporting Object pages.

Create Script

If the **Create** button is clicked in the **Install** property page, then a **Create Script Wizard** will be displayed that allows us to define details about the script. We start by defining how the script will be entered. The **Create from Scratch** attribute enables custom SQL commands to be entered from scratch, while the **Create from File** attribute enables an existing file with SQL commands to be uploaded. The **Script Type** attribute is used to determine whether the script being created is used to install, update, or deinstall the application. This is useful as the Create Script Wizard can be accessed from the Install, Upgrade, and Deinstall property pages of Supporting Objects.

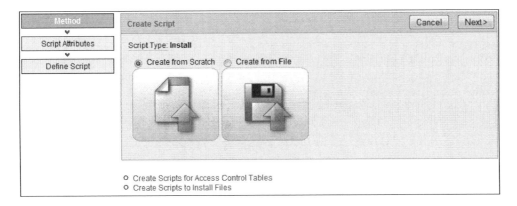

Script Attributes

Once we have defined how the script will be entered, we are then prompted to enter details about the script and when it will be run using the **Script Attributes** page. The **Name** attribute defines a unique name to identify the script. The **Sequence** attribute determines the order in which the script will be run. This is important if you have multiple scripts and there are dependencies in the order in which the scripts must be run. For example, a script to a create table would need to run before a script to create a trigger on the table.

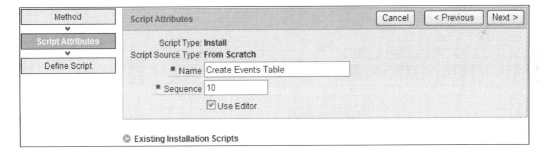

 We can also define a condition that determines if the script will be run. This can only be entered using the **Update Script Attributes** page. If a condition has not been specified, then the script will always be run.

Define Script

If we have selected the **Create from Scratch** attribute in the **Create Script** page, we are then prompted with the Script Editor page. The Script Editor page enables us to enter custom SQL, DML, and DDL commands for the script. Clicking the **Apply Changes** button will create the script.

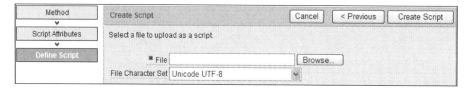

Otherwise, if we have selected the **Create from File** attribute in the Create Script page we are shown a page to upload a script file. The **File** attribute is used to select the actual script file that we wish to upload. Clicking the **Create Script** button will create the script based on the uploaded file.

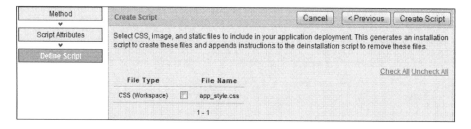

Create Scripts to Install Files

A useful function from the Create Script page is the **Create Scripts to Install Files** link. This enables CSS, image, and static files defined in Shared Components to be included as scripts in the installation.

Upgrade

The **Upgrade** property page is used to add SQL scripts containing DDL and DML statements that are used to upgrade database objects for the application. The page displays the name, the sequence order the scripts will be run in, and the source code to upgrade scripts using the **Name**, **Sequence**, and **Script** attributes. We can add a new script by clicking the **Create** button and modify an existing script by clicking the edit icon next to each script. We define multiple SQL scripts just like we did in the **Install** property page using the Create Script Wizard.

The **Upgrade** property page also enables a query to be entered to determine if the upgraded scripts have already been installed by using the **Query to Detect Existing Supporting Objects** attribute. If the query returns at least one row, then an error will be displayed and the upgrade scripts will not be installed. For example, if an upgrade script has been defined to create a table named customers, then the following query could be used to check if the customers' table already exists:

```
SELECT object_name
  FROM USER_OBJECTS
 WHERE object_name = 'CUSTOMERS'
```

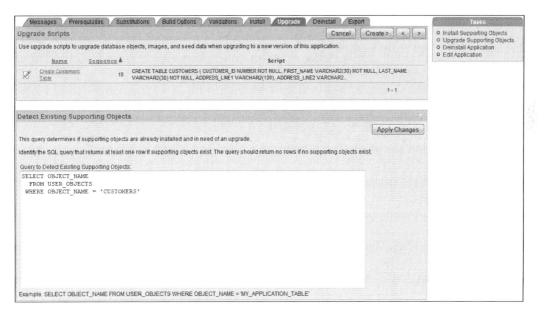

Deinstallation

The **Deinstallation** property page is used to define SQL scripts containing DDL and DML statements to remove database objects used by the application. SQL scripts are added and modified just like we did in the **Install** property page using the Create Script Wizard.

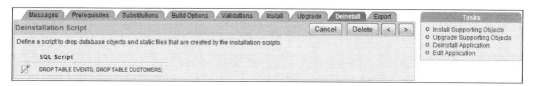

Export

The **Export** property page determines if Support Object definitions, like install, upgrade, and deinstall scripts, are included in the export of the application by default. This is entered using the **Include Supporting Object Definitions in Export** attribute. In the next section we will see how this attribute can be overridden when exporting an application.

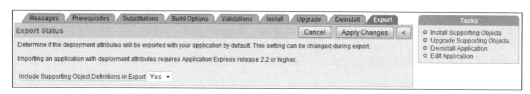

 APEX version 2.2 or higher is required to import and install an application that includes Supporting Object definitions.

Once we have defined Supporting Object definitions or created relevant SQL scripts, we are now ready to export the application. In the next section, we will look at how the application, including Supporting Objects, can be exported into a single file.

Exporting an Application

To create the necessary install files for our application we use the Export function. The Export function creates a single SQL script file that contains all our application pages, regions, items, and templates. If our application has style sheets, images, or static files uploaded in Shared Components, then these will need to be exported separately. The Export function is accessed from the Application Builder page. Alternatively, it can be accessed from the Supporting Objects page as well.

In the application export page, we can select which application to export from the workspace by using the **Application** attribute. The export file can be generated with line feeds for UNIX or carriage returns for DOS. This is specified using the **File Format** attribute. The **Owner Override** attribute determines which database schema to use as the application owner. We can control whether the application can be modified by developers using the **Build Status Override** attribute. Setting the **Build Status Override** attribute to **Run Application Only** prevents the application from being modified in the Application Builder, while setting it to **Run and Build Application** enables the application to be modified in the Application Builder.

The **Debugging** attribute determines if debugging is allowed in the application. This should only be set to Yes in development environments. The **Export Supporting Object Definitions** attribute determines if the Supporting Object definitions we looked at earlier in this chapter are included in the export like SQL scripts and messages. The **Export Saved Reports** attribute determines if saved Interactive Report customizations are included in the export. The **Export Comments** attribute determines if developer comments, entered in APEX property pages, are included in the export. We can also use the **As of** attribute to export the application from a particular point in time. This can be useful if something has accidently been deleted and we wish to retrieve the deleted source.

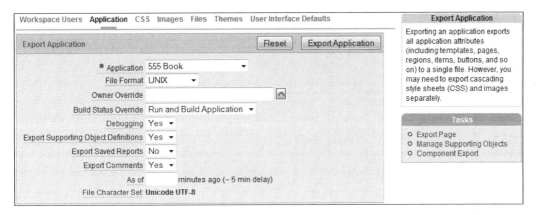

The Export function can also be used to export workspace users, style sheets, images, static files, themes, and User Interface Defaults individually in a SQL script file. Depending on how your APEX environment has been configured, you may need to copy images, style sheets, and other theme files to the Apache web server used by APEX. This is an alternative to storing files in APEX Shared Components.

Exporting a page

We have seen how to export an entire application, but what if we only wish to deploy a specific page? APEX provides an **Export Page** screen that enables us to export just a single page. This can be useful if we have made changes to a specific page and only wish to deploy the specific page, rather than deploying the entire application. It can also be useful when developing, as we can take a backup of the page we wish to work on prior to making any changes. Having a backup then makes it easy for us to undo our changes or even compare the changes we have made to a previous version. The **Export Page** screen can be accessed from the Action Menu in the Page Builder page (down arrow icon) or the task menu in the Export Application page.

In the **Export Page** screen, the **Page** attribute is used to select which page in the application we wish to export. Clicking the **Export Page** button then allows us to download and save the export file containing only the page selected.

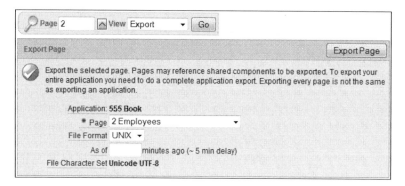

 To export a page and then import it into another APEX instance, the Workspace IDs in the source and destination APEX instances need to be identical.

Exporting components

The Component Export, like the Page Export, enables us to selectively choose specific components of our application to export, rather than exporting the entire application. Components can include things like Pages, Templates, Application Items, List of Values, Lists, Shortcuts, Tabs, and other Shared Components. The Component Export enables us to be very selective in exactly what we wish to export.

By being specific in what we export, we only need to select the pages, templates, or shared components that have been modified. This can reduce the amount of testing required as we are only deploying functionality that has changed. It can also simplify deployment, especially if you only need to deploy a change to a list of values for example. It can also be useful to backup specific components so they can be reapplied at a later stage if changes have been made.

The Component Export page is accessed through the task menu in the Export Application page we saw previously. The Export Components page displays four main tabs: Components, Components by Page, Application Attributes, and Build Option Status. We will start by looking at the **Components** tab.

Components

The **Components** tab is used to select components in the application that are to be included in the export file. This export file can then be used to deploy the selected components to another APEX instance.

The page lists all components in the application including the type of component, the name of the component, when the component was last changed, and who last changed the component. These are displayed in the **Component Type**, **Component Name**, **Last Updated**, and **Developer** attributes.

To make it simpler to find the component we are after, we can use the **Find** attribute to filter the listing of components based on the name entered. The **Component** attribute also enables the listing of components to be filtered based on the type of component; for example, selecting a Region Template will only display Region Template components.

The **Components to Export** region lists all the components we have selected to include in the export, including the name and type in the **Component Type** and **Component Name** attributes. To add a specific component to the export, we select the checkbox alongside each component and click the **Add to Export** button. We can use the remove icon to remove a specific component from the export if it has been accidently selected or is not required. The **Remove All** button will clear the list of components to export.

We can either use the other tabs like **Components by Page**, **Application Attributes**, and **Build Options** to further select components to export, or if we have selected all required components, then click the **Next >** button to generate the export.

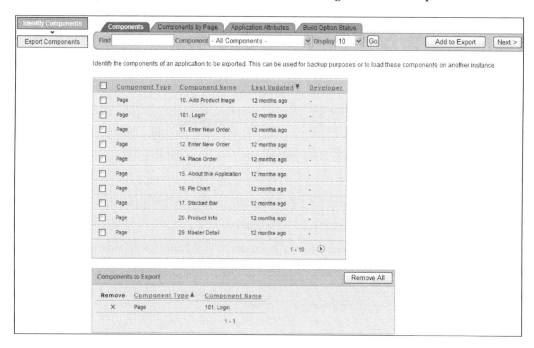

Components by Page

The **Components by Page** tab works in much the same way as the **Components** tab, except the listing of components are per page. Therefore, if we are working on a particular page, we can see the components that make up the page and select only those that have been changed. The **Components by Page** tab also enables us to filter the listing of components by a specific page by using the **Page** attribute.

Application Attributes

The **Application Attributes** tab enables the Application Definition attributes defined under Shared Components to be exported to another APEX instance. Application Definition attributes include attributes like application name, application alias, logo, and many others. We simply select which attributes to export and use the **Add to Export** button to include them in the export.

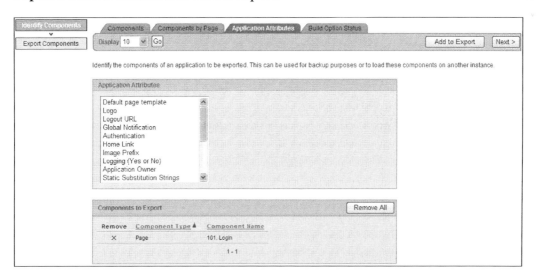

Build Option Status

The Build Options tab enables specific Build Options and their status to be exported to another APEX instance. This can be used to turn functionality on or off in another APEX instance of the application. We simply select the Build Option to export and use the **Add to Export** button to include them in the export.

Export Components

Once we have selected the components to export, we can then generate the export file using the **Export Components** page. The page lists all the components we have selected to export, including the name and type in the **Component Type** and **Component Name** attributes. We can customize the export file to be generated with line feeds for UNIX or carriage returns for DOS using the **File Format** attribute. We can also use the **As Of** attribute to export the components from a particular point in time. Clicking the **Export Components** button then allows us to download and save the export file containing only the components selected.

Once we have created an export file by performing an Application, Page, or Component Export, we are now ready to import (or deploy) the application. In the next section, we will look at how the application can be imported into another APEX instance.

Importing an application

Once we have exported the application, we can then install it in our destination APEX instance. We install the application by using the Import Wizard. The Import Wizard will guide us through the installation of our application and any Supporting Objects defined in the export file. In this section, we will walk through the steps required to install an APEX application using the Import Wizard.

Start the Import Wizard

The Import Wizard is accessed from the Application Builder screen. Click the Import option to start the wizard.

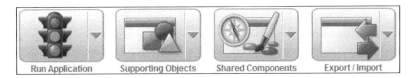

Specify File

The first step to install an application is to select the export file to install using the **Import File** attribute. We also need to specify what type of file we are importing by using the **File Type** attribute. Typically, we will be importing an Application, Page, or Component Export, but we could also import style sheets, images, static files, themes, or UI defaults. Click **Next** to continue.

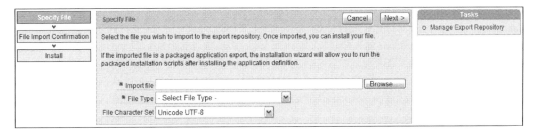

File Import Confirmation

In the next step, APEX confirms that the export file has been imported into the Export Repository. The Export Repository keeps a copy of all export files imported and enables an export file to be installed or re-installed if the application already exists. This essentially provides a history of all installed versions for our application. We can either click **Next** to install the file now or we can decide to install the file later on from the Export Repository.

Install

Once the export file has been imported into the destination APEX instance, we then need to specify details about the installation. The **Parsing Schema** attribute tells APEX which database schema to use for the application. We can control whether the application source can be modified by developers using the **Build Status** attribute. Setting the **Build Status** attribute to **Run Application Only** prevents the application source from being modified; setting it to **Run and Build Application** enables the application source to be modified. Once the **Build Status** attribute has been set to **Run Application Only**, it can only be changed by an APEX Administrator.

Each application in an APEX instance must be assigned a unique Application ID. This enables APEX to internally reference the application. The **Install As Application** attribute is used to determine how the Application ID is allocated. The following options are available:

- **Auto Assign New Application ID**: This lets APEX automatically allocate an available Application ID.

- **Reuse Application ID from Export File**: This uses the same Application ID as the source APEX instance. A warning will be displayed asking you to replace the existing application if the Application ID is already being used.

- **Change Application ID**: This enables a custom Application ID to be entered in the **New Application** attribute.

We can also install APEX export files using Oracle SQL Developer or by running the export files in SQL*Plus.

Supporting Objects installation

After importing and installing the application definition, if the export file being installed contains Supporting Object definitions, then we will also be prompted to install the Supporting Objects. The Supporting Object installation screen will be customized based on the messages defined, such as welcome messages and license agreements. It will also display error messages if any of the prerequisites or validations have failed. We will also be prompted to enter Substitution Strings and any Build Options to apply. Once the Supporting Object's installation has completed, our application deploys in the destination APEX instance. We can now run the application to ensure that the deployment is successful.

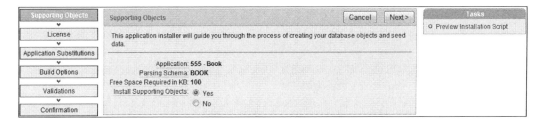

Use the **Preview Installation Script** link in the task menu to view further details about the installation, such as prerequisites and script contents, before you run the installation.

Command line export utility

A hidden utility in APEX is a Java program that is provided with the APEX installation files, and can be used to export APEX applications via the command line. This enables us to export applications without needing to log into the APEX Web interface. Being accessible from the command line means we could automate the export of applications on a regular basis for backups.

The export utility is named `APEXExport.class` and can be found in the utilities directory of the APEX installation files.

To use the export utility, we need to ensure that a JDK version 1.4 or higher is used and the Oracle JDBC libraries are in your CLASSPATH. To set the CLASSPATH in a Windows environment, we would use the following command:

```
Set CLASSPATH=%CLASSPATH%;.\;%ORACLE_HOME%\jdbc\lib\classes12.jar
```

We can then run the export utility by issuing the following command from the APEX utilities directory:

```
java oracle.apex.APEXExport -db -user -password -applicationid -
workspaceid -instance - skipExportDate -expSavedReports -debug
```

The export utility accepts the following parameters, which determine the applications or workspaces that will be included in the export:

Parameter	Description
-db	The JDBC database connection string used to specify the database where APEX is installed. The JDBC connection string is in the format "IP Address: Port:SID", for example:
	`127.0.0.1:1521:ORCL`
-user	Database username to connect as.
-password	Database password.
-applicationid	The ID of the application to export.
-workspaceid	The ID of the workspace to export. This will include all applications from the workspace in the export.

Parameter	Description
-instance	This will export all applications in the APEX instance. The database user account APEX_030200 needs to be unlocked to export all applications in the instance. Be sure to lock the account once the export has been completed.
-skipExportDate	This determines if the export date is included in the export files.
-expSavedReports	This determines if Interactive Report definitions saved by users, such as highlighting and conditions, are included in the export file.

To export an individual application, the following command can be used:

```
java oracle.apex.APEXExport -db 127.0.0.1:1521:ORCL -user book -
password book -applicationid 101
```

Summary

In this chapter, we have learned how to deploy APEX applications to another APEX instance. We have seen how Supporting Objects can be used to create a Packaged Application. Packaged Applications simplify our installation as we only have one file to deploy, which contains both our application and database changes. We have also learned how to export the application into a file and import the file in another APEX instance. The export and import functions in APEX make it very simple and quick to deploy our applications to another APEX instance.

In the next chapter, we will look at the APEX runtime environment.

21

The APEX Runtime Environment

When setting up a technical infrastructure to run our production applications, it is important to have an environment that is both secure and locked down. This is even more important when our applications can be accessed from the Internet, as this can expose our applications to many more security threats. In this chapter, we will see how the APEX Runtime Environment is one method we can use to help provide a more secure environment to run our applications. Specifically, we will be looking at:

- What the APEX Runtime Environment is
- Setting up an APEX Runtime Environment
- Managing the APEX Runtime Environment

What is the APEX Runtime Environment?

So far in this book, we have seen the APEX Full Development Environment. This environment provides web-based screens to build, manage, and deploy our applications. This provides features such as the Application Builder, SQL Workshop, Utilities, and Administration. In a production environment this exposes a number of functions via a web browser that can be used to modify applications and access database schemas.

In APEX 3.1, an APEX Runtime Environment was introduced to provide a more secure and locked down environment for hosting production and test applications. The major difference in the runtime environment is that there is no web interface to manage our environment. The runtime environment is also cut down to only contain the minimum database packages required to run applications. This reduces the APEX footprint and the database privileges required to run APEX.

Setting up a Runtime Environment

When APEX is first installed, we can choose whether to install the APEX Full Development Environment or the APEX Runtime Environment. This can be changed at a later stage by running the SQL scripts provided with the APEX install. We can convert from an APEX Full Development Environment to an APEX Runtime Environment by running the SQL script `apxdevrm.sql` using the SYS user with the SYSDBA role. We can also convert a runtime environment back to a full development environment by running the SQL script `apxdvins.sql`. Converting the environment will leave our applications unchanged, and they can be run using the exact same URL. Now that we have seen how to convert to a Runtime environment, let's look at how we can manage the environment.

> The Oracle SYS user is a special user that is automatically created when the Oracle Database is first installed. It contains all base tables and views for the data dictionary, and is critical for running the database. Never create or modify objects in the SYS schema.

Managing the APEX Runtime Environment

You may start wondering how we can deploy applications and perform other administration tasks in an APEX Runtime Environment when there is no web interface to use. To perform these administration tasks, we can use Oracle SQL*Plus or Oracle SQL Developer. In this section, we will look at some common administration tasks and how they can be performed in an APEX Runtime Environment.

> Oracle SQL Developer is a free GUI-based tool for database development, similar to the SQL Workshop in APEX. It can be downloaded from the Oracle SQL Developer website:
>
> http://www.oracle.com/technology/products/database/
> sql_developer/index.html

Installing applications

The most common administration task we need to perform when managing our environment is to deploy new or updated applications. In the previous chapter, we saw how to export our applications into a SQL script file. We can install our applications and other export files such as pages in an APEX Runtime Environment by running the export file in Oracle SQL*Plus. To do this, we need to connect to the database as SYS, SYSTEM, APEX_030200, or a user with the APEX_ADMINISTRATOR_ROLE assigned.

Alternatively, we can use Oracle SQL Developer to deploy an export file. Oracle SQL Developer provides a wizard very similar to the APEX Import Wizard that can be used to install our application. In the following screenshot, we can see how import options can be entered for the install once an export file has been selected:

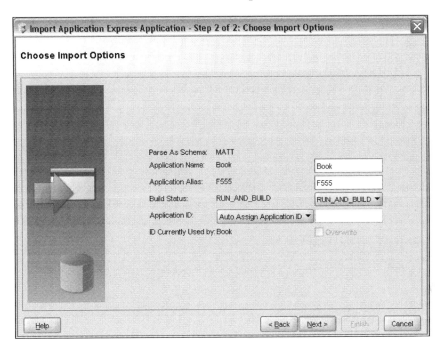

APEX_INSTANCE_ADMIN API

Another common administration task is the ability to set environmental settings and manage workspaces. APEX provides a PL/SQL package named APEX_INSTANCE_ADMIN that can be used to administer our environment. To execute the package we must log in in as SYS, SYSTEM, APEX_030200, or a user with the APEX_ADMINISTRATOR_ROLE assigned. The APEX_INSTANCE_ADMIN package provides the following functions and procedures, which we can use to manage our environment:

Function/Procedure Name	Description
SET_PARAMETER	Sets the value of an APEX instance parameter in the runtime environment such as e-mail and reports server settings.
GET_PARAMETER	Gets the value of an APEX instance parameter stored in the runtime environment.

Function/Procedure Name	Description
GET_SCHEMAS	Gets a list of database schemas mapped to workspaces in the runtime environment.
ADD_SCHEMA	Adds a database schema mapping to a workspace in the runtime environment.
REMOVE_SCHEMA	Removes a database schema mapping from a workspace in the runtime environment.
ADD_WORKSPACE	Adds a new workspace to our runtime environment.
REMOVE_WORKSPACE	Removes an existing workspace from our runtime environment.

Viewing APEX reports

The APEX Full Development Environment provides many reports to retrieve various details about our applications and environment. Reports range from installed applications and workspaces to activity logs and login attempts. These can be very useful when managing our environment. This information can still be accessed in the APEX Runtime Environment by writing SQL queries using Oracle SQL*Plus or Oracle SQL Developer.

APEX helps make writing SQL queries to retrieve information about our APEX environment simpler by providing a number of common database views. Details of these views are defined in the APEX Views function in the Utilities section of an APEX Full Development Environment. This feature not only explains the view and its columns, but also helps us to construct the SQL source required to query the APEX view. To demonstrate APEX views, the following SQL query can be run using the APEX_APPLICATIONS view to query all applications for the current user or workspace:

```
select workspace, application_id, application_name
  from apex_applications
```

Oracle SQL Developer

We may not have a web interface to manage our environment when using an APEX Runtime Environment, but Oracle SQL Developer can be used to help assist with the administration of our environment. Oracle SQL Developer is a free tool that we can use to manage and develop Oracle database applications. With Oracle SQL Developer, we can perform the following APEX tasks:

- Browse APEX applications, pages, and other application details
- Import and export applications and pages

- Run reports about the APEX environment

- Modify basic details about the application

In the following screenshot, we can see how SQL Developer displays a node for APEX under the database connection on the left:

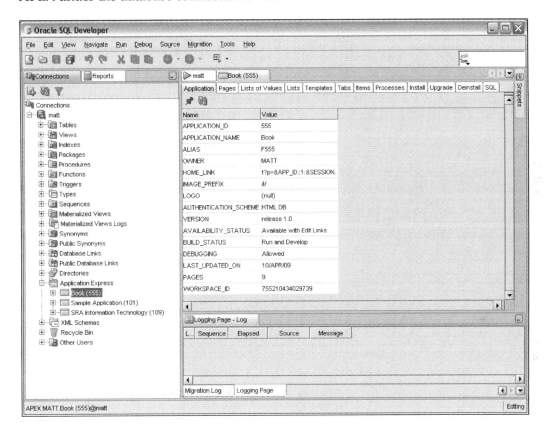

Right-clicking the APEX node displays a menu to perform functions such as importing an application. Expanding the APEX node will display all applications to which the database schema is linked. We can click an application and view further details about the application on the right. A number of tabs are displayed that enable us to view information about our application, including pages and templates.

Summary

In this chapter, we have learned about the APEX runtime environment and how it can make our production environments more secure. We have seen how we can change an APEX Full Development Environment to an APEX Runtime Environment. We have also seen how we can manage the APEX Runtime Environment using Oracle SQL*Plus or Oracle SQL Developer to perform tasks such as deploying applications, setting parameters , managing workspaces, and accessing common environment details through APEX views.

In the next chapter, we will look at Security and how it can be used in our applications.

22
Security

Security is an important feature when building applications, as it enables us to prevent unauthorized access and activity in our applications. Not all applications require security; a public website doesn't for example. However, for many applications, we need to be able to control who can run and gain access to them. Once a user is logged into our application, we also need to further control what functionality they have permission to access. In APEX, these security features are implemented through the use of Authentication and Authorization Schemes. These schemes enable us to declaratively define security for our applications quickly and easily. In this chapter we will explore how to use these and other features to implement security in our applications. Specifically, we shall be looking at:

- Authentication Schemes
- Authorization Schemes
- Session State Protection
- Security Attributes

APEX security features overview

When implementing security in our applications, there are many features we need to have in place, such as authentication, authorization, and auditing. In APEX, these and other security features can be found in the **Shared Components** section of our application. This section provides a central point where we can define and apply security settings for our application. In the following screenshot we can see links to the security functions provided by APEX, which include the following:

- **Authentication Schemes:** These are used to determine the identity of users and control who can access our applications
- **Authorization Schemes**: These are used to control what functionality a user can access within our applications once they are logged in

- **Session State Protection**: This is used to prevent tampering of application URLs and session item values stored in APEX

- **Security Attributes**: This is used to enter security attributes for the entire application

In this chapter we will walk through each of these features and explain how they can be used in our applications. First we will look at how we can authenticate application users by using Authentication Schemes.

Authentication Schemes

The first task when implementing security is to determine the identity of the user trying to access the application. This is commonly achieved via a login page where a username and password are entered. A login page may also include a digital certificate or secure key as an additional measure, in order to verify that the user is who they actually say they are. The login details are then validated against a user repository to check whether the user account exists and the password entered is correct. If the user passes these checks they are allowed to access the application.

In APEX, we implement this authentication process through the use of Authentication Schemes. Authentication Schemes are a standard way to handle the processing of a login page and managing if a user's session is active. There are a number of ways we can store user accounts that influence how login processing needs to be handled. APEX makes our life easier by providing a number of preconfigured Authentication Schemes to interact with many common user repositories. This makes implementing authentication quick and easy, all without having to write a single line of code. The following preconfigured Authentication Schemes are available:

- **Show Built-In Login Page and Use Open Door Credentials:** This scheme enables all users to access the application just by entering a user name in the login page.

This can be useful when building a prototype or demo application. We can implement a basic login without needing to worry about the implementation details for authenticating users, such as where users will be stored and how they will be validated.

- **Show Login Page and Use Application Express Account Credentials:** This scheme uses the built-in APEX user repository to store and mange user accounts. This lets APEX handle our entire authentication and is the quickest and easiest way to authenticate our users.

This scheme should only be used for development or personal environments and is not recommended for a production environment. APEX also comes with a database package APEX_UTIL that can be used to manage APEX user accounts programmatically.

- **Show Login Page and Use Database Account Credentials:** This scheme authenticates users against the username and password of a named user in the database. This requires each user to have a database user account created. Connections to the database are logged in as the APEX_PUBLIC_USER.

- **Show Login Page and Use LDAP Directory Credentials:** This scheme authenticates users against a **Lightweight Directory Access Protocol (LDAP)** user repository.

- **No Authentication (using DAD):** This scheme authenticates users by using the user credentials supplied in the PL/SQL Database Access Descriptor (DAD) configuration file. If no user credentials are entered, then a basic authentication screen is displayed (separate to APEX) and you are logged in as a database user, not as the APEX_PUBLIC_USER.

- **Oracle Application Server Single Sign-On (Application Express Engine as Partner App):** This scheme authenticates users by using Oracle Application Server Single Sign On (SSO). The APEX engine must be registered as a partner application in SSO.

- **Oracle Application Server Single Sign-On (My Application as Partner App):** This scheme authenticates users by using Oracle Application Server Single Sign On (SSO). Our application must be registered as a partner application in SSO.

Once our Authentication Scheme has determined the identity of a user in our application, the username is stored in a built-in substitution string named APP_USER. This can be referenced in our application to retrieve the username of the current user. This is useful in page processes or conditions where we may need to reference the current user as part of our logic. In the next section, we will see how we can quickly and easily add a pre-configured Authentication Scheme to our application.

Adding an Authentication Scheme

In the following screenshot we can see the Authentication Schemes page, which can be accessed from **Shared Components**:

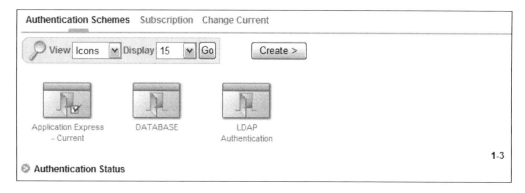

The screen displays all the existing Authentication Schemes that are defined for our application. We can select an Authentication Scheme to modify or, alternatively, we can create a new Authentication Scheme. The screen also enables us to see any Authentication Schemes referenced from other applications by using the **Subscription** tab. We can also switch which Authentication Scheme is currently active by using the **Change Current** tab.

To create a new Authentication Scheme, APEX provides a wizard which will guide us through the process of creating a new Authentication Scheme. To demonstrate, we will use the wizard to create a new Authentication Scheme that uses LDAP to authenticate users. Now, let's walk through the steps involved to create an Authentication Scheme. To begin, click the **Create** button to start the Authentication Scheme wizard.

Creation method

The first step of the wizard is to define how we would like to create the Authentication Scheme. We can base the new scheme on an APEX preconfigured Authentication Scheme, a copy of an Authentication Scheme from another workspace application, or code our own scheme from scratch. For our example we will select the **Based on a pre-configured scheme from the gallery** option and click the **Next** button:

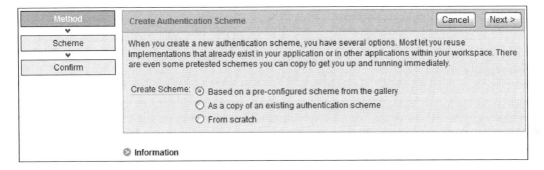

Selecting a pre-built Authentication Scheme

As we have selected to create our Authentication Scheme on a preconfigured scheme, we are now prompted to select which preconfigured scheme we wish to use. These preconfigured scheme options were covered earlier in the chapter. For our example we will select the **Show Login Page and Use LDAP Directory Credentials** option and click the **Next** button:

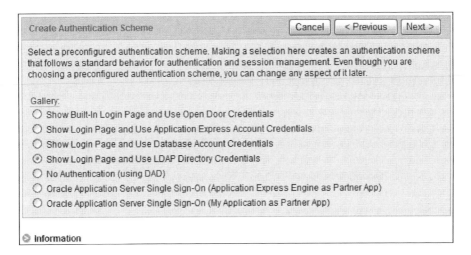

Adding a login page

In the next step we need to specify a login page that will be used for the Authentication Scheme. We can select to create a new login page for our application or use the default APEX built-in login page. If we need to customize the look and feel of the login page, then create a new login page, as the built-in login page cannot be modified. If our application already contains a login page, then the wizard will provide an option to select the existing login page. Select the **Create New Login Page** option and click the **Next** button:

 Make sure you clear the session state for the username and password items in your login page once authentication is complete. You don't want these items being kept in the session where they could potentially be accessed.

Specifying LDAP settings

As we have selected to create an Authentication Scheme based on the preconfigured LDAP scheme, we are now prompted to enter details about the LDAP server we wish to use. We specify the address and port of our LDAP server by entering the **LDAP Host** and **LDAP Port** attributes. We also specify a distinguished name string in the **LDAP Distinguished Name (DN) String** attribute.

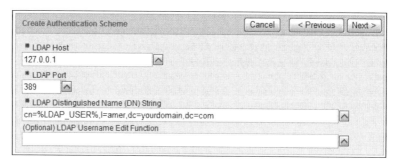

Authentication Scheme name

The final step is to provide a name for the new Authentication Scheme using the **Name** attribute. At this point, we have now entered enough information for the wizard to create our Authentication Scheme. Click the **Create Scheme** button to add the Authentication Scheme to our application. Now that we have added a new Authentication Scheme to our applications, we need to make it active so that it will be used when users log in to our application. In the next section we will see how to change the current Authentication Scheme of an application.

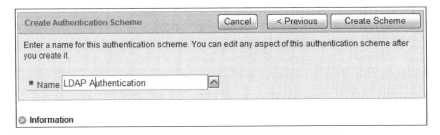

Changing the current Authentication Scheme

In our applications it is possible to have multiple authentication schemes defined. We can only ever have one authentication scheme active at a given time. The Change **Current Authentication Scheme** page enables us to switch between Authentication Schemes defined in our application. This can be useful in a development environment, where we may want to use a separate authentication method than in our production environment. The Change Current page makes it very easy for us to change how users are authenticated in our applications.

In the screenshot we can see the Change Current page. We simply select the Authentication Scheme we wish to use from the **Available Authentication Schemes** attribute and then click the **Next** button. APEX will then display a confirmation page to which we accept. The Authentication Scheme selected will now be used to authenticate users when they log in to the application.

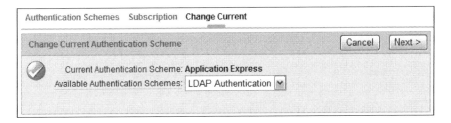

This is very useful where an Authentication Scheme used in an application is not available from another APEX instance. In this scenario we can use the in-built APEX Account Credentials to be able to run the application without being dependent on having security infrastructure in place.

Custom Authentication Scheme

We have seen how APEX provides a number of preconfigured Authentication Schemes that enable us to quickly and easily add authentication to our applications. But what happens if there is no preconfigured Authentication Scheme to handle how we wish to implement authentication for our application? To solve this, APEX enables us to create our own custom Authentication Schemes. To demonstrate, we will create a custom Authentication Scheme to verify users against a database table that stores usernames and passwords for our application users.

Before we can create the custom Authentication Scheme, we first need to build a PL/SQL database function that will validate the user login details. APEX requires that the database function accepts two parameters—a username and a password. APEX will pass these parameters based on the username and password entered in our login page. The database function is also required to return a Boolean result—TRUE if the user details are valid and FALSE if the user details are invalid. The following is a simple example of a database function to check if a username and password entered in our login page exists in our database table:

```
create or replace function valid_user (p_username in varchar2,
                                        p_password in varchar2)
  return boolean
as
  l_pw_check varchar2(1);
begin
  select 'x'
    into l_pw_check
    from users
   where upper(username) = upper(p_username)
     and password = p_password;
  apex_util.set_authentication_result(0);
  return true;
exception when no_data_found then
  apex_util.set_authentication_result(4);
  return false;
end valid_user;
```

In the code example we query a table named users to check if a record exists with the username and password supplied as parameters. If a record exists, then the function will return TRUE to indicate the login is correct, otherwise we return FALSE to indicate the login is incorrect. The code also logs the authentication result into the APEX activity logs by calling the database procedure APEX_UTIL.SET_AUTHENTICATION_ RESULT. We can use this later to run reports about the login attempts to our application. The following are the result codes and description to use when calling the APEX_UTIL.SET_AUTHENTICATION_RESULT procedure to audit logins:

- 0: Normal, successful authentication
- 1: Unknown User Name
- 2: Account Locked
- 3: Account Expired
- 4: Incorrect Password
- 5: Password First Use
- 6: Maximum Login Attempts Exceeded
- 7: Unknown Internal Error

Once our database authentication function has been created, we can then create a custom Authentication Scheme using the Authentication Scheme wizard shown previously. In the **Creation Method** step of the wizard, we need to select the **From Scratch** option. This will guide us through the steps to manually define our own custom authentication code. The main step in the wizard is the Authentication Function. The Authentication Function enables a PL/SQL function to be specified that will be used to authenticate user details entered from a login page.

In the following screenshot, we select the **Use my custom function to authenticate** option and enter the name of our database function in the **Authentication Function** attribute. This needs to be entered in the format return followed by the name of our database function. Once the wizard has completed, we can then change the current Authentication Scheme to use our newly created custom Authentication Scheme. APEX will now authenticate users against our database table when users log in to our application.

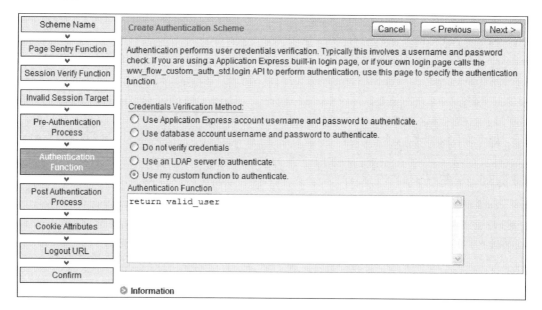

When creating your own custom Authentication Schemes, be sure to consider security features such as maximum login attempts, password expiry, and having to change the password on first use. Also, make sure passwords are not stored in clear text. These features can help make our application logins far more secure.

Authentication reports

Once our Authentication Scheme is being used to authenticate users in our application, it's important to regularly monitor login activity. APEX records the results of our Authentication Scheme in its activity logs. Using these activity logs, we can access a number of reports that can be used to detect any suspicious login activity and also provide details of login attempts. These reports are accessed from the Monitor Activity page in the Administration section of APEX. These reports are useful when administering security in our applications.

Authorization Schemes

Now that we are able to identify users of our applications, our next security task is to control what functionality the user can access within our application. In APEX this is implemented through an Authorization Scheme. An Authorization Scheme is a security condition that will either pass or fail. A pass enables the user to access functionality, while a fail denies the user access to the functionality. Multiple Authorization Schemes can be added to an application, which are then assigned to functionalities within our application, such as pages, regions, items, or buttons to restrict access. This means the user must pass the Authorization Scheme condition to be able to view the functionality. In this section we will see how to add an Authorization Scheme to our application and assign it to a page or item.

Authorization Schemes are very similar to a role. Roles are physically granted to a user, but with an Authorization Scheme a condition is defined using SQL, PL/SQL, or other condition types to dynamically evaluate if the user is assigned to the Authorization Scheme.

Create an Authorization Scheme

In the following screenshot we can see the Authorization Schemes pages, which can be accessed from **Shared Components**. The screen displays all existing Authorization Schemes defined for an application. We can select an Authorization Scheme to modify, or alternatively we can create a new Authorization Scheme. The screen enables us to see which Authorization Schemes are referenced from other workspace applications by using the **Subscriptions** tab. We can also view where in our application the Authorization Scheme is being used by clicking the **Utilization** tab.

To create a new Authorization Scheme, APEX provides a wizard that will guide us through the process of creating a new Authorization Scheme. To demonstrate, we will use the wizard to create new Authorization Scheme that will check if the current user is an Administrator for our application. It will do this by checking a user's table to see if an administrator flag column is set. Now, let's walk through the steps involved in creating an Authorization Scheme. To begin, click the **Create** button to start the Authorization Scheme wizard:

Creation method

The first step of the wizard is to specify how to create the Authorization Scheme. We can create the Authorization Scheme totally from scratch by selecting the **From Scratch** option. Alternatively, we can base it on an existing Authorization Scheme in the current application or from another workspace application by using the **As a copy of an Existing Authorization Scheme** option. This option creates a copy in our application that we can then refine and customize, rather than creating the whole scheme from scratch. In our example, we will create the Authorization Scheme from scratch by selecting the **From Scratch** option and clicking the **Next** button.

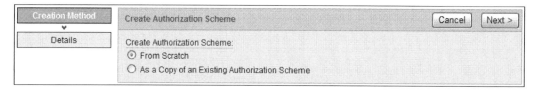

 If we have an existing Authorization Scheme that is similar to the one we need to create, then use the **As a Copy of an Existing Authorization Scheme** option. This can save us time and effort as we don't need to create the scheme totally from scratch, and we can re-use a scheme that already exists.

Authorization Scheme details

Now that we have selected to create the Authorization Scheme from scratch, we need to define a condition to determine if the user belongs to the scheme. We first allocate the scheme a name using the **Name** attribute. We then define how the scheme is evaluated using the **Scheme Type** attribute. The **Scheme Type** attribute is similar to display conditions and lists a number of types we can use, including **Exists SQL Query, PL/SQL Function Returning Boolean,** and **Item in Expression 1 Is Not Null**. We then use the **Expression 1** and **Expression 2** attributes to define SQL, PL/SQL, or an item name to be used in the scheme type.

If the Authorization Scheme condition fails, or returns false, then we can define an error message to display using the **Identity error message displayed when scheme violated** attribute. To finish, we need to specify when the Authorization Scheme condition will be evaluated using the **Validate Authorization Scheme** attribute. Selecting the **Once per page view** will evaluate the scheme every time a page is accessed. The **Once Per Session** option will evaluate the scheme only once during the user's session and store the result in the user's session.

Use the once per page view only if your condition is likely to change during the user's session. Otherwise, use the once per session; this is more efficient as the condition does have to be re-evaluated every time a page is accessed.

In the screenshot we can see our example Authorization Scheme to check if the user is an administrator. A SQL query is used to check if a record exists in the users table with an administrator flag set for the current user. This scheme will only be evaluated once during our session and will display an access denied error message if the user is not an administrator.

We have now entered enough information for the wizard to create the Authorization Scheme. Clicking the **Create** button will add the scheme to our application and enable it to be used. Now let's see how we can assign the Authorization Scheme to our application to restrict user access.

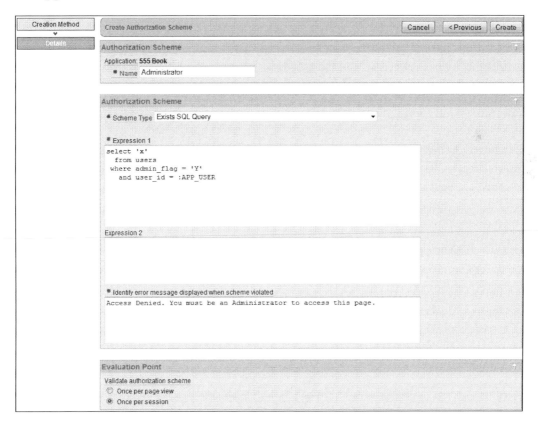

Assigning Authorization Scheme to pages, regions, and items

Once we have created an Authorization Scheme, the scheme will not restrict access to the functionality until we assign the Authorization Scheme to pages, regions, items, or buttons in our application. To do this, we need to access the properties for a page, item, or any other object we wish to protect. In the following screenshot we can see security properties for a page. The **Authorization Scheme** attribute specifies which Authorization Scheme the user must belong to in order to access the page. The **Authentication** attribute determines if the page is public or requires the user to be authenticated. The **Form Auto Complete** attribute will prevent the browser from automatically completing fields based on previously entered values.

In the following screenshot we can specify security properties for a page item. The **Authorization Scheme** attribute specifies an Authorization Scheme that the user must belong to in order to be able to view the item. If the user does not belong to the Authorization Scheme, then the item will not be displayed on the page. The **Session State Protection** attribute is used to prevent the item from being tampered with inappropriately in the form or via a URL. The **Store value encrypted in session state** attribute determines if the value of the item is encrypted when stored in the user's session.

A common problem encountered when assigning Authorization Schemes to restrict access to pages, regions, or items, is that only one Authorization Scheme can be selected. If we need to select multiple Authorization Schemes, then we have to create an additional Authorization Scheme that combines each of the Authorization Schemes into one. Then we can just select the one scheme that will evaluate if the current user belongs to the multiple schemes.

Also, if we need to define an Authorization Scheme for all items in a region, simply assign the Authorization Scheme at the region level. This will save having to apply the Authorization Scheme to every single item in the region.

Resetting Authorization Scheme results

We have seen when defining an Authorization Scheme that we can select to have the Authorization Scheme validate only once per session. This means the Authorization Scheme is only evaluated once and the results are stored in each user's session. We may encounter a scenario in our application where we need to reset the authorization result for the user due to a data change that changes this result. In this scenario, we can call the database procedure `APEX_UTIL.RESET_AUTHORIZATIONS` to clear Authorization Scheme results for the user's current session. After calling this procedure, next time the user tries to access a page, it will cause the Authorization Schemes to evaluate and store the result in the user's session.

Authorization Reports

Once we have assigned Authorization Schemes to functionality in our application, such as pages, regions, items, and buttons, we need a way to document what privileges have been assigned. This helps us to review and check what functionality users can access in our applications. We can access the Utilization tab from the Authorization Schemes page to view where in the application an Authorization Scheme is being referenced. We can also run Security reports from the Application Reports page to help us to easily know how the Authorization Scheme is utilized.

Session state protection

Earlier in this book we looked at how buttons and branches can populate page items and application items via the APEX URL. We often use this technique to pass unique identifiers or other items in the URL to customize the page we are calling. An example of this is when we have a search page that calls an update page; we want the update page to display the record selected in the search page. As these items are passed in the URL, it could be possible for a user to tamper with the URL and add, remove, or modify items and their values.

To demonstrate URL tampering, let's assume we have an edit employee screen that accepts an employee number parameter to determine which employee record to edit. The following URL will display employee number 222:

```
http://myserver:8080/apex/f?p=101:10:12345::::EMPNO:222
```

Let's now modify the employee number parameter in the URL to display employee number 999:

```
http://myserver:8080/apex/f?p=101:10:12345::::EMPNO:999
```

As we can see, we have changed the employee number displayed in our edit employee screen. Modifying the URL directly can potentially lead to errors in the processing of our page, enable session state items to be incorrectly modified, or even enable restricted data to be displayed.

To prevent the tampering of URLs in our application, APEX provides a security feature called Session State Protection. Session State Protection works by including checksums in the APEX URL. Using these checksums, APEX can detect if the URL has been tampered with or if the session state has been altered. In this section we will see how Session State Protection can be applied to our application to make it more secure.

In the screenshot we can see the Session State Protection page, which is accessed from **Shared Components**. In the Session State Protection page, we can use the **Set Protection** button to enable or disable Session State Protection for our application. For enabling Session State Protection for our application, we have a configure option that can be used to apply protection settings to all pages, page items, and application items in our application. Otherwise, we need to use **Page, Item,** and **Application Item** buttons in the Session State Protection page to individually apply protection settings to a page, page item, or application item.

 APEX will not display checksums and protect URLs if Session State Protection has been disabled, even if Session State Protection settings have been entered against pages, page items, or application items.

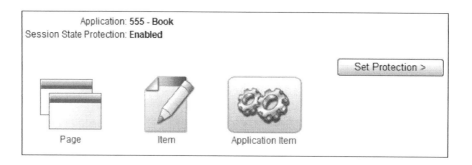

When setting Session State Protection for an individual page, we can define settings for both the page and its items. In the screenshot these can be entered through the **Page Access Protection** and **Item Session State Protection** attributes. The **Page Access Protection** attribute can be assigned one of the following options to determine how URLs accessing the page are protected:

Page Access Protection options	Description
Unrestricted	This option enables the page to be accessed by a URL without any checksums required.
Argument Must Have Checksum	This option requires a checksum to be provided in the URL if any parameters such as item names, item values, and clear cache have been specified in the URL.
No Argument Allowed	This option enables a page to be accessed by a URL, but no parameters can be specified in the URL.
No URL Access	This option prevents the page from being accessed by a URL. The page can only be accessed when it is defined as a target in a branch.

The **Item Session State Protection** attribute can be used to assign one of the following options to determine how each item in a page can be assigned a session state from a URL or form:

Item Session State Protection options	Description
Unrestricted	This option enables page items to be set from a form or URL without a checksum required.
Checksum Required — Application Level	This option only enables a page item to be set from a URL if a checksum has been provided that is specific to the workspace and application.
Checksum Required — User Level	This option only enables a page item to be set from a URL if a checksum has been provided that is specific to the workspace, application, and user.
Checksum Required — Session Level	This option only enables a page item to be set from a URL if a checksum has been provided that is specific to the user's current session.
Restricted — May not be set from browser	This option prevents the page item from being set by a URL or form.

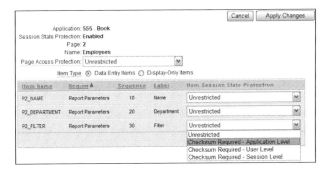

Security Attributes

The Security Attributes page provides a handy way to apply security settings across our entire application, rather than having to apply settings on individual pages or items. In this section we will explore security settings that we can apply to our entire application.

Authentication

The Authentication section enables details about the home page, login page, and public user to be entered for our application. We can define a URL or procedure to display the home page for our application using the **Home Link** attribute. This attribute is stored in the HOME_LINK substitution string. We can also define a URL to display the login page for our application using the **Login URL** attribute. This attribute is stored in the LOGIN_URL substitution string. These substitution strings can both be used in page templates to place links for accessing our home page and login page.

In this section we can also define the username that is used for a public user in our application using the **Public User** attribute. The username is determined by the actual database user that is connected through the Database Access Descriptor (DAD). The public user for the application is normally defaulted to ANONYMOUS, except when we are using the Oracle Database Express Edition where the public user is defaulted to APEX_PUBLIC_USER. This user is stored in the APP_USER substitution string. The **Define Authentication Schemes** button also enables us to create or modify Authentication Schemes, as we have seen earlier in this chapter.

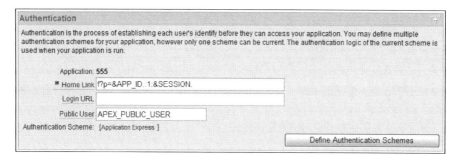

Authorization

The Authorization section enables an Authorization Scheme to be applied to the entire application. Selecting a scheme in the **Authorization Scheme** attribute will check if the current user belongs to the selected Authorization Scheme when accessing any page in the application. The **Define Authorization Schemes** button enables us to create or modify Authorization Schemes, as we have seen earlier in this chapter.

Database Schema

This defines the database schema any SQL or PL/SQL commands will run against for our application.

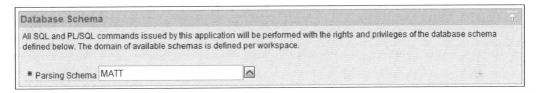

Session Timeout

The Session Timeout section enables us to control how long a session can remain active. The **Maximum Session Length in Seconds** attribute determines how long a session in the application is allowed to exist for. To allow a session to exist indefinitely, set the attribute to null. APEX sessions older than 12 hours are automatically deleted. The **Maximum Session Idle Time in Seconds** attribute determines how long the application can be left idle before the session is expired. Once the session has expired, the user will be required to log in to the application again.

Session State Protection

The Session State Protection section enables Session State Protection to be turned on or off for the application. This is entered using the **Session State Protection** attribute. Session State Protection helps application URLs from being tampered with, which could lead to problems in our application. The **Manage Session State Protection** button navigates to the main Session State Protection page that we have seen earlier in this chapter.

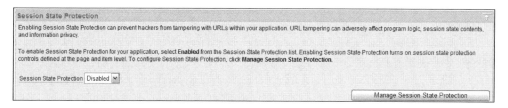

Virtual Private Database

Virtual Private Database (VPD), also known as Fine Grained Access Control, is an Oracle Database feature used to provide row-level security when accessing data from tables. VPD automatically filters data rows based on predefined conditions that have been configured. If we are using VPD, then we can specify a PL/SQL procedure that sets the security context or row filter conditions to be used.

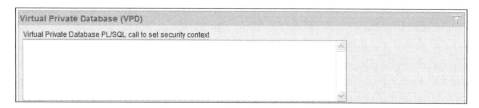

Summary

In this chapter we have learned about APEX security settings that we can apply to make our applications more secure. In particular, we have seen how to create Authentication Schemes to control access to our application and Authorization Schemes to control access within our application. We have also seen how to protect the session state of our application and apply application-wide security settings using security attributes. APEX makes it very easy for us to quickly apply security settings to our application and prevent unauthorized access to our applications.

In the next chapter we will look at how we can convert Microsoft Access and Oracle Forms applications to APEX.

23
Application Conversion

In many organizations it is common to find a number of Microsoft Access applications. These applications are often created by users to capture simple information, but they end up growing into important business applications. Often, they are not backed-up, not designed well, and not secure, and duplicate data is stored in other systems. Organizations may also have many very large Oracle Forms applications that contain many screens. Often, these applications will need to be consolidated and converted into newer browser-based technologies to simplify the deployment, management, and maintenance of these legacy applications. Converting these applications can be a costly and time consuming process. To assist us, APEX provides a number of conversion features that help us to quickly and easily convert Microsoft Access and Oracle Forms applications to APEX. In this chapter, we will discuss how to convert applications to APEX. Specifically, we shall be looking at:

- Converting Microsoft Access applications to APEX
- Converting Oracle Forms applications to APEX

APEX application conversion

Before we begin to use the APEX conversion tools it's important to note that the tools will not always convert our application perfectly, nor will they emulate the exact functionality of Oracle Forms and Microsoft Access. There are many differences between how a Web application like APEX behaves as compared to Microsoft Access and Oracle Forms applications. Some functionality in these applications may not easily translate, or even be applicable, in a Web browser environment. But the APEX conversion tools can generate the core functions of our applications such as forms, reports, master-detail forms, and tabular forms. This provides a significant jumpstart to the conversion of our applications. Even though the APEX conversion tools may not automatically convert all the functionality of our application, it still provides features to help track and manage the manual conversion of these tasks. This helps us to ensure that we have converted all the required functionality and not missed any important business rules along the way.

Planning and understanding the application

Before we rush in and try to convert the application, we need to plan the approach and take some time to understand the application we are converting. We need to be clear about the scope of the functionality to be converted and if there is any functionality that is no longer required. Converting the application could also be a time to enhance the application and add additional features or maybe even tidy up areas that are not implemented well. The conversion process provides an opportunity to make improvements to the application. Although the conversion will convert the majority of our applications, we still need to factor time in to our planning for enhancing the application, completing manual conversion tasks, testing, and training both users and developers.

APEX Application Migrations

To begin the conversion of Microsoft Access and Oracle Forms applications, we start with the Application Migrations page. This can be accessed from the task menu on the right-hand side of the APEX home page and is shown in the following screenshot. The Application Migrations page provides a central location to access resources on converting our applications and also provides a work area to perform the actual conversion of our applications.

In the Application Migrations page, we can find information about converting Microsoft Access and Oracle Forms applications to APEX by using the **How to Migrate Microsoft Access Applications** and **How to Convert Oracle Forms Applications** links. We can also download utilities such as the Exporter for Microsoft Access, which will assist in the conversion of Microsoft Access applications. The Exporter can be downloaded by using the **Download Exporter for Microsoft Access** link. The Application Migrations page also has a link to download **Sample Files**, which we can use to try out the conversion capabilities of APEX.

The Application Migrations page also enables us to create new Migration Projects by using the **Create Project** button. Migration Projects are used to help us track, manage, and convert our applications to APEX. If we have any existing Migration Projects, then they will be listed together with the following details about the conversion project:

- **Edit**: Enables the Migration Project details to be modified
- **Project Name**: Links to the Migration Project page, which enable us to track, manage, and convert an application

- **Type**: Displays whether the conversion project is for a Microsoft Access or an Oracle Forms application

- **Schema**: Displays the database schema used to store database objects for the converted application

- **Application**: Links to the Application Builder page to enable the generated application to be run or modified

- **Forms**: Displays how many forms need to be converted

- **Triggers, Blocks, Program Unit, PLLs, OLBs**: Displays how many Oracle Form triggers, blocks, program units, PL/SQL libraries, and object libraries need to be converted

- **Reports**: Displays how reports need to be converted

- **Update and Update By**: Displays when the Migration Project was last modified

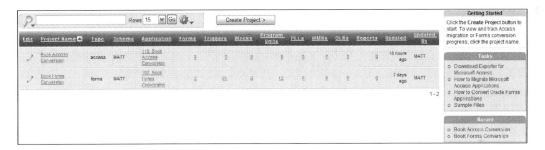

Creating an APEX workspace

To begin the conversion of a Microsoft Access or Oracle Forms application we need to set up an APEX workspace. This will be used to perform the conversion of the application and store the final generated application. In the workspace we need to create administrator and developer user accounts for those involved in the conversion process. When creating a workspace we need to define the database schema that will be used for the converted application. An APEX workspace needs to be created by an APEX administrator.

To demonstrate the conversion capabilities of APEX, we will walk through the process of converting a Microsoft Access application and then an Oracle Forms application. First, we will explore the steps required to convert a Microsoft Access application.

Converting Microsoft Access applications

In this section, we will walk through the steps required to convert a Microsoft Access Application to APEX. Converting Microsoft Access applications to APEX involves the following main steps:

- Exporting the Microsoft Access metadata
- Migrating the Access database to Oracle
- Creating an APEX Migration Project
- Reviewing and editing application metadata
- Generating the application

In this chapter, we will take a closer look at each of the steps required to convert Microsoft Access applications to APEX. We will begin by exporting metadata about our application using the Exporter for Microsoft Access.

Exporting Microsoft Access metadata

The first step in converting a Microsoft Access application is to export the application metadata that will be used to convert the application. APEX provides an Exporter tool that can be used to extract metadata from Microsoft Access versions 97 through 2007. The Exporter tool can be downloaded from the Application Migration page of APEX or from the migration menu in Oracle SQL Developer.

In the following screenshot, we can see the Exporter tool. The Exporter tool provides the following options to determine exactly what type of metadata we would like to export about the application:

- **Export for Oracle SQL Developer**: This option will export metadata about the database objects in the Access application including tables, views, and integrity constraints. This will generate an XML file, which we will use in Oracle SQL Developer to convert the Access database objects to an Oracle database schema.

- **Export for Oracle Application Express**: This option will export metadata about the forms and reports that make up the Access Application. This will generate a SQL file which we will use to generate the forms and reports for the application in APEX.

- **Export for Both**: This option enables metadata to be exported for both SQL Developer and APEX.

To demonstrate, we will export metadata to convert both the database objects and user interface that make up the Access application using the **Export for Both** option and click the **Next** button.

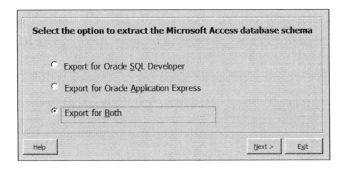

The next step of the Exporter tool is to select the Microsoft Access files (MDB files) we wish to convert. Multiple Access files can be converted and are selected by using the ... button. If there are multiple files with the same name we will need to define a unique name for each file using the **Unique Name** attribute. If security is configured for the Access application we can also specify the password in the **Password** attribute. The **Status** attribute displays one of the following statuses to determine if any action is required:

- **Ready**: Indicates the file is ready to be converted
- **Password Required**: Indicates a password must be specified for the Access file
- **Alternative Name**: Indicates the unique name entered is already in use and that an alternative name needs to be entered
- **Unique Name Required**: Indicates multiple Access applications with the same filename have been selected and need to be assigned a unique name

We can then control the location where the SQL Developer XML and APEX SQL files are created using the **Output Directory** attribute. If we wish to export data from the Access Application we can select the **Export Table Data** attribute. This will create DAT files for each database table in the output directory, which can be loaded later by using Oracle SQL Loader. To start the export of the metadata files, we click the **Export** button.

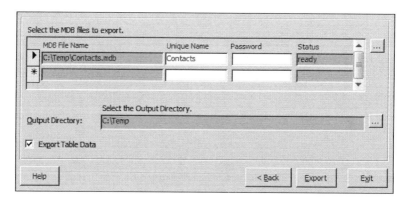

While the Exporter tool is gathering information about the Access application, be sure not to interrupt it. It may take some time, especially if the Access application contains many tables, forms, and reports. The Exporter tool will display a confirmation message when it has completed or if there is an error processing the information. Also, disable any macro security warnings before exporting as this can affect how well the utility determines the details about your application.

Migrating the Access database to Oracle

At this stage, we have now gathered metadata about the Access application and can begin to convert the application. Before we can convert the application forms and reports we need to convert the Microsoft Access tables, views, and constraints to Oracle. This is done by using the migration features in Oracle SQL Developer version 1.2 or later. Oracle SQL Developer migration functionality can be accessed from the Migration menu. In this section, we will explore the steps required in Oracle SQL Developer to generate an Oracle database schema.

In this section, we will show how to convert a Microsoft Access database using Oracle SQL Developer, but it is possible to perform the following steps to convert other databases such as Microsoft SQL Server and MySQL.

Creating a repository

First we need to create a migration repository in SQL Developer. We select a database connection in the **Create Repository** attribute where database tables for the repository will be created. These tables will be used to store details about the migration of the Access database.

Capturing Microsoft Access exported XML

Once a database migration repository has been created we can specify the database metadata XML file generated by the Exporter tool. This is specified in the **File Path** attribute. Clicking the **OK** button will then load details about the Access database objects into the migration repository.

Converting to an Oracle Model

Now that the metadata about the source Microsoft Access database has been loaded into the repository, it can be displayed in SQL Developer as a Captured Model. The Captured Model enables details about the tables, views, and other objects that were captured from the source database to be displayed. At this stage, we can rename objects such as table and column names and modify any data type mappings. After making any modifications, we then select the **Convert to Oracle Model** menu option to take the Captured Model information and represent it as a final Oracle database schema.

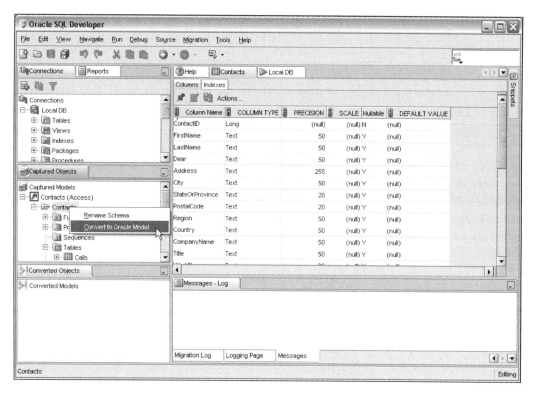

Generating schema

Creating a Converted Model now represents the Captured Model in a structure that shows how it will be created in an Oracle database. The Converted Model enables details how database objects will be implemented to be displayed. It also enables any final modifications to be made, such as renaming database objects and changing data types. Creating a Converted Model will have also converted any triggers and stored procedures to PL/SQL. The database is now ready to be converted, and we can select the **Generate** menu option to create a SQL script that will create the Oracle database schema.

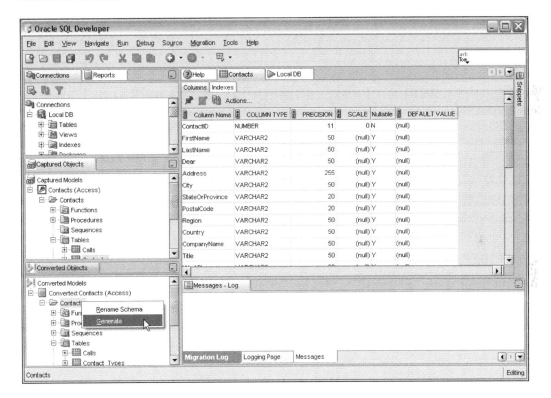

 Creating a Converted Model will have also converted any triggers and stored procedures to PL/SQL. If these items are unable to be converted, then their original code will remain as the source, and we will need to modify these in the generated schema creation script.

Creating an Oracle database

In the following screenshot, we can see a generated SQL script that can be used to create the Oracle database schema for the application. The script can be altered and then run to create the required database objects. The database schema needs to be run before we can convert data and the application forms and reports.

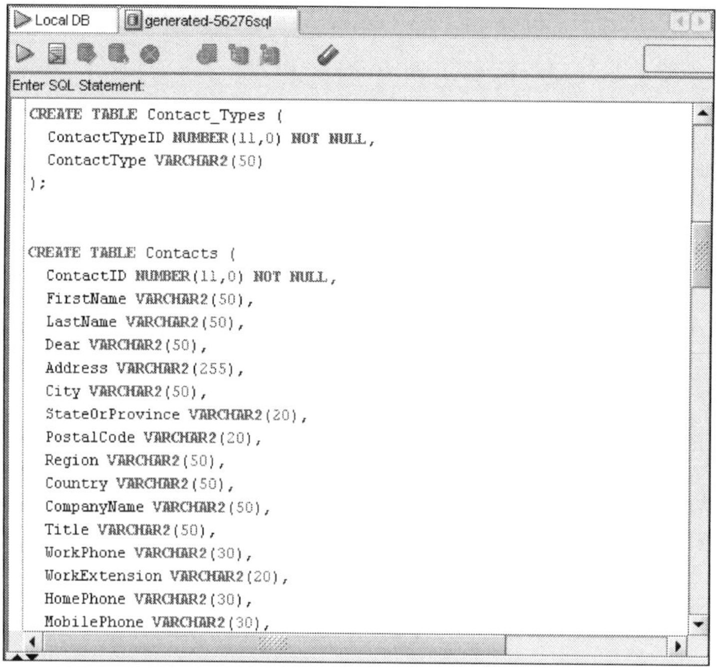

Creating a Migration Project

Now that we have created an Oracle database schema for the application we can convert the forms and reports that make up the application. To do this, we create a Migration Project in APEX. A Migration Project is an area in APEX where we can view, monitor, and perform the conversion of applications.

To create a Migration Project we assign a name to the Migration Project by using the **Project Name** attribute, while the **Type** attribute defines what type of application is being converted. The **Type** attribute contains options **Access** for converting a Microsoft Access application or **Forms** for converting an Oracle Forms application. The **Description** attribute enables any relevant comments or notes to be entered about the migration.

As an APEX workspace can be associated with multiple database schemas, we need to select which database schema contains the converted database objects for the application. This is entered in the **Schema** attribute. We use the **Migration Export File** attribute to select the application metadata SQL script generated by the Access Exporter tool. This provides information about the application forms and reports we wish to convert. Clicking the **Next** button will display a confirmation screen asking to confirm the creation of the Migration Project. Click **Finish** in the confirmation screen to create the Migration Project.

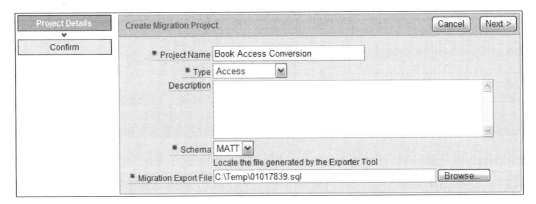

The Migration Project page

Once a Migration Project is created, we can view the Migration Project page. The Migration Project page displays a conversion summary of objects that make up the Access application including tables, forms, reports, and modules. The page displays the following summary columns:

- **Objects**: This breaks down the conversion summary into the different objects that make up the application such as tables, forms, reports, and modules.

- **Count**: Displays how many items of the object type exist in the project, for example, the number of forms that are in the Access Application.

- **Valid**: Displays how many objects are ready to be converted.

- **Invalid**: Displays how many objects have issues or errors that need to be resolved before they can be converted. Tables will appear invalid if no primary key exists. Forms and reports will appear invalid if the required database tables or views are missing or if they contain SQL with Access-specific code.

- **Included**: Displays how many objects have been selected that are to be converted in the project. Objects not selected will not be converted. The object must be valid before it can be selected to include in the conversion.

The Migration Project page also provides access to common migration functions in the tasks menu. The migration functions available in the tasks menu include:

- **Delete Project**: Removes the Migration Project from APEX
- **Edit Project Details**: Enables Migration Project details to be modified
- **About Access Migration**: Provides help information about converting Microsoft Access applications to APEX
- **Set Application Defaults**: Enables tab, authentication, theme, and globalization settings to be defined that will be applied to the application when generated
- **Generate Application**: Creates an APEX application based on the application objects selected for inclusion
- **Generate Maintenance Application**: Like the **Generate Application** function, this can be used to generate a separate application that can be used to handle the administration and maintenance of the application like maintaining lookup data

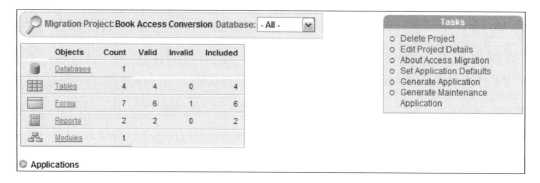

In the following screenshot, we can see the page that is displayed when the **Forms** link in the Migration Project page is selected. This page enables details about the form to be displayed and modified. The following details are displayed:

- **Checkbox**: The checkbox at the beginning of each form listed is used to select if the form is to be included in the converted application.
- **Access Form**: This links to a page where additional details about the form and its fields are displayed.
- **Source Type**: This displays whether the form is based on a **Table** or **SQL Query**. The Source Type is displayed as a link that, when clicked on, will provide details about the table or enables the SQL query to be modified.

- **Source Name**: Displays the database table name the form is based on if the **Source Type** is **Table**.

- **Status**: Displays whether the form is valid or invalid.

- **Start Up Form**: Displays if the page is displayed when the application is first run.

- **Parent Form**: If the form is used in a master detail drill down, then the name of its parent form is displayed.

- **Migrate To**: Determines how the form is implemented in APEX. We can select to display the form as a single record **Form, Tabular Form,** or **Report and Form**.

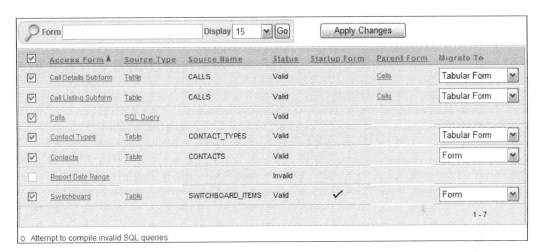

Generating the application

Once all required application objects have been selected for conversion, we can then generate APEX pages for the selected forms and reports. APEX provides a wizard that will guide us through the application generation process. The wizard can be accessed from the task menu in the Migration Project page. In this section, we will walk through each step of the Generate Application Wizard.

Select Application Objects

The **Select Application Objects** page displays which pages will be generated in the application. We can remove a page by using the **Delete Page** icon. We can also enter additional details about the page, such as headings and the page name, by using the **Page Name** link. This will display the Page Definition page.

There is also an option to add extra blank pages to the application using the **Add Page** button. When adding a blank page, we can specify if the page is used to drill down to provide additional information from a parent page using the **Subordinate to Page** attribute. We can also define a name for the blank page using the **Page Name** attribute.

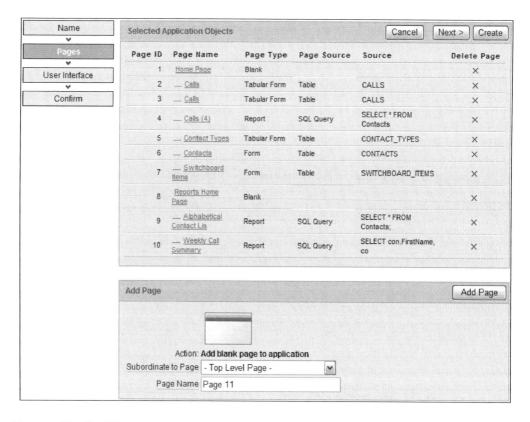

Page Definition

The **Page Definition** page enables additional details to be specified for a page. It is accessed when clicking the **Page Name** link in the Select Application Objects page. We can define a name for the page using the **Page Name** attribute. The **Parent Page** attribute is used to define a parent child relationship between the page and other pages in the application. This page relationship is used to render tabs, breadcrumbs, and other navigation in the application.

We can also select an icon to associate with the page. This icon will be used in menus by using the **Page Icon** attribute. The flashlight icon next to the attribute can be used to preview and select from the available icons. Also, on the page, we can enter headings and format masks for each item in the page using the **Heading/Label** and **Format Mask** attributes.

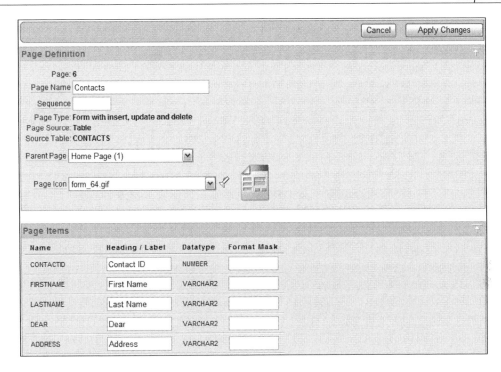

User Interface

In this step, we define a theme for the application. A theme will control the entire look and feel of the application. Select a theme option and click the **Next** button.

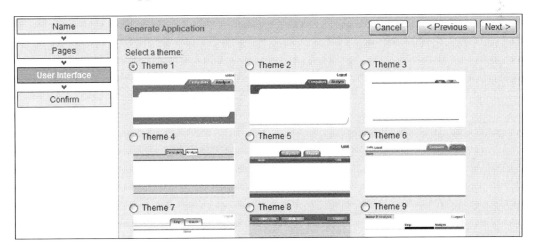

Confirmation

The wizard has now gathered enough information to generate the APEX application. Clicking the **Create** button will generate the application. Once the application has been created we can use the Application Builder page to run and modify the converted application.

Converting Oracle Forms applications

So far, we have seen how to convert Microsoft Access applications. However, in this section we will look at how to convert Oracle Forms applications to APEX. Converting Oracle Forms applications to APEX involves the following main steps:

1. Converting Oracle Forms to XML.
2. Setting up an Oracle database schema.
3. Creating an APEX Migration Project.
4. Reviewing and editing application metadata.
5. Generating the application.

In this chapter, we will take a closer look at each of the steps required to convert an Oracle Forms application to APEX. We will begin by converting Oracle Forms to XML.

Converting Oracle Forms to XML

Earlier, we saw how the Exporter tool for Microsoft Access is used to export metadata about the application. When converting Oracle Forms applications we also need to export metadata about the application. However, this time we will use the Forms2XML utility provided in Oracle Forms 9i and 10g. The Forms2XML utility will create XML files for each Oracle Forms source file (FMB file) using the same filename as the form. This XML file will provide details about each Oracle Form including blocks, items, and triggers, which are used by APEX in converting the application. The Forms2XML utility can be used to convert not only Form source files, but also Forms Menu and Object Library files as well.

It is possible to convert Oracle Forms 4.5 and 6i using the Forms2XML utility, but there is no guarantee that the utility will work correctly for these versions. If the utility does not work correctly, Oracle Forms will need to be upgraded to Oracle Forms 9i or 10g to use the Forms2XML utility.

Database

The next step is to ensure we have an Oracle database schema for our application. As Oracle Forms applications will already have an Oracle database schema in place, this step is made very simple. The only thing we need to ensure is that the database schema for our application exists in the same database instance as the APEX environment being used to perform the migration. This is to ensure that our forms can access the required tables, views, and stored procedures.

APEX Migration Project

Now that we have the metadata for the application and can access the database schema we can convert the forms and reports that make up the application. To do this, we create a Migration Project in APEX like we did when converting a Microsoft Access application. The only difference is that we select **Forms** in the **Type** attribute and select an XML file generated by the Forms2XML utility in the **Forms Module XML File** attribute. This will provide information about the application forms and reports that will be used to convert the application.

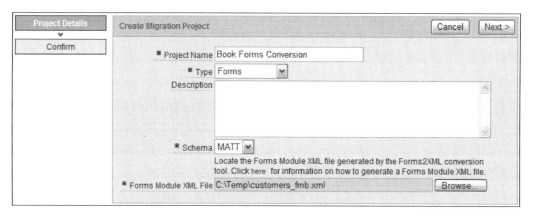

In the next step of creating a Migration Project, we can select to upload additional files by using the **Upload Another File** button. Alternatively, we can click the **Finish** button to create the Migration Project. Additional Forms Module XML files can be uploaded after the Migration Project has been created.

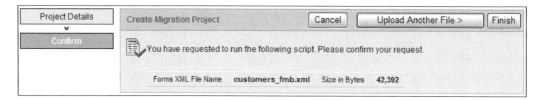

The following screenshot is displayed if we select to upload additional files. Additional metadata files are selected using the **File** attribute. We also need to define the type of metadata file we are uploading by using the **File Type** attribute. The following types of metadata files can be uploaded:

- **Forms Module (_fmb.XML)**: This uploads Oracle Forms XML files generated by the Forms2XML utility

- **Oracle Report (.XML)**: This uploads Oracle Reports that have been converted into XML by Oracle Report Builder

- **PL/SQL Library (.PLD)**: This uploads PL/SQL Libraries that are saved as a PLD text file

- **Forms Menu (_mmb.XML)**: This uploads Oracle Forms Menu XML files generated by the Forms2XML utility

- **Object Library (_olb.XML)**: This uploads Object Library XML files generated by the Forms2XML utility

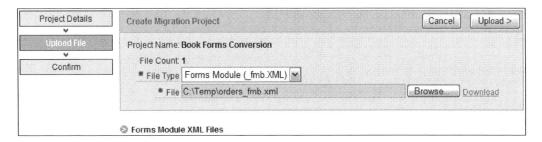

Reviewing and editing application metadata

Once a Migration Project is created, we can view the Migration Project page. The Migration Project page displays a conversion summary for each Form Module XML file we have uploaded into the Migration Project. The conversion summary is displayed in an Interactive Report that makes it easy for us to perform searches and other analysis of the objects to be converted. The Migration Project page displays the following summary columns:

- **Edit**: Links to a details page where overall conversion details can be entered for the type of Oracle Forms metadata file that has been uploaded.

- **Type**: Displays the type of Oracle Forms metadata file that has been uploaded, such as Forms Module, Oracle Report, PL/SQL Library, Forms Menu, or Object Library.

- **File Name**: Displays the name of the Oracle Forms metadata file that has been uploaded.

- **Blocks, DB Block, Items, Triggers, Record Groups, List of Vales, Alerts, Program Units**: Displays how many blocks, database blocks, items, triggers, record groups, lists of values, and/or alerts were uploaded in the Oracle Forms metadata file. Clicking the links against each of these columns displays a page where we can select whether the item is to be included in the conversion. When selecting, for example, the Items link we can also define the field prompts for each item in the form.

- **Component Count**: Displays how many components are in the Oracle Forms metadata file that requires conversion.

- **Completed Components**: Displays how many components in the Oracle Forms metadata file have completed conversion.

- **Percent Complete**: Displays the overall conversion percentage of the Oracle Forms metadata file that has been uploaded.

The Migration Project page also provides access to common migration functions in the tasks menu. The migration functions available in the tasks menu include:

- **Delete Project**: Removes the Migration Project from APEX

- **Edit Project Details and Applicability**: Enables Migration Project details to be modified and specific types of components and triggers to be automatically marked as applicable for conversion

- **About Forms Migration**: Provides help information for converting Oracle Forms applications to APEX

- **Set Application Defaults**: Enables tab, authentication, theme, and globalization settings to be defined that will be applied to the application when generated

If we need to upload additional metadata files, then we can use the **Upload File** button. This works in the same way as when we uploaded a metadata file to create the Migration Project. Once we have reviewed the metadata and selected objects to include in the conversion, we can click the **Create Application** button to launch the Application Generation Wizard. Once the application is generated, we can use the **Run Application** button to run the application. The Migration Project page also provides a conversion status for the overall application in the **Components**, **Completed**, and **Percent Complete** attributes displayed on the right-hand side of the page.

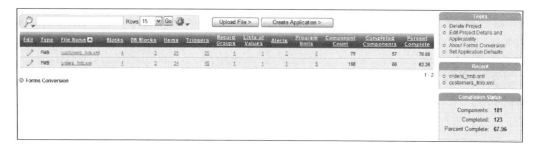

Annotations

Annotations are used to track and manage the conversion of any objects in our Migration Project such as forms, blocks, and triggers. The **Applicable** attribute determines if the object needs to be converted. The object can be assigned to an APEX user and assigned a priority by using the **Assignee** and **Priority** attributes. We can also determine if conversion of the object is complete by using the **Complete** attribute. Any relevant notes or tags regarding the conversion can be entered in the **Notes** and **Tags** attributes.

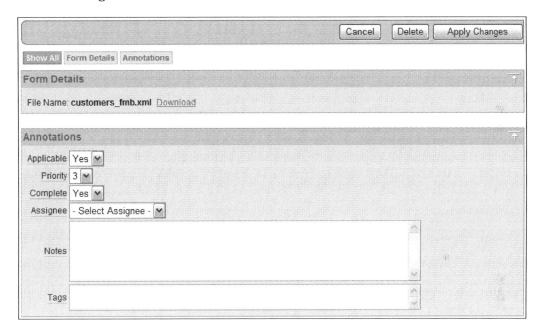

Including objects in conversion

Before we can generate the APEX application we need to select which objects from the uploaded Oracle Forms metadata files need to be included in the converted application. In the following screenshot, we can see the page that is displayed when the **Items** link in the Migration Project page is selected for an Oracle Forms metadata file. This page enables details about the items in the form to be displayed and modified. The **Include** checkbox is used to select if the item is to be included in the converted application. We can also enter a label for the item using the **Item Prompt** attribute. Clicking the **Bulk Changes** button will save any changes made.

Generating the application

Once all the required application objects have been selected for conversion we can generate APEX pages for the selected items. APEX provides a wizard that will guide us through the application generation process. The wizard can be accessed from the **Create Application** button in the Migration Project page. In this section, we will walk through each step of the Generate Application Wizard.

Application name

The first step of the Generate Application Wizard is to specify some basic details about the application. We enter a name for the application in the **Name** attribute. The **Application** attribute displays the Application ID that will be assigned to the application. The **Creation Method** attribute determines if design details will be re-used from a previous application generation. This saves time by not having to re-enter property values in the wizard. This is selected by using the **Based on existing application design model** option. Selecting the **Based on Migration Project** option enables property values to be manually entered for pages. The **Scheme** attribute displays the database schema where database objects are located for the application. Click the **Next** button to continue.

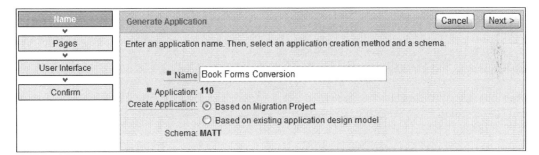

Create Pages

The Create Pages screen displays which pages will be generated in the application. We can remove a page by using the **Delete Page** icon. We can also enter additional details about the page, like headings and the page name, by using the **Page Name** link. This will display the Page Definition page.

The Create Pages screen also enables additional pages to be added to the application. The **Select Page Type** attribute can be used to select the type of page to add such as **Blank**, **Report**, **Form**, **Tabular Form**, **Master Detail**, and **Report and Form**. Depending on the **Page Type** selected, we will be prompted to provide additional details, such as what table to base the page on. If the page is used to drill down and provide additional information from a parent page, then we can specify the parent page by using the **Subordinate to Page** attribute. We can also define a name for the page by using the **Page Name** attribute. Click the **Add Page** button to add the page to the application.

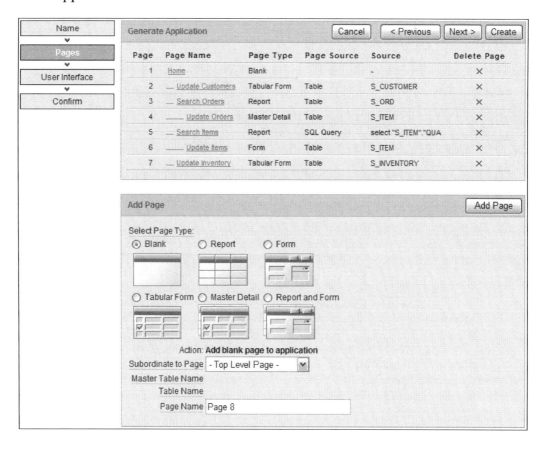

Page Definition

The Page Definition page enables additional details to be specified for a page. It is accessed when clicking the **Page Name** link in the Select Application Objects page. We can define a name for the page using the **Page Name** attribute. The **Parent Page** attribute is used to define a parent child relationship between the page and other pages in the application. This page relationship is used to render tabs, breadcrumbs, and other navigation in the application.

We can also select an icon to associate with the page, which will be used in menus by using the **Page Icon** attribute. The flashlight icon next to the attribute can be used to preview and select from the available icons. Also on the page, we can enter headings and format masks for each item in the page using the **Heading/Label** and **Format Mask** attributes.

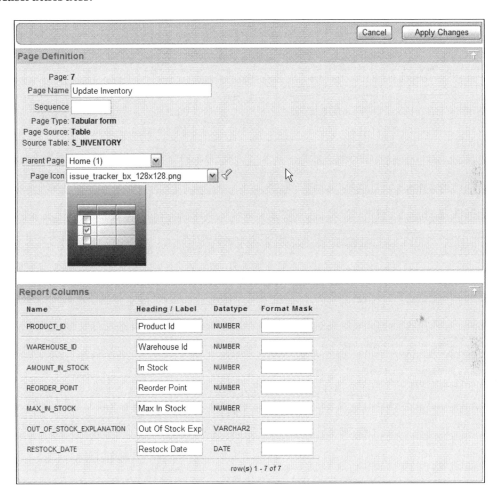

User Interface

In this step, we define a theme for the application. A theme will control the entire look and feel of the application. Select a theme option, and click the **Next** button.

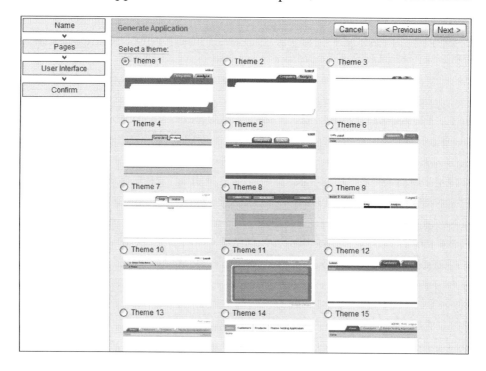

Confirmation

The wizard has now gathered enough information to generate the APEX application. Clicking the **Create** button will generate the application. Once the application has been created we can use the Application Builder page to run and modify the converted application.

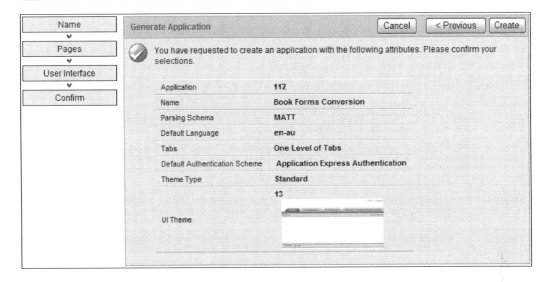

What's left to do?

We have now converted the core of our Microsoft Access and Oracle Forms applications to APEX. The conversion tools are not perfect and will not have converted all the functionality from our previous applications. For example, **Visual Basic for Applications (VBA)** code in screens will not have been converted for Microsoft Access applications. Also, a number of form triggers will not have been converted for Oracle Forms applications. A major reason for this is the difference between how a Web application like APEX behaves as compared to Microsoft Access and Oracle Forms applications.

To finish off our conversion, we will need to complete the remaining tasks that the conversion tools could not perform. It is also a great opportunity to implement the many great features APEX has to offer. We have seen throughout this book how features such as JavaScript, AJAX, Interactive Reports, List of Values, Themes, Templates, Globalization, Security, and more can be implemented to enhance the application. We will also need to thoroughly test the generated applications and train users how to use the new application.

Summary

In this chapter, we have learned about converting Microsoft Access and Oracle Forms applications to APEX. We have seen how we can obtain metadata from our existing applications and use it to create Oracle database schemas and APEX Migration Projects. We have also seen how we can use Migration Projects to track, manage, and perform the conversion of an application. Once converted, we can complete remaining conversion tasks and enhance the application using the APEX Application Builder. The APEX conversion tools will not completely convert our applications, but enable the core of our application to be converted quickly and easily while providing a good foundation to build upon.

In the next chapter, we'll review our APEX best practice, and how they can help you while developing in APEX.

24
APEX Best Practices

Best practices are a set of rules, advice, tips, and tricks that are collectively formed by the development community and are based on previous knowledge and experience. Best practices are not only aimed at helping us to develop our applications faster and easier, but also help to ensure consistency, readability, and maintainability. As a result, a high standard of quality is achieved in our applications.

Best practices are not carved in stone and should be used as guidelines at your own discretion. They can be subjective and vary between organizations. They can be dependent on the general development environment (such as developing in a Windows versus Unix/Linux environment, single developer versus team of developers, and so on), and greatly influenced by the enterprise culture. However, by nature, *best practices* should fit the widest common denominator possible.

As a novice developer, they can help you to build high standard applications right from the start, while reaching a high degree of productivity faster than you'll be able to do all by yourself. As you gain more experience, or as an expert developer already, you should review them, challenge them, and adopt what you see fit. If necessary, you can change them to fit your specific needs or to reflect your own knowledge and experience. In these cases, you are encouraged to share your best practices so others will be able to benefit from your wisdom and experience, just as we hope you'll benefit from ours.

Using best practices while designing, building, and maintaining APEX applications can help lead to a higher degree of uniformity and consistency, both within a specific application, and across all your other applications. While doing so, don't be afraid to adapt them to your own specific environment, and even add and expand them based on your own experience. This can help make the development and maintenance of your applications much simpler.

In this chapter, we will share with you some of our own APEX best practices.

 The order in which the *best practices* are displayed is quite arbitrary and does not reflect, in any way, the importance, usefulness, or productivity enhancement of them.

Don't re-invent the wheel

APEX is a declarative development tool. Use it.

APEX provides many great built-in features that help us to rapidly develop our applications with little or no coding. These features are implemented in the form of wizards and property pages and allow us to refrain from worrying about the "how to" implement details, but focus more on "what we want" to achieve from the application details (the business logic, as we call it).

Sometimes, as developers, we do need to write custom code to achieve certain functionality, but we should always be mindful to build it within the APEX framework and not to avoid or replicate functionality that already exists.

 This is especially true with the built-in APEX validations and the conditions mechanism. Wherever possible, you should use these built-in features rather than your own custom code. Most likely, they will perform better and be easier to maintain.

On top of APEX wizards and property pages, APEX also provides a number of built-in JavaScript and PL/SQL APIs. You should try to familiarize yourself with these libraries and APIs (and we tried to use them as often as we could throughout this book) and use them wherever possible. Remember, the APEX development team enjoys intimate knowledge of the APEX engine and it does its best to tailor all the code components in the best and optimal ways. It can only help that while doing so, it has the Oracle knowledge and experience resources at its disposal.

Moreover, as APEX runs inside the Oracle database, be sure to take advantage of the wealth of PL/SQL packages and other features the Oracle database provides. This can greatly simplify and reduce the code we need to create when developing applications.

Be innovative when necessary

Having said all that, it's important to remember that with all the advantages the APEX development team has, they are still responsible for developing a product that should be supported on as many Oracle platforms (database versions) as possible. APEX 3.2 (the latest version when writing the book) can be installed on Oracle database 9.2.0.3 and above. This implies that the development team can't use all the new and advanced features that were introduced in later versions (although some of the existing code does take advantage of the improved and optimized code of the newer database versions, so even for APEX, it's always best to run the latest database version). If you think such an advanced feature can help you improve your application and its performance, you shouldn't hesitate to use it. Actually, this brings us to one of the best things about APEX—even though APEX is a declarative development tool by nature, it doesn't prevent you from expending its original capabilities and fully exploit all your programming skills.

Learn the APEX IDE

You should learn your way around the APEX IDE, which provides many features that can be used to assist and save time when performing everyday tasks. Often these features are tucked away and not always obvious, but when used they are real time savers.

Spend some time to save even more time. Knowing your way around the APEX IDE can save you a lot of time, not to mention tedious hard work, and learning it is well worth your while.

The Drag and Drop Layout wizard

A good example of a productivity enhancer utility is the **Drag and Drop Layout** wizard, which can be used to adjust the layout of existing page items, as well as adding new items to the page. The editor can be accessed from the **Drag and drop** icon, which is located in the *Page Definition* **Items** section, near the region names:

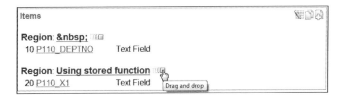

The **Drag and Drop Layout** wizard that can be seen in the next screenshot makes item-related tasks, which usually require manual coding/input over multiple item property pages, very simple and quick.

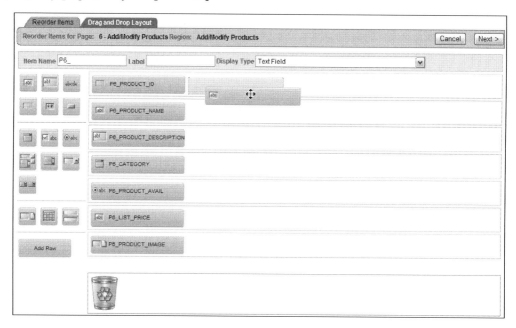

The Action Bar

You should pay special attention to the **Action Bar** on the *Page Definition* page, which can be seen in the following screenshot:

The *Action Bar* includes several very useful icons that lead us to some productivity enhancer APEX wizards and functionalities. We'll review some of them throughout this chapter.

The Page Definition view options

One of the less utilized features of the *Page Definition* page is its **View** options, as can be seen in the next screenshot. The page view options includes reviewing database objects related to the page, the history of the page development actions, and locking/ unlocking the **Export Page** wizard, the *Page Groups* it belongs to, and a list of pages that reference it.

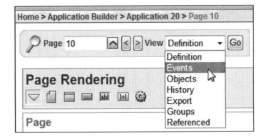

My favorite view option is **Events**. This option can display all, or just the existing, APEX events on the page in the order for their evaluation by the APEX engine. It's a great way of looking at the "big picture" of the page, the way the APEX engine sees it. The following screenshot is a fragment of such a view, which displays all the events that pertains to the *Page Processing* phase.

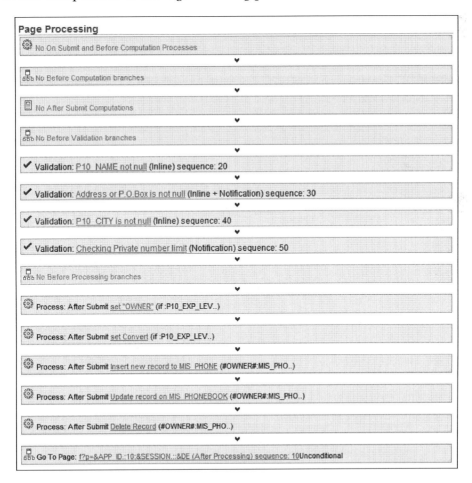

Setting up workspaces

The APEX import mechanism allows us to import any full application export to any APEX workspace we need. However, when dealing with individual application components, for example a single page or a shared component, it only allows importing it into an identical workspace as the component's original workspace. This means that if we want to easily port applications and application components between several APEX instances, like our Development, Test, and Production environments, we must define identical workspaces in all of them.

Workspaces in APEX are allocated a unique number ID (referenced in the code as `security_group_id`). To setup identical workspaces across all our environments we first need to create the workspace that we'll use for development. Then, we can use the **Export Workspace** wizard to generate a script that includes all the necessary statements to create a new APEX workspace (including its defined users). This script can be used by the **Import Workspace** wizard to create a new APEX workspace on a new/different APEX instance. The newly created workspace will have the same features as the original workspace, including the same workspace ID.

In the following screenshot, we can see how to access the **Import Workspace** and **Export Workspace** wizards. These wizards can be accessed by an APEX Workspace Administrator.

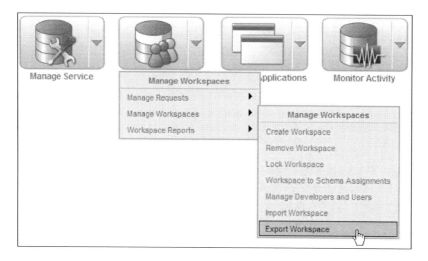

After creating the initial development workspace, be sure to create individual workspace users for each administrator or developer that will work on this workspace. Never share workspace user accounts, as it makes it difficult to track user activities and hides accountability. By not using individual user accounts, some of the APEX built-in *Application Reports*, which were designed to help us track and manage the various development activities (e.g. page update, page locking, etc.), might become useless, as we can't differentiate between the developers working on the same workspace. When working as part of a development team, this kind of information can be very useful and helpful.

When managing workspace users, be sure not to make all developers equal to administrators, and disable user accounts when access is no longer required. As I have mentioned before, when we are importing a workspace into a new APEX instance, its original defined users are created with it. Make sure to delete all the accounts for the users that are not needed on the new instance.

Application ID

Every APEX application is assigned a unique ID number. This number must be unique for the entire APEX instance, and not only for the workspace in which the application is defined.

The APEX development team has reserved the range of 3000-8999 for itself, but other than that you can choose any (integer) ID number you want. Because of the unique constraint of the application ID, within a specific APEX instance, the **Install Application** wizard allows us to manipulate the application ID while deploying our application.

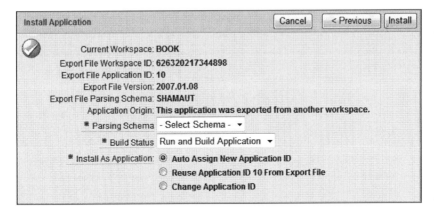

As can be seen in the above screenshot, we can allow the wizard to allocate a new application ID, we can retain the current application ID, or we can assign our own application ID. These options give us a great deal of flexibility with our application ID.

Unfortunately, this flexibility doesn't exist when it comes to translated applications. As mentioned in Chapter 18, when we dealt with the APEX translation mechanism, we must retain the original translated application ID, otherwise it will not work properly. In order to avoid possible problems with the unique application ID constraint, we should try to assign our translated application a unique application ID by using high and random number. I usually use a seven or eight digit number without any noticeable digit pattern.

This best practice advice is especially important for commercial translated applications that are going to be deployed outside the development environment, where we don't have any control over the existing APEX applications and their IDs.

Page numbering and page groups

When building applications, it can be common for an application to be made up of many pages. Often, multiple pages are related and belong to common functional areas of the application. This can make it difficult to view and find required pages if they are not organized in a logical sequence. To simplify this, be sure to keep related pages together through the use of *page numbering* and *page groups*.

Page numbering is where we designate a range of page ID numbers for similar functionalities in our application. For example, pages 1 to 50 could be reserved for customer related functionalities, pages 51 to 100 for sales related functionalities, and so on. Be sure to document the page ranges so it can be communicated across the entire development team.

It is also a good practice to leave some free numbers between the current defined pages, just in case we would like to insert a new page between two existing ones and still maintain the grouping logic and sequencing.

Page Groups enable us to implement our page numbering policy, by logically grouping pages with similar functionalities. In the following screenshot, we can see an example of how **Page Groups** are displayed on the *Application Builder* page. We can browse the **Page Groups** much like if we were browsing files in a file explorer. Clicking a **Page Group** displays only the pages assigned to this group, making it easier to locate all the pages with a similar functionality.

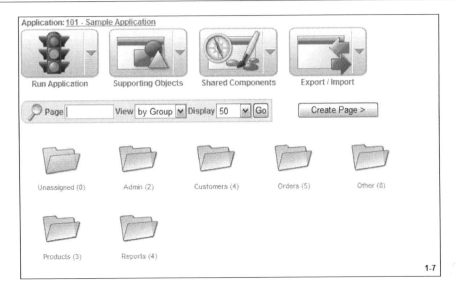

Use Oracle naming conventions

This could have easily been the first best practice on our list. You should use the Oracle naming conventions and rules for all the APEX objects and components, but especially for item names.

Although the APEX engine supports item names of up to 255 characters, Oracle bind variable names are limited to only 30 characters. At this point you should already recognize the importance of using bind variables in APEX applications, and the flexibility it gives you as a developer. It can only happen if you adhere to the proper Oracle naming rules.

Use bind variables

As we have just mentioned bind variables, let's sharpen this issue. You should use bind variables in SQL and PL/SQL code to help improve performance and scalability of the Oracle database. Bind variables enable the Oracle database to cache and reuse identical SQL statements. The database checks if the query is already parsed in the shared pool, and if so, it can immediately execute the statement. Otherwise, it will need to perform a *hard parse* of the statement, which is CPU intensive and increases statement execution time.

> Using bind variables is also a very good way to be guarded from possible SQL Injection attacks.

Don't hardcode, use Substitution Strings

You should use *Substitution Strings* to store system parameters and other constants. It will give you higher degree of flexibility, portability, and more maintainable applications.

Using hardcoded parameters and constants is considered to be a bad development practice (even outside APEX), and it can cause problems, should they ever need to change. Finding all instances of the parameter in an application can be difficult and there is a risk that some instances may be overlooked. To avoid hardcoding and to make our applications more maintainable and portable, APEX provides us with some built-in *Substitution Strings* (some of them we reviewed in Chapter 3) and enables us to define our own twenty *Substitution Strings*. If twenty is not enough for you, I remind you that you can always use the *Substitution String* notation with application level items. As those are not limited in numbers, you should not have any problems implementing the policy of not using hardcoding.

Use PL/SQL packages

You should use PL/SQL packages to store application logic and large PL/SQL code. PL/SQL packages provide an effective way to group similar functionality. Using stored procedures and functions, instead of inline PL/SQL code, is not only faster—since the packaged code is already compiled—but it also helps to make the application easier to maintain by avoiding duplicate code in multiple spots. It also makes it easier to debug and test the PL/SQL code by using external tools like the Oracle SQL Developer, which has some specific built-in APEX integration, and it's distributed free of charge.

PL/SQL packaged code can be accessed from any relevant APEX component, e.g. *Computations*, *Validations*, and application/page level *Processes*, and as such can be shared (re-used) across a specific application or across multi APEX applications.

Protect your business logic secrets

Using PL/SQL packages for the application logic has another very important advantage. While the APEX in-line PL/SQL code is saved within the APEX metadata tables as open and clear text, and as such can be seen by any database user with the appropriate privileges, PL/SQL packages can be wrapped. The wrapped package code retains its obfuscating state regardless of the user database privileges. Although not 100 percent foolproof, a wrapped package is still the best way to hide your business logic secrets from the public.

Re-useable code

Re-usable code can save you time and coding effort. Using the same code over and over again can help you maintain unified functionalities and the same look and feel throughout the application—for example, using the same code to validate a date in a specific format, using the same query to display a select list, or using the same unique color scheme with the application *Theme* are just a few possible examples.

Another advantage is that the re-useable snippets of code are usually concentrated in specific and known locations. That makes application maintenance easier.

Shared Components

The *Shared Component* module includes several sections that allow us to re-use specific APEX components. Whenever you need to use the same APEX object or functionality more than once, you should check if you can define it as a shared component. Notable examples are the **List Of Values** (LOV), **Application Items**, and of course, the **Templates**.

Shared Components can easily be accessed from the *Action Bar*, using the cogwheel icon — ❀ — the second icon from the right.

Page Zero

Application **Page Zero** is also a special option to share APEX objects like page regions, buttons, items, etc. Every component that is defined on *Page Zero* will be automatically added by the APEX engine to all the other application pages (pending object conditions). This is a very simple and effective way of sharing APEX objects throughout the application.

Page Zero is not created by default as part of creating a new APEX application. If you need it, you should create it yourself.

Pre-defined and built-in resources

We already asked you, at the beginning of this chapter, not to reinvent the wheel. In this context, it means that you should prefer using the pre-defined and built-in APEX resources such as the *Conditions*, *Validations*, *Computations*, and DML *Processes*. It will save you a lot of time and will almost always be more optimal than using your own code.

User Interface Defaults

Use **User Interface Defaults**, under the **User Interface** section of the *Shared Components*, to set labels, item types, and other settings for database tables and their columns. A little time spent up front defining the user interface defaults can save a lot of development effort later when building the application. When using the APEX wizards to build a form or a report region, **User Interface Defaults** will automatically be applied to save us time by not having to modify item types and labels. It will also help you to easily maintain a unified look and feel for the entire application.

Never change the provided APEX resources

You should never change the original provided APEX resources like Themes, Templates, graphical files, the JavaScript, and CSS provided libraries. Always create duplicates of the provided resources and work on them.

Themes and Templates

APEX allows you to easily duplicate any *Theme* or *Template*. Use it to create your own modified resources.

Every major version upgrade of APEX includes an updated Images directory, which must be copied to run over the existing one as part of the post upgrade procedure. This means changes that you have made to the APEX-provided resources in the old version will not be there for the new version and you will have to repeat them. Creating your own resources, based on the provided ones, can prevent that.

The APEX upgrade process does not change the application *Theme* and *Templates* of existing applications. This means that the existing applications will continue to use the *Theme* and *Templates* from the old version. In some cases this is an advantage, as all our own resources will continue to be available, as is, to our existing application, even after the APEX upgrade. On the other hand, new features of the *Theme* and *Templates* from the new version will not be available to us, out-of-the-box, for these applications.

If you want to utilize the new *Theme* and *Templates* features, and you are using the original APEX *Theme* number—meaning you didn't create a new *Theme* as a duplicate of a provided one, just added your resources to the original *Theme*—you should change the current application *Theme* number to a new one. You can do that with the **Change Theme Identification Number** task on the **Theme** section of *Shared Components*.

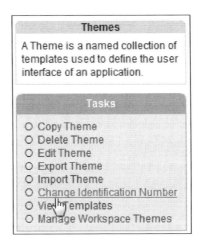

Now you can use the **Create Theme** wizard, and by choosing the **From the Repository** option, you will create a new copy of the provided APEX *Theme* in its new version. This *Theme* will not include your own resources, but as you created your own distinguished resources in the previous version (following our best practice advice), it will be quite easy for you to port them into the new *Theme*. You can read more about creating new *Themes*, and switching the current application *Theme*, in the Appendix, in the section that deals with APEX upgrade.

JavaScript and CSS

APEX also allows you to create external JavaScript and CSS files and load them to every page of the application, just like the provided resources. If possible, store these files on the local OS filesystem of your database server. It will give you the best performance, regardless of the APEX version you are using.

 Make sure to load your own CSS file(s) after the APEX provided files in order to use the CSS cascading effect. Usually, it should be located after the #HEAD# *Substitution String*, in the page templates.

Never trust the end user

It may seem like harsh advice, but given the nature of the Web environment, it's an absolute must.

You should always inspect, filter, escape, and validate every piece of input made by the end user. The criteria should not only pertain to the application business logic but also to the security and safety aspects of the data itself. Make sure to scan the input for possible malicious code and protect your application from possible code injection attacks. Wherever possible, work with secured applications that require registration and/or authentication. Be careful when delegating privileges and access control rights to the end users, and when applicable, implement an auditing mechanism.

Client-side validation

Client-side validations are great to enhance the end user UI experience. However, they can't replace the server-side validation in any way. Due to the open and accessible nature of JavaScript code in the Web browser, it can be very easily manipulated and made to lose its validation value. Use server-side validations, which are out of reach for the end user, to perform the real validation functionality.

Don't rely on database constraints

You should strive to catch all the database constraints violations using APEX *Validations*. It will give you much more control over the error messages and will allow you to instruct the end user on how to act in order to resolve the error situation.

Create your own restore point

APEX doesn't have an undo function, per se. While developing, you should create your own restore point, which will allow you to easily go back in case something bad or unexpected happens (like accidently deleting something), or you just don't like the new code.

A very simple and effective solution can be to create an export file of the page you are going to work on. By importing this file into the application, you'll be able to go back to the time and version the export file was created on. Besides being very simple, it will also free you from being dependent on your DBA, as all the involved actions are within your privileges as an APEX developer. The **Export Page** wizard can be accessed by clicking on the down arrow icon — ⇩ — which is the second icon from the right on the *Action Bar*. This icon leads you to the following screen:

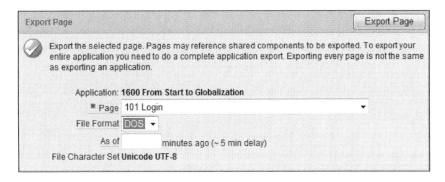

I want to draw your attention to the wizard's third field: **As of ___ minutes ago**. This option, which is also available in the **Export Application** wizard, gives us the option of exporting the page (or application) as it appeared in the APEX metadata tables, a specific number of minutes in the past. This option can be very useful in cases where we didn't generate a proper application/page export that we can go back to, or the export file we do have is too far in the past and we want to go back to a more recent point in time.

This option relies on the database initialization parameter UNDO_RETENTION, which is set to 15 minutes by default. This is probably too narrow a time window for our purpose, so you should adjust it according to your needs and your database environment. As this parameter influences the behavior of the entire database and it has a cost of retaining data history, you should set it carefully (or ask your DBA to do it for you).

Multi-user environment

Running the application in a multi-user environment requires us to take special precautions to ensure our data integrity and consistency. Most novice developers, and also many of the experienced ones, aren't always aware of issues like concurrency control, lost updates, and locking mechanisms. Even if you are aware of these potential problems, you may not always know what to do about them.

In the Web environment we are usually using a locking mechanism called **optimistic lock** (which we reviewed in chapter 14). All the APEX built-in DML processes are implemented using this locking method. However, as we reviewed in Chapter 9, about *APEX Processes*, these built-in processes are not always suited to our needs and demands so we need to code our own DML processes.

I want to remind you that the option of using the *Object Browser* to create PL/SQL packages includes all the necessary functionalities to perform all the necessary DML operations on specific database tables of your choice, while implementing optimistic locking when it is needed. Use this option whenever you need to generate your own DML code. It will save you a lot of time and tedious manual coding, but more importantly, by implementing the optimistic locking, it will help you maintain the integrity and consistency of your data.

Multi-lingual environment

Chapter 18, which deals with APEX Globalization, specifically claims that multi-lingual support can be added in any phase of the development process. We are not taking it back, of course, but if you know in advance that you are going to develop a multi-lingual application, it would be wise of you to start planning it right from the start and not wait for the primary language development to end. Using translatable supported components, such as shortcut (the message type), defining Globalization parameters and validations (e.g. date format, local currency, etc.), and taking translation into account in your external JavaScript code can save you a lot of time and effort when you reach the translation phase.

Team development

One of the features we are missing the most in the APEX IDE versions, until now, is a built-in support to facilitate a multi-developer environment. That's going to be changed in APEX 4.0, but for now, it's important to be familiar with what APEX does give us.

Lock your pages

The *lock pages* feature is a much underutilized feature of APEX and should always be used when there are multiple developers working on the same application. The *lock pages* feature enables developers to place a lock on a specific page that they are going to work on, which prevents other developers from modifying it. The other developers will still be able to view and run the page, but are not able to make modifications. This prevents developers from changing the same code and interfering with each other. The *Lock Pages* feature can be accessed by clicking the padlock icon— for unlocked pages, or for the locked ones. It's the third icon from the right on the *Action Bar* of the *Page Definition* page. Another access option is from the **Lock** column of the application page listing, on the application home page of the *Application Builder*.

When locking a page, a developer must enter a comment (mandatory field). This comment should be about why the page is locked. This is useful for other developers to know what is being changed in the page and which developers have the page locked. APEX also provides wizards and reports to view and manage all the locked pages, including allowing a workspace administrator to unlock any locked pages.

Version control

The APEX IDE doesn't include a real built-in version control mechanism. However, the **Edit Application Definition** page (in the *Shared Components* module) includes a mandatory field for **Version**. This field can be tied into a date format (look at the field help) and can supply a very crude version tracking. Personally, I find it more useful to handle this field manually, to differentiate the versions of the same application on the various APEX environments, such as development, QA, production, etc.

Just so you know, there is a wealth of experience in using external VCS systems with APEX. If you are working on a complex APEX project in a multi-developers environment, you can search the APEX OTN forum for additional information.

Document development standards

When building APEX applications, be sure to document and communicate development standards to the entire development team. Development standards help to ensure that pages are developed consistently and help to make development and maintenance of applications easier. Even though the core development in APEX is done through wizards and property pages, proper development standards should still apply, such as naming and formatting. Development standards should cover various areas such as the following:

- APEX naming standards—items, validations, processes, and other APEX object names should be informative and indicate their origin, location, or functionality. For example, item name should include the page it's defined on, the database column it may associate with, etc. The P12_EMPNO item name indicates that the item is on page 12 and associates with the EMPNO column.

- Oracle database naming standards
- PL/SQL coding standards
- Common code
- Deployment Procedures

Include your development standards in the application documentation and, if you are part of a development team, make sure that everyone on the team is aware of these standards and acts upon them.

Thou shall enter comments

Commenting is a standard practice when developing any application and it is no different when using APEX. Comments should be entered to help explain programming logic, business rules, development history, and any other useful information for developers. Almost every APEX component/object, definitely on the *Page Definition* page, includes a **Comments** field. That includes the page itself, items, computations, validations, processes, and almost any other APEX component.

On top of that, the APEX IDE supports a **Developer Comments** system, which allows us to document application-level issues and associate them with a relevant application page(s). The **Developer Comments** wizard is accessible through the *Action Bar*, using the balloon comment icon — 💬 — which is the second icon from the right. In the following screenshot we can see that the wizard tab allows us to define a developer comment. We can also see that other tabs of this wizard allow us to view and manage the existing developer comments.

By consistently using all the comments options provided by APEX we can create a very good documentation of our APEX project as we go along. Using the **Developer Comments**, all comments entered against pages, items, and other APEX objects are stored in the APEX metadata tables. Using the provided APEX views (APEX dictionary) we can query these comments and use them to form the basis of our documentation.

The following query can be used to display comments entered against pages by using the `APEX_APPLICATION_PAGES` database view:

```
SELECT workspace, application_id, application_name,
       page_id, page_name, page_title, page_comment
  FROM APEX_APPLICATION_PAGES
```

We can also view comments entered against page items by using the `APEX_APPLICATION_PAGE_ITEMS` database view:

```
SELECT page_id, page_name, item_name, component_comment
  FROM APEX_APPLICATION_PAGE_ITEMS
```

APEX views (APEX dictionary)

The APEX dictionary is a very powerful tool. It enables us to access various details about our applications by querying database views supplied by APEX. Further details of these views can be found in the Application Express Views page in the Utilities section. Be sure to explore these views and take advantage of them in your applications. A demo application that allows you to explore the APEX dictionary will be attached to this book demo applications.

APEX Application Reports

The APEX Application Reports module includes numerous pre-defined reports that include vast information on all the development aspects of the application, and is divided into four major categories: **Shared Components**, **Page Components**, **Activity** and **Cross Application**. It can be accessed from the **Tasks** window on the application home page, or by clicking on the page sheet icon— — which is the third icon from the right on the *Page Definition Action Bar*.

I want to draw your attention to the **Database Object Dependencies** report, as part of the **Application** section of the **Shared Component** category. This can be seen in the following screenshot:

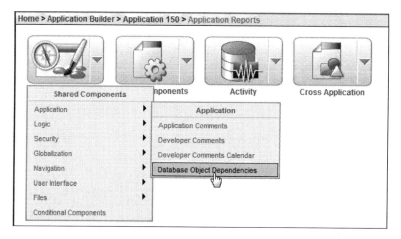

This report, which for large APEX applications can be quite "heavy", lists all the database objects that our APEX application depends on, how many times these objects are referenced within the application, and where (drill down to the **Reference Count** column in the following screenshot):

Application 1600			
Database Object Dependencies			
Owner	Referenced Name	Referenced Type	Reference Count
BOOK	COUNTRIES	Table	8
	CUSTOMERS	Table	11
	CUSTOMERS_VIP	Table	3
	DEMO_ORDERS	Table	7
	DEMO_ORDER_ITEMS	Table	6
	DEPT	Table	2
	DEPT_SEQ	Sequence	1
	DML_CUSTOMES	Package	1
	EMP	Table	4
	EMPLOYYES	View	2
	EVENTS	Table	2
	STATES	Table	5
	TESTING	Table	2
FLOWS_030100	HTMLDB_ITEM	Package	1
	V	Function	1
	WWV_FLOW_GLOBAL	Package	1
Public	APEX_APPLICATION	-	2
	APEX_APPLICATION_GLOBAL	-	1
	APEX_ITEM	-	1
	APEX_UTIL	-	7

Besides a great documentation value, this report would be very useful in helping us gather all the **Supporting Objects** we need as part of the application deployment scheme.

Moreover, after the dependency report table, it also includes a list of all the PL/SQL parsing errors it encountered during the preparation of the dependency report. This process includes scanning all the PL/SQL snippets of code, including those generated by the APEX engine itself, in order to locate all the dependent database objects. This is a great QA test for our applications at the final stage of development.

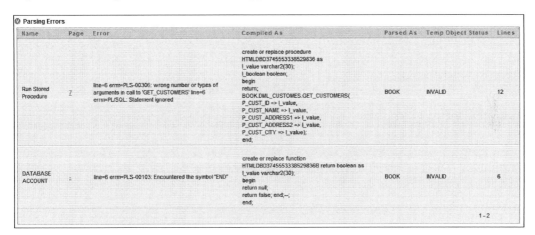

APEX Runtime-only version

When relevant, especially for commercially deployed APEX applications, the APEX Runtime module can be a very effective solution to maintain a high degree of security for the application. The runtime environment prevents access to the APEX development modules but doesn't impair, in any way, the functionality of the application itself.

Backup, backup, and more backup

Last, but definitely not least. Although almost every professional book, every instructor in a professional course, and probably every mentor you had constantly told you that backup is one of the most important tasks and responsibilities you have as a developer we keep encountering repeating backup disasters. Most often it is all because we don't have any backups.

We can not over estimate the importance of having a comprehensive and workable backup. Don't count only on your DBA and the database level backups they run. Use all the means APEX provides you to backup your developed application. Constantly and periodically, export copies of your APEX workspace and the applications in it. APEX includes, in its distribution files, a command-line, Java-based export utility called `APEXExport.class`. This utility allows you to automatically export all the applications in your APEX workspace. If you can't handle application by application exports, you can use this utility.

Remember, having backups is a good start but it's not enough. The backups — in our context the exported APEX files — must be in working order. From time to time, you need to verify your backups by using these exported files and importing them into an APEX instance. This is the only way to make sure that in times of need you have the proper tools and resource to overcome the crises.

Summary

In this chapter, we reviewed some of our *Best Practice* tips, tricks, and advice. These should help you to ensure consistency, good design, and high quality in your applications, right from the start.

Best practices should not be a fixed list of issues but rather a dynamic list that continually evolves and changes. Business requirements, technologies, APEX, and many other factors keep changing through the life course of a project, and it's important that we continually maintain the best practices list and the issues/procedures it contains, and always propagate it around.

APEX Installation, Upgrade, and Configuration Tips

We find the APEX documentation regarding installation, upgrade, and configuration to be very good – simple, clear, and thorough. As such, we don't see much point in reviewing these actions from scratch. In this chapter, we'll discuss and highlight some important pointers and tips we find useful and important.

Obtaining APEX

APEX is distributed (actually embedded) in Oracle XE and Oracle 11g. In both cases, the embedded version is not the latest, but it can be upgraded to it.

The latest version of APEX, as a standalone tool, can be downloaded from the APEX home page on `http://www.oracle.com/technology/products/database/` `application_express/`.

You can use APEX, free of charge, as long as you are using it on a valid licensed Oracle database (starting with 9.2.0.3), Oracle XE, or under the development terms of OTN.

Reading the relevant documentation

I know that there are users who think that reading the relevant documentation prior to installation is just a waste of time. If there is a setup installation program or a script, it's good enough for them. WRONG! Reading the relevant documentation can ultimately save you a lot of time and grief.

The APEX installation is very simple and straightforward, provided you are following all the guidelines in both the release notes and the installation guide. Both documentations are included in the APEX distribution file, so they are accessible right from the start.

The Installation process includes some pre-installation tasks, dedicated mainly to make sure that your database environment meets all the required conditions for a successful installation. It also includes some post-installation tasks, which are very important to complement the main installation and properly configure it.

In all my working days with the various versions of APEX, starting with HTML DB 1.6, I never had to deal with a faulty installation or upgrade of the tool mainly, as I believe, because I strictly followed the documentation instructions and guidelines.

Back up your database and APEX applications

Another important step that many users tend to overlook is the backup stage. As I said, the APEX installation/upgrade process is very simple and straightforward. However, it's still a major operation on your database and things might go wrong, and it doesn't have to be your fault.

You should back up your database prior to any installation or upgrading of APEX. In case of the latter, I strongly recommend that you also export all the APEX applications, so in case of problems in the upgrade, it won't be necessary to restore the entire database.

Use AL32UTF8 in your DAD

The character set segment of the `PlsqlNLSLanguage` parameter in the DAD (Database Access Descriptor) file must be set to **AL32UTF8**. This setting is mandatory regardless of your database character set. This setting is crucial for the correct and smooth operation of both the APEX IDE and the applications we are developing with it, especially (but not only) if we are using AJAX (and the APEX IDE massively uses AJAX).

Oracle recommends using the `AL32UTF8` character set as the default choice when installing a new database. If you have plans to develop for a multi-lingual environment, then this is the obvious and simplest choice. Using `AL32UTF2`, in both the database and the DAD, will save you a lot of character set conversions in the way in and out of the database.

APEX is using AL32UTF8 (**Unicode UTF-8**) as the default encoding for all the exported files from the *Application Builder*, and won't even give you an option of changing it.

Bear in mind:

Using any other character set in your DAD, especially one that matches your (local) database character set will not stop APEX from working, and in some cases, it can even appear as it works well. In all likelihood, this is a false and misleading, and it's only a question of when problems start to emerge. Installation and configuration problems are hard enough to diagnose and solve as it is. Don't add another hardship by using a faulty configuration from the start.

PL/SQL Web Toolkit

APEX requires version **10.1.2.0.6** or later of the PL/SQL Web Toolkit.

The version of the PL/SQL toolkit doesn't necessarily correlate with the database version you are using. To find out your current version, you can run the following:

```
select owa_util.get_version from dual;
```

If your current version is older than the required version, you should install the newer version prior to installing APEX.

The necessary PL/SQL Web Toolkit files can be found with the APEX distributed files, under the apex/owa directory. The directory also includes a readme file that instructs you regarding installation.

Bear in mind:

Similar to the AL32UTF8 issue, not using the correct version of the PL/SQL Toolkit will not stop the installation process and will not yield an error message. However, inappropriate (older) versions of the tool might create problems in generating the HTML code for the application pages. A typical error is when snippets of the HTML code itself appears on the page or the page doesn't include all its elements.

EPG – Embbeded PL/SQL Gateway

This option is the default installation option on Oracle XE and Oracle 11g database. It replaces the use of the OHS (Oracle HTTP Server).

Unlike the OHS, which we need to install and configure manually, the EPG is installed by default as part of the installation process of Oracle XE and Oracle 11g, and all we need to do to complete the installation process is to run a SQL script that is provided to us with the APEX distribution file. The process is very well documented in the APEX installation guide.

The EPG is also using an alias - /i/ by default that points to the images directory; only this time we are not talking about an OS filesystem directory. All the files in the images directory are uploaded into the database (into the XDB that hosts the EPG) in a manner that mimics the hierarchical structure of the images directory. You can see the files with any Web browser that supports WebDAV (an extension to the HTTP protocol) and most of the modern Web browsers are. Using a similar URL to the following should display the files:

```
http://127.0.0.1:8080/i
```

Enabling FTP on EPG

If you want to manipulate the images directory files that were uploaded to the XDB or add files of your own (like CSS or JavaScript external files), you can use an FTP client. However, you should first enable the proper port in the EPG. The default FTP port is 21, and to enable it, you can use the following from SQL*Plus (connected as "SYS as SYSDBA"):

```
exec dbms_xdb.setftpport(21);
```

To verify the setting you can use:

```
select dbms_xdb.getftpport from dual;
```

Enabling remote access to EPG

By default, the access to the EPG is restricted to the local machine. If you want to enable remote access, you can use the following from SQL*Plus (connected as "SYS as SYSDBA"):

```
exec dbms_xdb.setlistenerlocalaccess(FALSE);
```

EPG versus OHS

EPG is only (officially) supported on Oracle XE and Oracle 11g database. There are some hacks that allow the use of EPG on a 10g database, but they are not recommended.

It can be very simple and comfortable to use EPG on the supported platforms, but experience shows us that, performance–wise, it is slower than the OHS. As such, we recommend using it only for the development environment.

 The APEX license agreement stipulates that you can use the OHS, free of charge, as long as you are installing it on the same server as your APEX instance. In most cases, it should be good enough to serves the APEX needs.

Utilizing static files caching

As was mentioned in Chapter 3, while discussing where to store our external CSS or JavaScript files, APEX 3.1 introduced the use of a new set of HTTP Header parameters, allowing the Web browser to also cache static files that were uploaded into the database.

These parameters will not necessarily be available to us through the (OHS) mod_plsql DAD, and most likely will not be available through the EPG DAD. In order to be sure, we should define them ourselves.

If you are using OHS, enter the following into your DAD, and restart the OHS:

```
PlsqlCGIEnvironmentList HTTP_IF_NONE_MATCH
PlsqlCGIEnvironmentList IF_MODIFIED_SINCE
```

If you are using EPG, you should run the following in SQL*Plus, connected as "SYS as SYSDBA":

```
BEGIN
  DBMS_EPG.SET_DAD_ATTRIBUTE (
    dad_name    => 'APEX',
    attr_name   => 'cgi-environment-list',
    attr_value  => 'HTTP_IF_NONE_MATCH'
  );
```

```
        DBMS_EPG.SET_DAD_ATTRIBUTE (
            dad_name     => 'APEX',
            attr_name    => 'cgi-environment-list',
            attr_value   => 'IF_MODIFIED_SINCE'
        );
    END;
    /
```

Obfuscate your DAD file

Your DAD file, which is basically a clear text file, includes the name and password APEX uses to connect to the database. A typical entry will look similar to the following:

```
    PlsqlDatabaseUsername APEX_PUBLIC_USER
    plsqlDatabasePassword apex1234
```

This is a serious breach of security. You should at least obfuscate the APEX password, and a very simple way of doing it is to use the dadobf.exe utility, which should be available on the same directory as your DAD file. The utility accepts the password as the parameter and returns its obfuscated value, as can be seen in the following screenshot from a Windows CMD window:

Now you should copy the obfuscated value into your DAD file and restart the OHS.

Upgrading an APEX Instance

APEX supports direct upgrade from any major old version, starting with HTML DB 1.5 to the newest version. No special measures should be taken for upgrading the Instance. The process starts the same as a new installation, and a new APEX owner schema is created—in the case of APEX 3.2.x, it's the APEX_030200 schema. If an older instance of APEX exists on the database, the installation script will detect it, and all the relevant metadata from all the existing applications in the old instance will be copied into the new version instance. If the process was successful, a proper message will be displayed on the screen, similar to the following image:

```
-- Now beginning upgrade. This will take several minutes.--------
-- Ensuring template names are unique -------
-- Migrating metadata to new schema -------
-- Switching builder to new schema -------
-- Recompile WWV_DBMS_SQL -------
-- Migrating SQL Workshop metadata -------
-- Upgrading new schema. -------
-- Copying preferences to new schema. -------
Upgrade completed successfully no errors encountered.
-- Upgrade is complete --------------------------------------------
timing for: Upgrade
Elapsed: 00:00:36.58
...End of install if runtime install
...create null.sql
timing for: Development Installation
Elapsed: 00:10:12.51
Disconnected from Oracle Database 10g Express Edition Release 10.2.0.1.0 - Production

C:\Apex321\apex>
```

After completing the post-installation tasks, all the existing applications will be available to you in the new version of the *Application Builder*.

Backward Compatibility:

APEX fully supports backward compatibility. This means that any application exported file, from any older APEX version, can be imported into your new Instance, and it will be available to you immediately.

Bear in mind:

The APEX upgrade procedure doesn't delete the schema of the old APEX instance. In case of problems in the upgrade process, you can choose to go back to the old version. The reverse procedure is documented in the installation guide, alongside the process of how to clean (completely remove) a faulty installation.

Copy the new images directory

An important part of the upgrade process is to copy the new `images` directory from the new APEX version distribution file into the location of the `images` directory. If you are using OHS, we are talking about a simple OS copy operation. If you are using EPG, the APEX distribution file includes a script called `apxldimg.sql` that will do it for you.

```
SQL> @apxldimg.sql c:\apex321

PL/SQL procedure successfully completed.

old   1: create directory APEX_IMAGES as '&1/apex/images'
new   1: create directory APEX_IMAGES as 'c:\apex321/apex/images'

Directory created.


PL/SQL procedure successfully completed.


PL/SQL procedure successfully completed.


PL/SQL procedure successfully completed.


Commit complete.

timing for: Load Images
Elapsed: 00:22:10.18

Directory dropped.

SQL>
```

As you can see from the screenshot, the script is quite a silent one, and it doesn't report its progress. Depending on your machine, uploading all the `images` files can take a while (in the example, it took about 22 minutes), so you should be patient.

Themes and Templates in the Upgrade process

The APEX upgrade process creates a new *Themes* repository, but it doesn't change any of the *Themes* and *Templates* currently assigned to the existing APEX application. That makes all the existing applications immediately available to us in the upgraded version, while still supporting all the changes that we made to their *Themes* and *Templates*.

In some cases, however, the new *Themes* include new features that we would like to use in our application. Past examples include the region **Static ID** or the **Weekly** and **Daily** views in the *Calendar* templates. In these cases, we should replace the existing *Theme* with the newer version, and this is a manual process.

First, we need to change the ID of the current application *Theme*. We can do that through the **Themes** section of the application *Shared Components*. On the **Themes** home page, we should choose the option of **Change Identification Number** from the **Tasks** window. In the following screenshot, we can see an example of assigning a new *Theme* number – **118** – to the current *Theme* – **18**.

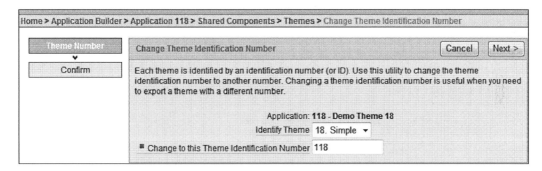

Next, we are going to create *Theme* 18 from the APEX repository. As this repository is part of the APEX upgraded version, the new *Theme* will be created with all the new features that the new APEX version includes.

From the *Themes* home page, we should press the **Create** button, and that will lead us to the **Create Theme** wizard, which we can see in the following screenshot:

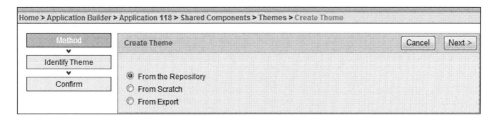

Choosing the option of **From the Repository** will lead us to the next wizard screen where we'll be able to choose the *Theme* to create. In our example, we chose to regenerate the built-in **Theme 18** with all its new features.

As we can see in the following screenshot, our application includes two *Themes* now—the current **118** *Theme* and the newly created *Theme* **18**. After making all the necessary changes into the new *Theme* **18**, including utilizing the new features we wanted to use, we can press the **Switch Theme** button.

The **Switch Theme** wizard verifies that the new *Theme* includes all the *Templates* that the application uses, as can be seen in the next screenshot:

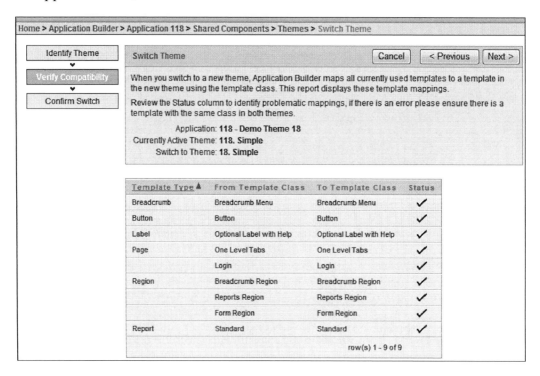

If everything checks out, the new *Theme* in our example **Theme 18**, will take control, and we'll be able to enjoy its new features in our application.

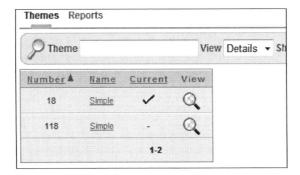

Summary

In this appendix, we have reviewed some issues related to an APEX installation, upgrade, and configuration.

The best and most important tip we can give you is to strictly follow all the instructions in the APEX release notes and the installation guide and perform all the pre and post installation tasks.

Index

Thank you for buying
Oracle Application Express 3.2

About Packt Publishing

Packt, pronounced 'packed', published its first book "Mastering phpMyAdmin for Effective MySQL Management" in April 2004 and subsequently continued to specialize in publishing highly focused books on specific technologies and solutions.

Our books and publications share the experiences of your fellow IT professionals in adapting and customizing today's systems, applications, and frameworks. Our solution based books give you the knowledge and power to customize the software and technologies you're using to get the job done. Packt books are more specific and less general than the IT books you have seen in the past. Our unique business model allows us to bring you more focused information, giving you more of what you need to know, and less of what you don't.

Packt is a modern, yet unique publishing company, which focuses on producing quality, cutting-edge books for communities of developers, administrators, and newbies alike. For more information, please visit our website: www.packtpub.com.

About Packt Enterprise

In 2010, Packt launched two new brands, Packt Enterprise and Packt Open Source, in order to continue its focus on specialization. This book is part of the Packt Enterprise brand, home to books published on enterprise software – software created by major vendors, including (but not limited to) IBM, Microsoft and Oracle, often for use in other corporations. Its titles will offer information relevant to a range of users of this software, including administrators, developers, architects, and end users.

Writing for Packt

We welcome all inquiries from people who are interested in authoring. Book proposals should be sent to author@packtpub.com. If your book idea is still at an early stage and you would like to discuss it first before writing a formal book proposal, contact us; one of our commissioning editors will get in touch with you.

We're not just looking for published authors; if you have strong technical skills but no writing experience, our experienced editors can help you develop a writing career, or simply get some additional reward for your expertise.

Oracle Application Express Forms Converter

ISBN: 978-1-847197-76-4   Paperback: 172 pages

Convert your Oracle Forms applications to Oracle APEX successfully

1. Convert your Oracle Forms Applications to Oracle APEX

2. Master the different stages of a successful Oracle Forms to APEX conversion project

3. Packed with screenshots and clear explanations to facilitate learning

4. A step-by-step tutorial providing a proper understanding of Oracle conversion concepts

Oracle User Productivity Kit 3.5

ISBN: 978-1-849680-16-5   Paperback: 540 pages

Build high-quality training simulations using Oracle UPK 3.5

1. Create engaging, high-quality training simulations for any Windows-based application leading to reduced training time, increased knowledge retention, and improved user acceptance.

2. Harness the full functionality of UPK 3.5 to add value to your documentation and training materials.

3. Re-purpose your simulations to create multiple document types, including business procedures, test documents, and job aids, and learn how to extend UPK by defining your own output types.

Please check **www.PacktPub.com** for information on our titles

Oracle Essbase 9 Implementation Guide

ISBN: 978-1-847196-86-6   Paperback: 444 pages

Develop high-performance multidimensional analytic OLAP solutions with Oracle Essbase

1. Build multidimensional Essbase database cubes and develop analytical Essbase applications

2. Step-by-step instructions with expert tips from installation to implementation

3. Can be used to learn any version of Essbase starting from 4.x to 11.x

4. For beginners as well as experienced professionals; no Essbase experience required

Oracle Warehouse Builder 11g: Getting Started

ISBN: 978-1-847195-74-6   Paperback: 368 pages

Extract, Transform, and Load data to build a dynamic, operational data warehouse

1. Build a working data warehouse from scratch with Oracle Warehouse Builder.

2. Cover techniques in Extracting, Transforming, and Loading data into your data warehouse.

3. Learn about the design of a data warehouse by using a multi-dimensional design with an underlying relational star schema.

Please check **www.PacktPub.com** for information on our titles

8551475R1

Made in the USA
Lexington, KY
10 February 2011